SPORT FISHING USA

Sport Fishing USA

DAN SAULTS *Managing Editor*

MICHAEL WALKER *Editor*

BOB HINES *Illustrator*

REX GARY SCHMIDT *Photo Editor*

THE UNITED STATES DEPARTMENT OF THE INTERIOR

Bureau of Sport Fisheries and Wildlife • Fish and Wildlife Service

Foreword

It is fitting that we mark the centennial year of Federal efforts to conserve our fishery resources with publication of a book about the fun and frustrations, mysteries and rewards of sport fishing. For truly, fishing is the great American outdoor sport, luring millions of us with the wholesome beckoning of ocean, lake, and stream.

As we face together the new conservation challenges that lie ahead may the pleasure of "wetting a line" be equaled only by the pleasure of reading about it in *Sport Fishing—U.S.A.*

Rogers CB Morton

Secretary of the Interior

Acknowledgements

The Bureau of Sport Fisheries and Wildlife is deeply grateful to the authors who contributed their thoughts to this book. Though many are outside the Federal agencies—some earning their living by freelance writing—they generously contributed their talents to this book. Chosen for their special knowledge on key subjects, all were encouraged to write freely.

A committee headed by Dr. Joseph P. Linduska helped plan the book and reviewed manuscripts for factual correctness. The committee included Dr. Willis King, Paul E. Thompson, Ben Schley, Dan Saults, Keith R. McCarthy, and Dr. Raymond R. Johnson. Robert J. McKendry of the Government Printing Office created the design of the book. Gail McCathen copy edited and typed manuscripts and read proofs. Peter A. Anastasi coordinated the production work.

MICHAEL J. WALKER
Editor

A QUESTION
EVERYONE ASKS

Why People Fish

by Curt Gowdy

I can still remember those days. I must have been 8 or 9 years old. My father and I used to fish the small streams of Wyoming in the spring while the snow runoffs were roiling the bigger rivers. We used to crawl along the banks on our hands and knees and drop a worm into dark, pocketed pools hemmed in by willows. The trout of those days seemed like monsters to me—they were probably in the 8- to 12-inch class, but that is how it all started.

CUTTHROAT TROUT

SOMETIMES I would walk along an open irrigation ditch dragging a worm on the end of a flyrod and to my delight would sometimes jerk a fat, flopping native trout onto the grassy banks while my dad with more patience would fight the bush and obstacles and work his way into the better holes.

Then the summer would move along. After the runoff, the Little Laramie, Big Laramie, and Encampment Rivers would start to clear before the then awesome Platte River, and the fly fishing would start. I would still be using a worm or spinner on a flyrod (spin casting was not used in this country in those days), and I would troop along marveling at how my father would catch fish and I could not. My flyrod in those days was collapsible and made of steel.

On my 10th birthday, I was presented my first bamboo flyrod and started fly fishing. Somehow I would slop that line and fly out into a fast moving riffle and feel bump after bump as the wild hungry trout would hit my fly, but I had not learned yet how to set the hook on the sunken artificial. Then it started to come, as I learned the reflex action, and soon I was catching trout on a fly. I was hooked for life on a beautiful, passionate hobby.

My uncle, Fred Smith, was a railroad executive in Ogden, Utah, and used to come to Wyoming every summer for a couple of weeks of fly fishing. Uncle Fred was a dry-fly man and to me this was the wonder of wonders. Now it was August and early September. The streams were low and clear, especially the North Platte River in the Saratoga, Wyo., area. To me in those days it was a gigantic river that could be frightening. I was constantly warned about wading in the swift riffles and long, deep pools. The rocks were slippery and treacherous, so I did not wander too far from my dad or uncle.

I would follow my uncle and watch him in awe as he worked upstream. His casting was effortless, as he would lay 50 feet of flyline out in a tight loop behind, and then flick it forward so it would gently settle in a long, slow glide. It was quite a show to watch that tiny artificial fly come bobbing along the surface and then be sucked in by a big brown or rainbow trout. My uncle's 8-foot flyrod would bend in a deep bow, because these were native, wild trout in superb condition which were lying in swift currents to make the fight even more challenging.

That is how it all began for me. I was a lucky youngster. The population then was only 225,000 in that big magnificent State, and we had miles of rivers and lakes to fish. It was a rare day when you ran across another fisherman on the particular stream you would be fishing—you almost had it all to yourself. Every spare summer day would be spent fishing. When I went to college at the University of Wyoming in Laramie, I could slip out in the spring and fish the nearby creeks and beaver ponds after a 4 o'clock afternoon class. In September when college would start again, I was fishing in the mornings and afternoons because the Little Laramie and Big Laramie were just minutes away from the college campus.

It was not only the challenge and fun of getting trout to take a fly or spinner that made me fish; it was the atmosphere. The streams held a fascination, especially the bouncing riffles which smoothed out into bubbly dark pools. From meadow creeks to the big treacherous Green, Snake, and Platte Rivers, the

2

roar and mystery of the waters started a lifetime fascination. The big cottonwood trees and bushy willows, the quaking aspen, especially when they were golden in the fall—these added to the enjoyment. The sweet smell of the meadows and the morning dew bathing my waders as I walked from the ranch house down to the stream were delights.

So the fun, challenge, and beauty combined to make me start fishing, but then as I grew older the hobby increased in its intensity and pleasure. Now, I no longer live in Wyoming but travel around America and the world as a sports broadcaster, and in recent years the hobby has become part of my business as I have become host for the hunting and fishing television program called the American Sportsman on the ABC–TV network. The show has been the surprise hit of television sports programs. Many television executives and advertising agency men are amazed at the huge audience the show attracts.

Twenty-million Americans tune in each week. Why? Sure, the filming is handsomely done and the great outdoors lends itself to modern color television. The exotic places we visit around the world give the average viewer a vicarious chance to live these adventures himself. But more than anything, people like to fish and hunt in this country—they always have and always will.

As a participant in these outdoor television shows, along with my other sports broadcasting assignments over the years, I have been very lucky getting to know and fish with some of the finest anglers in the world. I have had a chance to learn, improve my own fishing, and also gather observations from these angling greats and learn why they fish.

For instance, I was broadcasting the Boston Red Sox games when Ted Williams was the biggest name in baseball. Ted was just as good a fisherman as he was a batter. He took me out with him on the Florida Keys, and we spent many hours in planes, hotel rooms, and dugouts during the baseball season talking fishing. Williams is a perfectionist, which is undoubtedly why he was so explosive and controversial a ballplayer. He has to be good at anything he tries. He wants to know all about it and will go to everyone to find out.

There are not many men in the world as versatile as Ted Williams in fishing. He has caught big billfish, he is outstanding with the spinning and plug-casting rods, and he is one of the best for distance and accuracy with the flyrod. Then he can sit down at his fly-tying bench and with those big powerful hands that nearly ground so many baseball bats to pieces, turn out the daintiest little dry flies imaginable. He knows tackle of all types and what makes them good or bad.

I remember one day in the 1950's when the Red Sox were playing a series against the Senators in Washington, D.C. We had a night game scheduled, and Ted had noticed that the national casting tournaments were being held at the reflection pool on the mall. The best casters in America had gathered to compete in the distance and accuracy events.

We were watching some of the events, when one of the participants recognized Ted and invited him to try his gear. Ted stepped out on the platform, stripped the shooting monofilament line on the deck, and with that strange outfit cast a fly just 5 feet shorter than the man who that week won the national distance fly-casting championship.

4

In the cab on the way back to the hotel I asked Ted why he liked to fish: "Gee, for a lot of reasons, I guess," Ted said. "Living in San Diego as a boy I was around water and got interested then. But I like the challenge it offers me. It's a real relaxation for me. I like to get away from crowds—off by myself. It's a chance to relax and not have some fan or writer getting on me. I like the competition of going for records on all different types of tackle and line test. Fishing offers so many different things I enjoy that I can't single out one particular reason why I like to fish—but boy, it's been great for me."

Ted Williams introduced me to another champion angler, Joe Brooks. Reared in Baltimore, Joe has fished ever since he was a boy. His love has always been fly fishing, but he is excellent at every type of fishing he tries. He is one of the kindest and most understanding men I have ever been around—an all-around top athlete but very gentle and beautifully mannered.

I was supposed to go bone fishing on the Florida Keys with Ted one February day in 1952, but Ted had to go to a fishing tackle convention, so Ted called up his neighbor across the road in Islamorada, Fla., and asked him if he would take me out. Ted then called me and explained the situation. I was disappointed in not going with Ted but was delighted to meet the great Joe Brooks because I had just finished reading his book on saltwater fly fishing, a field that he helped pioneer.

My wife and I drove up to Joe's home shortly before noontime and were greeted at the door by a handsome, smiling gray-haired man who said: "Come in. Mary has lunch ready. Then we'll head for Key Largo Sound and see if we can't get you a bonefish on a fly. The tides should be just right." We were received with such hospitality that we felt we had known Joe and Mary Brooks for years instead of a matter of minutes.

There is no one who is better with a

"I want fish from fishing, but I want a great deal more than that, and getting it is not always dependent upon catching fish."

flyrod or who knows more about fly fishing than Joe. He has fished everywhere in the world for every type of fish. He has written umpteen books on fishing, and his articles in the monthly outdoor publications are avidly followed. Joe started me after bonefish and tarpon on a fly. The saltwater angling opened an entirely new vista and made my fishing season 12 months instead of 3. He took me to Cuba, the Bahamas, Bermuda, British Honduras, Yucatan, and Argentina. I could not return the favor of taking Joe to my native Rockies for trout fishing, because Brooks spent 6 weeks every year in Montana, one of his favorite fishing areas in the world.

The one area I did bring Joe into was television. He made appearances with me on Wide World of Sports and the American Sportsman. His feat of casting a fly 75 feet into a 50-mile an hour wind is still talked about by TV sports buffs. The best trip of my life was to a remote mountain lake on the border of Argen-

tina and Chile—Lago General Paz—where Joe and I lived in sleeping bags for 3 weeks. We filmed a trout fishing contest against two native fishermen for Wide World of Sports. The show was received so well, that the idea for the American Sportsman series was born.

It was high in the Andes Mountains one night under the stars that I asked Joe why he liked to fish. Bear in mind that this was a man who acted like he had not been fishing for months and who every day seemed to be pent up with excitement to get on the water.

"Just because of this," Joe answered as he waved at the beautiful night. "I like to get away from the turmoil of the city and modern life. I like sparkling waters, the wind in the pines. I like the feel of my fly tackle. The feel of a fine instrument is a joy to me. I just like to get away."

Another all-time angling great I have had the pleasure of fishing with is Lee Wulff, considered by many to be the

6

greatest salmon fisherman in the world. His book—*The Atlantic Salmon*—is still the bible on fishing for this marvelous game species.

This tall, whipcord type of man is unbelievably versatile in the out-of-doors. He fishes, paints, writes, photographs, and creates. It was Lee who tied what is now the most used dry fly in the world—the Wulff fly in its various patterns. Lee created this fly on the trout streams of New York, but it is now used everywhere.

Lee was born in Alaska and spent his boyhood on the West coast. He has always been in the out-of-doors and has loved it. Gradually his fishing led him to the Atlantic salmon in Maine and the Canadian Provinces, because he wanted the ultimate in his freshwater fishing with bigger fish in bigger streams.

Lee is also an excellent pilot. In fact, he learned to fly so he could get into the good fishing of Newfoundland and Labrador. He flew me into the Minipi River back in the bush country of Labrador where we filmed a show on eastern brook trout fishing. The fish averaged 5 pounds, and this area is probably the last frontier of the beautiful, big brookies.

One rainy day when we were confined to camp, I leaned back against a tree watching Lee tie a big Wulff dry fly without a fly tying vise. I was held in fascination by the skill of those large, sun-tanned hands as he created the cream and black imitation. I suddenly asked him why he liked to fish.

"I think it was born in me," Lee answered. "There were few things to do in a small Alaskan town so I turned to fishing. I think you either like the people who fish—like to be with them—or you like to get away from tension. Doctors fish and fish hard, because they like to get away from human problems."

Lee grew more serious as he continued: "I think also a real important thing is dealing with something that has a mind of its own like fish and game. It puts you in touch with nature—takes you away from the man-oriented cycle. I also feel a lot of people fish because father and son or expert and novice can do it together. The novice stands as good a chance as the expert in hooking a big fish."

Bernard "Lefty" Kreh is a short, moon-faced man who is always smiling but is usually happiest when he is either fishing or teaching someone else how to fish. Lefty has been fishing for the last 25 years, first in his native Maryland, then along the Eastern Shore, and now in Miami. He runs the best fishing tournament in the world—the Miami Metropolitan Tournament—sponsored by the Miami Herald. He is an artist with the flyrod but can use any type of tackle like most pro anglers and enjoys all kinds of fishing.

Lefty spends much of his time now touring the country and putting on fishing clinics for youngsters and adults who want to learn how to fish. He can cast either left- or right-handed and is so simple and good with his instructions that he can have you whipping out a fly 40 feet with only a half-hour of teaching.

One day while we took a break for lunch on one of the flats of the Florida Keys, I asked Lefty why he fished. That engaging smile lit up his round face as he said:

"It's just pure fun. No better relaxation, and I never get tired of it. There are so many ways to fish—ocean, bass mill ponds, trout streams, big lakes. They all offer a special problem, and solving these problems is 90 percent of the fascination fishing has for me. I also believe there is very little luck in good fishing. The best angler is the one who solves the problems."

These famous anglers have been fishing since they were youngsters. But golfer Jack Nicklaus just started fishing seriously about 5 years ago, and he is getting to be as good with the fly and spinning rod as he is with the golf club.

Jack and I fished together in the San Juan River in Nicaragua for tarpon in a freshwater river. We spent 4 days together in a johnboat where you can get to know a man in a short time. I found him completely different than his image on the golf course. He was friendly, talkative, and considerate. I could see he loved fishing.

"Why do you like it, Jack?" I asked.

"It's great for me to get away from the pressure of tournament golf," Jack answered. "I love the fly casting and the tarpon. I moved to Florida where there are so many opportunities to fish. I bought a new boat, and can't think of any more fun than taking my two little boys out fishing."

These men I have talked about are all famous fishermen who spend most of the year making fishing their life or their living. They all give different reasons why they like to fish. But I have also stopped on bridges, piers, seacoasts, lakes, and rivers and asked other fishermen why they fished. Some go for a giant tuna and billfish. Others use bait casting rods, cane poles, spinning rods, flyrods, and even bow and arrow. They fish in ponds, streams, lakes, or the ocean. They fish deep or on top. They use everything from live bait to dough balls to a number 20 dry fly. They all talk about the challenge, the trophies and prizes, the delicious healthful food for the table, the relaxation, the atmosphere, the uncertainty, and all the other joys of fishing.

I think though that Rodrick Haig-Brown sums it all up best. Rod was English born but now lives in the Pacific Northwest. He is not only a top fisherman, but his writings on fishing and nature are so moving that they become sheer poetry.

In his book, *A River Never Sleeps*, he has a chapter titled "Why Fish?" He answers thus:

"I do not fish, as I understand some people do, for fresh air and exercise; no doubt I pick up a share of both when I go fishing, but they are unearned increment—I am not really looking for them. I do not fish for fish to eat; having to eat fish is one of the penalties of having been out fishing. With this penalty in mind I probably fish a little less often and less painstakingly than I otherwise would. I do fish to catch fish—at least, that is an idea not too far in the back of my mind while I am fishing; but I have fished through fishless days that I remember happily and without regret. I want fish from fishing, but I want a great deal more than that, and getting it is not always dependent upon catching fish.

"All this brings us back to the original answer—I fish to please myself."

No one can say it better than that.

THE FISH

Outside and In

by Frank J. Schwartz

*Those who seek the challenge are puzzled
by this strange creature—the fish. From the biologist, they expect
answers to such questions as: What is the fish like,
outside and in? What type of water does it prefer? What food does it eat?
Where does it go? Why does it do what it does?
I shall attempt to answer briefly the first question while succeeding
chapters in this section will delve into the others.*

LIONFISH

W HAT BOTH impresses and puzzles many people is the shape of the fish—its obvious streamlining. Most—except for such as the goosefish and the seahorse—are torpedo shaped, as if carved by a sculptor to enable the fish to move more readily through its world of water. It has evolved this shape after many, many millions of years, and today it benefits by the ease with which it darts here and about or as it wanders far and wide.

Many, like the sunfish, are flattened on the sides; some are elongated, like the ribbonfish; a few are short, like the ocean sunfish; some are globular, like the puffers; others are tubular, like the eel; and some are flattened, like the rays and skates. But all of these are streamlined from head to tail and take advantage of this shape.

People are also fascinated by the fins of the fish. These are governed by muscles and help move the fish through the water much like our limbs move us across the land.

The caudal or tail fin, along with sinuous body movements, is the prime propellant in most, but its function may be replaced by an elongate dorsal or back fin, as in the bowfin, when it maneuvers for position. Where body rigidity (cowfish, trunkfish) prevents the tail fin from functioning well, dorsal and anal fins double as the propelling fins.

Dorsal, anal, or caudal fins can propel a fish forward, backward, or keep it stationary. Wrasses and parrotfish row their way through water by using their pectoral or chest fins. In the shark these fins elevate the fish since it lacks a swim bladder and tends to sink. In swim bladdered fish (most bony ones), pectoral fins help in turning an upward moving fish or serve as braking devices. Pelvic fins also help in close maneuvering and position adjustment.

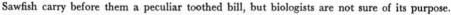

Sawfish carry before them a peculiar toothed bill, but biologists are not sure of its purpose.

As with most vertebrates, eyes in fish are paired and occupy a prominent position on the head. They are most often on each side of the head, but in some, such as the deep-sea idiacanths, they are on stalks some distance from the head.

Vision ranges from blindness, as in cavefish, to excellent for underwater conditions. For the most part, eyes are lidless.

Both eyes can focus on the same object, and thus fish have binocular vision like humans. However, some can move each eye separately. And in some deepwater types (giganthurids), telescopic forward looking eyes are present. We don't know what purpose this serves.

Experiments have definitely established that most fish can detect colors; however, the range of colors that can be perceived varies. Eyes are more like cameras, in that the fish can adjust the position of the lens depending on how close is the object focused on.

Flounders swim upright with an eye on each side when young, but as adults they swim on one side. With this change one eye migrates across the head, so both lie on the same side.

Eyes are positioned so that fish can see rearward. They also tend to be larger in fish living at depths of 2,000 feet, but then decrease in fish living still deeper, only to increase in such very deep bottom dwellers as ratfish.

Much more developed in the fish is the sense of smell. Present just above the mouth are paired openings or nostrils. Lampreys and hagfish have only a single nostril. In most fish a structure is present at the nostril opening to guide the water into the cavity so that it can be analyzed.

Most nostril openings lie flat on the head, but bowfins, moray eels, and others have them on the ends of tiny projecting

Adult winter flounders have both eyes on the same side of the head.

stalks. In globefish a pair of solid nasal tentacles serve as nostrils. In lungfish and other more primitive types the nostrils open internally into the mouth cavity.

Smell influences the fish profoundly, guiding many of its movements and also directing it sometimes to food. It is so highly developed in fish that they can detect greatly diluted substances, as low as several parts per billion in water.

Fish mouths also vary in shape, size, position, and function. More primitive forms have sucking, circular, jawless mouths, like the lamprey. More advanced types have jaws which may or may not be filled with teeth. Some, like the paddlefish and marlin, have the upper jaw elongated. Needlefish, pike, and gar have both jaws extended, while halfbeaks have only the lower one developed outward.

Sturgeon jaws are soft, pliable, and protrusible. Shark, skate, and ray jaws are cartilaginous and are often protruded. Bony fish have jaws that vary in size from small apertures (ocean sunfish) to large (deep-sea gulper eels, which are almost all mouth), and those that may or may not be movable.

Jaw position often suggests a fish's preference for feeding habitat. For example, jaws opening downward, as in skates, croakers, and sturgeons, are associated with bottom-feeding fish. A forward-opening mouth, as in trout, swordfish, and many others, suggests that any water level of feeding may be occupied. An upward-position mouth like that of the guppy suggests surface feeding or fish that rest on the bottom and feed on organisms that pass above, as in the stargazers.

Furious leap of largemouth reveals mouth and gills.

Armature of the mouth, whether teeth or bony plates on the jaws, throat, or tongue, enables the fish to eat or crush food items—from algae to hard coral. And as you will see in a later chapter, each type of fish has a distinct preference for certain types of food.

The skin covering a fish is a relatively tough structure that is continuous with the lining of all body openings and transparent where it covers the eye. It consists of two layers, the outer one known as the epidermis and inner as the dermis. When you skin a fish you see many of the fibers, blood vessels, etc., that terminate in the dermal layer. This layer binds the skin to the underlying muscles and bones and is also important in that scales and related structures have their origin in it.

The outer layer contains mucus gland cells that produce the slippery or slimy substance that covers the outer surface of most fish. This slime not only helps lessen drag as a fish swims through the water, but also prevents infection from micro-organisms. Hagfish are notorious for producing copious amounts of mucus. Two or three in a bucket can soon fill it with their slime.

Most fish possess scales which vary in type, structure, and size, but some like the catfish are scaleless. Those that are not scaled often have other derivatives of the skin to protect them. These may be prickles, electric producing organs or cells (electric eels), venomous glands, (lionfish, madtom catfish), and glands for odor (trunkfish). Some have varying amounts of body scale covering in the form of plates (sturgeon and sticklebacks).

Such items as teeth are derivatives of scales in sharks, while the barbs of stingrays are modified scales. Bony plates of seahorses or tropical South American catfish are modified scales.

Scales are usually arranged like the shingles of an overlapping house roof, with the free edge pointing to the rear. (Imagine what the reverse position could do to the swimming ability of the fish.) These scales may be thin or thick. Gars have primitive diamond-shaped types, while true bony fish are covered with one of two basic forms: a smooth disclike, thin, circular shape with no outer projections (minnow) or a back-toothed edge scale (yellow perch). Trout-perch and some freshwater bass can possess both of these types.

It is noteworthy that the skin and scales of gar are so tough that American rice farmers once used them to protect their wooden plowshares.

Age of many temperate-water fish can be determined by observing the ringlets or annuli which occur on scales. Even their past history can be revealed by the spacing of these annuli, indicating periods of good or poor growth, as a result of perhaps inhabiting good or bad environments.

Few things are so striking as the brilliance of the dolphin, with colors of yellow and green and spots of blue, or the spotted sail of the sailfish. Trout in all their finery or tropical-sea fish with their myriads of colors are artistic wonders to behold. Yet a fish's coloration can reveal much about him or the habitat in which he lives. Bottom dwellers are usually darker above and pale or silver below (flounders). Mid-water forms may have many varied color patterns, whereas surface or open-water swimmers are usually silvery or white colored on the sides and belly with blues and greens prevailing on top.

Countershading is an important fac-

tor for many fish. When those that are dark colored on the back and lighter on the belly are illuminated by sunlight, they in effect change color and blend in entirely with the background.

Color is caused by two types of pigment cells: chromatophores and iridocytes. Chromatophores lie within the dermis of the skin, either outside or beneath the scales and have pigment granules imparting the actual colors. These granules are red and orange, yellow, and black but by dispersal and expansion of these cells most color combinations are produced. The silvery coloration is the product of the iridocyte cells. Control over color cell size is through nervous or hormonal action.

Often changes in color enable fish to blend in with the background—actual camouflaging. Rapid color changes to achieve this are governed by the nervous system, whereas slower color changes, such as occur when day passes into night, are controlled by hormones.

Many times color changes tell us whether the fish is alarmed, frightened, or aggressive. And color serves to attract attention to the fish, as when spawning. Vivid flashes of colors may attract another fish to a parasite cleaning station (brilliant goby fish). Camouflages, of course, help conceal the fish or prevent its being eaten.

The oceans have often been referred to as the silent depths, but actually they are alive with sounds originated by fish and other animals. Fish have ears to detect certain sounds and will respond to some of them; thus, ears in fish are rather well developed. They are not external, however, as with humans, but

An adult wrasse colorfully different
from yellow young.

16

are positioned on each side of the head internally.

Most mysterious of the outer body fish structures is the lateral line system and its associated components. This system is the dotted or dashed line that runs along each side of the fish, connected to the brain near the inner ear. We still don't know much about this structure, but we suspect that its prime function is the detection of low frequency sounds. This may help the fish in schooling and in locating prey.

In another strange system, special cells or photophores produce luminescent "light" by means of endocrine action in some fish. For example, some deep-water sharks and rays, the fragile lanternfish, or the bulkier midshipman can produce their own luminescence.

Other fish (grenadiers) possess cells in which light producing bacteria reside and which are under no central control. Some such as the deep-water angler or goosefish have luminous "baits" to lure prey to their doom.

Sometimes the light producing structure is so complicated that light is produced, concentrated, and directed by a lens, as in a flashlight.

Internally, a fish is just as interesting. The most basic structure, of course, is the skeleton. Sturgeons, lampreys, hagfish, sharks, and rays possess cartilaginous skeletons.

Important hard structures lying within the skull in chambers near the inner ear are the ear bones (otoliths), which help determine balance. They are also useful in determining the age of a fish, if one examines the ringlike markings that are produced as the fish grows.

Numerous muscles give shape and substance to the body of a fish and help control movement and function of other body organs. In general, the side muscles are W shaped for best movement and efficiency. Important to fast-swimming fish like the tunas is a dark muscle band underlying the lateral line system, providing fish with energy and permitting it to maintain high swimming speeds over long distances and periods of time.

Like humans, fish have a complex internal digestive tract which begins with the mouth cavity, extends down a varying length of esophagus to a stomach area, and then leads into a varied length intestine. Powerful acids help break down chunks of food in the stomach. Some fish swallow food whole, while others may grind it and then swallow. Meat eaters usually have a shortened intestine, while that of algae or herbivorous eaters is lengthened.

Of special interest in the mouth cavity is the gill chamber. In primitive fish such as the lamprey, external gill openings lead into gill pouches into which water is pumped in and out before reaching the pharynx. In sharks and their relatives water enters the mouth and passes over gill rakers which filter out food items, and gill arches with filaments where exchange of vital life-giving gasses occurs before passing to the exterior via several gill openings.

Bottom dwellers such as rays and skates and some sharks have an opening on the back—the spiracle—through which water enters, instead of through the mouth, before passing out the sides. Bony fish pass water from the mouth cavity over the gill arches and filaments out to the exterior through a single pair of gill slits.

In addition to gills, some fish have developed accessory breathing structures which enable them to live in oxygen

Scorpion fish, excellent at camouflage and with poison spines.

depleted waters or even out of water for short periods (climbing perch).

A tubular to heart shaped structure called the swim bladder is found in many fish. Generally it is a long tube on top of the digestive tract just below the backbone. The more primitive lampreys, hagfish, and sharks and some of the more evolved ones resting on the bottom like the darters lack the swim bladder.

Various concentrations of oxygen and nitrogen and in some fish even fat fills the bladder. Its function varies, but it often serves to help the fish maintain buoyancy. Toadfish and drums have muscles associated with the bladder which can be twanged to produce sounds. Catfish and minnows have extensions of the bladder into the four modified vertebrate located just behind

19

Sand shark and its replaceable teeth.

the skull where sound waves may be registered.

The blood of fish is colored by red cells called erythrocytes. Some antarctic fish possess colorless blood, as do young eels. The blood system is an elaborate system of tubules operated by the pumping of the heart, which pumps blood forward to the gills and then to all organs and parts of the body. In the heart, blood passes through two chambers on its journey to the gills.

Very important to fish are the kidneys and the other parts of the excretory system. This system enables the fish to survive the many stresses in his environment. Those in freshwater, for example, are struggling to keep dissolved salts within and to eliminate the excess water they are exposed to or which "seeps" in. Marine fish lose water and gain excess amounts of salts "drinking" seawater.

In marine fish, nitrogenous wastes are eliminated via the gills, while salts are secreted through the gills and intestines, a little through the urine. In freshwater fish gaseous waste elimination is accomplished mainly by the kidney.

Imagine what transpires in a fish and the physiological and anatomical changes that must take place in the kidneys if it is a salmon migrating up from the sea into freshwater to spawn. Eels experience and survive the reverse problem when migrating from freshwater to the sea to spawn. Most fish do not transfer easily from salt to fresh water or the opposite, yet some do.

The reproductive organs of fish are varied as are the methods of reproduction. There are egg layers and those that bear live young. I shall leave a more detailed discussion of this complex topic to a later chapter.

20

Governing the functioning of all these systems as well as the external actions of the fish are the brain and its nerve extensions. Located in the head, the brain is much smaller and much more primitive than that of mammals, but it governs behavior and functions that are just as— and possibly even more—complex than those of humans. It even enables the fish to remember and learn and guides it on gigantic migrations and through minute color changes. It enables the fish to seek out food, mate, and build nests. Everything the fish does is triggered by the nervous system.

There are fish like the electric eel that are able to produce electricity for either defense or capture of prey. Various body tissues like the muscles and nerves are specialized to produce the electricity. In fish where only low voltage is generated (knifefish), they are able to guide their movements by obstructions that disrupt the electrical field that surrounds their body.

So we have seen that, outside and in, a fish is as complex and efficient an organism as land-based vertebrates, including man. It is adapted to its world of water, just as we are to the world of air. It must remain in intimate contact with its environment to obtain oxygen, food, shelter, a place to grow and reproduce, as we must in ours. Nor can it seek a world outside of water, just as we cannot forgo the world of air. When it is unable to seek a better, cleaner habitat, it simply perishes—as we would die if our environment became fouled.

Zip Code H₂O

by Charles H. Walburg

Water covers three-fourths of the earth's surface—and fish are found almost wherever there is water. They live in Arctic waters near the freezing point, in hot springs where temperatures exceed 100° F., around brilliantly illuminated ocean coral reefs, and within the perpetual night of underground limestone caverns. Fish are swimming in Lake Titicaca, 3 miles above sea level, and finning along at a depth of 7 miles in the deepest oceans. They live in the pure, soft water of mountain streams and in saltwater lakes several times more saline than the oceans.

MOUNTAIN LAKE FISHING FOR BROWN TROUT

Most evolutionists believe fish originated from ancestors that lived in the sea. Some became adapted to freshwater over millions of years, and thus today we find them all over the globe in inland waters. There are at least 20,000 species—most living in the oceans. Some have worldwide distribution, while others are limited to a single lake or stream. They live wherever they can complete their life cycle. The requirements are quite different for the various species, and therefore many different kinds are found in various types of waters.

There are those living permanently in freshwater, in saltwater, in estuaries or coastal areas where fresh- and saltwater mix, and in both salt- and freshwater, migrating from one to the other.

Freshwater types can be divided into those that live in streams, rivers, lakes, and ponds. Saltwater types can be grouped into those that live on or near the Continental Shelf out to a depth of 100 fathoms (600 feet), open-sea or oceanic forms, and deep-water forms living in depths greater than 100 fathoms. Most found in estuaries are able to live, at least for short periods, in either fresh- or salt-water.

Water temperature is the most important factor limiting the distribution of fish in freshwater streams, which may be cold or warm depending on source and local conditions of shade, depth, and current. Cold streams, where summer temperatures do not exceed 70° to 75° F., are best for trout.

Brook trout cannot tolerate summer temperatures in excess of 75° F., brown trout 81° F., and rainbow trout 83° F. A trout stream must also provide adequate volume of flow and current; suitable pools, riffles, and shelter; minimum turbidity and erosion; plus shade, aquatic vegetation, and food.

Warm streams may be swift-flowing or sluggish with many deep pools. The bottom usually contains some silt, and the water is less clear than in a typical trout stream. Fish in such a stream include largemouth and smallmouth bass and other sunfish, channel catfish and bullheads, various species of suckers, and minnows.

Larger warm streams and rivers are more turbid, containing quiet water and many deep pools. Common inhabitants are catfish, buffalofish, gars, carp, freshwater drum, walleye, sauger, and various sunfish.

With increase in temperature, turbidity, and unstable water levels, fish that feed by touch and taste or smell rather than sight, such as carp, suckers, and catfish, become dominant.

Cold, infertile lakes with rocky bottoms and steep shorelines are inhabited by trout. These waters are very clear, low in mineral and organic content, and relatively infertile. The surface may warm in summer, but deeper water is always cold. Large, deep lakes usually over 100 feet in depth are the typical habitat for lake trout, but northern pike, suckers, lake herring, and sometimes walleye and smallmouth bass are also present.

There are lakes that are 75 to 80 feet deep, relatively infertile, and with water that is moderately cold. Their bottom waters lack dissolved oxygen in summer. Common fish in them are northern pike, walleye, suckers, yellow perch, smallmouth bass, and a few lake trout.

The warm lake often is quite fertile with sand and mud on the bottom. Some

A southeastern swamp is home for many kinds of fish.

24

are from 8 to 15 miles across, and may range in depth to 200 feet. Because these waters are rich the cold deeper layers lack dissolved oxygen during the summer, and fish are confined to the warm upper areas.

Other lakes are relatively shallow, from 35 to 40 feet. Dissolved oxygen in these is adequate at most depths because wind and wave action mixes the waters. Walleye, yellow perch, northern pike, and suckers are common inhabitants.

Comparatively small lakes with numerous bays and inlets, often are rich in organic matter and have large amounts of vegetation. The shores and bottoms are usually mud and sand. These lakes are usually over 20 feet deep and some exceed 100 feet in maximum depth. When they are deep enough, bottom stagnation with loss of bottom oxygen occurs. Common fish are largemouth bass, crappies, other sunfish, northern pike, suckers, perch, and walleye.

The typical prairie lakes are fertile, with mud bottoms and shores that are lined with cattail and other types of aquatic vegetation. Usually 6 to 20 feet deep, they contain bullheads, buffalofish, carp, and sometimes walleye, northern pike, crappies, and other sunfish. Winter fish kills are common in these shallow lakes because the dissolved oxygen in waters beneath the ice is used up by fish and decaying vegetation.

Warm farm ponds, usually ½ to 1 acre in size, are stocked with largemouth bass and bluegill, or channel catfish, while several kinds of trout are stocked in cold-water ponds.

Reservoirs formed by dams on streams and rivers over the past 40 years have created some of the largest lakes in the United States. Their fish populations are often quite different from those in the river before impoundment. Lake species common to the region become dominant and river species decrease in

Reefs attract great schools of fish.

Fishing off Alaska in waters that support many fish and a few people.

Stripers caught in eastern estuary through which they swim to spawning grounds.

27

Largemouth bass prefers quieter, warmer fresh waters.

numbers. Spawning conditions necessary for river fish, such as spring flooding of shore vegetation, usually do not occur in reservoirs.

Ecologists have divided the ocean into three general zones, each with its characteristic fish. The zones include the shore out to the edge of the Continental Shelf to a depth of 100 fathoms; the open sea beyond the Continental Shelf from the surface to a depth of 100 fathoms; and the deep sea or waters deeper than 100 fathoms.

The most characteristic fish of the open waters over the Continental Shelf are the herring, barracudas, sharks, mackerels, bluefish, needlefish, tarpon, tunas, marlin, sailfish, butterfish, kelp bass, groupers, snappers, grunts, porgies, and seatrout.

Bottom dwelling fish of the Continental Shelf are also numerous and include those that live near shore and are influenced by the tides and those that live in deeper waters. Among the better known are stingrays, several flounders, bonefish, eels, morays, croakers, kingfish, drums, hakes, and pollacks.

Coral reefs, found in warm seas, support some of the most colorful fish in the world, including the many species of butterflyfish. Other common inhabitants are surgeonfish, filefish, triggerfish, parrotfish, blennies, and certain sea basses like the grouper.

The open sea beyond the Continental Shelf has fewer fish than the inshore area. Seasonal variations in temperature, water chemistry, and other environmental factors are not as great. Light and temperature are important in determining distribution. Included in this zone are oceanward migrants from the inshore area, including mackerels, bonitos, albacores, tunas, dolphins, flyingfish, marlin, and sailfish.

Deep-sea waters have little seasonal variation in environment and fish numbers decrease with depth. Temperatures range from 35° to 50° F., light from dim to complete darkness, and pressures are very great. Some fish, such as the lanternfish, have light organs. Some are nearly or totally blind, an example being the Mexican cave characin.

Bottom fish found at depths between 100 and 500 fathoms include halibut, cod, chimaeras, and hagfish. Those found at greater depths include the grenadiers and brotulas. Little is known about those occurring in the deepest parts of the sea.

Estuaries mix freshwater from a river with saltwater from the ocean. Most are drowned river mouths, ranging in size from small ones that receive a single river to large ones that receive many rivers. An example of the latter is the Chesapeake Bay on the Atlantic coast—one of the largest in North America.

These waters are characterized by extreme fluctuations of salinity, currents, turbidity, and siltation. Shorelines are often sand, silt, and mud and they are often bordered by various types of aquatic vegetation. Many species of marine and freshwater fish are found in them.

Some use these waters primarily for feeding or nursery areas. Common species include many herrings, killifish, mullets, flounders, drums, silversides, and anchovies.

Estuaries are also travel routes for fish that live in the ocean but spawn in freshwater (anadromous) and for those that live in rivers but spawn in the sea (catadromous). Examples of anadromous types are sturgeon, shad, and salmon, while the American eel is a catadromous species.

Fish that pass regularly between salt- and fresh-water have to maintain a balance between the salts in their blood and body fluid and that of the surrounding water. A freshwater fish has a higher salt content in its body fluids than does the surrounding water, and since the water seeks constantly to dilute these salts by entering the body through its skin, gill membranes, mouth, and exposed body surfaces, the fish is under relentless pressure of water invasion. It must regularly excrete water to maintain proper salt balance.

Marine fish, however, have the opposite problem. They are constantly losing water to the saltier environment, and must take in water steadily to maintain body fluids. To cope with the salinity of the water they take in, they have cells in their gill filaments to excrete excess salts.

Most fish cannot survive movement between fresh- and salt-water because they are relatively intolerant to salinity change. Estuarine types tolerate these changes because their bodily functions compensate for salinity changes that occur.

The salt content of some lakes and ponds is so high that fish cannot live in them. These waters, often called alkali lakes, are found in the Great Plains and

29

the desert Southwest. No fish can live in Utah's Great Salt Lake where the salinity is seven times that of the oceans.

Fish need more than water to live. Each species is able to tolerate only a limited range of environmental conditions and this range commonly varies with the season, age, and activities of the individual. They often require a different habitat for eggs or young than for the adult, for resting than for feeding, for spawning than for day-to-day existence. Environmental factors that influence them are available food, temperature, dissolved oxygen, depth, salinity, turbidity, direction and strength of currents, bottom type, and shelter.

Exactly where fish live in water is influenced by what they eat. Some feed exclusively on plants, others on animals, and others on plants and animals. There are bottom feeders or ground fish like the flounder and open-water or pelagic feeders like the herring. Some like the bluefin and yellowfin tuna and the Pacific salmon travel great distances on feeding migrations.

Fish are cold-blooded and adjust their body temperature to that of the surrounding water. Many are tolerant of a limited range of water temperature, and temperatures outside this range are lethal. They are not only temperature sensitive, but they also seek waters in which temperatures are near their preferred range.

Knowledge of temperature preference by species has been used by fish management biologists to assist fishermen in locating fish to increase catch.

The effect of temperature is illustrated by distribution of fish on the Atlantic coast. Some are found only in the cold waters of the North Atlantic, others are found only in the warm waters of the South Atlantic, while still others are found in the intermediate waters between Cape Cod, Mass., and Cape Hatteras, N.C. Seasonal movement between these zones is also related to temperature preference.

Biologists agree that water should contain at least five parts per million of dissolved oxygen for normal activity of most fish. They remove oxygen from the water through their gills. In unpolluted water the supply is normally adequate, but it may be deficient or even lacking near the bottom of lakes and ponds because of natural decay of animal and plant matter. Polluted sections of lakes, rivers, and estuaries are often devoid of adequate dissolved oxygen, resulting in the elimination of many fish.

Decrease in numbers of walleye and other desirable fish in Lake Erie since the 1950's, for example, resulted from pollution.

Temperature and dissolved oxygen affect the seasonal depth distribution of fish. The waters of most lakes in the Temperate Zone deeper than 60 feet develop into three different temperature zones during the summer. The top layer, termed the epilimnion, has a water temperature range from 70° to 80° F. or more at the surface. The bottom layer, termed the hypolimnion, has water temperatures in the range from 39° to 55° F. The middle layer, termed the thermocline, has intermediate temperatures.

Dissolved oxygen disappears from the hypolimnion in many lakes during the summer months. This occurs because bottom deposits and suspended materials in the lake contain organic substances which undergo decomposition. This decomposition consumes dissolved oxygen, and if the volume of the hypolimnion in relation to the amount of organic decay is small, the oxygen eventually disappears.

One of several million ponds built since the thirties and stocked with game fish.

Lakes of this type, no matter how deep, can only support warm-water fish, which are necessarily confined to the warm, well-oxygenated epilimnion.

Deep lakes can support cold- and warm-water fish when the hypolimnion remains oxygenated during the entire summer. Cold-water types, like the trout, char, lake whitefish, and lake herring, remain in or beneath the thermocline, while warm-water kinds, like the large-mouth bass, crappies, and other sunfish, are restricted to the shallow upper layer.

Fish need protection from their enemies to survive in any water, as they are prey at some time during their lives not only to other species but often to their own kind. To avoid predation, many have developed a protective coloration pattern which tends to make them inconspicuous in their natural suroundings.

Free-swimming, open-water types possess simple coloration grading from whitish belly, through silvery lower sides, to upper sides and back that are irides-cent blue or green. Bottom dwellers and weed bed occupants are often strongly and intricately marked above and pale beneath. Color in oceanic kinds correspond to depth of habitat, as those inhabiting the upper zone are silver, while those in the middle zone are red, and those in the depths are violet or black.

Protective cover is also used to avoid enemies. Fish are often found near overhanging banks, brush, logs, weed beds, rocks, and coral reefs. The habit of some species to concentrate near protected places has been used by managers to concentrate fish for angling purposes. Brush shelters have been used under floating fish docks in southern reservoirs to increase crappie harvest. Artificial reefs are used in coastal waters to concentrate marine fish.

We have thus seen that there can be water without fish, but no fish without water. Conditions present in the water determine what kinds and how many fish are supported.

31

Food for Fish

by William M. Lewis

Like most animals, fish don't have such a highly developed taste for food as humans, but the water denizens do have definite preferences. Some feed exclusively on minute plants and animals known as plankton, while others thrive on animals living on and in the mud of the bottom—the so-called benthos. The predators—the nektonic feeders—take free-swimming forms, particularly other fish. Many accept food from a terrestrial source, such as insects that fall or are washed into the water. Aquatic vegetation serves as food for a few.

BLUEFISH AND ALEWIVES

PLANT PLANKTON consists primarily of single-celled algae which may be so numerous that they impart a brown or green color to the water, referred to as algal bloom. Algal blooms are frequently cyclic, with a period of abundance following a period of scarcity, and different species of algae may be prevalent during different seasons of the year. The algae require phosphorus, nitrogen, potassium, and other plant nutrients. This has given rise to the practice of fertilizing to increase the production of algae with the hope of increasing the food supply of fish.

While most fish don't use it directly as food, dead or live algae serve as food for other organisms which are then taken by fish. For example, many copepods ingest large amounts of algae and then are in turn eaten by many fish.

But while fertility of water and an associated abundance of algal growth contributes to an increase in fish food, an over-abundance may also worsen the environment. The decay of algae uses up large amounts of oxygen in the water, leaving less for the fish, so fertility is good only to a certain point.

Animal plankton of the freshwater environment is made up primarily of tiny crustaceans including *Daphnia* and related forms. In marine waters radiolarians, copepods, and krills are major contributors. The occurrence and abundance of these animals are associated with plant plankton, and they, too, have periods of great abundance and periods of scarcity. Within a given body of water they are concentrated in areas rich in plant plankton and organic matter upon which they feed.

In the oceans the density of plankton is greatest along the coastline of the continents and in areas where there are up-wellings that bring phosphorus and other nutrients to the surface. Naturally, areas supporting a rich plankton growth are major feeding grounds for fish.

The plankton feeders are adapted to their type of food by the presence of long gill rakers (fingerlike projections from the gill bars) which form a strainer by means of which they filter the tiny organisms from the water. These fish are not aggressive and often travel in large schools, feeding much of the time, and locating their food by sight.

Some of our most important commercial fish are plankton feeders, such as herring and whitefish. Tremendous numbers of herring, sardines, and menhaden are harvested for use as human food or as a source of protein meals for animals and oils for industry. This plentiful, rapidly reproducing food supply also supports dense populations of fish.

The young of many fish use plankton as food. One of the principal problems in the production of fingerlings of largemouth bass, pike, and walleye is maintaining an adequate supply of animal plankton.

Included in the benthos are a number of worms related to the earthworms; immature stages of insects such as the midges, dragonflies, stoneflies, and mayflies; and a number of the mollusks, including snails, clams, and their relatives. A square yard of the bottom of the ocean, a stream bottom, or the mud of a pond may contain hundreds, even thousands of these food organisms. The species of animals making up this community varies considerably from the marine to freshwater environment, from streams to lakes, and from infertile lakes to fertile ones.

In freshwater the abundance of bottom food is closely related to the amount of organic matter in the bottom material. In the oceans the benthos is concentrated along the Continental Shelves and other shallow water areas such as the North Sea. These latter areas, of course, support dense populations of bottom-feeding fish.

Members of the sunfish family of North America subsist primarily on benthic animals, and the benthos is also a significant item in the diet of trout. In streams, organisms are continually being dislodged from the bottom and form an abundant food supply referred to as "drift" organisms. Midges, mayflies, and other insects are benthic organisms when immature but rise to the surface and transform into adults before reproducing. At the time they are undergoing this transformation they are eaten in great numbers by fish.

Many benthic feeders have shorter, heavier gill rakers and locate their food by touch and taste. The mouths of some are directed downward, and some, like the freshwater drum, are capable of crushing the shells of mollusks on which they feed. A few have snouts that enable them to search for benthic organisms deep in the mud.

Both young and adult fish, crustaceans, aquatic insects, and free-swimming mollusks such as squid comprise the nekton food supply. These animals feed on the plankton and benthos, and they in turn are taken by the predacious fish. This dynamic relationship of one food supply using another is referred to as the "food chain."

The part which young fish play in the food chain of larger ones is particularly interesting. The young are produced in great excess, subsist on the abundant plankton food supply, and are subsequently taken by larger fish. This sequence is actually an adaptation where-

Copepod magnified many times—a plankton at the bottom of food chain.

by the large fish are able to use indirectly a part of the abundant plankton food supply.

Predatory fish or nekton feeders are aggressive, have large mouths, and large, well-developed stomachs. They can detect movement in the water by a sensory system on the side of the body, as well as by sight. They may lie in wait for their prey or actively pursue it. The bluefish, vicious predators, follow schools of smaller fish, dart into the schools, and kill and maim a large number of their prey while feeding.

In the inland waters of North America, the better known predators are the pikes, large- and small-mouth bass, and walleye, while in the marine habitat the barracudas, tunas, bluefish, and sharks are notable examples. By virtue of their feeding behavior, the nekton feeders are some of our most important game fish. As a group they are sight feeders and will most readily strike artificial lures.

Nekton feeders, like most other fish, select food items that they can swallow whole. There are, of course, exceptions. The piranha and many sharks are capa-

Minnows and other freshwater forage fish.

School of bait fish being attacked by marine predators.

This walleye didn't finish one meal before going after another.

ble of biting off pieces of large prey animals. However, the fact that most predators are restricted to a certain size prey places a limit on the food available to them. Thus all forage fish in the habitat are not suitable food items. Since many prey animals, including small fish, are not easily caught, the predators usually spend much of their time hunting. The meals they get are frequently large ones but must last 1 or 2 days until they are again successful.

The behavior and adaptation of the forage organisms play a significant part in controlling their use of the nekton feeders. The predators seek to capture the prey, but the prey is adapted to escape capture. In older reservoirs the adjustment between the largemouth bass and the prey species is such that the food intake of bass is often at a low level. In new reservoirs easily caught prey species, such as crayfish, frog tadpoles, young bullheads, and green sunfish, occur in abundance; thus bass maintain a high level of food intake and grow rapidly.

The more important terrestrial food available to fish is animal life that falls or is blown or washed into the water. Insects and a multitude of other invertebrates are important constituents of this food supply. The significance of this source of food is greatest in small streams and ponds.

Notable among the fish feeding on terrestrial insects are some of the minnows that have a set of sharp, bony structures (pharyngeal teeth) on the last gill arch. These structures function in shredding the food, thus making it more digestible.

Besides the minnows, trout in small streams and sunfish of both streams and lakes include a high percent of terrestrial insects in their diet. During rains great quantities of invertebrate life are washed into lakes and streams and are readily consumed by many fish present. It is not unusual following a rain to find a stomach of a fish filled with terrestrial forms. The poor fishing that follows rain is probably related to this occurrence.

Few fish take vegetation as food, but important exceptions are the tilapia of Asia and Africa and the grass carp of Asia. Vegetation is, of course, a less expensive food than animal life, and thus there is considerable interest in the possibility of rearing herbivorous fish for human food. Tilapia and grass carp have received considerable study for use as food in tropical areas. Aquatic weeds are often a nuisance, and the use of herbivorous fish for their control is an attractive possibility.

Herbivores have teeth suited for biting off bits of plants or for scraping plant growth from the surface of rocks or hard substrata. They have long intestines and digestive enzymes differing from those that feed on animal life.

Some fish may go for several days without food, particularly the predators having difficulty catching a prey, but usually they feed a great deal of the time, consuming large amounts of food. For example, an adult largemouth bass feeding on fish will eat the equivalent of 4 to 5 percent of its body weight each day. A young northern pike will eat several times this amount. And fish feeding on less nutritious food will consume even more. Predacious types generally require several pounds of fish flesh to produce a one pound gain in weight, while plant feeders require 30 to 40

Bluegill serves as forage for larger predators and as a joy for anglers.

pounds of vegetation to produce a single pound gain.

Temperature is of great significance. Warm-water fish feed mostly when the temperature is above 55° F., and thus they have a growing season which affects their annual production. A number of marine fish extend their feeding season by north and south migrations.

The abundance of food also plays a part. Thus where predators are concerned, forage organisms are scarce early in the spring season, then become very abundant, and again scarce late in the season. This affects fishing success, especially in inland waters.

Even though a fish may use more than one of the food sources, it is usually adapted to only one. But feeding habits change with age. Thus a fish may eat plankton while a fingerling, benthic forms as a young adult, and primarily fish in later life. There may also be seasonal changes. Cod feed on herring in the spring but change to benthic organisms in the summer.

Some will accept artificial feeds similar to those used for poultry and swine. Humans take advantage of this by selecting desirable species with this characteristic, notably rainbow trout and channel catfish, and grow them under controlled conditions. Thus channel catfish, which might be expected to occur at densities of one or two hundred pounds per acre when dependent upon natural food, can be produced at up to 2,000 pounds per acre with artificial food.

Fish have specific dietary needs, of course. Thus it is necessary to recognize the required amino acids, carbohydrates, fats, minerals, and vitamins. With the developing interest in fish farming, the manufacture of fish foods is becoming a significant industry, and highly satisfactory foods are being produced.

But as we have seen, most fish fend for themselves, developing natural preferences among the various food sources. Given proper management and use, our waters can be expected to support considerable populations of fish, including game types. Knowing the food preference of the game type you are after will help you catch it.

Migrations

by Clarence P. Idyll

Fish are famous for their wanderings. Of all the animals in the world, perhaps the birds exceed them in the complexity and length of their migrations—but as our knowledge increases, it appears that even the birds do not out-perform them in this respect. There are few phenomena in nature more spectacular than the migrations of salmon up a spawning stream or of eels from European rivers to the Sargasso Sea and back. And we are learning that other fish exhibit migrations which are little, if any, less extraordinary in character.

ATLANTIC SALMON

NEARLY ALL FISH are restless, moving about to some degree in pursuit of their food and satisfying other biological needs. But not all of them exhibit true migrations, and it appears that many—perhaps most—stay relatively close to home throughout their lives.

The term "migration" is usually reserved for regularly patterned movements of fish from one aquatic environment to another. These movements are commonly on an annual basis and are often associated with reproduction. Unpatterned movements in response to changes in the temperature or other water conditions, on an irregular basis and over relatively short distances, are normally not called migrations.

In Florida, for example, we found after extensive tagging experiments that most striped mullet undertake only small coastwise movements: over 90 percent moved less than 20 miles and most less than 5 miles from where they were tagged. Several other Florida species showed the same pattern. For example, gray snapper, sheepshead, and spotted seatrout were usually recaptured within a few miles of release points, even after considerable periods of freedom.

Reef fish also tend to stay close to home. Tagging experiments by Dr. John Randall in the Virgin Islands and by Dr. John Bardach in Bermuda showed that groupers, snappers, and others exhibited little movement. Some individuals were caught repeatedly in the same traps, even weeks or months after tagging.

But some species make migrations of hundreds or even thousands of miles, sometimes more than once during their lifetime. Long migrations require considerable time and expenditure of energy and they must, therefore, be of survival value to the fish. This is usually in terms of temporary residence in an area where conditions are better for reproduction and survival of the young, followed by residence in another area—perhaps far removed—where food suitable for older stages is more abundant.

Migrations may be horizontal, with members moving across a body of water, or vertical. Horizontal migrations are usually seasonal; vertical movements are commonly diurnal, the fish occupying deep layers of the ocean in the daytime and surface layers at night.

Among those exhibiting vertical movements are several kinds of small deep-sea dwellers, including lantern and viperfish. They spend much of their time every day moving to the surface and back from 1,000 feet or more. In this they may be subjected to significant changes in environment—pressure differences of 40 to 50 atmospheres and temperature changes of 20° to 30° F., the latter being equivalent to a surface journey from the coast of Iceland to the Equator.

In general, freshwater species tend to run upstream in their spawning migrations. Anadromous fish spend part of their lives in the sea but ascend into rivers and lakes as reproduction approaches. The most famous of the anadromous types are the salmon and trout; smelt and shad are others. Fewer species are catadromous, meaning that they exhibit the opposite spawning migration pattern in which the adult moves from freshwater into the sea to spawn. The eels are the most famous of these.

A remarkable aspect of spawning migration is the tendency of some species to return to the area where they themselves spawned. Both freshwater and marine dwellers exhibit homing. In experiments to test this instinct in cut-

44

throat of Yellowstone Lake, members were taken from streams which they had entered to spawn and then were displaced some distance down the lake and tagged. A high proportion returned to their original spawning streams.

A number of these fish had attached to them a polystryrene float, so that their movements could be observed directly by the motion of the float on the surface.

This showed that not only did the fish return eventually to their home streams, but they usually moved quickly in the correct direction.

Salmon exhibit the homing tendency to a marked degree; some 95 to 98 percent of sockeye salmon, for example, return to their parent streams. Many marine types, including cod and herring, appear to return approximately to the

Charterboat in a school of migrating fish near the surface.

same area of the ocean where they spawned, although this tendency is not known to be as precise as it is in some of the anadromous species.

Frequently, exceedingly large numbers of fish take part in migrations. Dr. Allan Hartt of the University of Washington estimates that in some years a minimum of half a million young sockeye salmon pass south of Adak Island in Alaska every day from late June through late August. In big years as many as 60 million adult sockeye salmon swarm back towards the Bristol Bay spawning areas. Immense numbers of herring and other oceanic species take part in migrations.

Some species migrate astonishing distances. A half century ago, some biologists doubted that salmon exhibited a true homing instinct, but instead that they returned to their home streams after short excursions into the ocean adjacent to the estuary. Now it is known that some salmon travel very great distances.

Chinook salmon move from the Columbia River to the Aleutian Islands, a minimum one-way distance of 2,000 to 2,800 miles. Pink salmon from southeastern Alaskan streams travel in enormous counterclockwise loops which sometimes take them far west near the Asian shore and south into the open Pacific.

Some pinks cover distances of 3,000 to 4,000 miles in 12 to 14 months of life. Sockeye salmon may make vast loops of the northern Pacific Ocean 2 or even 3 years in a row.

Certain sharks have exhibited migrations notable both in distance covered and in time at large. A Greenland shark moved 700 miles along the coast of Greenland in 8 years of freedom. Another individual was caught 152 miles from its tagging location after 16 years.

A dogfish marked near St. John's, Newfoundland, moved 900 miles south in 132 days; another tagged in the same place migrated 1,300 miles to Cape Henry, Va.

Dogfish in the Pacific also show remarkable migrations. One tagged off Ucluelet, British Columbia, went 700 miles to south of San Francisco Bay; another tagged off Willapa Harbor, Wash., was recaptured by a Japanese fisherman over 7 years later at the north end of Honshu Island, Japan—a minimum distance of 4,700 miles. A third was at large 10 years, but was recovered 8 miles from where it was tagged. It can only be guessed what travels it may have taken in the meantime!

Three Pacific sablefish tagged at Holmes Harbor, Puget Sound, were recovered between 6 and 7 years later by Japanese fishermen in the Bering Sea. They had moved 2,100 miles by great circle route, or a minimum of 2,700 miles if they moved along the coast, as is more likely.

Even when they have reached the mouth of their home streams, many fish still have a long distance to go. Chinook salmon are known to ascend the Yukon River through Alaska and into the Teslin River in British Columbia, a distance of well over 2,000 miles. An Asiatic relative of the herring runs up the Yangtse River 1,000 miles or more.

Eels carry out migrations opposite in direction to those of salmon. The adults spend most of their lives in freshwater and move back to the sea for reproduction. Virtually nothing is known about how this is accomplished—the route, the cues, the time required—since most adult eels leaving the streams are never seen again. We know, however, that they

Cohos leaping toward their destiny.

spawn eventually at considerable depths—350 feet or more—in the Sargasso Sea, an immense eddy in the western Atlantic. They may swim 2,000 to 3,500 miles during the journey.

This information was gained indirectly, through the capture of eels at young stages. The center of spawning is assumed to be where the larvae are smallest, and this was discovered by a Danish biologist, Johannes Schmidt, who gained permanent fame for the research that led to the solving of this age-old mystery.

Many questions of how the problems faced by the adults in finding their way to the Sargasso Sea and by the larvae in getting back to freshwater streams in Europe and America are still unanswered. The adults probably do not swim straight for the Sargasso Sea, but follow

the great arc of the Atlantic current system south, then west, and finally north. They have never taken this route before and the migration mechanism is unknown.

The movements of the young are hardly less amazing. Young eels destined for Europe appear to be carried north and east by the Gulf Stream, requiring 3 years to make the journey. During that time they transform from strange, leaf-like "leptocephalus" larvae to nearly transparent "glass eels."

But American eels, going much shorter distances, require only 1 year to get home. Remarkably, their transformation to glass eels takes place in 1 year instead of 3, and this is neatly timed to coincide with their delivery to the mouth of their own river.

Tagging a billfish to learn more about its migration route.

Some species of tuna exhibit long migrations. In the Pacific a bluefin tagged in 1965 off the coast of Japan was recaptured 10 months later off Baja California, Mexico, having traveled a minimum distance of 5,000 miles. In 1958 one tagged off Guadalupe Island, Mexico, was picked up more than 5 years later, 300 miles south of Tokyo. It had traveled a minimum of 5,800 miles, but it probably went a far greater distance.

Bluefin in the Atlantic exhibit spectacular cross-ocean migrations. Individuals tagged in the Florida Straits by Frank Mather of Woods Hole have been recovered in Norway 50 days later, a minimum of 4,200 nautical miles away. Two more tagged off Maryland were recovered off the Spanish coast.

The albacore also make transoceanic migrations. Some individuals move from the North American West coast to the central western Pacific, where Japanese fishermen catch them; some go farther westward to Japanese coastal waters, and some return to the American fishery the following summer. There is thus a regular loop pattern of movement from the North American to the Asian shore and back again over thousands of miles of water.

Migrations of white marlin also form an elliptical pattern. Tagging by Frank Mather in the western Atlantic shows that in summer they move north along the coast of North America as far as Cape Cod. The fish then turn offshore to the southeastern part of George's Bank and move south in offshore waters, swinging west again toward the Caribbean Islands or moving all the way to the north coast of South America before completing a great ellipse.

Much of the information about these spectacular oceanic migrations has come to light in very recent years, and it is entirely possible that as more tagging is done it will be revealed that many more species exhibit considerable oceanic migrations.

The mechanisms by which fish perform such extensive and complicated migrations are not clear, but they must be highly sophisticated. For many species, including the eel and the salmon, the adult makes its homing run only once in its lifetime and the young go off in the opposite direction. Hence no familiar landmarks are available to serve as guides.

Evidence is accumulating that in some species a remarkably acute odor sense serves to guide them back to their place of origin in the freshwater phase of migration. In other cases it has been established that fish can maintain a constant compass direction by dead reckoning, or more remarkably, that some navigate in the true sense, involving corrections of their course.

Some exhibit a fantastically high ability to smell odors in the water in extreme dilutions, perhaps as low as one part per billion. More than this, some can distinguish between two different, very dilute odors. This latter skill has been demonstrated for some freshwater species by Dr. Arthur Hasler and his associates at the University of Wisconsin.

Blunt nose minnows, for example, learned to distinguish between water from two closely located streams flowing into Lake Mendota, Wis. After a month of training, the minnows were able to recognize water from either Otter Creek or Honey Creek whose underlying rocks, soils, and plant associations were different. With one group of fish a reward (food) was offered when Otter Creek water was introduced into the aquarium and a mild punishment (a weak electric current) was administered when Honey Creek water was used. With another group of fish the reward and the punishment were offered with the opposite kind of water.

The minnows quickly learned when food was to be forthcoming or when to expect punishment—which means that they had learned to discriminate between the two kinds of water. Later, when the "reinforcement" in the form of food and current was omitted, the fish still showed the correct reaction to the particular water offered.

It seems likely that recognition of home water by its characteristic odor is one means by which salmon make their remarkable migrations upstream from the sea. The problem that the salmon faces after it arrives in the estuary is a formidable one. To reach its home tributary it may first have to breast mile on mile of murky tidal estuary where the waters are alternately salt then fresh. It may be unable to see more than a few feet in the muddy water, but it must nonetheless swim unerringly upstream, passing tributaries where it is faced with a series of choices. It makes the proper choice in nearly every case, even though it may be presented with scores of these before finally reaching its own spawning area, perhaps months after it has entered the estuary hundreds of miles away.

Evidence that salmon are using their olfactory senses in making this remarkable journey is supplied by work of Warren Wisby and Arthur Hasler in a stream near Seattle, Wash. Here coho salmon which had entered branches of Issaquah Creek were taken downstream again. The fish were released to repeat their migration, some without treatment and others with their nostrils plugged with cotton soaked in petroleum jelly. The normal fish chose the correct fork in nearly every case, while those whose olfactory sense had been blocked made many errors.

This theory of migrations proposes that the fish becomes "imprinted" with the unique odor of its natal stream and that it remembers this odor when it returns, sometimes after several years and thousands of miles of ocean migration. Since only the faintest possible traces of this particular water will persist in the lower reaches of the stream, which has been swelled by the addition of hundreds of other tributaries, the salmon must have a fantastically keen sense of smell.

But even this amazing sense cannot serve it in the ocean, a thousand miles or more beyond the mouth of its natal stream, and some other mechanism must serve here. One theory is that sun navigation is carried out by fish. It has been known for several years that the birds are able to guide their sometimes enormously long migrations navigating by sun and stars, and it now appears that some fish may be able to do this as well.

Laboratory experiments by Dr. Hasler and his associates showed convincingly that fish can use the sun's position to determine direction. A pumpkinseed sunfish was trained to choose a certain compartment on the south side of a circular tank. When the pumpkinseed nibbled at the correct disc on this compartment it received a reward of food. The only clue the fish had was the position of the sun. Eventually the fish made the right choice each time.

These experiments during the training period were conducted every day between 9 and 10 a.m. After the fish had shown that it knew it must nibble the south disc to get its reward, trials were run between 3 and 4 p.m. This is the time of day when the sun has moved across the sky far enough to make the azimuthal angle 90 degrees different from what it was in the morning. If the fish were setting its course to the rewarding south disc by the sun's azimuth, without compensating for the difference in this angle caused by movement of the sun, it should now nibble at the west disc instead of the south. But if it were compensating for this difference, employing some biological clock to tell it how much alteration to make, it should still choose the south disc. And it did.

But this mechanism may not work in the sea, at least not for all fish. There are considerable difficulties, for example, in explaining Pacific salmon migrations by sun navigation. This mechanism breaks down when the sun is hidden, and salmon must often have difficulty in seeing the sun, since the northern Pacific clouds and haze obscure it a great deal of the time, during the period when migration is underway. This is a stormy stretch of the ocean and the water is whipped into ripples and waves so that the sun must be hard to see, even when it does shine. Further, salmon migrate at night as well as in the daytime.

William Royce, Linwood Smith, and Allan Hartt of the University of Washington believe that the salmon may make use of electromagnetic currents. Seawater is an electrical conductor, and water currents generate small but meas-

Successful anglers—because they knew time and place of migrating blues along east coast.

urable electrical currents as they move through the earth's magnetic field. These electromagnetic currents are patterned enough that they may serve as a guiding network for the fish, if it can detect them. This has not been established positively for salmon, but certain kinds of eels have this ability, and other species may possess it too.

The more we learn about fish migrations, the more marvelous they seem, not only in terms of the distances involved and the precision with which the migrations are performed, but in the navigational skills exhibited. While evidence seems strong that freshwater fish navigate by odor discrimination and perhaps by sun navigation, we are still groping for a complete understanding of oceanic movements. It is probable that they do not use any single mechanism to bring them back to their native streams, but that they are using all their senses for this complex skill.

One Generation After Another

by C. Lavett Smith

*If we think of life as a fleeting, temporary condition,
we are thinking of individuals, the single units of existence who must
sooner or later pay back the materials they borrow to build their bodies.
In a broader view, however, we know that life is one of the more
permanent things on this planet. We can trace some groups of organisms
back over 500 million years, during which time much of the world's
surface has been torn down and rebuilt several times. Living organisms
owe their permanence to periodic replacement of old and worn-out bodies
through the wonderful process of reproduction
of one generation after another.*

SMALLMOUTH BASS AND ROCK BASS

REPRODUCTION also reshuffles the hereditary materials. Each individual receives half of its genes from its father and half from its mother. New combinations result in offspring that are not quite like either parent, and if the combination is a lucky one, the new being will have a better chance of surviving to produce the next generation than its less fortunate rivals. The very fact that hundreds of thousands of combinations are possible prepares the species for changes in its environment by assuring that there will more likely be members who can cope with the new conditions and survive to continue the line.

Fish reproduction is critically important to the fisherman—to say nothing of the fish—for it is the only way of creating more fish. Fish die from many causes, including injuries, disease, being eaten by predators such as bears and Cub Scouts, starvation, and just plain old age, but the only way their numbers can increase is simply through sex. Although much of the work of fish management is aimed at making reproduction easier, it is still up to the fish themselves, and it seems unlikely that it will ever be otherwise.

All fish reproduce sexually. In most species there are males and females, but quite a number of different kinds of fish are normal hermaphrodites in which each individual has both male and female reproductive organs. Some of the small sea bass produce eggs and sperm at the same time, but others—for example, the groupers and certain porgies—function first as one sex and then transform into the other sex. These normal hermaphrodites are not to be confused with the occasional abnormal hermaphrodites that can appear in almost any species of vertebrate.

Another unusual case is the Amazon molly, a small live-bearing fish that exists only as a female. This female must be inseminated in order to reproduce, but apparently the sperm of another fish activates the egg and stimulates it to develop while not contributing any hereditary material to the new generation. Males of any one of several related species can serve as mates. These unusual cases illustrate the tremendous variety of reproductive specializations that occur among the 20,000 or more species of living fish.

Fish produce their eggs in ovaries, which are usually located in the back part of the body cavity just below the swim bladder. The ovaries are hollow sacs in most fish, and the right and left ovaries join to form a common tube through which the eggs pass to the outside. Often the tube is only open during the breeding season and sealed at other times. Primitive types such as the trout have ovaries that are only partly covered by membrane, and their eggs are released into the body cavity, then swept into funnel-shaped oviducts. Some fish have only a single ovary.

Eggs vary in size from less than one twenty-fifth of an inch to more than a half-inch in diameter. Fish such as the cod that produce small eggs may lay 2 or 3 million eggs in a single season; others lay less than a dozen. Brook trout lay 200 to 3,000 eggs, depending on the size of the female; bluegills produce between 12,000 and 25,000 eggs per female.

Fish eggs are said to be pelagic if they float, or demersal if they sink. Eggs may be laid singly, in long strands, or in masses. Some eggs are sticky, so that they adhere to the bottom or to each other; others are nonadhesive. In shape, fish eggs are usually more or less spherical,

Fish low in the food chain overcome predation by being highly prolific.

but they may also be dumbbell-shaped or formed like tiny footballs. The eggs of flyingfish and their relatives are provided with many adhesive threads, and those of the beaugregory and sergeant major are attached to the bottom by a stalk.

Live-bearing fish have naked eggs that lack the covering membrane present on most, while the eggs of sharks and rays are enclosed in horny capsules. To top it all off, fish eggs vary in color from completely transparent to completely pigmented. The next time someone asks you to describe fish eggs, change the subject.

The male sex organs—the testes—are usually paired solid structures lying along the lower part of the swim bladder. In immature males they are pale and straplike, but in sexually active fish they will be swollen and white in color. Ripe males can also be recognized by the freely flowing milt and the uniform texture of the testes, whereas ripe ovaries are yellow or orange and granular in appearance. It is often difficult or impossible to determine the sex of immature fish even by microscopic examination.

Most fish have external fertilization—that is, the eggs and sperm come together after the eggs have left the body of the female. Fish that bear their young alive, however, must have some provision for introducing the sperm into the body of the female. Species like the guppy and the gambusia accomplish this by means of a complicated modification of the front rays of the anal fin. This structure, called a gonopodium, is sometimes almost as long as the body of the male. It is provided with hooks and flaps and a set of muscles for directing it into the genital tract of the female. Certain other groups of fish have evolved a fleshy penis, while sharks and rays use a specialized lobe of the pelvic fins as a sperm transfer device.

Secondary sex characters, such as bright coloration, elongate fin rays, body proportions, and even general color patterns, are features that are not part of the reproductive system but are peculiar to only one sex. Usually they appear only in the adult males; the females and juvenile males have the neutral condition. Not all fish show secondary sex characters; in fact, their presence is the exception rather than the rule, and in many species it is imposible to distinguish the sexes on the basis of external characteristics.

Sometimes these sex differences appear only during the breeding season, but often they persist after sexual maturity. A striking example of a transitory secondary sex character is the array of breeding tubercles that develop on the head, body, and fins of most minnows during the breeding season. These horny skin structures are used in defense of breeding territories and may serve to hold the females during the spawning act. After spawning these tubercles,

Bluegill males guarding their nests.

called pearl organs, slough off only to develop again the next year.

Sometimes sexual differences are so great that males and females have been thought to represent different species. In the late 1950's the number of species of parrotfish in the western Atlantic Ocean was suddenly reduced by almost half when it was discovered that the brightly colored forms are males and drab individuals are females.

Most species spawn once a year, usually when the water temperature is rising and the day length is increasing. A few fish have intermittent spawning periods often correlated with a particular phase of the moon or tide level. Some are sexually active throughout the year. As we have come to expect, with fish there are numerous qualifications and exceptions to these general patterns, and

56

Female rainbow trout deposits her eggs in nest.

it is likely that if we knew all about the spawning of every living fish species we would find a complete spectrum of spawning habits.

As the breeding season approaches, reproductive organs begin to function and secondary sex characters, if any, begin to intensify. Males develop their distinctive colors and start to move into the breeding areas. Sometimes this means shifting a few feet into shallow water as in the case of certain bass of the North American Continent; sometimes it means long migrations up the streams to traditional breeding grounds.

Nearly everyone is familiar with the spectacular migrations of the Pacific salmon that travel hundreds, even thousands, of miles to spawn up rivers, but this is just the extreme of the general phenomenon of moving onto the breeding grounds. Sturgeons, lampreys, ale-

wives, and shad also have pronounced spawning runs from the sea into freshwater; trout and suckers move into streams from lakes; and American eels migrate out to sea for their breeding activities.

It is in the nesting and courtship practices that fish display their greatest sexual virtuosity. Courtship ranges from simple pairing to elaborate displays by both partners, all serving to insure that eggs and sperm are released at the same time, to assure fertilization. Even among species that spawn in large aggregations, pairing is the rule within the schools.

This pairing does not imply any particular marital fidelity; fish change partners with a frequency that a Hollywood starlet might envy. But there is pairing.

Sometimes, as in the case of suckers, mating is polyandrous—that is, several males spawn with a single female at one time. Interestingly enough, even certain hermaphrodites that produce eggs and sperm simultaneously undergo courtship and pairing with one partner assuming female behavior and the other male.

Nest building among stream-dwelling fish can take many forms, but the brook trout will serve as an example of one type. They are fall spawners, as are most other trout except the rainbow, and it is the female who prepares the redd (nest) while the male stands by. This redd is a shallow depression in a gravel bottom, scooped out by the sweeping action of the fish's body and tail.

Then a courtship ritual takes place during which the male pushes the female into the depression and touches her with his body and fins. The pair then clasp, and the eggs and sperm are released. Immediately after this, the female

begins to cover the nest. The male soon leaves, but the female remains on the nest for several hours.

Some minnows build elaborate nests consisting of piles of gravel, sometimes a yard wide by several feet long and a foot high. These are used by several other species in addition to the original builder, which is one of the reasons that we sometimes encounter natural hybrids. When several species are spawning simultaneously, occasional interbreeding or miscegenation is almost inevitable.

Many North American sunfish spawn in shallow, quiet, or slow moving waters, and nearly all of them build similar nests. But here it is the male who builds the nest by fanning out a depression with a diameter approximately twice his length. When it is ready, he entices a female

Rainbow trout eggs about to hatch.

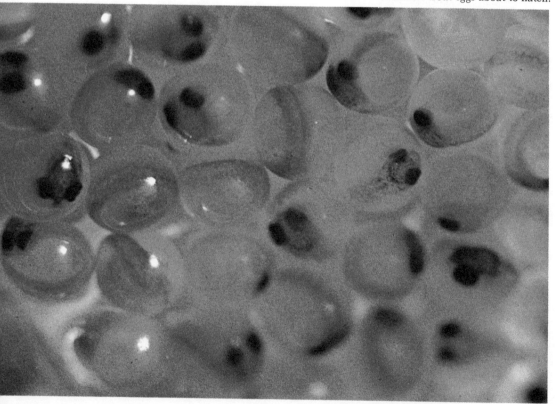

Fertilized eggs of lake trout.

Newly hatched sac fry of lake trout.

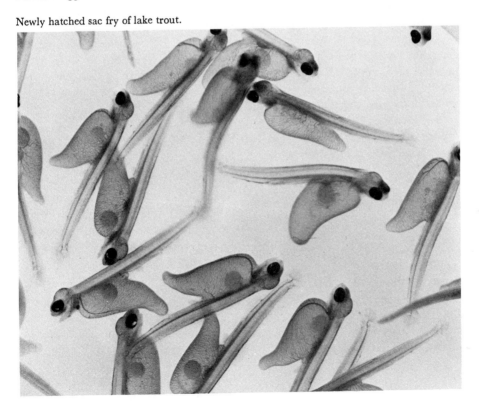

into the nest, and they spawn by lying parallel to each other and bringing their undersides together. Males may spawn with more than one female, and each female may contribute to more than one nest. After spawning, the male stands guard over the nest until the eggs hatch, and depending on the species, he may herd the young for a time after hatching.

The little North American freshwater sticklebacks build more complicated nests of bits of vegetation cemented together with a secretion from their kidneys. These nests are barrel-shaped, and when completed, the male entices a female into it by a series of courtship dances to which the female gives proper responses. This group of fish is a favorite subject for students of animal behavior.

There are many other kinds of nests, including the floating bubbles produced by some South American armored catfish and the labyrinth fish—the latter popular in aquariums. The male rises to the surface and takes in a mouthful of air, then expels mucous covered bubbles which clump together. After elaborate courtship the male picks up the eggs and puts them into the nest. The male is then stuck with the task of guarding the nest and later the young against hungry raiders (including the female).

Some fish have solved the problems of protecting their eggs against predators, insuring that they have sufficient aeration, and keeping them out of the silt at the same time by carrying their eggs around with them. One Indo-Malaysian species carries the eggs attached to a hook on top of the male's head, while seahorses and pipefish have a special brood pouch on the abdomen or the underside of the tail where eggs are kept until they hatch. Here again it is the male that carries the eggs and partakes of the joys of pregnancy.

Oral incubation—retaining the eggs in the mouth until they hatch—occurs in several unrelated groups of fish. Examples are found among the sea catfish, the cardinal fish, and a number of others. In some species the male carries the eggs; in others the female gets the job.

One group of African fish known as cichlids has an intriguing method of insuring fertilization. The male's anal fin has a series of spots the size and color of cichlid eggs. As the female picks up the eggs she attempts to mouth these spots, and in so doing she is sure of taking in sperm to fertilize eggs already in her mouth.

Another extreme case is the European bitterling. Ripe females develop a long tubelike ovipositor. Eggs travel down this tube and are introduced into the gill cavity of certain freshwater clams. The males release sperm where they will be picked up by the clam's respiratory currents. The eggs then develop on the gills of the clam—simple poetic justice, since clam larvae often develop on the gills of the fish. It is interesting to note that the bitterling has successfully been introduced into North American waters where it found clams suitable for its spawning.

The new generation starts when eggs and sperm come together. Fish life history is conveniently divided into embryonic period, larval period, juvenile, and adult. The embryonic period begins when a fertilized egg starts to divide into more and more cells that eventually arrange themselves into a complete fish. As the embryo grows it converts materials stored in the yolk into skin, muscles, heart, nerves, and all the other sundry parts that make up a fish. This is hard work, and many weaklings are culled out before hatching.

The embryonic period is also a critical time when slight environmental disturbances such as temperature or mechanical shocks can kill the embryo or cause it to develop abnormally. Siamese twins, pugheads, spinal curvature, fused vertebrae, and abnormal fins are a few of the results generally attributed to accidents during this sensitive period.

The fish ceases to be an embryo when it hatches and leaves the egg membrane. Most species then pass through some kind of larval stage before assuming their final shape. Sometimes these larvae bear little resemblance to the adults they will become, and the proper identification of fish larvae is one of the more difficult problems facing the fishery biologist.

By the end of the larval period the young fish more or less resemble their parents. They are then called juveniles until they reach sexual maturity. Few fish survive beyond their reproductive age, and some such as the lamprey and the Pacific salmon die after spawning so that the generations barely overlap.

Life history patterns constitute one of many adaptations to a particular way of life. Thus, coral-reef fish and those of the high seas have larvae that are specialized for survival near the surface of the open ocean. Such larvae often have transparent bodies and elongate fin spines. The larvae of bonefish and eels are elongate, flattened, ribbon-shaped affairs that are quite unlike the adults. These planktonic stages drift with the currents to new habitats far from their parent home, thus accounting for the rich fauna of reefs around remote islands that could never be reached by bottom loving adults.

Stream-dwelling fish such as the trout hatch while there is still a lot of yolk material left. These "sac fry" continue their development in the gravel bottom until they are able to maintain their position against the current. Quiet-water fish, by contrast, seek shelter among vegetation soon after they are hatched.

Another critical stage for all fish occurs when the yolk is finally used up and the larva must find its own food. This is the big barrier to the successful cultivation of most marine fish.

While adults are generally not known for their parental devotion, often dining on their own young, there are a few cases of highly developed parental care. As mentioned, the male largemouth bass guards its young, and the same is true of North American catfish and the very primitive bowfin. Some mouth brooders shelter the young for a week or two after they hatch.

As if to show that there is no end to the reproductive specializations found among fish, there are even forms that suckle their young. The discus fish, a South American cichlid, produces a nutritious skin secretion that is eaten by its young, and South American banjo catfish carry both eggs and young attached to specialized skin areas on the undersurface of the female. They too feed the young on specialized skin secretions.

Fish that lay pelagic eggs—cast out on the surface of the sea—obviously take no parental care, and for them the sexual rites end with the release of eggs and sperm. The same is true of many fish that broadcast their eggs over the spawning grounds—for example, northern pike, carp, and whitefish.

Thus, the production of one generation after another is accomplished with the help of many physiological and behavioral variations, and sex—as it is for humans—proves to be not simple, even for a fish.

Understanding Fish Behavior

by Warren J. Wisby

*A fish has problems to solve, just as we do,
and his involve most of the same things as our more basic ones.
He must eat, he must escape being eaten,
he must reproduce. In short, he must survive and ensure the survival
of his species. In so doing, he solves with his comparatively
simple nervous system, problems that even humans often find difficult.
But because of the similarity of many of our problems
with those a fish faces, our descriptions of his behavior are often
expressed in terms that should be reserved for humans.*

DIVING ON A REEF

F OR EXAMPLE, we may see fish suddenly begin to strike at one bait after ignoring all the other lures they have been presented. We tend, under these circumstances, to say they "like" that bait better or they "prefer" that lure. That these terms are inaccurate descriptions of what really happens can best be understood by taking a close look at certain aspects of a fascinating subject—the behavior of fish.

First, let us examine one complicated bit of behavior in a fish that has been much studied, the threespined stickleback. If we place in an aquarium a male and female stickleback, we may find that the male begins to construct a nest, using pieces of plant material that he cements with his saliva into a minature bird's nest with a hole in one side.

Arrival of a gravid female stickleback causes the male to begin a beautiful little courtship dance in which the female soon begins to participate. The end result of this activity is that the female deposits her eggs in the nest, where the male stands guard, fanning them at intervals, until they hatch.

A closer look at the whole performance, by Dr. N. Tinbergen, revealed the following: As the female approaches the male, he swims toward her until he receives a signal which causes him to assume a specific posture. She "accepts," and he then leads and she follows. He indicates the opening of the nest, and she enters and deposits eggs, whereupon he fertilizes the eggs and "guards" them.

In each instance, a specific action by one produced in the other a specific response which, in turn, became the stimulus eliciting the next response. Normally, the courtship proceeds without interruption. Should something distract the pair, however, we find that they cannot

simply resume where they left off. The whole process must start over from the beginning. This has been called "fall-back," and serves to illustrate one of the attributes of fish behavior—rigidity.

Also, the same pair of fish can serve to illustrate yet another principle—what is accomplished is irrelevant; responding in the proper manner to the presented stimulus is the important thing.

At one stage of the courtship the male inserts his nose into the nest opening, and the female responds by sliding past the male and entering the nest. Were we to ask the female, "What are you doing?", she would not reply "I'm entering the nest," but rather, "I'm pressing against the male and swimming past his nose."

We can prove this as follows. A dead male stickleback, or a model of a stickleback, is impaled on a wire and made to go through the motions of a normal male. The female responds as if a normal male were indeed present. If, at the crucial stage, we cause the model to place its nose against a rock or into the sand, we find that the female presses close against the model and makes frantic, unavailing efforts to enter a nonexistent nest.

One of the many aspects of this small animal's behavior may interest those of us who feel superior to fish. A male stickleback, it can be shown, responds to a model as if it were a male stickleback only if it has a red abdomen. It responds to a model as if it were a ripe female only if it has a swollen, silver-colored abdomen.

It now becomes possible for us to construct a model that has a far more swollen abdomen, and one that is more silvery, than any normal female. We find that such a model receives a far more

Even the ferocious moray eel sizes up the prey before striking.

frenzied response than would any normal female.

Modern man can easily identify with the male stickleback after a day of looking at redder than normal lips, slimmer than normal waistlines, and longer than normal eyelashes, to mention only certain of the possibilities.

Thus, the nervous system of fish functions in such a manner that the individual appears "programed" to respond in a certain way to a certain stimulus. Whereas flexibility of response is the rule in humans, rigidity characterizes the behavior of fish.

In fairness, it should be mentioned

65

that not all fish operate on as simple and direct a level as the stickleback. Some, for instance, can easily recognize individuals they know by sight, hearing, and smell—much as we do. This, however, merely implies a more complex set of stimuli and responses—not a different level of awareness.

Consider, for example, the angler who had a large number of flopping mackerel in the bottom of his boat and reflected on his good fortune. He was well aware that one reason for his good catch was his skill in spotting the water disturbance caused by the bait fish on which the mackerel were feeding. Having thereby located the mackerel school, the fisherman had only to lower a bare treble hook into the water, snap his wrist to impale one of the bait fish (pilchard), and a mackerel would immediately take the bait.

Had the angler been a bit more reflective, he might have wondered about another, more subtle, cause of his good fortune. The pilchards outnumbered the mackerel by hundreds of thousands of individuals. The chances that any individual pilchard would be struck by a mackerel at any given time were considerably less than the slim chance of filling an inside straight at poker. And yet, whenever the fisherman snagged a pilchard, this one out of all the others was immediately snapped up by a mackerel and the mackerel was hooked. Obviously, something more than pure chance was responsible. The reason for this catch was far from mere luck; a hooked pilchard is a much more likely victim than its free neighbors.

The mackerel, had they been thinking, articulate creatures, could have assured the angler that there are biological laws which govern predation, and which make it possible to predict with some certainty those conditions leading one animal to eat another. The mackerel had behaved according to those laws, responding in the unhesitating, unthinking, sterotyped manner of their kind, by slashing at the hooked pilchard in preference to a free one.

It may well have been an experience such as the preceding one which first prompted a biologist to wonder why a particular animal was devoured by a predator while other, perhaps more accessible, individuals were ignored. The study of predator-prey relations is of interest to various kinds of biologists. A fishery biologist might be interested in the effect of predation on the harvestable population of a prey species. Others, studying population dynamics, may concentrate on the relations between the number of the predator species and the number of the prey species. For example, it has been found that fluctuations in the number of Canada lynx follow closely the fluctuations in the number of snowshoe hare on which the lynx primarily feeds. Another phase of the study of predator-prey relations, however, is concerned with the interaction between individuals of the predator and of the prey species, and this is the special realm of the student of animal behavior.

While field observations of the activities of wild animals have yielded much information on their behavior and on the interaction between individuals, it remained for laboratory experiments to point out how delicate was the relation between prey and predator, and on what small, seemingly insignificant circumstances hinged the life of the prey animal.

One of the first experiments involved the well-known ability of fish to adapt their color to their surroundings. Sumner, in 1935, placed one group of small gambusia in a dark container and another group in a light container. He permitted them to remain in their respective environments, which were the same except for the difference in background, until they had adapted. Those in the dark container became darker, and those in the light container became lighter. Some individuals from both containers were then placed in an experimental tank which resembled the dark environment. When these fish were exposed to fish-eating birds and predator fish, it was found that the predators captured many more of the individuals adapted to the light environment than those adapted to the dark.

When the experiment was run in reverse (the dark and light adapted fish placed in a light tank), those from the dark environment were eaten. Under the conditions of the experiment, neither swimming ability nor agility could have accounted for the difference. The results showed conclusively that color differences alone were responsible.

In another experiment, largemouth bass and their natural prey, bluntnose minnows, were kept together in a large circular tank. Certain of the minnows, selected at random, were dyed unnatural colors, while others had small portions of their fins removed. It was found that the altered minnows were selected by the bass more often than would have occurred by chance. From other experiments with the same two species, it was learned that a minnow's chances of escaping predation increased with the length of time it remained in the tank. In other words, the newcomers were eaten, while the old inhabitants continued to survive. Also, strange as it may seem, a blinded minnow had a better chance of surviving, when placed in a tank with the bass, than did a normal individual.

With the possible exception of the last experiment, it is easy to see an underlying general principle of predator-prey relations. That is, an animal which is out of phase with, or not attuned to, its environment is more susceptible to being eaten than is an individual which is adapted to its environment of the moment.

The same statement applies in the case of the blinded minnow. When a young bass approaches a normal minnow, the minnow responds in typical prey fashion by producing a startled fright response and by fleeing. This, in turn, usually results in a typical predator response by the bass: chasing, catching, and eating. When a bass approaches a newly introduced and therefore slightly confused, blinded minnow, however, its seeming self-confidence vanishes. The prey does not flee, because it has seen nothing. In some cases, a minnow will perceive the movement of the bass by means of other senses, but perhaps owing to the traumatic experience of having been recently caught in a net and transferred to the new aquarium, its inability to orient properly may send it dashing toward the predator. In such cases, the pursuer may become the pursued, the minnow having inadvertently produced the stimuli normal to an aggressive and well-adjusted individual.

There is yet another situation in which bluntnose minnows have been seen to chase and repel their bass predators. During the spawning season, male bluntnose minnows are vigorous guardians of their spawning site. Attacks are directed against all intruders, including bass and the legs of snoopy biologists. Here again, the prey does not produce a typical flight response and is therefore, at the moment, not a prey animal.

The preceding examples illustrate yet another of the general principles of predator-prey relations. That is, predators which attack animals of nearly their own size, often exhibit fear of their prey. For example, a well-fed cat will usually not attack a rat; its hunger drive is not sufficiently high to overcome its fear. As its hunger mounts, a point will be reached where the two drives are in almost perfect balance. Such a cat will stalk and circle a rat with expressions of interest and excitement but will usually not attack. A starving cat, on the other hand, would not hesitate to attack, even though a rat is a worthy adversary for most cats.

That fish are not the only organisms which experience difficulties on being transferred to a new environment can be attested to by any small boy who has moved to a new neighborhood. "Been moved" would probably be more fitting because few would move voluntarily, having once experienced the sensation. In fish, as in small boys, the newcomer often experiences difficulties with members of its own species. Introduce a new individual into a happy community aquarium, and pandemonium reigns until the recent arrival has established its position of dominance with respect to the other inhabitants. Let one of the members become ill, and the symptoms of distress are immediately recognized and reacted to by the others.

Under certain circumstances, a normal individual in an aquarium can be induced to produce distress symptoms. When this happens, the rest of the aquarium inmates respond as though the individual were indeed in distress. For example, African synodontid catfish normally swim upside down, a position which is ordinarily assumed by other fish only when dead or dying. When in this position, the synodontid's belly is darker than its back. This coloration is the reverse of that found in fish which swim right side up, but the effect is the same; the surface which is on top is dark and the bottom surface is light. If food is placed on the bottom of the aquarium, it becomes necessary for the catfish to turn over in order to eat. When this happens, it attracts the attention of every other aquarium inmate. Larger fish nip at it and smaller ones stare.

As if to evidence its discomfort, this catfish soon reverses its coloration, and retains it until it again assumes the normal upside down position. Such fish were obviously not in distress. In fact, they were happily eating, which is quite a normal function. They were, however, exhibiting one of the prime symptoms of distress, appearing to swim upside down.

Symptoms of distress, then, become a mechanism for imparting information and can, therefore, be considered communication. When that mackerel angler cited earlier impaled a pilchard on his hook, that pilchard immediately appeared different from all of the other pilchards in the school. His frantic struggles and flip-flops were a clear signal to every mackerel that this individual was in distress and, therefore, vulnerable. The mackerel responded without hesitation, and the angler boated another fish.

It is obvious that fish may signal their distress by visual means. What other symptoms of trouble might a predator detect? Violent struggling may cause vibrations which are meaningful to a

Barracuda, the tiger of the seas, is a typical predator; the creatures it eats are typical prey.

More is being learned on how the individual fish responds to color variations.

Mackerel travel in schools, but each behaves as an individual in response to cues.

hungry predator, as in the case of the impaled pilchard. These signals are probably detectable at a much greater distance than that over which vision alone would be effective. Also, if any injury occurs which releases blood into the water, the incident could be detected by any predator with a good nose.

It is possible for the angler to profit from the information gained in the laboratory. On a day when the fishing is slow, try putting the bait on upside down. Remember the catfish? Or when trolling for deep-water species, try using a shallow-water fish for bait. Get him out of his environment, and he may be in trouble.

Also, if the live bait does not seem to be working, try fishing with one that has been kept in a white or black baitwell, depending on the color of the water. Remember the gambusia? Some bait fish are able to change color so rapidly as to

be quite inconspicuous in the water. They become darker when a shadow passes over them or when swimming over a dark bottom, and lighter in sunlight or over a sunny bottom. Try fishing with a dead one that cannot change color, and hook him in such a manner that, when jerked, he darts and turns like a wounded or severely frightened fish.

A little blood in the water wouldn't hurt either, when fishing for certain species. Your primary aim during these experiments should be to cause your bait to produce as many distress symptoms as possible. There is plenty of food in the sea, but it is usually the erratic or distressed individual that gets eaten first.

There is another aspect of behavior which should interest fishermen. Certain animals, including some fish, respond with increased fervor to stimuli of ab-

70

normally high value. Thus, for example, a herring gull will sit on, and attempt to hatch, the largest egg-shaped object in its vicinity, even though this means abandonment of its own egg.

In a similar manner, a stickleback, which responds with sexual behavior only to females swollen with eggs, will produce a frenzied response to a misshapen model—provided only that it have an abdomen more swollen and more silvery than that possessed by a normal female. Were a fisherman to produce, in his lure, distress symptoms of supernormal stimulus value, his fishing success might also be of supernormal proportions. Remember that one of the most successful and most famous bass lures is called, by its manufacturer, an "injured minnow."

And remember also—to catch fish, understand fish behavior.

By Any Other Name

by Homer Circle

*There is a good possibility that the first question
about the name of a fish arose back in primordial days when one
cave man said: "It's a fish." 'And Og, the intellectual,
said: "Yep, but what kind?" Then he got drummed out of the tribe.
Donnybrooks over the names of fish have been going on
ever since and no doubt will continue so long as colloquial names are used
by fishermen. And the opposition to changing fish names
remains a constant challenge to those who would bring order out of chaos
by settling on one common name for each species.*

BLACK CRAPPIE AND WHITE CRAPPIE

IT HAS BEEN my pleasure to serve as chairman of the Fish Nomenclature Committee for the Outdoor Writers Association of America for the past 15 years. This committee was formed to spearhead a movement to strive for the adoption of an approved list of common names for North American sport fish.

The main hopes for success lie in three areas: the assistance and support of far-sighted fish scientists; the backing of fellow outdoor writers across the Nation; and future generations of fishermen who would adopt the common names used by scientists and the outdoor press.

Well, it hasn't been easy. Just as Lou Caine and Bill Ackerman, who initiated this program, found back in 1946—ordinarily broadminded men become amazingly narrow when they are asked to settle on one common name for their favorite sport fish. Obviously, the one they have been using for decades should be the only common name!

Crappie, known by 55 common—or uncommon—names.

To give you an example of what the committee found when it started compiling a list of common names being used across America—consider the following list, with "tip off names" left out:

bachelor	newlight
bachelor perch	papermouth
bachelor shad	perch
banklick	razorback
banklick bass	roach
barfish	sac-a-lait
bigfin bass	rockfish
bitterhead	sago
bride perch	sand perch
bridge perch	shad
calico	silver bass
calico bass	silver perch
calico bream	speckled bass
campbellite	speckled perch
chinquapin	speck
chinquapin perch	spotted perch
Dolly Varden	spotted trout
goggle-eye	straw bass
goggle-eye perch	strawberry bass
goldring	strawberry perch
grass bass	suckley perch
John Demon	sun perch
lake bass	tin mouth
Lake Erie bass	tin perch
lamplighter	white perch
Millpond bass	

Those of you who use any of the above colloquial names will recognize the fish. Those who have been calling this fish by its one common name would have difficulty recognizing—the crappie.

"Tipoff names" which should be added to the above list are: crapet, pale crappie, ringed crappie, and timber crappie. A total of 55 names for one fish—oops, watch it!—there are two species of crappies, the white and the black. And therein lies another keg of powder—similar species.

Take the three bass "cousins"—the largemouth, smallmouth, and spotted. These make up the most popular sport fish in North America because of their combined broad distribution. And, as you would deduce, these have a batch of colloquial names—most of which have the name "bass" involved. Like green bass, black bass, bronze bass, etc.

And yet—these really aren't bass at all but members of the sunfish family, which also includes the bluegill, rock bass, warmouth bass, crappies, and other panfish.

As a matter of fact, the only true bass are the white and yellow bass, and—hold your hat—the white perch! So it isn't only the fishermen who have been guilty of misnomers; the fish scientists who have been recognizing and using these names are part and parcel of the resulting confusion.

And the confusion will continue so long as a so-called authority in Arkansas calls a certain fish a jack salmon, while a writer in Wisconsin calls the same fish a walleyed pike, and a guide in Canada calls it a dore, pickerel, or pike perch. The common name is walleye.

Of course, it is a member of the perch family, together with its blood brother, the sauger, and also its more distant relative, the yellow perch. But the name walleye is descriptive of its main characteristics—white-opalescent eyes which make it instantly identifiable.

Other misnomers for the walleye are blue pike, glasseye, jackfish, Susquehanna salmon, and yellow pike. Maybe some day it will be simply and understandably just—walleye.

But settling on one common name is not easy, as the committee has found. A case in point is the popular and widely

Red drum—or do you call it a channel bass?

76

distributed northern pike. Why not just "pike?" Why any more northern pike than southern or eastern pike, where they are also found?

The committee agreed that the name pike would be sufficient and preferable—but not just yet. And here is its reasoning:

(1) A national poll of outdoor writers, game wardens, fishermen, and conservation departments showed only a small, but growing, minority favoring pike.

(2) Northern pike is a step forward from the name commonly used for so many years in the Great Lakes region, great northern pike—which sounds more like a railroad than a fish.

(3) Over simplification can bring needless confusion, and the committee patiently is awaiting the day when its national poll shows a majority preferring the single name, pike.

The committee was challenged by writer members on its using the same scientific name, *Salmo gairdneri*, for both the steelhead and the rainbow trout, pointing out that these two fish look completely dissimilar.

True, the committee agreed, they do look unlike each other, but only after the rainbow has returned to a stream or river after its migratory run into a large lake or saltwater. Aside from external appearance, these two fish are one and the same species.

And here is a point to emphasize. The Outdoor Writers Association of America's Fish Nomenclature Committee agreed to accept the scientific names adopted by the American Fisheries Society, knowing how conscientiously these scientists pursue the subject of proper scientific names for our multitude of fish.

Through its chairman, charged with the same task as I, Dr. Reeve M. Bailey, our committee has worked with the scientists toward a common goal. Much progress has been made through mutual effort.

But cooperation between, or among, people in authorative positions is not enough. There is the "man on the firing line" to be considered.

And each time a survey is made by the OWAA Fish Nomenclature Committee, the following are invited to voice their opinions on what are their choices of current, common names for our popular sport species:

Outdoor writers, outdoor radio and TV program directors, outdoor lecturers and photographers, game wardens, conservation agents, directors of all 50 State fish and game departments, magazine editors and writers, fish book authors, heads of various museums of natural history, the U.S. Bureau of Sport Fisheries and Wildlife, heads of various university fishery departments, and knowledgeable fishermen who have pursued their sport locally, regionally, and nationally.

Another survey is about due, and the same careful procedure will be followed. When concluded, a booklet will be published listing the most current, most popular, single common name for each species of North American sport fish.

The booklet will be distributed through the Outdoor Writers Association of America to all those who disseminate words spoken or written on the subject of fish or fishing. We will hope then, as in the past, that this list will be used as the latest (but not the last) word on what is the best available consensus of common fish names.

As in the past, the list will bring both

Brown trout are known as brook trout in Europe—but aren't the same as our brook trout.

Striper, also known as rockfish, is as large
either way.

Bream is one of many local names for the bluegill.

praise and heated criticism. And this will be accepted as part of the game. But each time a list goes out, more and more new-generation fishermen are heard using the suggested common names.

And that is sufficient encouragement to continue the quest, to one day reach the point where fishermen in all parts of North America will recognize the com-

mon name of each sport species. Once that plateau is reached, then perhaps most (never all) will use that one name, because it just plain makes good sense!

[EDITOR'S NOTE: Just to show that the authors and editors of this book can also confound the issue, in using common names, the list of the American Fisheries Society was followed rather than the Outdoor Writers.]

THE FISHERMAN

Who Fishes

A Photo Essay Edited by Rex Gary Schmidt

Fishing for fun or food, relaxation or science,
is an American pastime that has grown socially more correct
over the years and more popular on the wheels
of our mobile population. Millions fish—from ghettos and deserts,
farms and factories, schools and courthouses,
seminaries and military bases. Probably more than one person in eight
finds pleasure, excitement, contentment, and a chance
to unravel tight-knit souls by wetting a line. Places to fish are
surprisingly many—desert canyon reservoirs
and seashore surf, farm ponds and lakes, rivers and estuaries,
the open seas. The cost? Anything you want to pay—and
the dividends from the investment may be a longer, happier life.

GIRL WITH SNOOK

On a lonely Ozark stream . . .

. . . on the historic C & O Canal . . .

On the Gulf Stream . . .

. . . with a swift, brilliant colored, leaping dolphin.

Hauling in a Rainbow.

Saturday charter.

In a mountain lake.

Hurry, mom, light the stove.

Fish wrangler?

What's this?

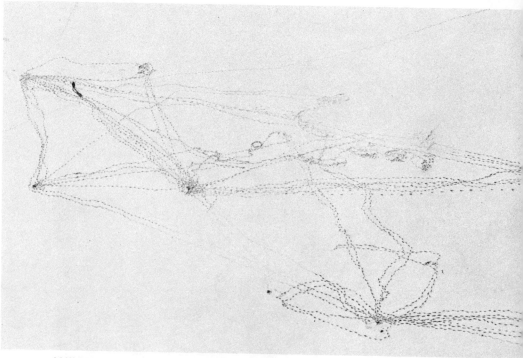

Ice fisherman creates a master doodle.

With underwater camera . . .

*In the
Indian Ocean*

91

Tools of the Trade

by Jack Randolph

*Tackle has improved so much in recent years
that fishing has become easier, not only for beginners, but for experts as
well. Please note that I said fishing, not catching.
Fortunately, the business of catching fish remains as challenging as ever.
But with much improved equipment the angler has more time
to concentrate upon fooling a fish, not just trying to get his line into
the water. As with most things in this age of
specialization, there are tools to meet most fishing needs. This is fine
for the expert who has many types of tackle.*

TARPON FISHING IN A FLORIDA BAY

Bᴜᴛ ᴛʜᴇ ᴀᴠᴇʀᴀɢᴇ angler tries to make one or two outfits do for all of his fishing. To him the proliferation of so many types of rods, reels, lures, hooks, lines, and accessories has greatly complicated the task of selecting the right outfit for his needs.

Whether you choose a spin, bait, or fly casting outfit is largely a matter of personal preference. Just about every form of equipment is available in so many sizes and models, and they all are more versatile than ever before. In selecting your outfit be guided by some important considerations.

Tackle is produced to fit nearly any budget, but because the manufacturers are in a fiercely competitive business, only those who make good equipment survive for several fishing seasons.

Browse through any catalog, and you'll pick up pointers on how to tell the difference between quality and inferior tackle. You'll notice that better quality rods, for example, are made with carboloy tips because this metal is very hard and resists abrasion by the thousands of yards of nylon lines that wear on it in its lifetime. Agate, a semiprecious stone that's almost as hard as diamonds, is just as good for this purpose except it is apt to be broken more easily. You'll also notice that rod guides, other than the tip, are made of stainless steel, agate, or tungsten-carbide. The guides receive less wear than the tip, but if they were made of softer metal the line would soon cut grooves into them which, in turn, will cut lines to ribbons.

With experience other indicators of quality become apparent. If you see rod windings where both "feet" of a guide are wound with one continuous strand of thread, you know immediately that you're looking at a poor rod. The use of metal stampings on the reel seat or low grade cork handles are other tipoffs.

A few fishing trips will teach you all about lines. To your sorrow, you may discover that those bargain lines on the nice big spools aren't such a good deal. If you really were stuck, you'll discover that the spool of your reel jammed or split for no apparent reason. When you haul the reel in for repair, you'll learn how a nylon line stretches.

Some inferior quality nylon lines will stretch quite a bit. When wound on the reel under tension, the line is stretched, but when the tension is removed the line returns to its original diameter, exerting tremendous pressure against the sides of the spool. All objectionable stretch has been removed from good quality lines.

If you're looking for a versatile outfit, try the open-faced spinning type. This, of course, is the standard spinning outfit that was introduced in this country in the midthirties, but never became popular until after World War II when it was married to nylon line.

An open-faced spinning reel is designed to hang below the handle of a matching spinning rod. The reel is placed beneath the rod to prevent the line, which spins off the end of the reel's fixed spool in wide spirals, from slapping the rod and reducing the length of your cast. Also to reduce friction and increase casting ease, spinning rods are equipped with large guides.

The smallest type of open-faced spinning outfit is known as ultralight. This is a tiny spinning reel mounted on a very light action rod, ranging from 5 to 6 feet in length. It's designed to cast very light lures, weighing as little as $\frac{1}{32}$ of an ounce on cobweb lines testing from less than 1 to 3 pounds.

Ultralight outfits became very popu-

Fly fishing outfit of President Eisenhower.

lar in the midfifties when many anglers tried hard to make little fish seem like big ones. Since bigger ones, like the coho salmon, striped bass, and muskellunge, have been so liberally stocked throughout the country, anglers are now becoming more big-fish minded, and the popularity of ultralight gear seems to be fading. I find the little outfits a pleasure to use on stocked trout and bluegills.

From ultralight, we step up to the standard-size spinning outfit, one of the more versatile of freshwater or light saltwater tackle. Outfitted with such standard-size reels as the Garcia 300, Zebco 830, Shakespere 2062, or the Heddon 280, the standard spinning rig is substantially heavier than ultralight gear. When matched to a suitable rod, the standard reel will handle a wide variety of lines ranging from 2- to 15-pound test.

Standard-size spinning rods are from 6 to 7 feet in length and are available in a variety of actions. The very light actions are fine for fishing light live baits and casting the usual trout-size weighted spinners. Heavier actions can be found to meet most any freshwater requirement.

The third largest spinning rig is known as the intermediate or heavy freshwater and light saltwater outfit. The reel is somewhat larger than the standard, and usually balances best on a two-handed spinning stick ranging from 7 to 9 feet in length. It handles lines in the 10- to 20-pound test class.

Although the intermediate is gaining in popularity among freshwater anglers, it's most commonly found along the surf where it's the preferred weapon of those who cast artificial lures for striped bass, bluefish, snook, tarpon, and smaller red drum. It's also popular on the West coast for anything ranging from surf-

95

perch to striped bass. In freshwater this is the spinning outfit with the guts to turn a determined muskellunge or stop a big striper.

The largest of the spinning reels is the surf-size outfit, which is really a bit large for many surf casters who prefer the intermediate for tossing artificial lures into the waves. The big surf types, with their huge line capacity, balance well on big, hefty two-handed surf rods running from 9 to 12 feet in length. This is the spin fisherman's reel for heaving heavy sinkers and large air-resistant baits far out beyond the breakers for big red drum, striped bass, sharks, tarpon, and other big surf fish.

Some anglers use the big reels for heavy trolling offshore. In my opinion the conventional offshore trolling reels, such as the Penn or Fin-Nor reels, are superior to spinning for this type of fishing.

A happy compromise between spinning and bait casting has been found in the relatively new pushbutton, or more correctly, spin-cast reel. Although this reel employs the fixed spool principle of the spinning type, the spool is enclosed in a steel nose cone and the reel, unlike the open-faced model, is placed on top of the rod handle. A button located at the rear of the reel permits the caster to control it with his thumb.

This reel must be matched to a spin-cast rod for best results. This rod is built like an old-fashioned bait-casting stick from the offset handle to the tip, except for the guides which are larger. Since the line leaves the spin-cast reel through an aperture in the nose cone, the spirals are smaller than those on the open-faced models. This permits the mounting of the spin-cast reel on top of the rod handle instead of below. Nevertheless,

larger guides are required to accomodate the tight spirals of line without creating excessive friction. A standard bait-casting rod, with the usual small guides, is not ideal for spin casting.

Modern bait-casting tackle has been tremendously improved during the past decade. There's really no comparison between our bait-casting reels today and those that were given such a tremendous shellacking by spinning reels at the end of World War II.

For a while it looked as if bait casting would fade into extinction with the passing of the "old school" anglers who had mastered the "devices created by Satan, designed to backlash at the most inopportune time." Then, from Sweden, came something radically new in bait-casting reels.

To begin with, the new Swedish reel was a handsome deep red color, a rash departure from the somber tones of American reels, but the differences were more than skin deep. The new reel borrowed from saltwater types, putting an efficient star drag and a free spool feature on the freshwater model. Best of all, it incorporated a completely different concept in antibacklash devices. This new centrifugal brake was unique in that it actually reduced backlashes. As a final touch the reel spool was designed so that no gap existed between the spool and the frame through which the monofilament line could creep and become entangled in the works.

This new reel was a great stride towards making bait casting easier for the average angler. It also influenced other reel makers to update their reels so that we now have a wide variety to choose from. These include one other type of reel which is refreshingly different and

96

Tying the fly, an art in itself.

Artistic touches should be to attract fish—not people.

a genuine pleasure to use——the light-weight, narrow-spool bait-casting reel.

The lightweight bait caster doesn't have a drag device but does have a free spool feature. The narrow spool is scarcely as wide as an average man's thumb. It balances beautifully on a light bait-casting outfit and is a terrific tool for freshwater bass and pickerel fishing.

Bait casting provides the angler with tackle that's suitable for fighting large, determined fish. The drag is comple-mented with a reel spool an angler can put a thumb to. It gives us more control over our tackle when handling a nice fish. Bait casting also gives the angler an entirely different sensation when a fish is on the line. If you've used nothing

but spinning gear, you'll appreciate it more when you've hooked your first fish on a bait-casting outfit. Somehow, the angler seems more directly involved with his fish than he does with a spinning outfit.

A bait-casting tackle is at its best when used to cast lures in the one-half to full-ounce weight class. It is also excellent for still fishing with live bait. In many ways, this type of tackle is directly competitive with spin casting. The difference be-tween the two is that while spin casting enjoys a wide edge in simplicity of cast-ing, bait casting offers the angler some-what better control over a good fish.

As you would suspect, bait-casting

reels are used with bait-casting rods. These, like spin-cast rods, have offset reel seats. But many bait casters prefer to use spin-cast rods which balance just as nicely. The larger guides on a spin-cast rod are suitable for bait casting, but spin-cast reels do not perform well on bait-casting rods.

Because bait-casting reels employ a revolving spool, they are also known as conventional reels. This category also includes many saltwater boat, surf, and trolling reels, which featured star drags and free spools long before they were used in freshwater. They come in various sizes ranging from the smallest 100-yard capacity types, used for taking saltwater panfish such as croakers, flounders, and spot to huge winches used offshore for giant game fish.

A popular saltwater reel is the wide spool surf model used with surf rods for striped bass and red drum. These outfits are popular, particularly for throwing heavy sinkers and large natural baits.

The performance of all tackle depends heavily upon the choice of lines. Monofilament line is just about the only type used for all forms of spinning and it is popular for bait casting, trolling, and still fishing. While the type of line is important, the proper weight or size has equal influence on the success of your casting.

Once I was asked to look at a spinning reel that "wouldn't cast." One problem was that the owner had mounted his open-faced spinner on a bait-casting rod. He also compounded his problem by loading the freshwater reel with 30-pound test line—so heavy and stiff that it would have taken 2 ounces of lead to pull it off the reel. The rule of thumb is: the heavier the line, the heavier the bait must be to cast it.

Two things govern the choice of lines: the weight of the lures and the type of fishing. Sometimes you must compromise for the best results.

Ideally, a spinning line used in a pond for bass and pickerel should be about 8-pound test. Under normal conditions, this will cast most lures well and be sufficiently strong to handle a good bass. Unfortunately, we seldom fish under ideal conditions. If, for example, the pond is full of heavy weeds or snags, the 8-pound test isn't strong enough to horse a bass up out of trouble. You may have to sacrifice some casting distance and settle for 10- or 12-pound test. I know some expert bass fishermen who use lines testing 15 or 20 pounds. On the other hand, if the water is very clear and the fish appear to be shy, much lighter lines are required.

In addition to monofilament nylon, bait casters also prefer braided nylon lines. Some like the hard braided type that resist abrasion but are somewhat stiff, while others prefer the soft braids that are far easier to handle. The soft ones, however, are not the best for all conditions because they are easily weakened on sharp rocks or stumps.

Dacron is often favored for offshore trolling because it has less stretch than nylon, but better nylon lines have most of the stretch removed and are quite competitive with the softer dacron.

Wire and lead core lines are specialties used for trolling in very deep water. Wire enjoys an advantage here because it has less diameter and sinks more readily, but it does kink if handled carelessly, a reason why some anglers continue to favor lead core.

No type of fishing depends more heavily on the line than fly casting. In fact, the fly fisherman casts the weight of his

The gear of some surf fishermen includes an assortment of contraptions to move up and down the beach.

line, not the weight tied to the end of it as in all other forms of fishing.

The secret of fly casting is starting off with a well-balanced outfit. Some novices buy a good rod and reel and just any line, then wonder why they can't cast.

Plan your tackle to match the fishing you intend to do. If, for example, you'll be specializing on trout with standard trout-size flies, you'll probably want a medium to light action flyrod with a matching line. On the other hand, if you'll be using your flyrod mostly for large, air-resistant bass bugs, you'll need a heavy weight-forward flyline and a rod

Is there a better place to stow extra lures?

sufficiently powerful to handle it. As a rule of thumb, the larger or more air resistant the lure, the heavier the line. This also means that the heavier the line, the more powerful the rod.

Flyrods range in size from light 6-footers designed for fishing tiny, brushy streams to husky 10-footers made for anything that will hit a fly. Rods are now marked as to what size line they require.

Of course, in most fly casting, the reel is nothing more than a place where excess line is stored, except for fly fishing for large fish as in saltwater. Here the reel with its drag plays a big role in wearing down a fish.

Most freshwater fly reels are small, narrow, single-action reels with a click device instead of a drag. Few anglers need anything more elaborate. Slightly better reels are made with a drag device for larger fish. There are also automatic types that work on a spring action and retrieve the line automatically at the touch of a finger. While some experts frown upon the use of automatics, mainly because of their weight, they are fine for bass bugging from a boat. With the auto you can keep excess line policed up and avoid stepping on it or crushing it against the deck.

Most modern flyrods are made of hollow fiberglass. Great bamboo rods are still available and favored by those who have a real appreciation for flyrodding, but the glass types are fast overtaking the bamboo in action and balance and can't be surpassed for durability.

The lethality of fly fishing is one of the best kept secrets in fishing. In the hands of an expert, a flyrod can be used in nearly any fishing situation. Flies are tied to match a wide variety of fish foods ranging from tiny insects to large minnows or even a swimming mouse. No one other type of fishing equipment is capable of representing such a wide variety of baits.

The selection of tackle for one end of the line is but half the job. Picking out the right bait or lure for the other end is what makes or breaks anglers. Choosing the right bait for the right fish is very tricky, because the fickle fish can change their desires from hour to hour.

Regardless of the lure you use, it must be rigged and manipulated by you. Contrary to many of the claims of lure makers, few artificials will catch fish if merely cast out and reeled in.

Among artificials there are three general categories: deep, shallow running, and surface types. Have a variety of each in your tackle box. Both deep and shallow running lures have optimum running speeds. You can discover the proper one for each lure by working it where you can watch it closely to see at what speed it produces the most appealing action. Try various speeds and rod tip actions to see how it behaves. Once you know how it feels through the rod when it is working properly, your chances of fooling a fish are better.

If you commonly use the lure for sharp-toothed fish and usually fish with a wire leader, you should test the lure on the same leader. The weight of the hardware at the end of the line effects the action of the bait.

Surface lures should be thoroughly checked out to see how they work with various tackle. Some baits are so delicately balanced, they won't work properly if fastened to the line with a snap swivel. Instead they must be tied directly to the end of the line. As a rule, surface lures perform best if worked in an intermittent, jerky manner.

Largemouth bass fishermen have been enjoying success with soft, plastic worms which can be fished almost as slowly as their live bait counterparts. An accepted method of using these worms is to select the floating types and impale one on a size 1/0 weedless hook, running the point through the nose of the worm and bringing it out a couple of inches below. This allows the point and bend of the hook to be exposed while the shank of the hook is within the worm. To complete the job, a large split-shot sinker is pinched on the hook shank next to the eye.

The weighted worm is cast towards a likely hangout and allowed to sink to the bottom, then the angler starts a slow retrieve. Whenever the angler has reason to suspect that something has grabbed his bait, he gives slack and waits for the fish to run with the bait before he attempts to set the hook. Strips of pork rind—known as pork chunk eels—are also effective when used in this manner.

In saltwater the plastic worms are also earning a reputation for catching redfish in the Gulf of Mexico. On the surf in Jersey, I've used red plastic worms to "stretch" a couple of dozen expensive bloodworms. Instead of baiting with two 10-cent bloodworms, I put one on the hook with a plastic red worm. The stripers weren't a bit fussy about taking my plastic offerings along with the natural.

Another new lure that has proven lethal in both salt- and fresh-water is the balsa minnow and the plastic copies that have followed it. These lures, with their bouncy action and realistic finish, are good when fished in a jerky manner.

The balsa minnow makes an effective bass and pike lure when worked as a combination surface and shallow running bait to represent a wounded minnow. The best technique is to bob the lure right on the surface with twitches of the rod tip. In saltwater for striped bass, the bait is good if reeled fast and given lots of rod tip action.

As spinning became popular in the United States, the weighted spinner gained popularity. Now available in a multitude of brands and finishes, this lure will surely be ranked as one of the alltime great fishing baits. It is effective on just about all freshwater fish and does fairly well in saltwater too.

Because the weighted spinner can badly twist fishing lines, it is habitually used in connection with a good snap swivel. A small sinker placed above the swivel is an extra precaution against line twitch.

The spinners seem to do their best work in running water, when fished deep, and with the current. They are also tremendously effective on largemouth bass if fished deep, slow, and with a strip of pork rind on the hooks.

Concerning live bait, check with local anglers to learn the best types used in that area. The trick with any natural bait is to present it in the most lifelike manner possible.

Despite all the fancy gear we use these days, our efforts lead to the same objective—to put a hook through a fish's jaw. Essentially, hooks have remained the same for many decades. What change there has been can be credited to an American company that came up with a design of a hook to give the most certain penetration and made to hold what it hooks. This hollow-point hook has about become standard among bait fishermen.

A common mistake is to select a hook that's too large for the fish you're seeking. It's better to err in the other direction; you can usually land a big fish on a small hook. Look for a short point-to-barb distance. The longer the distance from point to barb, the deeper a hook must penetrate to be secure.

For saltwater fishing, hooks must be stainless steel or plated to protect against rust. And they must be sharp, so carry a small stone and touch them up before you use them.

A fisherman's kit doesn't consist of tackle alone. He may also have a boat and an outboard motor. Both are more dependable than ever. The old cranky outboard is a thing of the past.

Besides tackle and a boat, the angler may have such fancy gear as an electronic device that finds fish and also tells him the depth of the water. He will certainly have a net or gaff to land his fish, a stringer or creel to hold his catch. He'll carry tools for cutting line and fixing gear. He should have life preservers and a first aid kit for emergencies, and if he's a bait fisherman, he'll have something to carry his bait in.

The size of your kit depends upon where you fish and how much you care to invest. Your outfit may be elaborate and worth thousands of dollars, or it may be a cane pole. Fortunately, the size of the kit is no indication of the pleasure you derive.

Tricks of the Trade

by Wheeler Johnson

You can have all the basics about angling down pat and still come home with an empty creel. Often this is because you failed to learn the tricks of the trade—the special techniques— along with the basics. All veteran anglers have their pet tricks, learned through bitter experiences, or by observation and conversation with other fishermen. There are knacks that help in taking a particular species—but usually you have to fish a long time to pick them up. Let's consider what trade secrets I can pass on.

YELLOW PERCH AND WALLEYES

ONE OF THE TRICKS of the expert is to learn some of the peculiar habits of the particular fish he seeks. It is obvious that if he is going to be successful, he must fish where the fish are likely to be and offer the most attractive bait. A little research and observation can save much time in locating the quarry and avoid the embarrassment of returning home and uttering those sad words: "Skunked again!"

The value of studying the species the angler hopes to catch was graphically demonstrated to me at an early age. My father was a busy dentist with only 2 weeks out of the year when he could enjoy his only recreation—fishing the tidal estuaries near his vacation cottage on the Georgia coast. In those days nothing seemed as sophisticated as now, including fishing equipment.

The main fishing outfit was 100 yards of hard-finished cotton line wrapped around an 8-inch section of scrub palmetto branch. At the business end of the line one tied a 6- to 10-ounce sinker, then attached a big hook to a braided "strap" of about 8 inches—the hook being fastened so that it fell about even with the top of the sinker. This was to attract the bottom feeders. A similar "strap" and hook was tied to the main line so that this hook fell some 12 inches above the sinker. This was for the fish that fed slightly above the bottom.

My father liked to catch sheepshead. When he first started fishing on the coast, he wondered why more of these husky, broad, hard-fighting fish weren't taken, and why no one liked to fish for them. It didn't take him long to figure out why. Sheepshead like to feed around barnacle-covered pilings or under the branches of oak trees that have fallen into the water. To consume the barnacles, fiddler crabs, and hardbacked shrimp that are its staples, the sheepshead has sharp incisors to snap the barnacles from the pilings and tree limbs and heavy molars to crush the shells. But it also has a tiny mouth in comparison to its size.

The local anglers all insisted on using heavy hooks with big bends and long shanks. They never had a line with a hook smaller than what now would be a 3/0. My father quickly reasoned that the reason they couldn't catch them was because the hooks they were using were so big the sheepshead couldn't get them in their mouths—although the fish could steal the bait.

Being an old freshwater fisherman, he discarded the hand line used by everyone else, got himself a sturdy cane pole, heavy line to resist the branches of the fallen trees and barnacles on the pilings, and at the end attached a very light sinker and a small but stout hook, very much like the ones he used to catch sunfish in the waters of his native central Georgia. Soon he had established a reputation as the finest sheepshead angler in McIntosh County and enhanced it by taking, on one of his little hooks, a 13½-pound specimen, which stood as a record for those parts for years.

Just as important as studying the habits of the fish and determining the type of tackle best to take it with is research on where the prospective prey lives and why. This also pays off handsomely.

Let's say your objective is largemouth bass and you're working a river that has tree-shaded banks, fallen logs, big boulders, a few riffles, and some deep holes. It's well to study this terrain before starting out. You will soon learn that bass may be taken at times in all of these places, but it may take you a little longer

The right size hook and a fiddler crab could get you a sheepshead—if you set the hook right and bring him in.

to discover that certain conditions enhance your chances of finding the quarry at any one of them.

For example, the banks are good places to fish in the early morning and late afternoon, when bass are moving about in search of food. They like to find an undercut bank and lurk there waiting for insects that might be blown into the water near their lair from the leaves of overhanging trees. Fishing close to the banks also is likely to be better in early

With knowledge comes the ability to match lure to specific fish.

spring, because that is the spawning season. Bass and other members of the sunfish family usually like to make their beds in the shallows near the banks.

Observation also reveals that logs submerged in water for some time are favorite hiding places for lunker bass. These old fellows conceal themselves in the shadows underneath a log and lie in wait for bait fish attracted by the moss and aquatic life that attaches itself to a water-covered tree.

Boulders that stand out in a river should be explored because bass often lie behind them in the quiet water where the current divides behind the rock. They wait there for the current to sweep food down to them, so a well placed lure behind the rock often will bring them out. The riffles are not so productive for largemouth bass, but in localities where they are found, smallmouths use riffles as a feeding area. Largemouths often station themselves in the deeper water at the end of long riffles.

Deep holes will also contain bass at times, particularly when the weather turns hot; the fish are lying inert there, fanning their fins, and trying to escape the heat.

If you have worked the banks in early morning, when the temperature rises and the water warms, it is time for you to turn to the deep holes. Though the fish might not be as eager as they are when their appetites are keen in early morning and later afternoon, they will respond if properly approached.

Which brings us to another point in our thesis that study of the species always pays off. You soon learn that bass will smash at top-water lures, such as floating propeller types, poppers, and others, more readily in the early spring and fall. But occassionally they will hit on the surface at any time, particularly in early morning and late afternoon. They also are likely to take surface lures at any time, when they are found in shallow water. So these would be good baits to use when working shorelines near overhanging trees. And in working such waters, you will soon learn that you can't cast the lure too close to shore. You'll be surprised how many rod-jolting strikes you'll get when you place the lure right at the bank.

But when bass have moved back to the cooler deep holes, another technique must be used. You need something to dredge the very bottom in most cases. The plastic worm, gaining in popularity among anglers every year, is ideal for these situations. Even the most phlegmatic bass will respond when one of these is slowly dragged past his nose.

But don't make the mistake of striking back as soon as the fish clamps his jaws on the worm. He needs time to work it into his mouth. When the line grows taut let him move off a few feet—then strike hard! Vigor is needed because his mouth is tough and power is necessary to set the hook properly.

Other deep running lures that bring strikes are the divers, spinners, and those subsurface baits that now are remarkable reproductions of minnows. Another excellent lure for probing the deep holes is a spoon dressed with a piece of pork rind.

The only reason for going so exhaustively into methods for taking bass in a discussion of fishing techniques is that general rules applying to bass can be applied to other fish. For instance, the bass angler who visits saltwater will find that fishing for snook can be very much like his favorite freshwater sport. He will get smashing strikes by casting as close to mangrove roots as he can get without snagging his hook, and he will have the same problem of shooting his lure underneath the overhanging mangrove limbs that he does in trying to probe under tree limbs on his favorite lake or river. (Incidentally, if you don't lodge a lure in these branches once in a while, you're not getting nearly close enough to the fish.)

As an example of how ideas useful in one type of fishing can be transferred to another, one of the tricks used by snook fishermen—and many other saltwater anglers—is the "sweetener." A favorite artificial used on snook is a white leadheaded jig or bucktail that is marked by two red-dyed groups of hairs on both sides of the white bucktail. Snook will take this lure as it is, when it is worked with a retrieve featuring short jerks with the rod tip, but they will take the lure much more readily when the hook is sweetened with a small piece of fresh-cut shrimp.

This idea can be transferred to many species of fish. I have used it successfully in fishing in Maryland for yellow perch. The accepted bait for these fish is live minnows hooked through the lips. But I found I could out-fish my live-bait friends by using a small bucktail dressed with a small minnow, retrieving this rig very slowly with a jerky action of the rod tip.

This idea works in reverse in a technique for taking flounders that I learned from Claude Rogers, Director of Virginia's Salt Water Fishing Tournament. Flounder fishermen on Virginia's Eastern Shore mostly use either live or frozen bullhead minnows, drifted over the edges of channels where flounders lie half-buried in sand while waiting for their prey. The bait, taken to the bottom by a small sinker, stirs up puffs of sand very much like a minnow scooting along the bottom, and arouses the flounder to action. But Rogers found that he could add to his catch of flatties by embellishing the hook and minnow with a 3-inch strip of shark belly.

The white of the shark's underside seems to help flounder see the bait; at any rate, they bite more readily with this addition to the rig. Any white strip of fish would do as well as shark belly, but sharks are usually available on Virginia's Eastern Shore. I can testify to the efficacy of this trick, because the first time I used it while fishing with Rogers, I landed a 6-pound 2-ounce flounder that was worth a citation in Roger's fishing tournament.

There are many other ways of making additions to ordinary baits and artificial lures that will bring more strikes. As most fishermen know, spoons are generally more effective when dressed with a piece of pork rind. The same goes for

109

bucktails when they are being trolled for many species. I have even increased the strike ratio by using small bits of pork rind on spinners.

But there are other effective additions that are not so well known. For instance, the bucktail or jig used in combination with a plastic worm or eel can be a great fish-getter when big largemouths are lying deep. The jig should be worked slowly and bounced along the bottom, or in cases of rocky shores such as in many man-made lakes, it can be dropped from ledge to ledge. A limber plastic worm also can be cut and the tail end hooked to a spinner or spoon to make a more effective lure when the fish are not responding.

Many anglers now are dressing up bucktails, streamers, and even flies with strips of mylar or tinsel to add extra flash to these lures. Some old school fishermen say that these materials add too much flash and reduce the effectiveness of lures that work well by themselves, but the silvery flash adds something when the fish are not readily taking unadorned lures.

Another trick is ordinary aluminum foil from the kitchen, wrapped around the leader ahead of the hook, wet fly, or streamer to add extra flash that will attract fish. Many anglers use spinners and red beads in front of bottom rigs for perch, on the theory that dashes of color attract fish to the minnows used as bait.

While extra flash certainly does attract fish in certain circumstances, my feeling is that extra flash caused by snaps and swivels, so admired by some anglers, tend to make fish more wary. Naturally, there are circumstances where these items of terminal tackle must be used to rig a line properly for the species sought. But for the most part, our motto is, "The less hardware the better"—

An introduction to sport fishing—known to many a boy.

110

The trick is to start upstream and let the current carry you down—otherwise known as float fishing.

Teamwork is vital for landing large muskellunge.

particularly in freshwater. I prefer to tie the lure directly to the line when possible.

There are lures, however, that work better when they move freely. Tying them tight to the line restricts their action that simulates natural bait. Among these are jigs, bucktails, and minnow-type plugs. Some anglers believe that snaps allow this natural action and are willing to gamble on the possibility of spooking fish to get better action from the lure. But an end loop in the line not only gets rid of the unnecessary bit of metal, but also allows the lure to wiggle through the water much more easily than the snap does. A good end loop can be made with a simple bowline knot and a half hitch above it.

Knots are most important to a fisherman. His rig is no stronger than the knot he can tie, and the terminal tackle, affixed by a knot, is his last link with any fish he might hook. Fortunately, you can get by with a half dozen simple knots that will stand you in good stead for most standard fishing. Many fishing tackle manufacturers have booklets that show the most common knots used by fishermen.

Making a sound knot, however, has become more important in recent years with the rise of monofilament. In the days of my youth on the Georgia coast, such heavy line was used that the knot employed to fasten line to hook or leader didn't make much difference since there

112

Handling this much line in fly casting is an art.

was enough reserve strength in the line that even a poor knot would be sufficient.

Introduction of light spin tackle and monofilament line brought problems along with some of the advantages. Monofilament is nearly frictionless and knots which would hold with braided or twisted lines just won't do. Certain knots also cut the strength of monofilament by half, so new ones had to be developed.

One of the most useful is the improved clinch knot, for affixing hooks or lures to line or leader. Five turns are taken about the standing part of the line, and the running end is passed through the loop at the end of the standing part. The running end is passed through the bigger loop left when the line was brought to the end loop. The line then is brought slowly tight to form the clinch. You always should work monofilament knots slowly, and keep in mind that five turns around the standing part makes the strongest union possible. More or less turns weaken the line and the knot.

An important knot for the user of monofilament is the blood or barrel knot. This one is used to unite two pieces of mono, such as a leader to the line or to a shock line. First take five turns of line A around line B. Then take five turns of line B around line A. Push the running end of line A downward through the loop at the point where the first hitch was started with line A. Push the running end of line B upward through the same loop. Pull tight, slowly and evenly.

This knot is extremely important for saltwater fishermen. In trying to capture certain species, it is mandatory to have a strong section of line as a leader or shock line. You may get by in fishing light line for these species, but a heavier leader from line to hook is necessary because the fish have rough mouths that soon would fray and part a lighter line. Such fish are tarpon, barracuda, and snook in saltwater and members of the pike family in freshwater. Heavier leaders also will help the angler pull big bass out of weeds and from under logs, when he is forced to fish in this rough territory.

And speaking of fraying lines, a final tip is to closely inspect tackle before starting on any fishing trip. Line guides often become roughened for many reasons, and nothing will fray a line quicker than a few retrieves through a roughened guide. This is a common cause of broken lines and lost fish.

I could go on like this to fill an entire book, but I think my point has been made: Like a good craftsman, the expert angler learns the tricks of the trade to assure him success. These aids build up over a lifetime until the angler has accumulated a vast storehouse of knowledge peculiar to each fish and each situation. These become stock in trade at fishing "bull sessions" and lead to an exchange of tips that will make your future angling trips more successful.

Preparing clam chum to attract stripers or blues—a trick of the trade.

The Right Time

by Robert B. Whitaker

A sage has said, "The time to go fishing is when you have time."
Any fisherman will agree who has cleansed his soul and tranquilized his
troubles beside a sluggish catfish creek, in the predawn
mist on a bass lake, or with a heavy trout stream pressing on his waders.
For many anglers the esthetic values of being outdoors
are paramount to a full stringer. Yet anglers—skilled in their
trade—realize much more is involved in selecting the best
time to fish than just getting out whenever the spirit moves them.

FISHING, EVENING

CERTAIN FACTORS combine into a magic formula making it possible for novice and expert alike to fill limits, while the absence of one or more of these elements can doom any trip to failure.

Season, time of day, water temperature, barometric pressure, and tides are some of the variables influencing the feeding habits of fish. And you can add to the dilemma by including the legends that play on superstitious minds.

Fishing has added science to art. The more adept a student becomes in learning time and place, the more filets he will put in his freezer. Also interstate highways and jet air travel open horizons unknown to the barefoot boy of yesteryear, who seldom strayed far from his local fishing hole.

The most obvious and important consideration for the angler is season of the year. There is a tremendous range in climatic season within the United States. During winter months, fur-clad anglers from Montana to Maine drill holes in the ice to get at fish, while shirt-sleeved counterparts in Louisiana and Florida are flipping casts beneath moss-draped cypress.

The importance of climate in fishing isn't based on human garb because fish couldn't care less whether the angler wears an insulated jacket or scanty bikini. But seasonal variations mean change in water temperature, a key influence on when fish bite.

We talk of cold- and warm-water species—a general way of defining the fish's water temperature preference. For example, trout, northern pike, and walleye prefer cooler waters, while largemouth bass and catfish are semidormant during cold months and only become active when water temperatures rise to about 60 degrees.

Fishing comes alive in much of the United States with the first sign of spring. To anglers, a robin's call and blossoming dogwood herald the advent of another fishing season.

Although more and more States are going to year-round seasons, many fishermen still like to oil reels and rig tackle in anticipation of a traditional opening day, which arrives at varying times across the country. In the South, fishing fevers soar about March 1, but it likely will be May before warm-water species stir from northern depths.

From the fish's standpoint, spring is an active season, a time when anglers can often reap a harvest. The fish have come through the winter when their metabolism was low. Spring, however, revives body functions, creating greater demands for food in such species as bass and trout.

Spring also stimulates reproductive activities in many species, which means they will be searching for places to spawn and thus be more vulnerable to the lure. Rainbow trout may move out of lakes into streams, and largemouth bass swim out of deeper waters into sun-warmed shallows.

Saltwater action also picks up in spring. Striped bass arrive in force from Maine to Maryland, with red drum seizing the spotlight on down the coast. Silver-sided gladiators—tarpon and snook—account for much of the excitement in Florida's inshore and brackish waters, with bonefish nearing a peak on saltwater flats. Party boaters are having a ball along the Gulf of Mexico catching bottom fish; yellowtail take command off the southern California coast; and Northwest anglers are challenged by coho and chinook.

Summer is vacation time for most

Americans; their mass exodus from cities and suburbs comes during the hottest part of the year. During July and August, millions of anglers head for the northwoods in quest of smallmouth bass, northern pike, and walleye; to the Rockies for trout; south to float rapid streams for smallmouth or fish for largemouth in a growing number of reservoirs; and along both coasts where surfcasting and offshore angling reach fever tempo.

In the Northwest, summer brings ideal conditions for trout fishermen. By late July and August, rivers are clear and mountain lakes accessible by foot and horseback. Early summer often is most productive for wet flies, but low, clear water conditions in late summer makes the fish more wary; thus more skill is required to catch them.

Elsewhere summer heat simmers surface waters in lakes across much of the Nation causing largemouth bass, northern pike, walleye, and other quarry to seek cooling depths. To catch them, fishermen must change tactics and either go deep or time the day's outing when fish most likely will be roaming the shallows.

During these hot summer months, stripers dominate the saltwater scene from New England to Dixie, but anglers also can match their skill against tuna, bonito, marlin, bluefish, mackerel, and other prize species. In southern Florida, the tidal flats will be buzzing with bonefish, a species unsurpassed for sizzling runs on light spinning and fly tackle.

Off the beaches of Georgia, Alabama, Louisiana, Mississippi, and Texas, king mackerel, cobia, and billfish lure anglers out in the noonday sun. On the Pacific coast, ship-to-shore radios will be flashing news of albacore schools moving in off San Diego and Long Beach during late July with party-boat passengers now

Alone on the lake at sunrise.

"Summertime and the livin' is easy."

enjoying a double-barreled bonanza of albacore and yellowtail.

Even more favored by gourmets, however, are chinook and coho salmon which school at the mouths of many Oregon and Washington rivers. At the same time, San Francisco anglers should score heavily on summer-run striped bass.

Few fishermen will deny that autumn is the most beautiful season of the year. As leaves begin to fall, water temperatures drop, and across the land, fishing action picks up even as the tourist-angler drops off.

For example, fall in New England turns the fly fisherman's thoughts to brook, brown, and rainbow trout, which go on active feeding forays prior to winter. Where regulations permit, anglers can take advantage of this.

Walleye, northern pike, and muskellunge also gain new vigor in the fall, moving into shallows no longer plagued with splashing kids. Even bullhead and carp feed heavier in the fall.

In the Ozarks, rolling hills are ablaze with color. The autumn spectacle is unmatched along such famed float streams as the Current, Jacks Fork, and Buffalo, where fishing for bronze-toned smallmouth will make floating these rapid rivers an unforgettable experience.

Largemouth in southern reservoirs also feel new ambition as they ease out

120

Amid the color of fallen leaves, the angler dwells in beauty.

of the depths within range of top-water lures. The same is true of farm-pond bass which also sense a rebirth of spirit in the fall.

Some of the hottest Indian summer action comes in the West where trout streams are low and clear. September and October are peak months for fly fishermen. Puffy imitations of grasshoppers and other floating insect life account for many trophy catches.

Saltwater species, too, tingle with excitement during fall months. Cod and pollock are welcome additions to the angler's bag in New England, with bluefish and stripers holding at or near a peak. You'll also find billfish along the southern coasts, and snook fishing lively in the Florida mangroves. Seatrout action may be best of the year around Florida and along the Gulf of Mexico beaches.

Albacore and yellowtail continue to fill party-boat sacks on the southern California coast, with striped bass setting the pace farther north. In Oregon and Washington salmon fishing begins tapering off, but limits of these pink-fleshed beauties still are being taken by anglers fishing the ocean and tidal rivers.

Not too many years ago, December, January, and February were months when anglers worked out fishing frustrations by tying flies and tinkering with

121

For the hardy, frozen lakes are a challenge.

122

tackle. But today new techniques and ease of travel have opened greater opportunities for winter sportsmen. Even northerners living across the "snow belt" have learned to cope with ice and snow—and still catch fish.

Ice fishing has soared in popularity through the Dakotas, Iowa, Minnesota, Wisconsin, around the Great Lakes, and into New England. Northern pike, walleye, and yellow perch fill most stringers, while trout lakes also produce some catches. In fact, some of the biggest trophies in all these species are taken through the ice.

Even the ice houses themselves are becoming sophisticated. Some feature insulated walls, battery-powered stereos, carpeted floors, and self-contained heaters that keep the hut toasty warm.

Peering through the hole, fishermen see into another world. Although a sheet of ice may create a dormant setting topside, there is an exciting show going on below. In singles and schools, fish scurry about, occasionally darting over to gobble up a well-placed fly, jig, worm, or minnow.

Moving south, the sprawling reservoirs across the midsection of the Nation won't freeze in winter, but fishing for the most popular species—largemouth bass—slows as water temperatures hover in the 40's and 50's. One popular way of spicing up the action is catching crappies from heated docks such as you'll find at Grand Lake in Oklahoma and Bull Shoals Lake on the Missouri-Arkansas border.

But for faster winter fishing, anglers must head deeper into Dixie. Here, for example, they can fish some of the 29

Early spring sometimes has its snow, but anglers will find the fish hungry.

major reservoirs in Alabama, where daytime temperatures averaging 64 degrees keep spirits high for both fish and fisherman. Much the same holds true in South Carolina, Georgia, Mississippi, and Louisiana, with Florida freshwater angling probably the Nation's best during January and February. Prospects also are good for lunker bass in Arizona, southern Texas, and New Mexico reservoirs.

On the saltwater scene, winter fishing slows to a snail's pace along the upper Atlantic seaboard, but sailfish move on stage in the Gulf Stream, with king mackerel, bluefish, jacks, ladyfish, pompano, groupers, and snapper providing excitement in other southern waters.

Fishing also slackens along the Pacific coast, with cold weather putting a damper on action from California to the Pacific Northwest. Nevertheless, toughened anglers dressed in rain gear and waders will be battling some of the best steelhead trout of the year on the Deschutes, Rogue, Umpqua, Russian, and other top rivers.

Leaping back to summer, Alaska offers fantastic fishing for a variety of species. But in this angling paradise, the question of when is as important as where. Steelhead trout muscle their way into hundreds of streams during spring and early summer, while late July and August bring in silver-flanked coho salmon. Arctic char, shaking salt from their tails, also move up freshwater rivers along Berring Sea and the Arctic Ocean in summer. The little-known sheefish or inconnu also is a midsummer visitor to several watersheds in Eskimoland.

Cutthroat, Dolly Varden, brook, lake, and rainbow trout can be taken with less critical timing along with northern pike, grayling, and other nonmigrating spe-

cies. Best time for Alaska angling generally extends from May through September.

Time of year means little to those who fish among the pineapple fields and smoking volcanoes of Hawaii. Saltwater action also is consistent throughout the year in this island State.

U.S. possessions in the Caribbean and Pacific offer various mixed-bag sport, with the maximum appeal in winter when snowbound citizens board airplanes and steamships for such exotic hinterlands as Puerto Rico, Samoa, and the Virgin Islands.

One final seasonal fact is that the whole pattern can be disrupted by elevation. In Western States the elevation of lakes and streams has a marked influence on water temperature. Consider Arizona where the elevation span amounts to nearly 12,000 feet. This means largemouth bass and crappies in desert reservoirs may be sulking in early summer heat, while mid-elevation lakes are reaching their prime, and waters above 10,000 feet are fringed with predawn ice.

After deciding the best season for a particular species, the next determination is what time of day to wet a line.

In saltwater angling the most productive hours are related more to tides than time of day. Inshore waters produce the best action about 1 hour before high tide and continuing through the first hour of ebb tide.

Many game fish move close to shore with the incoming tide to feed on churned-up crustaceans and gorge on sardines, anchovies, and other forage fish that ride in on the breakers. This is when the surf caster should be showing his wares.

Lacking the influence of tidal move-

124

ment, the hour of day becomes paramount in fishing freshwater lakes and streams. Early morning and late evening hours are customary chow times for a number of species, including the most widespread of all American game fish—largemouth bass.

In summer these bass prowl the shallows during these hours. Unfortunately, too many anglers ignore such magic moments and do their fishing at the hottest time of day when summer bass are deep. It's a matter of mind over body, but getting out on lake or stream before dawn pays off. Most fishermen start too late and quit too soon—fishing when they should siesta.

Fishing success in early morning and late evening hours is minimized during spring, fall, and winter months. In fact, during the late fall, winter, and early spring, largemouths in ice-free lakes are more likely to enter the shallows at mid-

day when sun-warmed surface waters bring the fish upstairs.

Night also can be a productive time to fish. Some species are nocturnal and do much of their feeding after dark. For example, the ultrawary brown trout may stay hidden in a deep hole or beneath an undercut embarkment until darkness lends a sense of security. Walleye and channel catfish also are voracious nighttime feeders.

During summer "dog days," surface waters likely won't cool enough to draw big bass into the shallows until several hours after dark. If you can avoid wrapping a flyline around your neck in the blackness of an August night, you'll find this an excellent time to clobber bass on flyrod poppers, while avoiding heat rash.

When I was a youngster growing up at Lake Okoboji, Iowa, we rarely went fishing in the heat of summer until an hour or so after sunset. Our catch in-

"Now fades the glimmering landscape on the sight."

cluded both large- and small-mouth bass, bluegill, walleye, freshwater drum, and even an occasional northern pike.

Another "moonlighting" group of species common to midwest ponds and lakes is the bullhead, which consistently bites best after dark. A majority of saltwater species also hit well after dark, with snook, tarpon, and striped bass getting most of the attention.

But all these rules about time-of-day come to naught if there is a sudden change in the weather. A rising barometer is generally believed to increase feeding activity, yet I recall many instances when feeding was sparked by a nose-diving barometer, moments before a storm struck.

The matter of wind and rain can affect surface fishing and also has a bearing on when fish enter shallows. Although the lee side of a lake is more pleasant on a windy day, you will usually find fish feeding on the windward side, where wave action stirs up morsels of food.

Largemouths, northern pike, walleye, lake trout, and a variety of other species lurk just back of these turbid, shoreline waters waiting for food stirred up by wave action. It may be wet and cold, but results usually far exceed those on the more comfortable lee side of the lake.

Rain washes food into streams and lakes causing fish to feed. I recall many instances of this occurring in the Ozarks, when a slowly rising river sent small-mouths on a rampage. The same is true in lakes where game fish move into shoreline waters following a downpour of rain.

Cloud cover also plays a part in selecting the best time of day to fish. During summer months a cloudy day lengthens the more productive morning and evening fishing hours, but in winter it likely will hold fish back from rising to warmer surface waters.

Trout and other fish are responsive to yet another factor affecting the best time to fish—insect hatches. When a hatch occurs, it's the same as ringing the dinner bell.

During the hatch, immediately check the insect for size and color. Whether fishing deep with a nymph or on top with a dry fly, the key to success is "matching the hatch." This doesn't mean a trout fly must be a perfect imitation of the natural insect, but it should approach it closely in size and color. Collecting several hundred different flies is fun for the fly tier, yet it isn't essential to fishing success.

Some anglers even go as far as to utilize a wristwatch in determining the best time to fish. Several years ago I fished with Howard Kelsey, operator of a dude ranch in Montana. Howard showed me a solunar watch that, he claimed, would tell the time of day when fish were most active.

I'd heard of the solunar theory but, until that time, put little stock in it. During the next 3 days, Howard put the watch to work with uncanny results. The best action with our flyrods started almost to the minute of when the watch indicated, and fishing slacked off at almost the exact moment when the watch signaled us to quit.

The Solunar Tables were developed by the late John Alden Knight, based on theories originating during market hunting days in the swamps of Georgia and Florida. The tables depend on the sun (solar) and the moon (lunar) and their relationship to the feeding rhythm of fish.

The tables indicate 4 solunar periods

One trick of night gigging is to keep feet anchored firmly on the bow of the boat.

of active feeding during each 24-hour day. There are two major periods, each lasting about 2 hours, and two minor periods of 45 minutes to an hour and a half each.

From my experience, I believe stream trout react more closely to the Solunar Tables than species inhabiting lakes. However, this could be explained by the fact that stream feeding areas are much easier to locate than those hidden beneath the surface of a lake, and thus streams become a better testing ground.

By now you realize that deciding when to go fishing can be a very complex matter. But, if all this subject matter seems overwhelming—rest your fears! The best philosophy still is to go fishing whenever you find time and wherever you find the place.

Any Fish Is a Good Catch

by Charles E. Most

*In an excellent little book entitled "Fishing for Fun and to
Wash Your Soul," Herbert Hoover referred to angling as a discipline
in equality, "for all men are equal before fish."
Having been politely shunned by species ranging from bullheads to
bonefish, it's clear to me Hoover had a point.
But what of the reverse—are all fish equal before men? Among most
fishermen I know, such a question is ridiculous,
for anglers have preferences—and prejudices—concerning the fish
they like to catch. But this doesn't change the fact
that any fish is still a prize worth the effort needed to catch it.*

BONEFISH ON FLORIDA FLATS

THE EFFORT required in bringing a fish to hand is undoubtedly one of the characteristics that gives a fish a preferred status. Some are simply tougher to catch than others, and the sporting way dictates that such fish become the most eagerly sought.

I believe this is as it should be.

The brown trout, noted for its wariness and probably the most prized trout among fly-fishing advocates, is a good example. I recall a stream in Pennsylvania, primarily brown trout water, where the fish are so "educated" that to have one or two just examine your offering during a day's fishing seems ample reward. Tiny flies, gossamer leader tippets, and great finesse in casting are believed vital to success on this beautiful stream. Just because I caught a 16-inch brown trout on a monstrous grasshopper imitation the first time I fished there has nothing to do with it.

Or does it?

Actually sport involves overcoming obstacles of our own making, and some fishermen tend to make their sport more demanding with tighter and tighter ground rules. If an angler feels that fairy-wand rods, microscopic flies, and leaders like spider webs are necessary to his success (and I can't say they are not), then those are the rules under which he chooses to play, and more power to him. But let's not forget that our objective is still a fish—a rather primitive creature, with a well-developed instinct for survival, but far from human intelligence.

A fishing teach-in.

I'm not saying that brown trout aren't difficult to catch. They do require extra effort, but the same goes for carp, a species reviled by many anglers. Those in the know realize how frustrating fishing for carp can be. These fish are so spooky that any clumsiness by the angler is likely to ruin the fishing for hours.

One of the cagiest anglers I know has developed his carp fishing to an art. He spends hours concocting various doughball baits designed to be the undoing of the huge carp that patrol the river near his home. I suspect he even goes through a few strange chants as part of the bait-making ceremony.

Whatever he does, it works; some of the scaly monsters he lands are downright frightening. This man realizes that carp are wary, that their small mouths, in relation to overall size, make them hard to hook, and that they are finicky about which baits will entice them to bite. He uses light lines to prevent frightening the fish and small hooks that aren't likely to be detected inside a doughball.

A 20-pound carp caught by this old riverman, who devotes much effort to his fishing, is as great a prize to him as a hefty brown trout would be to an angler using the most refined tackle. If you can't believe this, then the effort required to catch a fish is not a suitable measure of its value.

There are other attributes of various species that perhaps increase their value to anglers. Some taste better than others. Trout and large- and small-mouth bass are among our most popular freshwater fish and are delicious table fare. On the other hand, catfish are not overly difficult to catch, they are hard to clean, and they would hardly win any beauty prizes. Yet many people with a taste for fish—myself included—consider the lowly catfish as tasty as any American freshwater species.

Then there's the fast-stepping bonefish, one of the most prized fish sought by light-tackle saltwater anglers. I've never seen a mounted catfish, but almost everyone catching a bonefish wants it mounted so he can brag about it later. Yet bonefish are not considered edible at all. It doesn't seem that the table qualities of a fish are a good yardstick for measuring its value to anglers.

Perhaps it's the fighting ability of a fish when hooked that determines its sporting qualities and consequently its value to the angler. Strength that can put a strain on modern tackle is a factor that adds value to a catch. We all like to boast about the great skill needed to subdue a strong fish. Chinook salmon, the various tunas, lake trout, and red drum are good examples of fish noted for the strength they can pit against an angler's rod.

And yet a bluegill, for its size, can throw tremendous strength against a fisherman by turning the broadside of its body against the pull of the line. A professor of mine once described the fighting quality of bluegills as "holding onto the water as though they had claws." Many knowledgeable fishermen think bluegills, particularly when tackle is scaled to suit, are adversaries worth any angler's interest.

Neither can we discount the carp in any discussion of strength in fish. These brutes are not flashy fighters, but stopping their bull-like runs with anything less than heavy saltwater tackle is practically impossible. If bluegills and carp are not considered prize catches by sportsmen, then strength alone is not the basis for judging sporting qualities of fish.

131

The bowman meets a carp.

Speed is one attribute that the more popular species of fish seem to have in common, to a varying degree. Salmon and trout, including the rambunctious sea-run steelhead, display considerable speed when hooked. The elusive bonefish, which ghosts across the shallow flats of the Florida Keys, the Bahamas, and other tropical areas will, when spooked, turn on an awesome burst of speed to reach deeper water. I have heard that big billfish, particularly marlin, are the speediest of game fish. I frankly can't say—I've never fished for marlin or sailfish.

I remember, as a little boy, accompanying my grandfather on a sucker-snagging trip to an Ozark creek. Redhorse suckers were moving upstream to spawn, and grandfather would toss a line strung with alternating hooks and sinkers across a narrow part of the stream and wait for a big one to swim by. When the fish moved over the line, grandfather would give a violent yank, and more often than not, snag the fish on one of the hooks. I helped by keeping watch for fish moving toward the line.

Strangely enough, the one thing I remember best about this trip was the fish grandfather missed. I couldn't tell if they swam upstream or down because they simply disappeared. Several years later I tried my own variation of sucker-snagging, by lowering a weighted hook into a spring-fed Arkansas stream, to see if I could snag a big sucker resting on the bottom. As soon as the hook touched the fish, there was an explosion of speed as it moved to the lower end of the pool. I was younger then and more impressionable, but the speed of that fish impressed me just as much as that of the last bonefish I spooked in the Florida Keys.

Many fish sought by sport fishermen leap when hooked, and this certainly adds to the thrill of catching them. The noble Atlantic salmon is prized for its jumping ability as well as other sporting qualities. Probably the most aerial-minded of all trout is the rainbow, whose sea-run version, the lordly steelhead, is particularly notorious for wild leaps. Both largemouth and smallmouth bass tend to jump when hooked, with the smallmouth, in my experience, taking to the air more often.

The tarpon is probably the champion jumper of all fish sought by sportsmen. These overgrown herring throw themselves around with an unholy abandon when hooked and have broken overhanging, broomstick-size mangrove limbs during their frenzied leaps. Should one happen to land in the boat after one of its jumps, discretion calls for immediately abandoning ship. Their tremendous strength and total wildness makes them a threat to life and limb at close quarters.

That certain something that makes a fish leap when hooked is highly desirable to sportsmen, but that doesn't explain the popularity of bonefish, walleyes, and cutthroat trout, which seldom if ever jump. And what about the flyingfish? Will we someday have a sport fishery for these creatures which seem to feel they are more bird than fish?

A big fish of a given species is always worth bragging about, and the lucky angler catching an unusually large specimen is sure to get his picture in the hometown paper. Such a fish has survived longer, under a barrage of fishing lures and baits, escaped more natural enemies, and has developed its protective instincts to a keener edge, than lesser members of its tribe.

But when we cross tribal lines and compare a species of fish that never gets very large with another noted for its bulk, size begins to lose some of its meaning. A 20-pound carp may be a prize to my doughball-mixing friend but it's not likely to be honored by an ultra-purist trout fisherman.

Some species of fish seem to have studied knot-tying. At least I've hooked quite a few that knew just how to tie a line around the most convenient underwater obstruction. Some anglers say these fish are smart, others that they possess animal cunning. But such fish are actually just seeking shelter; and rocks, brush, and other obstructions are an automatic choice. On finding that the pull of a fisherman's lure persists after reaching such shelter, a fish will usually move on to other cover, tangling the line in the process.

Fish, such as rainbow trout and their sea-going steelhead brethren, Atlantic salmon, or shad, capitalize on the strength of moving water to try and escape the fisherman. Any angler hooking a big steelhead above a long, fast riffle needs track shoes or lots of line. These fish seem to always run downstream when hooked, and the fisherman must either make a record-breaking dash down the bank or, with enough line on the reel, let the fish run to the next pool and then follow at a more leisurely pace.

The first steelhead I hooked headed downstream with a savage rush, while boulders and logjams on the shore prevented me from following quickly enough. The fish hit the end of the line going full tilt, and that was the end of that. Now when I fish steelhead there's plenty of line on the reel, and I try to pick spots with the fewest obstructions along the shore.

The fish may be tiny but the interest is great.

There are many species of saltwater fish that live in and around coral reefs. Snappers and groupers in particular like the reef habitat, and catching them midst such hazards can be a trial. Some of the groupers are extremely powerful, and when hooked, generally swim into one of the coral caves. A fisherman's line, even of heavy test, cannot last long against sharp coral.

Fish that use every advantage offered by their environment, be it snags, coral, or a heavy current, offer a challenge that enriches the fishing experience. I've hooked brown trout that wedged themselves so tightly in thick mossbeds I had to reach in and haul them out, moss and all. And just thinking of the

134

Catfish oblige on trotlines in the river.

Beaching a sandbar shark is a tough job.

largemouth bass I've lost to stumps and snags is enough to make me weep. When I do lead a fish through a series of underwater hazards, however, the suspense makes it a moment that lives forever.

Some fish are lovely to behold; others seem to be somewhat lacking in physical beauty. Most trout, for example, are colorful, especially at spawning time, and their streamlined conformity, evolved to breast heavy currents, gives them an overall attractiveness to sportsmen. The brookie is probably easiest of all trouts to catch, but it is also among the highest prized by anglers. I suspect the primary reason for this is the brookie's wild, exotic beauty. I consider it the most colorful among America's commonly caught trout.

Even fish that are not very colorful or otherwise attractive have their following. Northern pike, chain pickerel, and muskellunge are far from winning any piscatorial beauty contest, but hordes of fishermen travel thousands of miles each year to fish for them. These fish have been called "water tigers" from the way they pounce from hiding onto their prey.

Perhaps it's their wicked appearance and a reputation as efficient killers that attract anglers. Their vicious strike is a thrill few fishermen soon forget.

And then some fish just live in more beautiful surroundings than others. I've caught bluegill in Okefenokee Swamp, snook in Florida's Everglades, smallmouth bass in pastoral Ozark rivers, and trout in mountain streams of the West. In every case, I have thoroughly enjoyed both the scenery and the fishing.

There are anglers, however, who are more provincial. A southern swamp may appear foreboding to some, while a western stream, fishing across a sagebrush flat, lacks appeal to others. A river that's polluted or whose banks are littered with trash certainly detracts from any fishing experience there. So the esthetic qualities of a fish's home, as seen through the eyes of an angler, can add to the popularlity of a particular species.

Imagine, after all that hauling and pulling . . . a clearnose skate.

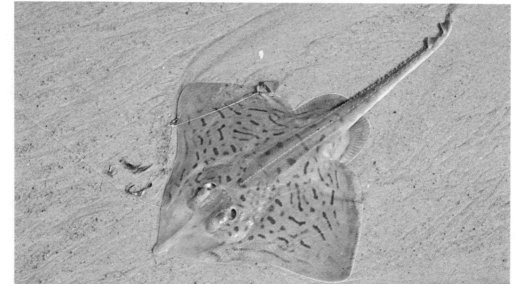

The green sunfish will challenge anything.

Why a certain species of fish should have greater appeal to a particular angler is a nebulous thing. The presence, or lack, of the various qualities I've discussed certainly influences such thinking, but there's no overlooking the personal attitude of the fisherman as a factor. And who can figure this out? I am not even sure I understand my own attitudes.

For example, I claim not to be particularly interested in eating fish—it's the sport of catching them that counts. Yet two experiences, one in freshwater and one in the salt, point up the hypocrisy of such an attitude.

Several years ago, while surf fishing on North Carolina's Outer Banks, I felt a sharp tug on the bait, and something powerful began taking out line. I was sure it could only be a good-sized red drum. After a lengthy seesaw battle, punctuated by moments of inactivity when I couldn't budge the fish, I finally landed the creature, and to my chagrin saw it was a big skate, a species of ray.

Sure I was disappointed—but why? The beast had given me a thrilling battle, and after all, I was certainly not interested in catching something to eat. Instincts are sometimes a better barometer of motives than thinking processes are.

Once while float-fishing Pennsylvania's Juniata River, I had a hard strike and saw a good-sized fish dash through a shallow area and into deeper water. I had apparently hooked a whopper smallmouth bass. After a hard fight that actually tired my arm, I boated a good-sized fallfish—a trash fish in most eastern streams.

Here was a fish that struck savagely at an artificial lure and then gave me a tremendous battle. Was my disappointment because fallfish are not as good to eat as bass? Perhaps I just wanted a fish I could brag about.

The soul-searching following these two experiences taught me not to be a fishing snob. I'm now convinced that any species of fish is a good catch—a prize worth the effort—and that an angler should go fishing when and where he can.

Because the finest fish I know just happens to be the one I'm currently trying to catch.

137

Escape to Reality

by Charles K. Fox

It is an unusual person who has not set aside his daily worries and at least once gone to the distant shore to wet a line. Indeed, doctors regularly prescribe this type of experience as a tonic for the weary. "Escape from reality; it'll do you good," they say. I wonder, is it such an escape? There is the story of the Wall Street broker who was quite an angler. He lived for his weekend and vacations so he could fish. A friend asked him whether he thought of it as an escape from reality? "Certainly not," he said. "It's an escape from the routine, humdrum, worrisome world, to reality. Fishing is more real to me than Wall Street."

FISHING, DAWN

IN ORDER that there be less misunderstanding of the outdoor-minded person and what it is that makes him tick, it is necessary first to reverse the direction of the march of time in the manner of an H. G. Wells. The time machine should be cranked back, way back, to the era preceding the dawn of civilization, then updated again, whereupon the answer to why a man chooses to fish and hunt comes through to all loud and clear.

From the beginning and throughout the Dark Ages there continued without abatement the conquest of man against the creatures of nature. Primitive cavemen depended upon wildlife for sustenance. Necessity forced him to catch, gather, and produce the things needed for food and clothing. The leader was called upon by the rest of the band for protection.

As a carnivore, man, by necessity, preyed upon the other creatures of nature. Such was life and he kept living it. The battle to survive was the only thing that counted. This was the story of early man in a period of time longer in duration than that of recorded history.

Now, today, there exists a latent desire to follow in the footsteps of progenitors. Each generation in turn produces a scion cast from the mold of his father. Each generation in turn hears the call which has reverberated through the years. As the angler answers this deeply ingrained and powerful pull out of the past, his blood is stirred most when he discovers a big actively feeding fish. He must follow his old leader who in the long ago led the band.

Let us investigate further this discriminating descendent of Cro-Magnon who waves a fairy wand as he wades a

"Fishing is more real to me than Wall Street."

stream or sits in a craft. Involved is a strange paradox, in fact the strangest for any sport and something positively confounding to the nonangler. He sets forth to catch fish, but he doesn't want to catch them too easily. He likes to catch large ones, but he doesn't want them all to be the same size. He doesn't like to have the experience of fish getting away, but he doesn't wish to be successful in landing all he hooks. Just because he is after fish, doesn't mean he must kill each in turn as it is reduced to possession.

Obviously, necessary requirements in his success formula are a certain degree of failure and considerable uncertainty. The yardstick of success for the regular angler is the degree of personal satisfaction which is realized. He revels in the challenge of natural problems and glories in the solution of some of them.

Stephen Gwynn, an Englishman who penned the *Happy Fisherman,* wrote: "Yet if all this experience has taught me anything, it's that a fisherman's best prizes are not accessible by any mechanical estimate. They have their own avoirdupois, which takes into generous reckoning, amongst other things, the fish we do not catch."

In our fishing, things are governed by the laws of relativity. What may be a giant of the species in one environment may be a pygmy elsewhere. The more hazardous the cast, the greater the challenge. The more complicated the landing, the more cherished the catch. All is measured in terms of personal satisfaction.

A comparison between a recreation and an athletic team sport is fair and in order. He who participates in the spectator sport has his great day in the morning; the chief satisfaction and reward—and they are great—stem from individual effort and coordination action, particularly if such activity wins the game or lifts the underdog above the favorite. Then it ends even before youth steals into middle age only to emerge into the world of make-believe to temporarily revert to the glory days. The old player just sits and watches and dreams.

The opposite is true of the angler, for he enjoys a lifetime of participation which continues through noon, then on into the sunset, and even into the eventide of life.

In writing about the one-hundredth college football game, the first such event between old rivals (Lafayette and Lehigh, 1964), veteran writer, Al Laney of the New York Herald Tribune, with the following words, may have reached the zenith in sports reporting:

"Returning to the scene of their youth with the mournful scent of burning leaves in the nostrils, they succumb to a melancholy brooding while making contact with a vanished day, envisioning themselves and others as they once were.

"Here for a few brief hours they touch a land of ghosts whence comes the breath of autumn days that are past, the rustle of silk long faded, the scent of flowers that are dust.

"For those coming from far away and long ago it is a game of an earlier vintage. The banners, the bands, and the crowds are the same. Only the date and the names are different."

This is not the way with the angler. He too returns to the scene of an earlier day and an earlier contest. But unlike the athletic has-been, the angler is better prepared, trip after trip, to contend with a worthy adversary. He is ever becoming a better observer, a keener analyst, and finer practitioner. By comparison his

141

"The angler . . . enjoys a lifetime of participation . . . into the eventide of life."

schedule is long, flexible, and of his own making. He enjoys a great day in the morning, a greater one in the afternoon, and the greatest in the evening of his life.

It is true that the regular angler forgets most of the fish he catches but he does not forget the streams and lakes in which they were caught. Brooklets, little rivers, big waters—all are rich in memory, rich in hope. Identical waters do not exist; similar ones are rare. The pools, too, vary as much as the streams of which they are a part, being different

142

"The love of nature was passed on to me, and I in turn am passing it along."

"One learns to love the dainty art for its own sake."

in size, setting, character, potential, and different in the fascinating problems they present. Streams merit the attention of the angler and artist alike, for all or in part, each possesses an attraction, a beauty, and nobleness of its own. Man cannot manufacture a stream; that is the work of the Creator; however, man

144

can make a body of water, a pool of almost any size above the appropriate dam.

Dr. James J. Waring of Denver, Colo., a fly fisherman and student of angling literature, touched his fellow doctor-anglers when he described in a speech to them, which he chose to call "The Anatomy of Angling," the following relating to the passing of an angler:

"Over 30 years ago, a friend and neighbor my own age, a passionate fisherman, lay dying of tuberculosis. During the last week of his life, continuously day and night, his devoted mother ran the water in the adjoining bathroom at his request. As his spirit hung between heaven and earth, his fevered imagination, prompted by the sound of running water, transported him to scenes and streams where he had fished, and he was comforted."

Progress in fishing continues, thus angling is a progressive pursuit. Each age has added its development and each age has had its say. Much is owed to anglers of past generations, but there is always up-to-the-minute information about fish, fishing, and fishermen. It is because of this that more writings on the subject are justified and each should have a value of its own.

The angling hobbyist combines a love of nature with the delights of angling. Beauty strews his path. There remains the difficulty of expressing the pleasure of it all, but some good men have done this well.

Rev. William Cowper Prime in *I Go A-Fishing*, 1873, contributed the following:

"The contentment which fills the mind of the angler at the close of his day's sport is one of the chiefest charms in his life. He is just sufficiently wearied in body to be thoughtful, and the weariness is without nervousness, so that thoughts succeed each other with deliberation and calm, not in haste and confusion. The evening talk after a day of fishing is apt to be memorable. The quiet thinking on the way home is apt to be pleasant, delicious, sometimes even sacred."

There comes a time when physique is falling, but mentality continues to climb. A master angler, Will H. Dilg, one of the founders of the Izaak Walton League of America, wrote:

"Those of us who have reached the half-century mark or more, and whose trail gently leads towards the setting sun, more and more value the yesterdays, especially the angling yesterdays. For doubtless we fishermen dream far more often of our favorite sport than other men of theirs."

Angling is the way to round out a happy life. There is romance in the knowledge that the naturals and the imitations are the same today as they were yesterday; even some of the pools, the hiding places, and feeding stations we know, our forefathers knew before us.

A man is the substance of the things he loves. The love of nature was passed on to me, and I in turn am passing it along. Maybe in their over-crowded world, my boy and my girl will discover escape from the concentrations and complications of people and revel in their own outdoors. Maybe they will be thankful for the wild strain in their blood and that I was their father. They deserve to inherit a stretch of trout water, which may remain sufficiently clean, along with a thicket and a swamp. And maybe, too, they will delight to be along a stream with a flyrod for company.

The stream, whatever the type and size, was murmuring, singing, or roar-

"The stream, whatever the type or size, was murmuring, singing, or roaring . . . even before the wildnerness was given a name."

"All is measured in terms of personal satisfaction."

ing in its wilderness even before the wilderness was given a name. Fortunate we are to be able to follow the trails of our fathers along a stream traveling toward the ocean and not too heavily charged with poison.

For generation after generation, angling has appealed to the highest type of mind. This is no casual pastime, it is inborn and instinctive, a pursuit reduced to a science. One learns to love the dainty art for its own sake and the little details become delightful.

Anglers come and anglers go, and the brooklet, the little river, and the big waters flow on. In man's brief passage through time he has wrought destruction and damage. The pertinent question is, will he take care of what is left so that fish thrive therein with the result that the sport of angling flourishes? The answer must be in the affirmative, for there must be clean water to sustain human life and that is where the fish will be.

Try the Unusual

by A. George Morris

To catch fish today, with all the angling pressure that we have on our streams and lakes, you have to give them something different, a bit unusual. Don't go down to the water and try to beat the fish to death with a lure like the ones they have already seen a dozen times that day. Either be smarter than the fish or try to think like one. Speakers tell a joke to get audience attention before starting the serious part of their talk. If you don't get the attention of a fish when you get to the stream, how do you expect it to take your hook—or even know you are fishing? The largest bass in the stream might be just on the other side of a log from your bait and starving for that particular morsel with which you are fishing.

CHANNEL CATFISH AND BROWN BULLHEAD

Get their attention

To try the unusual at least once. Instead of slipping down to the edge of the stream, being careful to make no noise or cast no shadow on the water, go all out! Walk down as if you owned the place. Pick up a big boulder and throw it out in the middle of your choice fishing hole. Then sit down and spend a little time lighting the old pipe and getting the tackle ready for fishing. Sure, you ran all the fish to the other side of the hole of water, but you got their attention, and soon they will swim back to see what caused the commotion. That is when you want to be fishing.

I have a friend who tries the quiet approach with his boat to his favorite crappie hole. He fishes for awhile and, if the fish don't bite, he gets out the oar and whams the water once or twice. It's hard to believe but sometimes it works. It's unusual!

On the market today are many lures that are supposed to attract the fish by giving off a noise underwater. Topwater baits make a burping noise that seems to get the fish's attention and at the same time aggravate them into biting.

Have you noticed the beautiful painting on the topwater lures? Well, that's to attract fishermen. The fish never see it unless they jump entirely out of the water and come down from above. The part they see is always a solid color, usually some variation of white, black, yellow, or red. Now, if the body of the plug could be turned upside down, I'm sure the fish would appreciate looking at your beautiful painting also. They might even reward your effort by taking a bite. So if the plug can't be reversed, get a little paint and try your luck at being an artist. You will be surprised, even though you are no great shakes as a piscatorial Reubens.

It's pretty common practice now for the fisherman to take along a transistor radio when he goes fishing. He can com-

150

Fishing with music.

bine listening to the ball game with fishing and the trip can't be a total loss. Try hanging the ear phone to the radio down underwater to attract fish to your location. It will work! I have done much experimenting with this method, but haven't yet found whether the fish prefer grand opera or a good hillbilly band.

Art for fish.

In fact, while I was experimenting to find out the kind that they really preferred, a curious bluegill took a nip at my ear phone and almost got away with radio and all. It might be well to equip your ear phone with a hook, just in case a 5-pound bass decides that the mechanism is a new kind of bug!

At one of those popular "put-and-take" rainbow trout fishing areas, it became well known by the best fishermen that several trout of very large size were in the stream. More than 100,000 fishermen fished the 2 miles of trout stream that year, where the usual fish released each night were 10 inches and over in length. But several trout had eluded the ordinary baits offered and turned to a diet of fish entrails that were thrown back in the stream by the fishermen when they cleaned their fish. (That practice was permitted on this stream.)

I don't know how much research and study a certain fisherman did, but I do

151

know that he finally came up with a bait like no other ever made. He took some white, cream, and red yarn and fashioned what resembled a minature mop. Unusual? It was a disgrace! He would plant a hook in the center of his mop bait, throw it out in the stream and permit it to roll on the bottom—the customary action of discarded fish entrails. He and his buddies were rewarded with many trout that weighed up to 10 pounds. It really worked—until the bait became usual. Then the catch of lunkers stopped.

Catfish, especially channels, usually have a given diet during the different seasons of the year. They do, however, like to pick up some other tidbits along with the regular diet. White laundry soap would not generally be considered a very good dessert, but channels sometimes think it is delicious. If you can secure fresh soap that hasn't been on the store shelf too long, it will be soft enough to be cut with a sharp knife without crumbling. A regular size bar of laundry soap will make a couple of dozen baits that will remain on the hooks of throw lines, trot lines, and bank hooks for at least 24 hours if the fish don't bother it.

One thing about using soap as a bait is that the fish caught will have clean mouths.

I noticed once, while dressing a couple of channel catfish, that they had some wild grapes in their stomachs. I figured they were not out climbing trees to get the grapes, so the fruit had to be falling in the water somewhere. I finally located a tree full of grapes hanging out over the water. By stringing a half dozen grapes on my hook I brought in several nice cats while fishing right where the

Try everything.

Soap bait.

152

Spoonbill fishing.

grapes were falling. Even when the wild ones were gone, tokay grapes worked very well; in fact the fish seemed to like the change.

Paddlefish don't seem to care much for the baits that you and I know about. They have an immense paddle-shaped snout which normally is half as long as the remainder of their body. The fish uses this bill to plow up the silt bottom of the stream and then, by straining the silt through its gills, which are almost like a net, it gets its food from the remaining small organisms. It must be a good diet, since paddlefish grow to 50 pounds and often more. I think these fish would bite a hook baited with chiggers or fleas, but it is a little tedious putting those mites on a hook. Probably that is why some sly person found paddlefish can be "grabbed" at certain times of the year.

On the Osage River in Missouri, people come from all surrounding States to grab paddlefish. Tons are caught each year. Your gear for this should be saltwater tackle, equipped with a reel having a drag and heavy line. Put a sinker on the end of your line and then tie from two to three treble hooks above the sinker about 1 foot apart. Cast out as far as possible, let the sinker drop to the bottom, and then start bringing it in with a series of jerks. It is a lot of work, but the struggle really starts when you hook a 40- or 50-pound paddlefish in the back or tail and try to bring it in to the creel.

The man who told me that a paddlefish tastes like a wet dog smells was all wrong. The fish is wonderful smoked. It is practically free of bones; even the spine is cartilage. If you should catch one containing roe, you've got first-rate caviar.

My grandfather told me—long ago, I'm afraid—about a man who knew where there was an extremely large catfish in the river that he wanted to catch. When catfish get ready to lay their eggs, they find a hole back in a bank or in a hollow log or under a large rock. This particular fish was holed up under a high bank. It wouldn't bite a thing that was offered on a hook, so the man decided to get it anyway. He made a hook with a barb on it, tied the hook to his wrist, went down to the river, and dived in. He paddled up in the hole where the catfish was and, after rubbing it on its back to quiet it down, he jerked the hook up under the catfish's jaw.

153

Some 2 weeks later, they found the man and the fish bound together about a mile down the stream, both dead. The fish had more strength than he had and held him under the water until he drowned, then finally the catfish died from pulling him down the stream.

That is noodling, but I never did want to catch a fish that way, and besides, in most States it is unlawful.

I guess the reason I never did like gigging is that everything connected with it requires that you be a perfectionist. First you have to obtain a gig, not any old gig that you can buy at the store, but one fashioned from the steel of a wood rasp. It must be tempered by the blacksmith so you can plunge it into a rock on the bottom of the stream without breaking it or dulling the point.

An amateur might be content with a gig made from a three-pronged fork, but not the expert, not the man that can stand on the end of a johnboat and go down a stream laced with rapids. He is the one that is not content with standing on the bottom of the boat either, but stands on the sides. By the light of a gasoline lantern, he can spot a fish out in the stream, throw the gig for 25 feet in 5 feet of water, and hit a fish running for its life. I am convinced gigging is a sport.

Once I tried gigging. Picture me (or yourself) at dark midnight, floating down a clear stream, standing up, looking for fish from the end of the boat. My helper, who was paddling, said, "Look at the wasp nest in that tree!"

Gigging.

Soft bait for pike.

I looked. While I was looking the boat moved to the other side of the stream. I didn't move with it. While paddling around in 10 feet of water with the temperature down near zero, I concluded that I didn't like to gig. It didn't seem the sporting thing then. Besides, nothing ever happens in connection with it that is really unusual!

I do like to catch northern pike. But they have a way of looking at you, as they follow an ordinary bait into your boat without attempting to bite it, that has always made me feel a little ashamed of myself for not furnishing them with a more interesting lure.

I never knew until a journey to Canada a few years ago that northerns shed their teeth during a certain part of the summer and can't bite a thing until their mouths heal up. My Indian guide told me that. "Dog days," he said. He was sorry I was there at the wrong time of year—northerns were in a deplorable state—"no teeth, no eat." Having had experience with dentures and knowing how painful a sore mouth can be, I spent the first night thinking about the poor fish starving to death, because they couldn't eat the usual hard plugs offered by the fishermen.

After staying awake half the night worrying about the deprived northerns, I took my guide the next day on a hunt for grass frogs. Fortunately, he knew where they were located. We caught 10 and put them in a small muslin sack. Then we caught 10 more and so on until I thought we had the required number. We wet the sacks to keep them cool.

That evening we started out in a lake where northerns were known to be in the majority among all fish present. We hooked a grass frog under the chin on the usual weedless silver spoon and then cast as we would have with any artificial bait. It's hard to believe how fast the gums of those northerns healed up. They forgot they didn't have teeth! The guide couldn't believe it.

When I returned home I did a little research and found that northerns shedding all their teeth is classed as a myth—like the belief that powdered northern jawbone will cure pleurisy. I am still convinced, though, that to catch fish, it does help to think like a fish.

Were you ever out topwater fishing when the fish came up to your bait, looked at it and swam off? Or jumped out of the water a foot from the bait? It was pretty obvious that you were attracting the fish up to where it should hit the bait but the offering just wasn't what it wanted. The usual thing to do would be to try another topwater bait and see if the change of color or action would make the fish more anxious to bite.

But instead of trying another bait, tie a foot-long piece of nylon to the back treble hook on the lure you have and equip that nylon with a hook. Then start baiting the hook with the various things that you think a fish might like. Cast in a normal manner. Try a live minnow hooked in the mouth, a frog, a worm— or, if you don't have any such baits, attach an artificial fly, or some small lure. Somewhere along the line you will hit the combination. This works especially well when you are trolling with a sink-

Try various baits.

Gourmet bait.

ing plug behind the boat, and the fish are following the plug but just don't seem to hit.

Baiting a hole is an accepted practice for taking warmwater fish. To do this you choose a spot in a lake or stream and build up a cafeteria attraction for finny diners, where you can return frequently—and catch fish. Game varieties, crappie especially, like to hide and feed around a submerged tree. Make sure that the tree you use has many branches. A lot of fishermen use cedar or pine trees, but a scuba-diving friend of mine on an impoundment where I fish said he noticed fish around all the submerged trees except cedar and pine. So, I use anything but cedar and pine.

Twice a week some sort of feed should be put in the water above the tree of your choice so it will sink down through the limbs. Trout feed sold by your local feed dealer is perfect. You are trying to attract crappie and largemouth bass, but really you must first lure small fish and minnows to your sunken tree. So bait the spot with the small size feed for little

156

fish. Then the larger bass and crappie will come to eat the fingerlings that are feasting on your fish chow.

Baiting a hole for carp, catfish, and suckers can furnish more enjoyment than you ever realized possible. Leave out the tree with these fish because you are going to need room for a battle. You want a clear underwater space; and you need to bait in water that is more than 5 feet deep, so your actions on the suface will not disturb the fish. Use canned corn (whole grain), or shelled corn that has been soaked for a few hours in warm water.

If available, one cotton-seed cake should be planted on the bottom of the hole each week. You can get cotton seed in a cake, about 1 inch thick, 12 inches wide, and 2 feet long. It will sink in the water, but to be sure that the fish eating it don't move it around, drill a few holes in it, run a cord through these, and attach some rocks. Don't make the mistake of putting the feed in a sack, even a mesh sack. You shouldn't expect fish to hang around just for the smell.

After you get the fish attracted to your spot, you have the sport of catching them. For the crappie and bass you naturally use minnows, but to take care of the ones that are already gorged on such fare, you will need a little something unusual. Try casting a small jig, say white or yellow. Let it sink to the bottom and reel it in slowly.

You will find that a number 3/0 gold plated hook, carrying two or three grains of corn, will produce fish in a hole baited for carp. If you prefer to make your own come-ons, try using some wheat flake breakfast cereal, moistened and worked into a stiff dough. Into this dough you can mix many things. Peanut butter seems to be like candy to some fish. I even know one man who put half a jigger of his favorite booze in the dough in place of an equal amount of water. He caught fish. You never can tell!

Since man invented sheer stockings for ladies, things in the fishing world have changed. If you are able to swipe a pair of your wife's hose—or you can always talk her out of a pair with runs in them—you are in business. Cut a nylon stocking in small squares, insert about any ingredient that you think a fish will bite, and tie it into a ball. Put this on your hook.

If you want to keep the bait clean, you can purchase a small bag of trout pellets from your local fish food dealer and tie a few in the nylon square. If you have a cold or just don't care about the smell, lay a shad out in the sun for a few hours, then mash it and put a large spoonful of the result into your ball. If you don't get their attention with that bait, it is because fish have lost their sense of smell. And you likely wouldn't want to eat a fish in that shape anyway.

Manufacturers of chlorine bleach sure helped anglers when they started putting their product in plastic gallon jugs. Jug fishing is an accepted way to catch catfish on many of our large rivers. It also will work on lakes. Get a dozen or so (or whatever is legal in your State) of the jugs. Screw the cap down tight, for this is your cork and you want it to float. Attach 5 or 6 feet, depending on the depth of the stream, of good strong monofilament line to each of the jugs by tying to the handle. Equip each line with a hook and sinker.

When you get to the stream, don't bait all of the hooks with the same thing; give the prey a little variety. Throw the jugs out in the water in a group and follow along with a boat that is equipped with a good easy chair. When you see a jug bobbing up and down, you have a fish; go get it. This kind of fishing is similar to getting money from home without writing for it.

There is always some way to catch fish, if there are fish in the stream. Try the usual—but also try the unusual. There seems to be only one fishing rule to which you can't find a new and better angle. That Golden Rule reads: "You will catch more fish if you keep your hook in the water."

Jug fishing.

A Memorable Day

by Anne H. Bosworth

You've had 5 days of slow water and slow weather,
and sharp as a lightning bolt, something goes tight inside of you.
You can feel it—there's a big day coming up!
Suddenly, on that hot, Hawaiian July night, the hurricane lamps on
the Kona Inn patio tables seem to flare nervously high,
and there's a sharper smash to the white surf against the seawall—
a different feel to the very air.
You tell this to your captain, who has just polished off a big steak dinner,
talking boats, baits, bad runs, and better ones.
You caught your first marlin with this man. He knows what you mean.
"Good," he says, pleased. "Real good. We'll run
early, then. Ha' past 6." And he's gone with a quick, "Good night."

PACIFIC MARLIN

YOU LEAVE as quickly, by-passing some beckons from the bar. "No, thanks" you say, stretching your arms fish-length wide. "Got a big date tomorrow." You get some raised "V" fingers, and some "Ho-ho-ho's" from the nonbelievers who have sat through the last 5 days. But you can feel your big one coming up, and for you, morning cannot come too soon.

In the dark of your room, you watch the torchlight flares spread weird palm frond shadows on your window. You're in for the night, your gear ready for the quick morning run, but sleep will not come. You go over in your mind other runs, other times.

You think about this captain, the man you are fishing with tomorrow. He's a charter man, and a bit of everything; a fine fisherman, who thinks like a fish, a fine boatman, who runs that sampan-hull of his as a teenager skips a skateboard. His boat is clean, his gear is clean, his lines are good, and his rods and reels suited to his game.

His greatest pride are his lures, most of them made to order, in special shapes and colors, expensively original, but on these big blues they work! He keeps them in top condition, cherishes them, and experiments with them like a scientist, with his better fishermen.

He loves his job, he loves the sea. He's a family man, a combination of icthyologist, oceanographer, sailor, teacher, adventurer, philosopher.

This man I am to fish with tomorrow taught me most of what I know of blue marlin fishing, patiently explaining the "why," cannily running a course that caught fish when there wasn't one to be seen. He gave me hard practice on the lures, the lines, the lengths, the split second to strike.

My old friend, Captain Juan, off Palmilla, Baja, sitting atop the cabin roof of his anciently creaking boat, eyes to sea, steering through the hatch with gnarled brown feet on the wheel taught me how to "snap-to" when black marlin swimming two-by-two in lazy circles ig-

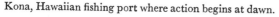

Kona, Hawaiian fishing port where action begins at dawn.

nore the bait. They'd still be there in twos, unless you fished as Juan advised you!

And finally, counting the catches like so many sheep, the crash-smash rhythm of the surf against the breakwater washes out today, and you are gone, gone, gone to tomorrow.

"Fi-thirty, lady," says your guardian angel of the wake-up crew. You stumble to the shower, dress, and go half-alert to the early breakfast line, with very few stragglers up.

The bay is mother-of-pearl, the palm fronds clatter in the early morning breeze. Several of the fishing boats ride at anchor, their night lights still ruby-red against dark hulls. Tide is out, the surf froths low out over the brown rocks, and suddenly the wind shifts slightly south. Oh, this is better than good!

Several of the early-up fishermen look at you, amusedly, indulgently—the only woman there at that hour.

"Who are you fishing with?" one asks.

"Alone," you answer. You don't add, "And I love it! The sea's all mine, the boat's all mine, and there's a big one out there, all mine!" But you know it and feel it. Today's the day!

At 6:20 your captain is at the inn door, and you clamber into the cab of the truck with him, to rattle down to the docks. The torches are still burning at Kona Inn and King Kam, the village is just waking. The south wind holds, and your Sampan-Hull-to-Heaven is rocking with a gentle surge at the docks.

Joe, the boat-boy who has slept at anchor, and brought her in for you to board, grins a welcome. He's an old friend, too. He cuts his eyes at the captain as you hand down lunch, gear, and your clean white slacks and shirt in a cellophane bag. You may start out in jeans and sweat shirt, but you're going to come home looking girl. It's 6:30 on the tick as you cast off, and all three of you can't wait.

Out of the harbor, the water chuckles along under the hull, the breeze holds south, the sky lifts to a lighter rose, and a lightening blue. There are scuds of white on the wave riffles, and a world that stretches endlessly, belongs wholly, purely to you. What a morning! What a day! You're out to sea!

Joe is busy bringing out the gear, three heavy boat rods, and your own light 50-pound test tackle with a lure these big blues can smash to bits at first hit. This is your own chance, for 80-pound test is about as light as your Pacific charter man wants to risk catch and gear with, and rightly so. These are all investments to him, too valuable to lose. If you want to run risks on light tackle, use your own.

Captain passes you a mug of steaming coffee, and Joe stops to show you the lures he's re-tailing. Color is important. It's early morning, so he's rigging two yellow and a light green, smooth, lively, gleaming, with a scatter of tinsel and glitter in their clear plastic bodies. He deftly attaches the slashed rubber skirts, test hooks honed to murder-point with a careful thumb, and snaps them onto the leaders. With solemn superstition you spit, and the game begins.

The lines go out, Joe hooks up the outriggers, and in the wake of the boat, the lures ride the froth, leaping, bouncing, diving, weaving. Beautiful action! The sun is up now, glinting bright edges on the small surface waves of the grey-blue water. You watch for the first sight of birds wheeling to feed on schools of small fish, skipping from the feeding larger ones. You hope your marlin fol-

A black marlin leaps, then line peels out as it makes a dash.

lows them. You can only wait.

For a moment, a frigate bird hangs motionlessly high above, and you watch the water behind the lures . . . no show. Rarely ever can you see a blue till he hits, but still you watch. You are superstitious about frigates. More than once this has meant a marlin below, but he drifts, and again you wait.

The frigate goes, and out of the sea by dozens, frolicking, diving, dolloping, a school of porpoises race around, under and ahead of the boat. The captain grumbles at loss of fishing time, but you love them. They're your good luck, they'll lead you straight to marlin. They have done it before, and will do it today. You lean forward over the rail, and can almost touch the nearest one, who swims persistently alongside. And then, with a last flip, they are all gone.

The sea is rising a little, you stretch and stand, easing to the long ground-swells running under the boat. Off to portside, a dark piece of flotsam shows, and your two friends humor you. Captain cuts over to have a look, and Joe hustles in two of the heavy boat rod lines, so you can have your light tackle fun.

You get it! There are dolphin around the old half-submerged freight box floating there, and on the first come-about, you get a beautiful smashing hit, and a breathtaking 5-minutes of fun. Another hit on the other line! Joe plays it, and you bring them both in, vivid and golden—the sea's best.

With lines wet, the day has really begun. Joe re-rigs, you have some more coffee, you begin to get the feel again. You want to see blue water, but the sea stretches out, an endless slate blue-grey. No birds in sight, no boil of small fish feeding. Wait for the turn of tide, your memory tells you. Wait.

Wait! That's the essence of marlin fishing, having the patience to find your game. The endless days when fish are scarce, and the weather is bad, and your luck seems gone—all are part of it. Wait,

Fury spent, the billfish lies exhausted and a guide applies the gaff.

Skipjack tuna's vertical markings indicate feeding frenzy.

for the slow tracking down of a fish you know is there, but won't hit your bait. Change your lures, change your bait, change your trolling speeds. Patience, patience, wait. Lose today, and go again tomorrow.

Marlin are hard to come by, a game fish prize, not alone for weight, the skill that goes into the catch of such a fighter, the thrill of his running, smashing, tremendous strength. Marlin have been played to the end of endurance, 7½, 11, 14½ hours on heavy 130-pound test line, stripped the gears on 16/0 reels, defied any boatman's maneuvers to run them down, and still got away!

Black, blue, striped and white—all are fantastic fighters, each one running differently and each strike differently made. Little is really known of the migrating, spawning, feeding, and lifespan of marlin. Like Indians, they live in strength and die in battle. It's almost impossible to bring one in green.

He has a thousand tricks, this sea tiger, from sawing lines with his bill, tailwrapping, tight turns, and charging the boat. Once hooked, he's maniacal. He will slam his powerful bill into a mahogany hull in fury, and the boat of a charter captain once was so attacked. A prominent Senator occupied the head at the time and was nearly impaled. The captain cut the bill off inside the head, polished it round, and it is quite the most famous utility holder afloat.

You tell your captain you'll settle for one caught that way today as a last resort. You're set on having your fish. He suggests lunch to break the slow streak, and it does. You're no sooner settled with the food out, than the water boils ahead.

Joe hurries out the light tackle for live bait. The bright jig scarcely hits foam when you're hit, fast, zing, more like a dolphin than the bonito you expected. What a little fighter! The light rod is a tight arc, you guess 50 pounds of fish out there, the way he feels.

And then you see him. Bonito! But a good bonito; he's a big one. So big that, when you bring him in, captain checks the marine records. He weighs him on the hand scales, and you find he beats the present line record by 11 ounces, at his even 31 pounds. You wrap him up tenderly in wet tarp, to keep his weight till you can get to the weighmaster, and tear hungrily into your lunch, temporarily a bonito world's record holder.

Someway, for you, if you haven't had a morning catch, 1 o'clock has been a lucky hour for you, off the Kona coast. You are about as far out as you'll go by then, and without a hook-up, ready to start the long run home. Anything can happen at tide-turn, and you'll usually strike a stream of blue water. Luck is with you today. The porpoise came out to meet you. You had that crazy bonito catch! Yes, anything can happen from now on in. You sit in the chair, to wait.

The far Kona coast lies green, with a white crest of clouds on Mauna Loa, and the sun lies hot on your back and shoulders. Joe has clambered up and sits Yoga-crosslegged on the cabin roof, watching aft, when far ahead captain sees birds. He makes a fast run, and circles their feeding spot. You're out of the chair, and half over the rail, trying to see.

Circle and wait, circle and wait. Tiger, where are you? Joe sees him first, raised in one wild leap, with one fast greyhound. There he is, feeding! Captain guns the boat over in that direction, and you see a streak of water, bluer than the rest. That's where he is, your tiger! Once more you bless the man at the wheel, who knows his boat, his fish, and

this fighter so well.

Now, to get him to hit, in hunger or anger, however he will! You watch the lures leaping, and pray. You wish, fleetingly, he'd hit the 80 line or your 50. It would rack up more points for your fishing club. You hope he'll hit anything, anything, any one of them! Hit, hit! Please, Neptune, just let him hit!

The lure on the big 130-line rod on the left out-rigger sails high in the air, you've had one flash of the sight of his bill. It's big, he's a good fish. Oh, hit, hit, hit again, tiger! Hit!

Captain comes about in such a tight turn you're nearly off your feet, the right out-rigger snaps, and the reel screams on the other big rod. You grab it, count back, and strike. Your fish hurtles out of the water, raging, tailwalks, greyhounds, and tears off 200 yards of line before he sounds.

Both men work the other lines in, your fish is tight on yours. You get in the chair, hook your harness, and start to work him. You take in 100 yards, when he surfaces in fury, tears them off your reel with a fast greyhound, and disappears. You can feel him rolling on the end of that tight line!

Again, and again, and again he shoots up, every tailwalk a threat. Just let him wrap that line, and he'll pop it like a thread. One sounding, if he can get under you, and he's gone.

He's tailwalked until you can't believe he could do it again, smashing the water, rising, shaking, thrashing to throw the hook. He's run again when you thought you had him, and twice you've worked him to within 20 yards of the boat. There isn't a muscle left unstretched in your body, and still his strength is terrific.

On that last run you felt as if he would

The expedition ends with the weighing in, when the angler learns how close he came to a record.

haul you right through the guides and out with the line! You ask captain how long you have been hooked-up, and he tells you, "Twenty-five minutes. You're doin' good." Twenty-five minutes! It feels like 25 hours.

Determinedly you work back the last run. He's tiring now too and surfaces for a last thrash, 100 yards out. You can feel

him coming toward you, though. Little by little, you're going to make it. And he runs again! Enduring, hanging on, you watch the line peel off the reel. Tight line, tight line, stay with it till he stops. And reel in again.

Joe has counted 11 tailwalks, and eight greyhounds. Somehow you've held this fish, and you still have a tight line.

166

Tired as you are, your reel-in is more rhythmic. He's slowly yielding and coming to boat. The great body surfaces now, with a flash of white belly. This time he stays up a little, still fighting you, but with less thrash. You are getting him in.

Easy, easy, 20 more yards to go, 15, 10, you can see your leader, and Joe and the captain are ready to gaff. He puts up one last fast, furious, lunging struggle at boatside, but he's deep hooked, and will die if you release him. The captain's grunted "Got him," finishes your tiger. Joe clobbers him.

They pull him over the boat roller, and into the boat. He measures 11 feet 9, tail to bill tip. You guess him at around 250 or 260 pounds, not big as Pacific blues go, but a fine fish, and he gave you a terrific fight. You can't believe it only lasted 40 minutes, strike to boat. It seemed much longer.

Captain shakes hands, Joe shakes hands, and you are shaking with exhaustion and excitement. Your marlin, so vivid a butterfly-wing blue in life, is rapidly turning a rubbery black. You mourn the fact that you couldn't bring him to boat, just measure and release him, a feat as tricky with a Pacific blue as it is to catch and kill him.

You go below to freshen up, put on your clean white shirt and pants, and cool again, girl again, you don't look as though you had just sweated out a man-day's work.

This time you sit down in the chair in a glow of happiness. There'll be a real rally at the dock! The nonbelievers will have to eat mahi-mahi tonight. The water chuckles under the hull, the wake boils white, and whirls behind you. Inland, the coastline is incredibly lush, green, and beautiful in the afternoon sun. You're too tired to talk, too content to care. You've had a memorable day.

Their Names Are Writ on Water

The Kienbusch Collection by Carl Otto von Kienbusch

*Carl Otto von Kienbusch has combined business, fishing,
and literature in his long life. He not only wet many a line; as an
amateur historian, he has collected and studied the world's
early literature on angling. His collection of angling literature has been
deposited at Princeton University Library, where anyone who wants to
savor the essence of the art-science can go. Although he was 83 years of age
and blind, he consented to write a chapter on his collection
for this volume. Men had thought and written about fishing for many
centuries before Izaak Walton; those who are dead speak to those who
are living from the age-yellowed pages of ancient manuscripts on angling.*

SHEEPSHEAD FISHING, NORTH CAROLINA

M Y COLLECTION of angling literature first went on public display in 1946 at an exhibit at the Princeton University Library, where 50 of the more than 1,300 works in the collection were exhibited and enjoyed by many in the angling fraternity. Subsequently I gave the collection to the University's Library for permanent residence for future generations to enjoy, as I enjoyed studying it during my lifetime. Many of the books in that original exhibit I consider among the greatest ever written on the subject.

The bibliography of angling runs to so many titles that a selection to show the progress of the art-science is difficult and a final choice open to endless argument. This is as it should be, for there have always been two (or twenty) sides to almost everything connected with this most controversial of sports,

and I devoutly hope there always will be; therein lies much of its charm.

There is one very early work—alas not in the collection—I must refer to. Who can fail to appreciate *De Matura Animalium* by Aelian, who in the third century watched Macedonians fishing in the river Astraeus with rod, line, and artificial flies dressed to imitate the insect hippurus. Aelian left a record of their method and described the pattern of their fly (body of scarlet wool, wings of feathers from a honey colored cock). I have tried this venerable confection, in various sizes, for trout and bass; it works as well here today as it did in Macedonia 1,700 years ago.

I begin my evaluation, however, with a work whose authorship is in doubt, but which offers advice on how, when, and where to fish. This is set forth in the rare incunabulum (1496) *Treatysse of Fys-*

Atlantic salmon angler and guide in Canada—still among the most rewarding of fishing expeditions since the 19th century.

Twentieth century anglers range even beyond the Arctic Circle.

shynge wyth an Angle, attributed to a possibly mythical English prioress, Dame Juliana Berners. The advice stands up even today, and my collection is fortunate to have in it a rare copy.

Oppian of Corycus wrote in the reign of Marcus Aurelius. His *Halieutika* (Aldine edition, 1517; Greek verse with a translation in metrical Latin) gives much information—and much misinformation— on ichthyology and the capture of fish. It is a valiant and ponderous effort, and I consider it an excellent addition to my collection.

To represent the early ichthyologies I have chosen Konrad von Gesner's folio, a fine copy with 706 hand-colored woodcuts. *De Piscium* (1558) is volume four of a portly set of five devoted to natural history. The scholarship and the patience of Gesner's research is beyond praise; he is justly called the German Pliny.

At the end of the 16th century the *De Piscinis et Piscium* (1552) of Janus Dubravius, Bishop of Olmutz, was translated into English; it is much quoted by later writers including Walton, who stood in awe of learned churchmen. Dubravius loved a good fish story. On page nine, for example, he tells how a large frog leaped on the head of a pike and by digging his feet into the pike's eyes blinded him for life. What a ride that frog must have had! Walton repeats the yarn as solemn fact, almost verbatim.

Some years ago, in London, I was offered a rather dilapidated little book, bound in vellum, called *The Arte of Angling,* the colophon giving the date

171

A representation of angling in the Middle East about 2,000 B.C.

1577. When the owner handed it to me to read, apologizing for the lack of the title page, author therefore unknown, I was startled to discover that I had found the source book for Walton's *Compleat Angler*. It told much of the Waltonian story about how Piscator met Venator, how they proceeded to the inn, and how they conversed together about fish and fishing.

This unique book (no other copy has ever been found) was of such importance that when I had a new edition printed and distributed by the Princeton University Library, the New York Times gave it first page publicity with reproductions of two of its pages. The article about it was headed: "Izaak Walton—Plagiarist." Newspapers here and abroad took up the cry, but after a while—until they became aware that in Walton's time it was considered rather flattering for one author to copy the work of another—adverse criticism of Walton ceased.

The Princeton edition of the book was quickly out of print. A second issue, with a new introduction, was put forth in 3,000 copies. This edition was also exhausted.

If Walton had read my copy of Taverner's *Certaine Experiments Concerning Fish and Fruite* he would have saved himself from several errors, about pike for instance, and about the breeding of eels. Taverner was far ahead of his time, took nothing for granted, "setting down onely what things my self have obserued and practised." His observations on trout stream insects are remarkably acute. The following passage might have been written by Ronalds, 263 years later:

"I have seene a young flie swimme in the water to and fro, and in the end come to the upper crust of the water, and assay to flie up: howbeit not being perfectly ripe or fledge, hath twice or thrice fallen downe againe into the water: howbeit in the end receiving perfection by the heate of the sunne and the pleasant fat water, hath in the ende within some halfe houre often taken her flight, and flied quite awaie into the ayre.

172

And of such young flies before they are able to flie awaie, do fish feed exceedingly."

The Art of Angling by Thomas Barker, first published in 1651 (I have the second edition, 1653), came off the press 2 years before the first printing of Walton's *Compleat Angler* and Walton, who had little experience fly fishing, was glad enough to lean heavily upon it in his fifth chapter: "I will next give you some directions for fly fishing such as are given by Mr. Thomas Barker, a gentleman that hath spent much time in fishing: but I shall do it with a little variation." Then he copies Barker for several pages and gives most of his patterns for the dressing of artificial flies.

Barker was a professional cook and as proud of his skill at preparing fish for the lordship's table as of his ability with rod and line. Once, on orders from his employer, Admiral Lord Montague, he fished all night and brought home a heavy basket of trout. Of them, for one meal, he prepared "trouts in broth, calvored trouts, marionated trouts, broiled, fried, stewed and roast trouts,

Sixth century B.C. view of an angler, by Chachrylion of Greece.

trout pies hot and cold, etc." How the Admiral's guests survived this culinary rodeo without benefit of Alka-Seltzer is not recorded.

Of Walton's *Compleat Angler,* the most famous book in all the literature of sport, little need be said. Dr. Bethune, editor of the first American edition, calls it "this darling book." Peter Oliver records 284 editions up to 1936. How many have read and loved it is anybody's guess, but I may safely say that, with the exception of the Bible, Shakespeare, and Bunyan, Walton's pages have had more readers than any book in all the English speaking world.

Five editions were printed in the author's lifetime, of which I have been able to purchase copies of each, plus a few later editions that seemed worthy. The fourth edition is the last of which Walton was the sole author.

In the fifth edition, *Part II, The Compleat Angler* by Walton's "spiritual son," Charles Cotton, is added (the first edition of his contribution, which John Hills considers "in many ways the best book on angling ever written") and also *Part III, The Experienced Angler* by a friend of theirs, Col. Robert Venables; the three parts combined being given the general title of *The Universal Angler.* Venables had first published *The Experienced Angler* separately (1662).

Subsequent editors dropped the Venables section as being out of key with the rest of *The Universal Angler,* retaining Walton's and Cotton's work as the permanent form of *The Compleat Angler.* Walton was 83 years old when *The Universal Angler* appeared, with the final and best version of the text. He had every reason to be proud of his masterpiece.

For 67 years after Walton's death the *Angler* was strangely forgotten. It was at the instigation of Samuel Johnson that Moses Browne finally brought out a new edition in 1750 and with that year began the popularity of what is not only the keystone of any angling library but one of the dozen best loved books in our language. The first Moses Browne edition, the first American edition, 1847 (a large paper, extra-illustrated copy) and the German edition of 1859, the only edition entirely in a foreign language, complete my collection of Waltons. Of them all

Earliest known illustration of a reel—13th century Chinese painting by Ma Yuan.

the German edition may well be the rarest, since only a few copies escaped a fire in the publisher's Hamburg warehouse.

The 18th century contributes little to the literature of angling. Not a book of primary importance came off the presses, but of important improvements in tackle there were many. Reels came into general use and the fact that the angler could now easily lengthen or shorten his line, made long rods (Cotton's were 15 to 18 feet) unnecessary. Silk lines were perfected, a great advance over those of braided horse-tail hair. Leaders of silk-worm gut are first mentioned by Saunders in *The Compleat Fisherman* (1724) who says they originated among the Swiss and the Milanese and that they are much stronger than hair of equal gage. By 1760 London tackle dealers were advertising the new discovery. Bowlker's *The Art of Angling* (1747) took the fly dresser's art out of its rut, set the fashion for up-stream fishing and added impetus to the study of trout stream insects.

Angling literature bloomed again in the first half of the 19th century. Sir Humphry Davy, Bainbridge, Ronalds, Pulman, Fitzgibbon, Penn (great-grand-son of the founder of Pennsylvania) angled and wrote with enthusiasm, wisdom, and success. I shall discuss only three of them here.

Bainbridge's *The Fly-Fisher's Guide* (1816) is still, after 150 years, one of the modern fly-fisher's textbooks; its colored plates have seldom been surpassed.

But to one far greater than he, to Alfred Ronalds, the modern angler is eternally indebted for a truly wonderful book, *The Fly-Fishers Entomology*, of which, from 1836 to 1913, 11 editions were published. My collection includes the first and the sumptuous memorial

edition of 1913, the latter in two volumes. On the pages of the second volume are mounted artificial flies dressed according to the author's patterns.

Ronalds was a profound student of trout stream insects, and since few books have been more widely read by thoughtful anglers or left a deeper impression on their minds, he became the patron saint of our present day school of "exact imitation," the men who insist that artificial flies must be dressed to resemble as closely as possible their counterparts in nature, especially if they are to be floated on the surface of the water as dry flies.

The man-made fly, fished so it barely touches the water, is as old as Aelian's false hippurus, but the development of the technique of dry fly fishing is a long story. The idea that the fly, to be effective, must be fished wet, offered to the fish under water rather than on the surface, persisted till recent times and it was not till the third edition of Pulman's *Vade Mecum of Fly Fishing* appeared in 1851 that this way of angling, now in such general use, was properly described. Pulman did it in one sentence:

"Let a *dry* fly be substituted for a wet one, the line switched a few times through the air to throw off its superabundant moisture, a judicious cast made just above the rising fish and the fly allowed to float toward and over them, and the chances are ten to one that it will be seized as readily as the living insect."

That sentence could not have been improved upon by Frederic Halford, the historian of the dry fly, the man who more than any other established its present cult. Of the fine books that came from his pen, the best known is, *Floating Flies and How to Dress Them* (1886). He carried the torch for the dry fly through five books—as rabid a reformer as ever was. Like most reformers, however, he hurt his case by over-enthusiasm. He and his followers became known as "purists" whose gospel was the sacredness of the dry fly. To them no other method of taking trout was ever respectable; anybody who disagreed could be classed only with the lower forms of animal life. They did not realize that the advent of the dry fly would bring further revolution; that knowledgeable anglers would invent still other ways of luring trout, ways that would be more effective under conditions of weather and water unfavorable to the dry fly.

Most of the food on which trout feed continues, in spite of Halford, to come to them under water, worms, grubs, shrimp, crustaceans, and winged insects, that have died and gone under after depositing their eggs. These last are, of course, imitated by the wet fly. There is another item on the menu, the nymph (pupa stage of the winged insect) which leaves its home on the bottom of the stream, rises to the surface and unfolds its wings as Taverner reported in 1600, "and of such young flies before they are able to flie away, do fish feed exceedingly." How long ago it was that anglers first began to dress their hooks with imitations of the nymph is hard to say. Early nymph fishers cut the wings from their wet flies and used the stump-winged bodies; these to some degree resembled nymphs. But nymphs accurately copied from the naturals are a recent development and the technique of handling them so they move as they should, slowly toward the surface, is newer still.

Eel spearing at Setauket, Long Island, painting by William S. Mount, 1845.

The gentle art according to Currier and Ives, 19th century.

The father of modern nymph fishing was G. E. M. Skues whose *Nymph Fishing for Chalk Stream Trout* (1939) is the new testament of the heretics who refuse to abide by Halford. Though there are some who will have none of Skues, saying he has led us into habits too closely akin to those of the pariahs who drown the lowly worm, we are beholden to this kindly English sportsman for showing us a way of angling that requires great skill and fills our creel when other honest methods send us home by way of the fish market.

In America, angling for sport had no literature worth mentioning till the third decade of the 19th century. For many years our forefathers, settling new lands, were too busy putting roofs over their heads and keeping body and soul together to waste time pushing a frivolous quill. They were "church people" with a stern code; imagine such a one admitting on paper that he had spent a day with rod and line not because his family needed a fish dinner, but just for the fun of the thing!

The Reverend Secomb in 1739 preached a sermon in a little church on the banks of a New England salmon river to the effect that angling for sport was sinless in the sight of God. This caused a tremendous sensation later when the sermon, in the form of a pamphlet, was published. It is among the rarest of American items on sport fishing, along with the broadside published in New York City, setting forth the penalties which would accrue to anyone contaminating the water of the Collect

Pond, once located where one of the city prisons now stands. The pond could furnish fish in case the town were besieged by Indians.

The Dictionary of American Biography gives the reason why Dr. Bethune dared not put his name, as editor, on the first American edition of Walton's *Compleat Angler:* "Owing to the public feeling against the propriety of such a book by a clergyman, it was published anonymously." And that was as late as 1847.

The first book printed in our country with any claim to importance as a practical guide to fishing for sport is a modest duodecimo in 1833 by Jerome V. C. Smith, M.D., *Natural History of the Fishes of Massachusetts, Embracing a Practical Essay on Angling.* The body of the book, the section on ichthyology, is poor and uninteresting, but the *Practical Essay* deserves to survive. Smith fished with flies for landlocked salmon in Maine and for brook trout on Cape Cod. He tells about it in an informal way; local conditions, tackle, methods—enjoyable reading and instructive.

In 1845 a tackle dealer on Fulton Street, New York City, put together, largely by means of shears and paste, the first American book to deal seriously and in detail with angling in America. It was very popular and went through seven editions. The rare first edition of this pocket size volume is in my collection— *The American Angler's Guide,* etc., *By An American Angler* (John J. Brown). It is packed with information from every imaginable source and gives an excellent picture of the American angler, his gear and his haunts, a hundred years ago. As head of a first-class tackle shop Brown knew almost every angler worth knowing. Their across-the-counter conversation is the basis of the best in Brown's book—what constitutes a good rod, the superiority of American reels, the patterns of hooks and flies, the newest thing in lines. He also fathered the first American angler's almanac, though it is doubtful if he wrote it. I have a copy of the first issue in my collection, *The Angler's Almanac for 1848.* Originally priced at 12½ cents, it is now among the rarest of Angling Americana, the ancestor of John Knight's Solunar Tables.

Till about 1850 no professional literary craftsman had appeared with the exception of Irving, Thoreau, and Cooper (there is a trace of angling in them here and there but it takes a long stretch of the imagination to call them angling authors) who could give a book on fishing the grace and charm of style. H. W. Herbert (pen name Frank Forester) could and did to some extent do this in *Frank Forester's Fish and Fishing of the United States and British Provinces of North America,* though that kind of book does not lend itself so well to artistry as *The Warwick Woodlands* and other titles among his numerous and varied productions.

Coming from England to this country as a grown man, he brought with him the experience of shooting and fishing at home and the British attitude toward the sport. He became therefore our earliest major prophet of the sportsman's code, of conservation, of the restocking of salmon rivers—all invaluable contributions and badly needed in a country whose people had, as yet, devoted little thought to such matters. *Fish and Fishing* was first published in England (1849); the first American edition (New York, 1850) is in my collection, along with its *Supplement,* printed the same year.

Herbert's style and his respect for

angling as sport colored the writings of the best of his immediate successors. A pamphlet of Herbert's, *Fishing With Hook and Line* (New York, 1858, the year he committed suicide) ranks nowhere near *Fish and Fishing,* but of this, the first edition, only two copies are known, which gives me an excuse to include it here as one of the rarest items in American angling literature. It attained a wide popularity, if I may judge by the endless reprints. Why only two copies of the original should have survived is a mystery.

Thaddeus Norris, writing some 14 years later, shows the influence of Herbert, but only to the extent that it could be assimilated by a very different man. Where Herbert was cocksure and sharply critical of others' errors, Norris, the Philadelphian, was modest, kindly, and wise enough to make allowances. He wrote a friendlier book than Herbert's *Fish and Fishing* and a better one, because he knew more about American conditions and because, as a tackle maker, he was an expert craftsman. His rods won a first prize at the Philadelphia Centennial (1876) ; one of the prize winners is among the treasures of the Anglers' Club of New York. A copy of the first edition of his famous *The American Angler's Book* is among my favorites. It may be out of date, but there is a certain something about it, perhaps the glow of "Uncle Thad's" personality, that keeps it always young.

From among the many volumes about American fishing clubs I have picked what, at first glance, seems rather an unimportant title: *Brook Trout Fishing. An Account of a Trip of the Oquossoc Angling Association to Northern Maine, in June 1869,* but with this little book began my acquaintance, on the printed page, with a club which still exists and on which center many fish stories of the Rangeley Lakes, as true as they are fantastic. The gentlemen of the Oquossoc Angling Association that June of 1869 kept a record of their daily catch. It is eye bulging to read; 6 pounders were common, now and then a 9 pounder. Those were the days.

Charles Hallock's *The Fishing Tourist* (1873) represents, at least in my collection, the "where-to-go books," a type which rolls endlessly off the presses. He was among the first to attempt an angler's Baedeker, scampering about from coast to coast, piling up information about local conditions, tackle, transportation, and costs. It leaves the reader a bit breathless but, in its day, it inspired confidence and gave many a fireside fisherman a vicarious thrill.

More of our people fish for what anglers in the old days called the "black bass" than for any other freshwater game fish. This group, which includes the large- and small-mouth bass, is more widely distributed than any other and manages to survive and prosper. Its devotees claim that "pound for pound it is the gamest fish that swims." It is worthy of respect and honor, and Dr. James A. Henshall was its prophet. To leave out of my collection his *Book of the Black Bass* (Cincinnati, 1881) would be worse than an oversight. It is a model of what a book on a fish should be and the spirit of it is such that to read it even once guarantees to make of any normal citizen a bass addict for life.

Horse racing is called the sport of kings because it takes a royal income to support a stable of bang-tailed nags, but Atlantic salmon fishing along the east coast of Canada is no cheap joy either. Few anglers can afford the best. In 1888 Dean Sage, who owned a long stretch of the Ristigouche and entertained his

179

A more realistic view of fly fishing in 19th century, by Winslow Homer.

guests royally at Camp Harmony, wrote and had privately printed in an edition of 105 copies a large quarto which could not be more characteristic of the plush era. It is probably the most sumptuous and expensive angling book ever issued in this country. To own a copy was at one time almost enough to prove that you belonged in the Social Register of *Salmo salar*. The paper is of the finest, there is a photogravure title page, 71 superb illustrations including engravings, etchings, etc., and in spite of all this grandeur the text is well worth reading, for *The Ristigouche and its Salmon Fishing* gives an excellent picture of the high and far-off times before commercial fishing began to cut down the annual run and "leaping silver" poured up the Ristigouche by the hundreds of thousands. My copy of Dean Sage's monument is in the original pictorial cloth binding.

The value of the dry fly for salmon in summer when the water is low and warm and the fish look biliously on standard wet fly patterns is a recent discovery. I first saw it mentioned in a letter (May 17, 1906) from Theodore Gordon to his English friend G. E. M. Skues. Gordon writes: "I have but one case in my own knowledge when a salmon rose and was killed with a dry fly. It was years ago when a good friend of mine was going to the Ristigouche for the first time. I tied for him a curiosity on a big number one Pennell hook—golden pheasant tail, yellow dubb, bronze peacock body, upright wings of two duck feathers, still as pokers, and a saddle hackle wound dryfly fashion. Late one afternoon my friend dropped this fly clumsily on the water with a lot of slack line. He said it looked like a little yacht under full sail. A 14½ pound salmon rose and made three efforts to get it in his mouth before he succeeded in doing so. My friend became wildly excited, struck fiercely and smashed his rod. He and his guide worked 2¼ hours to bring the fish to gaff. Think of a dry fly reminding a man of a yacht under full sail."

This may have taken place as early as 1900, to judge by what Gordon generally referred to as "years ago." It was 16 years after Gordon's letter that Edward R. Hewitt published the result of his experimental angling on the Patapedia and elsewhere in *Secrets of the Salmon,* a book which more than any other has influenced the present generation to take up dry-fly fishing for salmon.

Hewitt originated the bivisible dry fly, palmer tied of brown hackle with a few turns of white hackle at the head; this made it easy to see in almost any light. Leaders treated with silver nitrate are also a Hewitt invention. The chemical coating makes them less visible to the fish.

Two years after the publication of Hewitt's book, there came from the pen of George M. L. LaBranche *The Salmon and the Dry Fly* almost equally an angling reader's must. Chapter IV, "Casting the Curve," gives the first detailed description of how this all important cast is achieved. Hewitt and LaBranche were disputatious friends of long standing so I place their books side by side in this chapter.

But I also want to refer to a more famous title by LaBranche: *The Dry Fly and Fast Water* (1914). A second edition was issued in 1926. LaBranche set himself the task of recutting the slow English chalk stream cloth to fit the fast American mountain stream pattern and in so doing produced a classic. It is still the best thing on its subject and whether it can be improved upon remains to be seen.

The English dry fly purist waits for a hatch of insects to rouse the trout and put them on the rise; then he casts to a rising fish. LaBranche goes to a run, a pocket, or a pool where he is certain, from previous observation, that good fish lie and, by floating his fly over them many times, creates a hatch. The trout, seeing so many insects coming their way, finally take LaBranche's word for the authenticity of the phenomenon and begin to accept his offerings. Try it; it works.

In the early thirties there appeared in *The Sportsman,* a magazine now defunct, an article by John Alden Knight (I have the original manuscript) which set forth the author's conviction that the pull of the sun and moon, which creates the tides and thereby exerts so strong an influence on the feeding periods of saltwater fish, affects in like manner their freshwater relatives. Knight discussed the idea with other anglers, gave them tide tables corrected for longitude and asked them to keep records of the dates and the time of day when they had their best fishing. When the returns had been tabulated he was sufficiently satisfied with the result to put into a new book *The Modern Angler including the Solunar Theory* (1936) several chapters devoted to his findings and to promulgate a theory to which he gave the name "Solunar." Since then Knight wrote much, expanding his theory, and issued annually a pamphlet of *Solunar Tables* for the current year.

Knight's theory has gained so many converts that thousands of copies of the tables are printed each year to meet the demand. In using them it is essential to follow the author's directions properly correcting solunar time periods to the longitude of the location of the user. Where two or more anglers are gathered together and the conversational fire burns low, one has only to toss a *Solunar Tables* on the embers to kindle a nice, hot, lasting flame. For this, the most controversial, and for many other valued contributions to the expanding corpus of angling lore, our thanks to the late Jack Knight.

Let us end this bibliographical discourse on this controversial note, with the hope that all who read this chapter take the time to go to Princeton to partake of some of the many joys I experienced during a most rewarding lifetime.

Fish Are Fascinating

by Craig Phillips

One day in the summer of 1945 near the close of World War II,
I sat gazing into the depths of one of the many clear tide pools that fringe
the shoreline of Guadalcanal Island in the South Pacific.
Most of the varied and colorful members of the fish community
I was watching were new to me at the time,
and yet I could not help feeling that I had seen many of them before.

QUEEN TRIGGERFISH AND OTHER REEF DWELLERS

FISH-WATCHING had always been an engrossing occupation, and during a previous summer when I had worked at Florida's Marineland I had learned the movements and swimming behavior of various fish of the Atlantic coral reefs. Since the majority of these have close relatives in the Pacific, it was not difficult to assign many Guadalcanal specimens to their proper family status on the basis of their swimming behavior alone.

For instance, when young, many of the damselfish and angelfish look remarkably alike in shape and color pattern. But the former move about in fits and starts, with the body held straight, while the latter tilt the body at various angles as they swim, accompanied by flourishing movements of the tail and dorsal and anal fins.

The wrasses swim with a sinuous gliding motion that, once seen, is unmistakable, although imitated to some extent by the surgeonfish. However, the latter have highly compressed bodies that distinguish them at a glance from most of the wrasses, which tend to be cylindrical. Although the gobies and the blennies are an example of convergent form and difficult to tell apart by the novice, both of them behave much like the American freshwater darters in resting for periods on the bottom and moving forward with sudden jerky movements. Close observa-

The juvenile queen angelfish loses some of its glory as it matures.

tion, however, reveals that a resting blenny usually curls its tail to one side while a goby keeps its body straight.

The greater number of fish to be observed on any tropical reef, whether in the Atlantic or Pacific, fall into one of these six families, which may be recognized by anyone who takes the time to familiarize himself with their behavior.

Freshwater or marine fish of the temperate regions as a group are more generalized in form, color, and swimming behavior than those of the coral reefs.

Since swimming behavior is related to not only the form, but also the particular use a fish makes of its fins, let's look at these organs in a highly generalized example—the goldfish.

A normal fish has a full complement of seven fins (though the dorsal may be divided into a front and a rear portion), and they may be broken down into two categories, the paired and the vertical fins. The paired fins consist of the two pectorals, which are located behind the gill openings and the two pelvics located on the breast or belly, and these correspond to the fore and hind limbs of land vertebrates. The vertical fins are the dorsal, located on the back, the anal, located on the underside behind the pelvics, and the caudal or tail fin. In some (as in a few eels) all of these fins may be lacking, but in our goldfish example all are present.

In normal swimming activity, the main organ of forward propulsion is the caudal, assisted to some extent by paddling movement of the pectorals. The dorsal, anal, and to a large extent, the pelvics function mainly as stabilizers. When the fish turns, the dorsal and anal may assist to some extent by acting as vanes, and when the fish comes to a sudden stop or backs up slightly, this is aided by a forward bending of the caudal

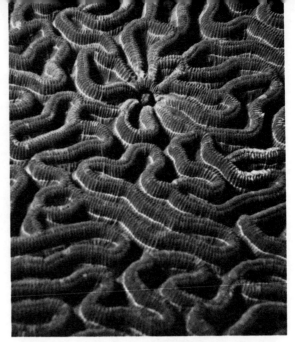

A blenny lives in the heart of the brain coral for protection from predators.

(sometimes of the dorsal and anal as well), but is accomplished mainly by a spreading and reverse paddling of the pectorals.

A very few fish (e.g., the knife fish) are able to move both forward and backward with ease. In the knife fish this is affected by a "conveyor belt" action of the very long anal fin (or more precisely, a movement like that of a long narrow curtain rippling in the breeze) while the body is held straight, in contrast to the similarly shaped eels which swim with a serpentine movement of the body. Other fish (including the eels) usually must turn around in order to go in the opposite direction.

One of the most unexpected forms of fish locomotion—unexpected because it occurs in several families of reef fish that are primarily adapted for normal caudal fin locomotion—is a type of progression that I call "rowing." In this type of locomotion, the caudal trails limply or simply functions as a rudder, while the fish

185

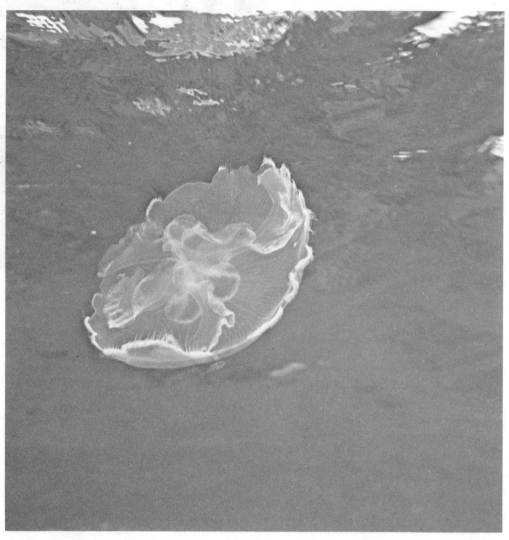

Small fish tag along beneath a moon jellyfish for protection.

propels itself along by stroking the pectorals in unison like a pair of oars. Just why this singular form of locomotion seems to have been adapted by several types (some quite unrelated to one another) of coral reef fish is a matter of conjecture, and I do not recall having observed it in fish from anywhere else. Primary among the "rowers" are the parrotfish, wrasses, surgeonfish, angelfish, and certain of the damselfish.

It must be understood that this "rowing" is a secondarily acquired form of locomotion, since, when any of these fish is suddenly alarmed, it swims away with the more rapid and efficient caudal sculling while the pectorals fold against the sides. An interesting side effect of "rowing" is that in some species it is attended by a flashing of the color of the inside of the pectorals, which reminds one of a similar phenomenon that ac-

186

How did that fish get into the visor?

companies the flight of some butterflies and moths, and which may possibly serve the function of recognition between individuals. A good example of this is the gray angelfish, which rhythmically flashes the bright yellow inner surfaces of the pectorals as it swims. No such flashing display, however, occurs in the closely related French angelfish, the inner surface of whose pectorals are, like the outer surface, black.

The "conveyor belt" sort of fin rippling is seen to a greater or lesser extent in a variety of fish. In the scrawled filefish, which is a common inhabitant of the Florida reefs, this occurs both in the long dorsal and anal fins which occupy a sizable section of the middle and rear sections of this fish's body. This method allows the fish to glide forward at any controlled speed with great smoothness of motion. It is interesting to note that a number of fish that employ self-generated electricity for (among other purposes) a sort of animal radar for the purpose of navigation in turbid water use the conveyor belt method of swimming. These fish include the famous electric eel, which is not related to the true eels, and its previously mentioned relatives, the knife fish, and also the Nile eel. Not only does this method of swimming permit the avoidance of objects in the simplest possible way, but its primary purpose seems to keep the body as straight as possible at all times,

which is necessary for the most efficient operation of the electrical sending and receiving apparatus.

I consider fish of this type among the most fascinating of all to observe swimming about a tank. The long anal fin which in the case of the electric eel and the knife fish runs along almost the entire lower side (in the Nile eel the dorsal performs this function) appears to be under remarkably precise nervous and mechanical control. Evenly spaced waves run continuously from fore to aft as the fish starts to move forward, then will abruptly reverse direction as the fish "shifts gears." Even when the specimen itself is stationary the fin may be in active motion, waves forming at either end and rapidly converging to cancel out at the center.

Certain triggerfish have evolved a propulsive mechanism that involves the

A sawfish would puzzle anyone.

joint use of the dorsal and anal, which are similar in shape and are raised to form points at right angles to the body when viewed from the side. Both fins bend to one side or the other at the same time; meanwhile their trailing edges are skewed by water resistance, transforming a winglike action into a rather propellerlike motion, although, of course, they do not actually revolve, but sweep from side to side, the tail meanwhile serving as a rudder.

This mode of swimming reaches its extreme perfection in the ocean sunfish, which may attain a vertical span of over 8 feet from the tip of the dorsal to the tip of the anal fin and a weight of 2,000 pounds. While serving as curator of the Miami Seaquarium, I had the fortunate opportunity of observing several of these giants in captivity, and I consider them to be the most intriguing fish in the world to watch, bar none.

In the ocean sunfish there is no true caudal fin—in fact, the foreshortened creature looks as if it consists almost entirely of head. The true tail atrophies very early in life and is replaced by a most improbable structure called a "clavus" which means rudder, and which it resembles in form and function. The clavus is rigid and is hinged along its base, serving to guide the ocean sunfish to the left or the right as the tall vertical fins make their massive sweeps. The fish is remarkably machine-like in its swimming behavior, and save for the great saucer eyes which indicate a certain alertness, there seems to be something singularly mechanical about the ocean sunfish.

These fish generally do not live long in captivity, perhaps because their natural food appears to consist largely of vast quantities of jellyfish and other soft-bodied forms of plankton which they suck in through their very small mouths, and a suitable substitute for this diet seems yet to be devised.

The first specimen we had at the Seaquarium I attempted, successfully, to feed some frozen squid, though these were never digested, perhaps partly because our ocean sunfish had been injured internally during capture. Feeding had to be done by hand and consisted of my donning a face mask and overtaking the creature underwater in our 80-foot circular tank, grabbing its small snout prominence with one hand, and shoving the squid in its mouth with the other. Despite its great size, ocean sunfish is usually a slow swimmer, though reliable witnesses have told me they have seen them break clear of the sea surface on occasion.

Although an aquarium may seem at first the ideal situation in which to observe fish, it has its limitations. In captivity fish do not always behave as they do in the wild (for instance, in the daily business of securing their natural food). Watching them in a tide pool (or better yet, through a glass-bottomed bucket in water of clear visibility, such as over a coral reef), will reveal many things of interest, but to really get a view of them in the proper perspective, one must use a face mask and snorkel, or better yet, an underwater breathing outfit.

If one is fortunate enough to live close to the south Florida reefs or along the southern California coast, he will find the best possible conditions for exploring underwater. Since the perspective is totally and unexpectedly different, the first glimpse beneath the surface may be an enchanting experience, but may also be awe-inspiring and something of a shock. Distances are magnified, objects,

Aquarium exhibits—fish and people get together.

particularly those seen at a distance, appear larger, and downward-sloping angles are increased so that a gentle slope may appear as a steep one, and a steep drop-off may resemble a precipice.

After one becomes oriented to this new environment, he makes an interesting discovery. Fish show far less fear of a human when he is swimming around among them than they do when he is wading or standing in a boat. In fact, with an underwater breathing outfit one can observe fish going about their daily activities and showing little or no concern toward the intruder, provided he does not venture unduly close. While diving about the Florida reefs, it is not an uncommon occurrence for me to be nipped on the arm or leg by one of the small damselfish when I happen to approach too closely to its particular territory, since these fish will often set up housekeeping in some rocky crevice or by a coral head, sponge, etc., from which they will vigorously drive away intruders many times their own size.

Although sharks occasionally and barracuda frequently are met on the Florida reefs, deliberate attack is most uncommon, unless one foolishly attempts to spear one while underwater. Any large shark or barracuda, or a medium-sized one for that matter, can be pretty dangerous when struggling on the end of a spear; hence, this sort of hunting is to be discouraged.

Barracuda (which are almost invariably present on the reefs) seem to have an insatiable curiosity, and they will habitually circle round and round a diver, often at the periphery of visibility, as if they were conducting a "war of nerves." I have to admit that this behavior of theirs can be somewhat disconcerting, but I have learned to ignore them as much as possible, keeping in mind the fact that unprovoked barracuda attack is, popular lore to the contrary, almost unknown.

On the other hand, I have seen what barracuda are capable of doing with their strong jaws and powerful teeth. Once in the live well of the Seaquarium's collecting boat, two 5-foot individuals managed to split open the skull of a third of like size during a trip across the Gulf Stream from Bimini. All of the specimens were so battered from fighting on arrival at Miami that they had to be subsequently destroyed.

Young barracuda under an inch in length are often found in the surf under floating seaweed during the summer. These little fellows are just as voracious as their elders on a smaller scale and will almost invariably take their victims tail first. This means that whatever fish the barracuda swallows has all its fins and spines pointing down the swallower's throat, but apparently this minor inconvenience doesn't appear to bother the barracuda.

Sharks are more of an enigma than the barracuda, since there are many more species, and the habits of some of these are highly unpredictable. Aside from the great white shark, which has been implicated in more unprovoked attacks on man than any other shark, the average one, even though it must be of considerable size, is unlikely to attack if the skindiver simply takes it easy and makes no sudden movement.

Movements of a distress-signaling nature can arouse a shark immediately, as I once saw demonstrated in a dramatic way. On this occasion Captain William B. Gray, who was then chief collector for Marineland, Florida, and I were angling for squirrelfish over a reef, using handlines and watching for our quarry through glass-bottomed buckets. Two small, 3-foot blacktip sharks were circling back and forth over the reef, paying little attention to the many species of colorful fish milling about (and who likewise did not appear to be particularly concerned over the presence of the sharks) as Gray and I carefully maneuvered our weighted, baited lines into the clefts in the reef where the squirrelfish were hiding.

The moment a squirrelfish was hooked and commenced to struggle the picture changed. Wherever the two sharks happened to be, they instantly turned and streaked toward the hooked squirrelfish with open jaws, and it became necessary for us to haul the fish to the surface with all possible speed in order to retrieve it unharmed. From this and similar experiences we have had, it would seem that the old advice about splashing and flailing the water in the presence of sharks might be the worst procedure to follow in such a situation.

Despite their size and apparent toughness, sharks are frequently difficult to maintain at an aquarium where they can be studied, since most of them require a great deal of room in which to move about, and some species (for example the great white, blue, mackerel, and mako) often will not stand confinement in an oceanarium-type tank, since they will ram themselves to exhaustion against the restraining walls. This problem has been partially solved through the construction of doughnut-shaped channels with a swift current of water which tends to keep the shark always headed in midstream. Under such conditions, difficult species will sometimes thrive for an extended period.

Under captive conditions lemon, tiger, bull, and various other types show themselves to have the most indiscriminate of feeding habits. Dead and long-defunct fish are taken as enthusiastically as fresh meat, and various objects such as a woman's plastic handbag, burlap sacks, rocks, dead conch shells, etc., may be swallowed when encountered and passed through the digestive tract in either changed or unchanged condition, depending on the particular material's resistance to the powerful digestive juices of the shark's stomach. Large bones, for instance, are rapidly decalcified and transformed to a rubbery consistency during their passage through the internal workings of a shark.

But despite their unsavory history and the vast amount of popular prejudice against them, I have always felt admiration and even empathy for these magnificently designed and wonderfully adapted members of the oceanic community.

Although the reefs remain the most fertile ground for the close-hand observation of wild fish, one's activities along this line have by no means to be confined to the sea. Florida, for example, has, in addition to a vast number of lakes, rivers, and streams, a series of giant freshwater springs, many extremely deep, crystal-clear, and navigable to their source by small craft. Most of these springs are the home of great hordes of fish, some of which like the crevalle jack, striped mullet, and the sheepshead are migrants from the sea. Some springs have become highly commercialized with glass-bottomed boat trips and underwater viewing chambers where the fish may be observed to great advantage, while certain others like Alexander Springs located in the boun-

daries of Ocala National Forest are largely unspoiled by man, and it is at this latter spring that my wife Fanny and I have done occasional diving with face masks and swim fins. The thrill of paddling over and looking straight down into the spring's main boil (which rises with considerable force during most of the year) is an experience that is difficult to describe to one who has never undergone it.

Native fish in this spring (like most of the others in north-central Florida) consist of longnose and shortnose gars, bowfin, golden shiners, largemouth bass, various other sunfish, and the white catfish, which is found in great numbers. Contrary to their common name, these catfish are nearly jet black above, although an occasional albino may be encountered. They all show a predilection for congregating in the spring boils by day, swimming head downward against the current, while at night they head for the downstream shallows.

Around the weedy edges of the springs are found many native "Florida tropicals"—mainly colorful members of the egg-laying and live-bearing topminnows and the tiny pygmy sunfish, chocolate brown in color marked with flecks of brilliant blue. The sandy bottoms of the springs are usually also inhabited by specimens of the 2- to 3-inch hogchocker sole, which rapidly adjusts the shade of its upper side to match that of the particular bottom on which it is lying and buries itself in the sand with a sudden flapping movement of the body, always an intriguing process to watch.

Schooling behavior in fish is an interesting phenomenon and is usually associated with species that inhabit the open sea, though many shallow water forms may also school. In the most highly organized groups the entire aggregation

Snorkeling with expert guidance opens up an aquatic world.

of individuals may at times behave as one, all members moving in unison in one direction or another. In such species as anchovies and pilchards this is especially true, all members of the group crowding together and forming a giant ball when threatened. Apparently the predators are less able to pick out the individuals when this occurs, and the entire school has the appearance of a solid object too big to swallow.

Under normal swimming conditions fish making up a school will often maintain a definite distance from one another. The lateral line receptor system, by means of which most fish are able to gage their distance from nearby objects by the reflection of low-frequency shock

The camera captures the under-sea world for many to enjoy.

waves (caused by their own swimming movements), is believed to enable them to do this. Other species may "ball up" on occasion. The little eellike plotosid catfish of the Indo-Australian region are probably the closest schoolers, as a group of them will often form almost a solid ball in an aquarium, weaving in and out of one another in such a way as to look as if they were trying to "knit" themselves together.

One of the best places to observe fish schooling is from a wharf or seawall when the tide is running. Under such conditions the school will often keep a constant position with respect to the shore while swimming against the current, and the various movements of the individual fish can be observed in detail.

I once was able to observe what was apparently the same school of young bumpers under a dock at Pass-a-Grille, Fla. for several days. These fish were always next to a piling partially under the shade of the dock, keeping pace with the tide and presumably capturing whatever planktonic organisms the current might bring their way. After the first couple of times I saw them (on an incoming and an outgoing tide), I made a point of being on hand at slack tide to see if they remained at the same spot, or whether they might go elsewhere at this time. To my surprise, I found that the bumpers formed themselves into a continuous doughnut-shaped school which revolved around the piling, remaining swimming in this fashion until the tide began to flow once more.

Often I am asked: "What is the most intelligent fish?" This is a question difficult or impossible to answer at the present time, because of the problems encountered in attempting a comparative evaluation of fish intelligence, much of which has to be guessed at from the nature of the creature's behavior. The African freshwater mormyrid fish are known to possess brains of considerable size in comparison to that of the fish, but nearly all of this bulk consists of cerebellum and seems to be related to the fish's system of electrical navigation and has nothing to do with intelligence proper.

From their behavior and responses in captivity, I would rate most of the plectognaths (with the possible exception of the ocean sunfish described earlier) as high on the fish intelligence scale. Members of this group (filefish, triggerfish, trunkfish, puffers, and porcupinefish) tame quickly, soon learn to eat from the fingers, and in general display a type of alertness in captivity that impresses most aquarists, whether it is actually true or not that they are smarter than the general run of fish.

For the present, the question of comparative intelligence in fish must remain unanswered until considerably more experimental work has been carried out using a number of species. For the present, it may just suffice to say that all fish are fascinating in one way or another, and their study is highly rewarding both in biological discoveries and just plain enjoyment.

Lip-Smacking Goodness

by John Dobie

The Wisconsin Fisheries Management Section organizes a good party,
and its gourmet hour usually consists of the famous Wisconsin fish boil,
which is delightful in a robust sort of way. The recipe
calls for one hundred pounds of fish, five-score pounds of potatoes,
and forty pounds of salt. An added gallon of kerosene is
a shock to the uninitiated.
A huge cast-iron kettle, filled with water
and seasoned with the salt, is suspended over an open campfire.
When the water comes to a boil, a wire basket
full of potatoes, skin on, is lowered into the kettle.
Twenty minutes later a basket of lake trout
or whitefish cut in cross-section slices is placed on top of the potatoes.

BREAKFAST OF TROUT AND EGGS

Lunch is ready.

WHEN THE FISH is cooked, the gallon of kerosene is thrown onto the fire to make the water boil so hard that fish slime from the kettle is boiled out onto the fire. Now the fish and potatoes can be removed without being coated with scum. The steaming fish and hot potatoes are usually served with a green salad and cold beer. It all adds up to lip-smacking goodness.

The American fish fry began in colonial days when settlers gathered along the rivers in spring to catch spawning shad, which were fried over open fires in salt pork drippings and were eaten with fried onions and potatoes.

In the early days of the Civilian Conservation Corps, when food in the evening mess was inadequate for some of us more hearty eaters, my companions and I would borrow a skillet, a pound of butter, seasonings, and a loaf of bread from the second cook and drive to a nearby bass lake. With five or six anglers working, we would have enough bass for a delicious fish fry by dusk. Freshly fried fish on a sandy beach in the evening is an experience to be long remembered.

A modern fry can have even more appeal because of the greater variety of methods available for outdoor cooking, improved cooking oils, and wider choice of tidbits to serve with the fish. They can be fried, broiled, or poached over an open fire or the hot coals of a charcoal burner.

Still, despite the variety of recipes, some anglers and their families do not like to eat their catch because of the "fishy taste." This unpalatable flavor

198

develops because the fish are not properly cared for from the time they are caught until they are eaten.

Some anglers throw their catch into the bottom of the boat where they die and deteriorate in the hot sun. Others use a stringer dangled in the water alongside the boat and often towed around the lake until the fish drown. A dead fish held in 70 to 75 degree water deteriorates rapidly. Those that have been neglected on the lake will not have a pleasant flavor no matter how they are cooked.

Only during cold weather can fish be left to die on the bottom of the boat, and even then it is not desirable because they soon become coated with grime and grease. The stringer is best used in cool weather, but even then the fish should be placed in a pail of cool water while the boat is in motion. The preferred stringers are the large mesh type that are designed to hold live ones.

In winter fish can be placed on the ice to freeze, but on cold windy days they should be covered so they will not dry out in the wind. The best method of taking care of them, winter or summer, is to place them immediately in a portable ice box, one-fourth full of crushed ice or ice cubes. Fish in an ice chest will often be alive when the fisherman returns home.

Freshly killed and cleaned ones will have a better flavor than those that have lain around awhile. Those that cannot be cleaned when fresh should be wrapped in a good grade of paper to prevent desiccation and placed in the freezer. When thawed in a pan of cold water, they can be cleaned almost as easily as if

Broiled catfish.

Fillet of walleye.

fresh, and the flavor will still be good. Those that have been cleaned or filleted can be preserved by freezing them in a milk carton of water.

Many people consider fish cleaning a horrible job; actually, it is quite easy. They associate panfish with a heavy scaler or knife that scatters scales over walls, floor, face, and clothes. My neighbor lady, whose husband is an ardent fisherman, showed me how to do the job with very little mess. Use a fork held with the tines pointing down and "rake" the scales off the sides and top of the fish.

Filleting is considered by many to be pure magic accomplished by only the professional cleaner or the local butcher. Actually, all that is required is a good filleting knife and a little practice. A good filleting knife has a thin, flexible, straight-edged blade. It is easiest to use when very sharp.

There are many ways of filleting, but

200

I believe this one is easiest for the amateur: Grasp the head of the fish, and hold the body so it points away from you. Make the first cut at the head end just behind the paired fins. Cut along (but not through) the backbone to the tail. Turn the fish and repeat. Remove the ribs from each fillet by running the knife under the ribs to the end of the ribs and then making a shallow cut along the end of the ribs.

To remove the skin, place the fillet skin down on the cutting board, so the tail end is toward you. Hold the tail end of the fillet with your finger tips and with the blade of the knife flat against the board, make a seesaw cut between the skin and the flesh. The pressure of the knife should be against the skin, but not hard enough to cut it.

Buffalo and carp are usually cleaned by "fleecing," whereby the scales are removed, leaving the inner skin to hold the fish together during cooking. Place a sharp knife at the tail end of the fish and make a cut under the scales between the inner and outer layers of skin. The scales come off in a big sheet, and the inner skin remains attached to the fish.

Bullheads are cleaned more easily than most fish. Start a cut behind the adipose fin (fleshy fin near the tail). Cut forward to the head and down to the backbone. Bend the head forward to break the backbone. Insert your forefinger over the end of the backbone into rib cage and hold. Pull the head backward and peel skin off the flesh. Entrails will come free with the head.

Another way to clean bullheads is to make a cut through the skin across the back at the base of the head. The skin is grabbed with a pair of pliers and is pulled off with one mighty tug. The

Slicing and deep-frying suckers softens bone.

201

Mullet roasting around a fire.

head is then bent down to break the neck and is pulled off with the entrails.

Some years ago I entertained a biologist from Java who was visiting fishery research stations in the United States looking for ideas. Javanese are great fish eaters and are not particular as to the variety, nor do they pass up a fish because it is too small or too large. My Java friend was surprised to find that many Americans do not eat much fish. He believed one difference was that most people in this country know only a few ways of cooking them.

I haven't the space to describe all of my favorite recipes, so I will cover the more general types of fish cooking, any of which you can use with good results, and offer one special recipe for each type of cooking.

The most common method of cooking fish in the United States is to fry them in oil or melted butter. A variety are prepared this way, including sunfish, carp, and bullheads. They are cleaned and the heads, fins, and entrails removed. Large ones are cut into slices or fillets. Each fish or fillet should be washed thoroughly and dried.

Some like their fish seasoned with salt and pepper and fried as is, but those dipped into milk or beaten egg and rolled in seasoned flour, cornmeal, or fine bread crumbs will brown better and become more crisp. The fish should be fried in $\frac{1}{8}$-inch layer of hot oil or melted butter fat and must be turned from time to time so both sides will brown. Total cooking time is 8 to 12 minutes.

202

In frying panfish, I use the following recipe:

> 6 to 8 panfish, cleaned and washed
> Salt and pepper
> 1 cup flour
> 3 to 4 lemon slices
> ¼ lb. salt pork, cubed
> 6 tbsp. melted butter
> 6 tbsp. water

Salt fish to taste at least one-half hour before frying. Roll in peppered flour, and fry in salt pork drippings until brown. Turn fish, add ½ slice lemon and 1 tablespoon of water to each fish. Cover and steam for 5 minutes. Turn again, add 1 tablespoon of melted butter, and fry until crisp on the outside.

Broiled fish are easier to prepare than fried ones, and are healthier for diet-conscious eaters. Fish for broiling, including walleye and perch, can be cleaned whole, as fillets with skin left on or removed. The simplest way is to place a fillet with skin removed on a broiling rack, brush with melted butter or oil, season with salt and pepper, and broil for 5 to 10 minutes. Turn the fillet and repeat. Fillets with the skin on do not need to be turned, but the cooking time must be increased to 15 minutes. Fish for broiling can also be dipped in seasoned milk and rolled in dry bread crumbs before being placed on the rack.

For broiled rainbow or lake trout, do as follows:

> 1½ lb. trout, filleted
> 2 cups of bread crumbs
> 3 eggs, beaten
> 2 cups dry sherry wine
> 1 tsp. salt
> ¼ tsp. black pepper
> 1 pinch basil
> 1 pinch garlic powder
> ½ cup melted butter
> ¼ cup chopped parsley

Soak trout fillets for 30 minutes in a marinade made by mixing the wine, salt, pepper, basil, and garlic powder. Roll in bread crumbs, then in beaten egg, and again in bread crumbs. Place in a broiling dish, broil 10 minutes, basting several times with the wine sauce. Turn and broil for another 10 minutes, basting several times more. Place fillets on a warm platter and pour on melted butter seasoned with chopped parsley.

Catfish, smelt, and others cut into fillets or steaks are usually used for deep fat frying. Pieces are washed and dried, and both sides are seasoned with salt and pepper. Each piece is dipped into a slightly beaten egg with 2 tablespoons of milk and is rolled in bread crumbs, cracker crumbs, cornmeal, or flour. A deep kettle and a frying basket are used with enough fat or oil to cover the fish, but the kettle should never be more than half full of fat. Heat the fat or oil to 375° F. Place one layer of fish in the basket and cook to an even brown, about 3 to 5 minutes. Raise the basket, remove the fish, and drain them on absorbent paper. Serve immediately. (Some cooks prefer to dip fish for deep fat frying in a batter made by mixing together 1 cup of sifted flour, 2⅔ cup of milk, and ½ teaspoon of salt.)

To deep fry smelt, I cook as follows:

> ½ lb. smelt per person
> 1 cup flour
> ⅔ cup beer
> ½ tsp. salt

Mix beer, flour, and salt into a smooth batter. Clean smelt, dip in batter, and fry at 400° F., until crisp.

The bones can be removed from a cleaned smelt by the following method: Place smelt belly down on a chopping block. Using the palm of the hand, press down hard on the back of the fish until the smelt looks like a butterfly shrimp. Turn fish belly up, take hold of the head end of the backbone, and lift the bones out in one piece.

Any large fish, whether lake trout, carp, buffalo, or catfish, can be baked for a delicious meal. Baking is a good method for cooking oily fish or those with soft flesh because the skin and binding will hold the fish in shape while it is cooking.

As most fish are baked whole, they are prepared to look good on the platter when served. Carp and buffalo should be fleeced, while trout need only to be gutted and cleaned, since the scales are so small they do not have to be removed.

After the fish is washed and dried, it should be seasoned inside and out with salt and pepper. The stuffing should be placed in the cavity, and the fish bound with string or fastened together with toothpicks. Cover the fish with strips of bacon that are held in place with toothpicks and place in a roaster or casserole. Place ½ cup of chicken broth, several sliced onions, 1 sliced carrot, and 2 tablespoons of dry sherry wine in the roaster or casserole. Cover the fish and cook in a moderate oven until tender.

To prepare bread stuffing, melt ½ cup of butter and add ½ cup finely chopped onion, ½ cup of chopped celery, 2 teaspoons of salt, ¼ teaspoon course ground pepper, and 1 teaspoon of chervil. Saute the vegetables for 5 minutes. Add 4 cups of bread cubes and toss lightly until all the butter has been absorbed. Pour the bread cubes and vegetables into a large bowl, mix together, and add enough hot water to slightly moisten the bread cubes. Press a small amount of stuffing between your fingers. If stuffing does not stick together, add more hot water.

For the topping for the baked fish, some people may not care for bacon. In that case, the fish can be basted periodically with cooking oil to prevent drying. Just before serving, the top side can be sprinkled with bread crumbs, moistened with wine, and placed under the broiler until the crumbs are brown.

One recipe for baked whitefish goes as follows:

1 whitefish, 2 or 3 lbs.
Salt and pepper
1 lb. fresh mushrooms, washed and dried
¼ cup melted butter
1 cup sour cream
3 tbsp. dry sherry wine

Scale the whitefish and remove head, fins, and entrails. Season with salt and pepper. Stuff cavity with whole mushrooms that have been seasoned with salt and pepper. Place fish in a pan or oven proof casserole with any surplus mushrooms. Brush fish with melted butter and cover with sour cream. Pour wine into the pan. Bake fish for 45 to 60 minutes in a moderate oven. Remove to a hot platter and serve.

Poaching is the process of boiling many types of fish or fowl in wine, milk, broth, or court bouillon, but not in plain water. Fish or fowl boiled in water loses flavor. In poaching, this loss is reduced to a minimum and the liquid imparts flavor in the cooking flesh.

To poach in the oven, place fillets, slices, or whole fish in a buttered shallow pan and cover with court bouillon. Cover the pan and place in a 350° F. oven until tender. Baste frequently with court bouillon. The remaining juice should be reduced until slightly thickened and used as a sauce when the fish is served. The court bouillon can be made by placing the following ingredients in a kettle: 1 quart of dry white wine, 1 quart of cold water, 1 tablespoon of salt, 2 small carrots, sliced thin, 2 medium-sized onions, sliced thin, 1 dozen cracked peppercorns, 2 whole cloves, 2 large bay leaves, and 1 pinch of thyme. Bring the liquid to a boil and simmer 30 minutes. Strain before using.

To poach large- or small-mouth bass, I usually use:

> 1 bass, skinned and filleted
> ½ cup dry sherry
> 3 tbsp. butter
> 2 tbsp. flour
> ¾ cup milk
> 1 tsp. tomato sauce
> Salt and pepper

Place bass in a well-buttered oven proof dish. Season with salt and pepper, pour on sherry, cover, and poach in a moderate oven for 25 minutes. Remove and place on a hot platter and keep warm until needed. Melt butter in a saucepan, season with salt and pepper, stir in flour, pour in the strained liquid the bass was cooked in, and thicken over fire. Add the milk and bring to a simmer. Pour sauce over the fish. Fish can be decorated with a mixture of 2 tablespoons of sauce and 1 tablespoon of tomato sauce.

In recent years people have had more leisure time for outdoor recreation such as camping, picnicking, and outdoor cooking. Consequently, the charcoal grill and barbecuing have become popular. This is the process of broiling or cooking food over an open fire in a highly seasoned sauce. Most barbecue sauces contain tomato sauce and various piquant spices.

Fish fillets are cut into serving-size pieces and are marinated in a sauce for 30 minutes. To make the sauce, cook ¼ cup chopped onion, 2 tablespoons of chopped green pepper, and 1 clove of finely chopped garlic in butter until tender. Add one 8-ounce can of tomato sauce, 2 tablespoons of lemon juice, 1 tablespoon Worcestershire sauce, 1 tablespoon of sugar, 2 teaspoons of salt, and ¼ teaspoon of black pepper, and simmer 5 minutes. Cool before using. Fish to be cooked on a charcoal grill should be wrapped in aluminum foil, while fish to be cooked in a home grill should be placed in an oven proof dish, so it can be basted occasionally.

This is my favorite recipe for barbecued sunfish:

> 6 panfish
> 1 egg
> 1 cup cooking oil
> ½ cup vinegar
> 1½ tbsp. salt
> 1 tbsp. poultry seasoning
> 1 tsp. pepper
> 1 pinch garlic powder

Beat egg, add cooking oil, and beat again. Add vinegar, salt, poultry seasoning, pepper, garlic powder, and beat again. Marinate fish for 30 minutes, wrap in aluminum foil, and cook over charcoal coals for 30 minutes.

Smoking is a method of preservation that will keep oilier fish, like carp, bullheads, lake trout, and herring, in edible condition for a week to 10 days. They may be smoked either in the round, gutted, split, and beheaded, or cut into pieces with or without the skin removed. Usually, small ones, such as lake herring, are gutted and washed. Larger ones, such as carp and buffalo, are usually gutted, beheaded, and split in half. Those with considerable body fat, such as trout, salmon, carp, whitefish, and ciscoes, make a better smoked product than do fish with less fat, because many of the smoky flavors are absorbed by the fat. Better moisture and texture qualities are also associated with higher levels of body fat in the fish.

Fish for smoking are washed thoroughly and placed in a 10 percent brine (⅘ pound of salt to 1 gallon of water) for an hour to remove blood and slime. Wash them again and place in 18 percent brine (1½ pounds of salt per gallon of water) for 2 to 6 hours, depending on the size of the fish and the amount of salt desired in the finished product. The color of the smoked fish can be improved by adding 1 tablespoon of saltpeter for every 2 pounds of salt in the brine.

After brining, they are washed in freshwater, placed on the smoking rack, and allowed to drain until the skin is nearly dry. At this point additional seasoning, such as garlic powder or onion chips, can be sprinkled over the skin. Fish should be smoked with hardwood or nonresinous wood chips or sawdust. Some folks like apple wood, others use ash, elm, or oak. Smoking can be of two types—cold or hot.

In cold smoking, after surface moisture has drained from the brined fish, place them in the smokehouse where temperatures range between 90° F. and 100° F. The smoke should be rather thin for the first 4 to 6 hours, thick for the last 16 to 18 hours. The length of smoking time is dependent on the color and flavor desired. Smokehouses should be constructed in such a manner that will permit the humid air of the first hours of smoking to be carried out of the smokehouse. This will allow as little condensation of moisture as possible inside.

In hot smoking, place drained and dried brine fish in a smoker with the internal temperature between 80° F. and 90° F. for 6 to 12 hours. Smoke density should be light during this period. During the last hour, smoke should be more dense. The temperature in the smokehouse should be held at about 180° F.

Fish preserved in spiced vinegar—pickling—hold for shorter periods than those preserved by salting or drying. Brine-salted fish may be pickled, but those especially cured for pickling will have better color and flavor.

Herring, pike, and many of the bonier fish for pickling should be scaled, gutted, beheaded, washed thoroughly, and drained. After being boned, the fish are cut into bite-sized pieces, packed loosely in a crock, and covered with a brine containing ⅝ cup of salt to 1 quart of water, mixed with 1 quart of vinegar. They are left in the brine until the salt has "struck through." But they must be removed before the skin starts to wrinkle or lose color. The average time of brining is about 5 days.

When they are judged sufficiently cured, they are packed more tightly. Sprinkle a thin amount of dry salt (not too much) over them. Cover with a salt and vinegar brine one-half the strength of that just indicated.

A spicier taste can be obtained by adding 3 ounces of whole allspice, 2 ounces each of bay leaves and mustard seed, 1 ounce each of black and white peppercorns, 1 ounce of small red peppers, 1 ounce sugar, and ½ ounce each of whole cloves and sliced onion to every 2 quarts of brine. Pickled fish can be stored in a cool place for 2 to 3 weeks, or in a refrigerator for 5 to 6 months. As far as spicing or seasoning is concerned, each family group has its own preference—but be sure you follow the preservation procedure carefully for quality eating.

Fish that have been properly smoked or pickled are, of course, ready for eating and do not require any other preparation or cooking.

Baked flounder.

The French believe every meal should be an adventure in eating. Fish can be the heart of an especially good meal; there are hundreds of pieces and thousands of recipes. In planning the meals, different species and various recipes can be chosen with a wide range of spices and sauces. The best rule to follow is to choose a fish of your locality and turn loose the imagination. You'll be surprised at how many appreciate your efforts, as few will fail to enjoy the lip-smacking goodness of a well prepared fish meal.

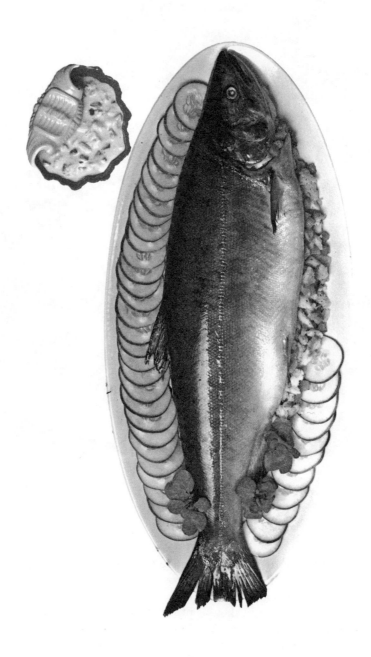

208

THE RIGHT PLACE

Somewhere a River Begins

by Ben Schley

If you're walking the old log grade between Timmins and High Rock, you hear the roar of Big Canoe Creek a long time before you actually see it. In the early spring, before leaves come out full on the trees, you can see the hard glint of the sun on a stretch of flat water, as you round the bend at the notch on the side of Taylor's Mountain. But in summer, when the woods are dense with leaf shadow, you'll nearly fall into the water before you get a good look at it.

BROWN TROUT

I NEVER KNEW WHY it was called Big Canoe Creek. No matter how you measure it, it still isn't very big—hardly large enough to float a canoe, except in the lower half mile or so and in an occasional quiet pool below Brenner's Falls. Maybe the "big" refers to the size of some long-forgotten canoe, not the stream.

Big Canoe first begins to show itself in the high, flat country to the north of Indian Head, then wanders along for a mile or so, hardly more than a yard wide, through old beaver meadows and sparse stands of birch and storm-shattered spruce.

As it moves to the edge of the plateau, the creek begins to draw water from a dozen icy little streams. Then, large enough to flow with authority, it begins a rather spectacular passage to the valley below and eventual juncture with the slow-moving Meander River some 7 miles away.

Like thousands of other obscure headwater streams throughout the country, the creek plays its part in helping to make up a vast river system. Big Canoe's cold, clear waters, gathered from many minor sources, are funneled together and eventually added to the already considerable flow of a major river. The relatively clear water from Big Canoe merges slowly with the turbid flood of the larger stream, then eventually loses its identity as the river moves toward the sea.

But all the water that comes from Big Canoe Creek, every drop of rain that falls on its watershed and works its way into the stream course, has an effect not only on the creek itself but on the miles of river that lie downstream from its mouth.

More through luck than good management, I suppose, the creek boasts a pretty stable watershed. It was first cut over in the eighties, then subjected to a continuing series of small fires until the

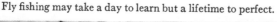

Fly fishing may take a day to learn but a lifetime to perfect.

early part of the century. Now the fire scars are healed. Dense hardwoods crowd the slopes, and dark stands of spruce outline the ridges.

No one lives in the upper part of the watershed any more. Only an occasional surviving apple tree or a crumbling stone wall remain to mark the existence of a forgotten farm. Deserted meadowland has given way to pale birch and summer fern.

Below the falls the old Brenner place still stands on a bend of the creek. Though it has seen better days, the big frame house continues to remain the home of a family that staked out its initial land claims in the area, before the Revolutionary War.

From there on down, the creek winds gently through hayfields and pasture-lands, slides under the old iron bridge at Cairnton, cuts behind the remains of Brady's Mill, and disappears into the river just above the new interstate highway.

Big Canoe Creek has always had a special kind of appeal for most fishermen. If there's any one stream in that part of the country that embodies most all the characteristics of a classic trout stream, Big Canoe is it. Somewhere in its 8 or 9 miles, you'll find about every type of water you've ever seen on an eastern trout stream.

High in the headwaters, the stream flows dark and quiet through abandoned beaver meadows and marshland thick with sweet flag and cattails. In summer tadpoles lie in the sun-warmed shallows, and tiny brook trout follow the cool channels as they search the water's surface for midges. Trout never get very big in this restricted environment, and it's a fortunate fisherman who manages to derrick a struggling 8-incher out of the cattails.

Below the marshland, Big Canoe ducks into dense hardwoods and begins to roar and splash, leaping from one shadowed moss-covered rock to another. This is pocket water where the current swirls and changes direction so often it's difficult to float a fly without drag. Here trout rise to insects trapped in the foam that traces the edge of the current.

Streamside alders, their branches interlocking, often exclude the sunlight and form a leafy tunnel, where only the most persistent fishermen can handle a fly with any success.

Many local people prize this section above any other. The fishing is demanding, but usually presents the advantages of solitude and an environment the way nature created it. The little brook trout that come from its shady pockets are abundant and beautiful beyond belief.

Once I watched Gil Brenner fish down through the pocket waters, his progression over the slippery boulders far more assured than his 74 years would indicate. He hauled out a couple of small brookies in rapid succession, then hung on to something which momentarily refused to be pulled out of the water. But Gil wasn't one to give up easily, and he shortened his grip on the rod and slid a flopping 14-inch rainbow trout out on the gravel.

"Danged scale fish," he said to me as he grabbed the gasping trout by the gills and slammed it hard against the unyielding side of a nearby boulder. The fish remained there on the sunlit gravel, as Gil rebaited his hook and started fishing on down the stream.

"I'd rather catch one 6-inch native than a dozen of those danged foreign fish," he said.

"Why, Gil, why?" I asked. "A rainbow is a beautiful thing, and many people consider them the gamest of all

213

Every headwater—a character unto itself.

trout. Why not be glad you were clever enough to land one?"

"It seems to me," Gil answered, "if the good Lord really wanted rainbows in this creek, he'd have put 'em here. This is native trout water, and I want to see it stay that way. Besides, did you ever see anything prettier than a basketful of brook trout—or anything uglier than a dead rainbow?"

I guess some questions were never meant to be answered.

Half a mile below the pocket water, Raccoon Branch joins the main stem at the head of the gorge. Here rock walls, seamed and lichen covered, rise steeply from the edge of the stream, and one narrow deep pool follows another to Brenner's Falls.

There are some good brook trout in this stretch—deep-bodied males with crimson fins, fish that test a man's control, when he's floating a #18 Ginger Quill on a 6X tippet.

I used to think that trout—brooks and an occasional rainbow—were the only fish above the falls. But in recent years, after the Muddler began to prove such a success, I discovered that the upper stretches of the creek were loaded with sculpins. These are odd looking, bony creatures with flattened bodies and widely spread pectoral fins. They spend most of the daylight hours under rocks and come out into the open only at nighttime. Local fishermen aptly describe their ludicrous appearance when they call them "chuckleheads."

Fish may be few and scattered, but other rewards include solitude and beauty.

215

An angler experiments with several flies to find the right one.

There's a good gravel road from Cairnton up as far as the Brenner place, and a narrow road over to the falls, and the public picnic area on the bank of the creek.

At Brenner's Falls the whole force of the stream is channeled into a narrow area, as it surges white with foam over a great limestone ledge to fall in shattered drops on the pool below. The falls are only about 20 feet high, but they make an effective barrier between two rather dissimilar fish populations.

Brook trout used to inhabit all of Big Canoe Creek, but now only an occasional one is taken below the falls. Brown trout were introduced in the thirties, and they must have found things to their liking, because they now constitute most of the catch from the falls to the mouth of the creek.

A canoe plus a fly rod and enthusiasm lead inevitably to a trip to the more remote reaches.

Each year Vermont stocks a few thousand 8- to 9-inch rainbows, most of them in the easy-to-get-at stretches from the falls to Cairnton. This usually brings in a big crowd from Somerset and Randall City, but most of the hatchery fish are caught in a week or two, and the serious fishermen can get back to working on the resident brown trout.

Smallmouth bass seem to work upstream a little higher each year, and once in a while a bug-eyed rock bass will spoil the float of a high-riding dry fly with a slimy rise. In the spring rosy cheeked suckers move up from the Meander River, bent on spawning in the creek's gravelly riffles.

Big Canoe Creek has never been noted for really big fish, though now and then somebody lucks into a 4- or 5-pound brown below Brenner's fence line. Here, deep-seated limestone springs swell the flow of the stream, as it moves through the floor of the valley, cutting its way through rich farmlands and wooded areas.

Most of the browns I take in the creek are from 8 to 12 inches long—beautiful golden things with rust-red spots and glistening fins. But now and then a larger one comes my way.

Once, on a warm gray evening in May, I landed a fine, fat 2-pound female brown, and except for rather unusual circumstances, I probably would have had another more than twice as large.

Duns were beginning to pop up all over the surface of the water, as I moved quietly into the lower end of what I call the sycamore pool. There's really nothing very spectacular about this little stretch, but it always seems to hold a few good fish. The water slides across a gravel bar at the head of the pool, is diverted toward the south bank by a big,

flat rock, and then goes into a long run under the exposed roots of a leaning sycamore before it flattens out into gravelly shallows. The road runs beside the stream at this point, with only the big sycamore and the remains of an old rail fence separating it from the creek.

A couple of 8-inch trout were beginning to skim mayflies off the surface of the lower end of the pool, and I managed to take both of them on a #12 Light Cahill, which seemed to approximate the hatching insects. After returning the fish to the water, I caught a glimpse of a heavy, swirling rise in the middle of the current and moved a few feet to my right to insure a better drift. I touched my fly with oil and made a looping cast well above where the trout was feeding.

On the third float the fish took firmly and began to move up and across the stream. I stopped it short of the tentaclelike sycamore roots, then gave line as the fish headed for the top of the run before coming out of the water in a clean, golden leap. I stayed below the fish and soon had things pretty much my way. I didn't have a net so I slid it out on the gravel bar, and after a couple of attempts, grabbed it behind the gills, and gave it a sharp blow on the head with a rock.

It was a beautiful brown, small headed and deep through the body. The tiny adipose fin was a brilliant orange. I climbed up the bank to the rail fence, hung the fish by its gills on a piece of rusty barbed wire, and photographed the still quivering trout against the late afternoon sky.

As I advanced the film I saw another heavy rise in the stream precisely where I had taken the trout. I hastily picked up my rod, scrambled back into the stream, and without bothering to re-dress the

217

fly, began casting over the now steadily rising fish.

My first few floats with the be-draggled Cahill were ignored, so I reeled in my line and changed to another fly of the same pattern but a size smaller.

The first float of the high-riding Cahill produced results, and a great head came out of the water and took the fly under. I could see the broad gleaming back and rudderlike tail of a male brown, as it turned in the clear water.

Mindful of my 5X tippet, I tightened up, then gave the big fish line, as it moved up into the head of the run and surged clear of the water in a great wallowing leap.

The late afternoon sun broke through thin clouds, as I stepped out on the gravel and began to put a bit of pressure on what I felt must be the largest fish ever hooked in Big Canoe Creek.

For 5 full minutes I worked the big trout. He never seemed very worried about the outcome of the battle, and every time I'd think I had him coming, he'd bull his way back under the sycamore roots and begin rubbing away at the tiny hook in his lower jaw.

Once I even got him up into the shallows, and for a moment he lay stretched out flat with the pale sun full on his scarred sides. For an instant I thought I had him, but as I reached out to grab him behind the gills he started thrashing. I relaxed the pressure a little to reduce the danger to my leader; he moved out of the shallows and, getting a powerful tail-hold in the water, went under the roots again.

About this time I picked up a movement in the corner of my eye, and turned my gaze from the water just in time to see a hand reach out of the brush and grab the brown trout I had left hanging on the rail fence along the road.

I couldn't believe my eyes. But the fish was gone.

My pulse pounded, and I began to see red. Who was stealing my fine, golden brown trout? I let out a mad yell, gave my flyline a couple of half hitches around a scrub willow, threw the rod into the branches of the tree, and set off in hot pursuit.

As I pulled myself up to road level, I could see a very small boy running hard in the direction of the falls, dragging my brown trout along the dusty road.

"Put down my fish!" I yelled, as I ran. "Put it down!"

Realizing my longer legs would soon catch him, the boy dropped the fish by the edge of the road and disappeared into the grass.

Puffing hard, I picked up the dirt-covered trout and watched as little Danny Brenner, eyeing me with fear, broke out of the grass as he headed across a plowed field for home.

Back at the sycamore pool, I found my line taut and throbbing with the current. With pounding pulse, I carefully picked up my rod and got the line back on the reel. There was no sign of life, no movement. I ran my hand beneath the old tree and under the water up to my arm pit, following the leader with my finger tips. The fly was solidly hooked in the tangled maze of sycamore roots and the fish gone.

Though we usually think of big fish being caught in big waters, yet some large trout are taken from relatively small streams in the complex of waters that make up a river system. Many small streams simply lack the space and basic fertility to produce large fish in great numbers, but sometimes large fish, which have achieved maximum growth in impoundments or in large rivers rich in food, migrate into the headwaters and

One of the rewards for treking to the headwaters.

are taken there by a surprised fisherman. There's no thrill quite like taking a really big fish in water which routinely produces only small ones.

Though very few of us spend the majority of our fishing time on the headwaters—living brooks and creeks that lace themselves together to form our major rivers—still there's an importance to our efforts far beyond mere participation.

All things must begin somewhere, and in the headwaters lies not only the beginnings of our vast and varied system of rivers but also the source of much of our angling heritage.

For it's here that the very essence of angling was born, where the art and ethics of the sport evolved, and where even today old traditions and practices are carried out. Much of the literature of angling concerns trout fishing in small waters, and there's little doubt in my mind that the consistently successful trout fisherman must possess greater skill, knowledge, and persistence than his counterpart on lakes, impoundments, or the ocean.

So that generations of anglers in years to come may help find their beginnings in the source of a river, we must strive to see that Big Canoe Creek and others like it remain in a relatively natural state and continue to rise and flow and become a part of great downstream rivers moving endlessly to the sea.

Downstream

by John L. Funk

*I stumbled over the jagged rocks of the wing dike,
burdened with rod and tackle box, slopping minnow pail, and all the
other things an angler carries. The setting sun
glared in my eyes, and sweat dripped off my nose. I hurriedly rigged a
minnow and cast out into the swirling current. Then as I began
the slow retrieve, I had time to take a deep breath and look around.
I listened to the slap and suck of the wavelets
against the riprap rocks. I watched the restless water of the great river
hurrying past on its relentless journey to the sea,
its path marked by frothy bubbles and floating bits of debris.*

URBAN FISHING, C & O CANAL

The meditative sport on a southern river.

A FEW FEATHERS of evening mist were rising; objects on the distant shore already looked hazy. It felt good; was good. You can have your lily-padded lakes or alder-bordered trout brooks; I'll take downstream fishing.

What are downstream waters, and where do you do downstream fishing? I am talking about the lower portions of big rivers, streams which meander wide and deep through a broad flood plain, seldom interrupted by riffles or rapids. Their gradients are low, but the current is strong because of the volume of water they carry. They are often turbid and polluted by wastes from cities and industries on their banks. Their waters are warm and they support only warm-water fish.

They are subject to periodic floods which all of the levees, dams, and other flood control structures have never brought entirely under control. These floods have important effects on fishing and fish production. Many are, or in the past have been, used for commercial traffic, and the navigation developments on them affect their fisheries.

I am talking mainly about the Mississippi, the Missouri, and the Ohio, and the downstream portions of their larger tributaries—the Wabash, the Cumberland, and Tennessee (both of the latter now dammed a few miles above their mouths), the Illinois, Des Moines, Osage, Grand, Kansas, Platte, St. Francis, White, and Arkansas. These are the streams I know best, and am best qualified to talk about.

But, what I have to say applies to the lower parts of the Ouachita, the Red, and the Yazoo, and much of it probably applies to the lower Pearl, Tombigbee, Alabama, Apalachicola, Suwannee, Altamaha, Savannah, Santee, Pee Dee, and Cape Fear. It may well apply to the Sabine, Trinity, Brazos, Colorado, and Nueces of Texas, although streams rising in the plains may be subject to extreme fluctuations of flow, and I don't know these rivers.

Farther up the East coast, the lower portions of streams like the Roanoke, James, Potomac, Susquehanna, Delaware, and Hudson are drowned in estuaries, although the Connecticut may have a downstream fishery. No West coast river appears to be of the type we are discussing. The Sacramento-San Joaquin ends in an estuary; the fishery of the Columbia is dominated by the salmon and steelhead runs.

In the streams I know best no fish except the American eel are truly migratory, although some make fairly exten-

Shad are dipped as they migrate upstream in the East.

sive seasonal movements. The Atlantic coast streams have runs of striped bass, American shad, and perhaps other less well known anadromous species which are important in their fisheries.

This brings us to the critical question: What kind of fish can you catch downstream?

Relaxed fishing for steelhead and salmon on the Columbia River.

A greater variety of fish species is available to anglers in a large river than in any other freshwater habitat. Most of the common game and panfish of the area will be present either in the main channel or in the connecting chutes, backwaters, sloughs, bayous, oxbows, overflow ponds, and blue holes. Besides these, there are certain species which are characteristic inhabitants of large rivers. Some are also found in other large waters; some seldom occur anywhere else.

Occurring almost exclusively in large rivers are the paddlefish, the shovelnose sturgeon, alligator gar, skipjack herring, blue sucker, blue catfish, and the sauger. Of these, the shovelnose sturgeon, alligator gar, skipjack herring, and blue sucker have declined greatly in abundance in the past 50 or 75 years. Dams, siltation, pollution, and overharvest are variously blamed for their decline.

The paddlefish, alligator gar, and blue catfish grow to large size and are responsible for most tales of giant fish told along the large rivers. An example is the "blue channel cat" weighing 315 pounds, reported by Captain Bill Heckman to have been caught near Portland, Mo., in 1866. No less an authority than Dr. D. S. Jordan reported an alligator gar reached 20 feet in length. Paddlefish up to 163 pounds in weight have been recorded, and the modern Missouri record is 110 pounds.

Also characteristic of large rivers is a group of forage fish which seldom occur anywhere else, including speckled chub, river shiner, mimic shiner, silverband shiner, silver chub, flathead chub, sicklefin chub, sturgeon chub, and silvery minnow. The range of some of these is limited, and all will not occur in all the streams, but where they do, it is likely to be in large streams.

Of more interest to the angler are the fish usually most abundant in the sloughs, backwaters, bayous, oxbows, and overflow ponds connected to the large river. Much of the habitat here is more similar to a pond or small stream than to the river channel, and the water is likely to be clearer, current greatly reduced or absent, and aquatic vegetation luxuriant.

It is here that largemouth bass, crappies, other sunfish, and bullheads are most likely to be found, although largemouths also occur, along with spotted and smallmouth bass, in the channels of the clearer streams, and all often are taken in the vicinity of navigation dams. Either black or white crappies may be present, but you seldom find both at the same place. The other sunfish will be the kinds most frequently found in similar waters in the region, but the chances are good that bluegills will be abundant in most pool-like areas.

Many of the fish typical of large rivers also are likely to be found in other waters. The lake sturgeon is one of these, having been common at one time in large rivers and lakes throughout the North Central part of the country, but now is very rare. It grew to a large size. Forbes and Richardson report that near the turn of the century, 40 or 50 lake sturgeon weighing 50 to 100 pounds were taken each year near Allton, Ill. It already had declined greatly in abundance when they wrote in 1920.

Typical of large rivers but also likely to be found in other waters are the carp and the three species of buffaloes—bigmouth, black, and smallmouth—which among them made up 65 percent of the total commercial catch from the Mississippi River and its tributaries in 1964, the last year of record. It may surprise some of you, but the carp is also of considerable importance as a sport species, sought by skilled and highly specialized fishermen on the large rivers. Because of abundance, it makes up a substantial part of the sport catch.

The freshwater drum is another species important to both the commercial and sport fisherman. It made up 8 percent of the 1964 commercial catch in the Mississippi drainage and is considered a prize by many large-river anglers. It is known by many names throughout its range, including croaker and grunter because of the sounds it makes.

The channel and flathead catfish, along with the blue catfish, are caught by both sport and commercial fishermen. They made up 20 percent of the 1964 commercial catch in the Mississippi drainage. If there is an elite among the big river fishermen, it is the angler who goes after catfish with elaborate equipment plus painstakingly prepared (and profoundly pungent) baits.

Some species typical of large rivers, but widely distributed in other waters, are protected against commercialization in most States and therefore reserved for the sport fishermen. These include the white and yellow bass, the walleye, and the sauger. Both the white and the yellow are prized by anglers, though the yellow is not as widely distributed in the large rivers and tends to be less abundant.

The walleye and sauger are limited to the more northern streams under con-

The armor-plated Atlantic sturgeon is an upstream migrant in Florida.

sideration, seldom being found south of Tennessee or southern Missouri. The sauger tends to be more abundant and more tolerant of turbid waters, while the walleye grows larger and therefore is more desired. Both are excellent table fish. In the Mississippi, above the Iowa line and in other northern rivers, the northern pike is an important sport fish, especially in the impoundments formed by navigation dams.

Other fish common in large rivers as well as other waters include the carpsucker, especially the river carpsucker, which frequently is very abundant. These members of the sucker family are soft-fleshed, bony, and of little value to the angler.

The mooneye and goldeye often are abundant and provide good sport to the angler with light tackle. Their flesh, though bony, is excellent when smoked. The gizzard shad is a favored forage fish for predatory species, especially its very abundant young. The species is susceptible to temperature changes, pollutants, and other stresses and is likely to be a chief component of large fish kills. The emerald shiner and spottail shiner are forage species which often are abundant in large rivers and other waters.

The gars, especially the longnose and shortnose, are common in large rivers. They prey on other fish, but probably do little harm to a healthy fish population, since their prey is most likely to be the injured, diseased, or otherwise unfit.

Most of the angling on big rivers is like that on other waters; most of the fish are caught on a cane pole with live bait. Every access point, boat dock, ferry landing, bridge abutment, or navigation dam has its quota of old men and kids, with less patience and expertise but more energy, who fish tirelessly. I am not going to say much more about them here, for,

by and large, their methods are traditional "still fishing" and very similar to those used by anglers throughout the country. Also, most of the anglers fishing for bass, crappies, other sunfish, bullheads, and such in the connecting waters use tackle and techniques which are common on other waters where these species are caught.

Let's talk about methods which are truly characteristic of large rivers. Jug fishing, described earlier in this book by my good friend, George Morris, is almost unique to downstream areas and seldom used anywhere else. Trotlining is another. Although outlawed in some States, it is legal in most which contain large rivers and always has been popular on them. The origin of the name is obscure; it may have started out as a "troutline." It is one of several forms of setline fishing in which a number of short "stagings" equipped with hooks and sinkers are attached at intervals to the main "trot" line. The trotline is stretched across the stream from shore to shore or to a snag or bar. If the outer end is attached to a sunken rock or similar anchor, it is a "throw" line, or at least was where I grew up.

Sounds fairly crude, but I've described only the bare bones. The finesse comes in the care with which hooks, sinkers, and stagings are selected and assembled, the elaborate methods of attachment to the trotline, and the imaginative devices to keep the hooks from fouling and lines from tangling in transport. Then, there is the selection of the most likely place to set the line, the anchoring of it, the devices to hide it from other fishermen, and the degree of tension to make it fish properly in the current.

Finally, there is the matter of bait.

Trotliners usually are after catfish, so baits tend to be on the pungent side, but

Jug fishing for cats on the Missouri River.

Giant catfish are caught by noodling in Mississippi.

the variety is endless—liver, beef or pork melts, mussel meats, cut fish, chicken entrails, cheese, squares of artificial sponge soaked in blood, and various forms of "stink" bait prepared from carefully guarded recipes. Canned whole-kernel corn is a favorite, likely to take carp as well as catfish.

The true trotliner doesn't set his line and then go away and leave it. It must be "run" regularly, fish which are caught removed, and hooks rebaited. Catfish bite best at night, so this involves cruising a treacherous river in the dark, fumbling with sharp hooks, and subduing fighting fish by the uncertain light of a lantern or flashlight. A campfire to wait by is almost a necessity on a trotlining trip, and since one thing leads to another, a fish fry usually develops before the night is over, the crisp catfish washed down with a suitable beverage. You can begin to see why trotlining is popular.

Another kind of fishing I want to talk about is common on the large rivers, although by no means limited to them. In fact, in spite of what most sports writers and many fish and game departments may say, it is common throughout much of the country. It requires a great deal of skill, and the reward can be a breathtaking battle and a succulent meal. I'm talking about carp fishing.

The carp fisherman is inclined to be contemptuous of people who go for things like bass or trout. He tends to be rather secretive about his methods, but he is a skilled specialist. This shows in his equipment. The rod may be a cane pole or a metal or fiberglass casting rod (telescoping "fly" rods also are popular), but whatever kind, it has been carefully selected for backbone to withstand the frenzied fight of the quarry.

The line, likewise, is strong. The hook will be small, to be readily taken into the carp's small, sucker mouth. A treble hook frequently is used, both because it holds the bait better and because it increases the chance of hooking the nibbling carp. A fairly heavy sinker assures getting the bait to the bottom, but is arranged so that it doesn't carry it below the surface if the bottom is soft mud.

A large bobber usually is used to signal when the carp starts to nibble and when he finally takes the bait and it is safe to set the hook.

As with most forms of fishing, the selection of bait involves the greatest skill. Many kinds are used in carp fishing. That old standby, a gob of worms, has many followers. Others swear by Velveeta cheese or whole-kernel corn. The most distinctive carp bait, however, is some form of dough. The simplest is made by taking a pinch from the inside of a loaf of baker's bread, rolling it into a ball between the fingers, and impaling it on the hook. It stays on remarkably well and will catch carp.

The real specialist, of course, isn't satisfied with anything this crude. He has his own recipe, makes up his dough to exactly the right consistency, and has aged it just the proper time. Most such recipes include some aromatic material such as oil of anise to attract the fish.

The carp angler selects his fishing place carefully, throws out his baited hook into just the right spot, and then waits—a prime requirement of carp fishing is patience.

Sometimes after endless minutes of inactivity, the bobber starts to move slightly. The carp fisherman is expert at interpreting this gentle bobbing, as the carp sucks and nibbles about the bait before actually taking it. He doesn't do a thing but watch intently. This may go on for some time, but when the carp ends up sucking in the bait the bobber responds with a violent plunge, the fisherman sets the hook solidly, and braces himself against the frantic rushes of the fish.

The fight may last for some time, and on light tackle the carp could furnish more sport than a trout or bass of comparable size. Unfortunately, few carp fishermen use equipment which permits playing the fish. They are likely to horse it in as soon as it can be safely done. They get their kicks from the delicate business of inducing the carp to bite and of hooking him safely.

Navigation structures are always favored fishing places: the trail dikes, pile dikes, and deflectors which are likely to cause a deep hole to be washed out. The navigation dams are especially favored, and people who know these waters maintain that no better fishing is to be found anywhere.

Note, though, that I comment about those "who know these waters." This involves knowing the area thoroughly, the type of bottom, direction and velocities of currents at various water stages, the effects of these on the behavior of the different kinds of fish, when and where the various species can be expected to be present, and so on. In other words, considerable expertise is required.

In the fall, at the right places and water stages, it may be possible to catch large numbers of saugers and walleyes on minnows, fished slow and deep or on leadhead jigs. At the right place and water stage, in the spring, the bass may bite like they have forgotten how to keep their mouths shut, smallmouth and spotted in the swifter current, largemouth where the water is quiet. When conditions are right, this is a good place to catch drum or most of the other species common in the big rivers.

Downstream fishing is here to stay, and there is reason to believe that participation is increasing. Twenty-four metropolitan areas with populations of 100,000 or over are located on streams of the Mississippi River system. Their combined populations exceeded 13,750,-000 in 1960, up by more than 2,300,000 since 1950. They are still growing, and the handiest place for these myriads of people to fish is in the large rivers at their doorsteps.

The big cities, of course, while inviting anglers to use the large rivers, also pose one of the greatest threats to the fishery through pollution by sewage from their homes, storm runoff from their streets, and industrial wastes from their factories. Fish are tainted for over 100 miles of the Mississippi below St. Louis. A single pesticide factory in Memphis caused fish kills extending to the gulf. Similar situations exist below other cities. It has even been suggested that the transportation of wastes be officially designated as a principal use of certain large rivers.

But this picture is improving, however slowly. The Ohio, a prime horrible example of a polluted river a few years ago, has been somewhat cleansed, and work is progressing on other rivers.

More and more steam and nuclear-powered generating plants are being built on large rivers, located here to use the water to cool their generators. But the heat they release can have very harmful effects on fish production. This kind of development must be watched closely. Present Federal legislation, if adequately funded and applied and enforced by the States, should go far to restore hundreds of miles of large rivers to productive fish habitat.

On a hot summer day in Washington, the Potomac beckons.

Some other parts of the picture are also not so bright. Men have been tinkering with these rivers ever since the first flatboatman floated down and chopped out snags and brush to ease his passage. The greatest changes have been made by the installation of levees and similar works in the name of flood control, and by dams, dikes, and deflectors put in to aid navigation. It is almost impossible, in this day and age, to get a clear idea of what any of these rivers looked like to De Soto, Joliet, and Marquette, Lewis and Clark, or any of the other early explorers.

I have pointed out how some navigation structures are beneficial to fishing. The net effect, however, is to reduce the total fish habitat the river provides. Of course, where navigation dams are built, a pool is created which increases the fish habitat, but conditions are changed to the detriment of the characteristic river species.

In undammed streams, to get the required depth, every effort is made to confine most of the water to the navigation channel. Wing dikes, trail dikes, and other structures used for this purpose have been made of piling in the past; now most have been replaced with rock. This seemingly minor change has affected the fishery, due to the profound effects on the scouring action of the water and deposition of silt. Pile dikes let water through as they slow and direct the current, but rock dikes do not. The effect is to cut off the flow through most of the connecting waters which provide much of the variety of habitat, spawning, and feeding areas for many species and much good fishing. These waters are left to dry up, silt in, or if they do maintain themselves, are likely to be inaccessible by either land or water.

Another violence done to rivers in the name of navigation is the cutting off of bends. The distance between two river ports may be shortened, but those miles of water are lost to anglers. If the old channel doesn't dry up, it will be drained by the riparian owners to whom title usually will revert. Dredges work continuously in critical sections to deepen the navigation channel; not only do they change the river's character, but the spoil which they dig up must be deposited somewhere. Too often it ends up filling in some backwater, further reducing fish habitat.

These then are the large rivers, perhaps not the most glamorous places to fish, but frequently the most available and the most productive. They are broad and deep with treacherous currents, no place for the timid or foolhardy, but producing some of the largest fish found in freshwater. They may be poisoned by pollution, but the builders of dams and levees and wing dikes have succeeded only in reducing the extremes of their tantrums, not in bringing them under control.

The men who fish them observe carefully the effects of varying river conditions on the ways fish behave and develop specialized methods to catch the species which frequent these large streams. By applying this knowledge and these skills they are able to take kinds and quantities of fish unheard of in other waters.

As I think about it, I believe I should take back my statement about big river fishing lacking glamour. If we let our imaginations run, we will discover that our great rivers have a glamour all their own.

Big Reservoirs

by Robert M. Jenkins

Today's view of mid-America from the air would startle our grandfathers. Reflections from sprawling reservoirs and myriad farm ponds create the illusion that the plane must have strayed over Alaska or Canada. Instead, it's over Texas, Oklahoma, or any of a dozen other States. These "artificial" impoundments now furnish one-fourth of all freshwater angling, amounting to a hundred million man-days of fishing, with over one-half billion dollars spent in the process.

WHITE BASS AND SAUGER

At the turn of the century, there were only about 100 big (over 500 acres) reservoirs in the country; by 1968, however, the total was 1,200, combining about 9.4 million acres at average levels—all with the ability to support fish and angling.

About 45 percent of the total area is in Corps of Engineers and Bureau of Reclamation reservoirs, with the remainder under private power and irrigation companies, and State and municipal water supply, power, and recreation agencies. Less than 2 percent of the area is closed to public fishing.

One-half of the total area is concentrated in 9 States: Texas, Arkansas, South Dakota, Oklahoma, Alabama, Montana, North Dakota, Tennessee, and California.

An annual increase in area of about 3½ percent has occurred in the past decade, and if this rate of addition continues, there will be over 12 million acres available in 1975.

About 5 million people did most of their fishing in these bodies of water in 1965, while an equal number tried their luck there at least once. By the year 2000, a threefold increase is expected.

Lunker largemouth bass, slab-sided crappie, voracious white bass schools, and trophy-size rainbow trout, northern pike, and walleye have made many big reservoirs nationally renowned. Fabulous catches of largemouth bass and pike usually occur in the first few years after impoundment. Good fishing for these battlers continues, but fewer 10-pound-plus catches are made after the first 6 to 10 years.

Crappie, other sunfish, white bass, and

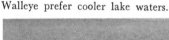

Walleye prefer cooler lake waters.

channel catfish are the staples for impoundment anglers, making up one-half to three-fourths of the harvest.

But over 50 species, ranging from sturgeon and gar to striped bass and sauger, and including rainbow, brook, brown, and cutthroat trout, pickerel, bullheads, white and yellow bass, white and yellow perch, and largemouth, spotted, redeye, and smallmouth bass, and 10 other kinds of sunfish, are caught, along with bowfin, carp, suckers, buffalo, and freshwater drum.

Not all of these species are present in each lake, but a wide variety is typical. A happy angler's stringer I saw on Bull Shoals Reservoir in May 1967 held largemouth, spotted, and smallmouth bass, white crappie, bluegill, white bass, walleye, and rainbow trout!

The average harvest from these lakes in 1967 was about 17 pounds per acre, varying from less than a pound to over 100 pounds per acre. With average luck, an angler took home three fish, each weighing 1½ pounds, after fishing about 4 hours.

An increasing store of information on reservoir fishing is being obtained by biologists to enhance the sport. Knowledge of angling pressure and harvest, fish populations, and the factors which cause them to fluctuate is improving.

The designation of large areas where high-speed boating is prohibited now enables anglers to continue their sport throughout the year. Zoning by management agencies, in both space and time, has eliminated some dangerous conditions and restored relatively undisturbed fishing on many reservoirs. As more zoning experience is gained, more improvements will be made.

Reservoirs vary greatly in their capacity to produce numbers and pounds of fish, having living conditions ranging from that of a sluggish river to a natural lake.

Most have higher rates of water exchange (flow-through) than natural lakes. They typically have greater shoreline lengths in proportion to surface area than natural lakes, and they age faster, due to the washing in of organic matter and silt from large watersheds.

Outlets in the dams are placed at various depths rather than on the surface. Density currents sometimes occur when turbid floodwaters flow through the reservoir toward low-level outlets. Water level fluctuations are usually of greater magnitude.

Large trees are often left submerged in the basin, and remain standing for 50 to 100 years, providing cover for fish and favorite fishing spots.

Changes in fish populations are more rapid and complex than in natural lakes. The loss of fish and fish food from reservoirs is higher because of greater water exchange.

Most lie in more fertile watersheds than do natural lakes, hence their production potential is greater. Geology, rainfall, soil type, and land use determine the fertility. The reservoir biologists' goal is to channel the existing fertility, high or low, into optimum sport fish production. Large waters cannot be fertilized as ponds are, due to excessive costs, but many are naturally "rich" and do not need fertilization.

All the habitats in which fish live are continually changing and especially so in reservoirs, where the trend is toward rapid aging and eventual extinction of the habitat.

Light is the source of energy in water, and the first step in fish production is the

The much-sought largemouth bass is taken in many impoundments.

harnessing of light energy by microscopic algae and diatoms—the phytoplankton. In muddy impoundments, light penetration is limited, and only a tiny fraction of the energy is ultimately converted to fish flesh.

Various chemicals are essential to fish production: carbon and nitrogen enter water from the atmosphere, and phosphorus is washed in from watershed soils. Phytoplankton are able to fix these elements into protoplasm, and fish that feed directly or indirectly on them convert the plant-fixed compounds into flesh. Waste products and carcasses of dead plankton and fish return the elements to the system for reuse, and in a series of reservoirs, they may be successively reused in downstream impoundments.

As in natural lakes, reservoirs stratify thermally when layers of water at various depths do not mix. In the spring, wind and wave circulation maintains uniform water temperatures from top to bottom. As summer approaches, wind velocities decrease, and the sun's rays warm the surface water, causing it to become less dense than the colder water below.

As the season progresses, warm surface waters mix to a depth of 15 to 40 feet, depending on wind speed, fetch, and outlet depth. Below this warm layer is a zone called the thermocline, varying from 5 to 50 feet, where temperature decreases rapidly.

In big fertile reservoirs, the water below the thermocline is cold (46–60° F.) and typically lacks dissolved oxygen.

236

Angling there is generally a waste of time, as there are few fish. In less-fertile waters, where fewer oxygen-consuming animals and processes are present, oxygen is not used up and trout and walleye are present at deep levels. In big, windswept prairie impoundments, no thermocline develops and the water remains in circulation from top to bottom, so fish thrive throughout.

Gradual cooling of surface waters in the fall to a temperature near that of the water below the thermocline, combined with wind action, results in fall turnover. In deep, southern waters, turnover may not be complete until December.

In winter, ice usually covers northern reservoirs, but it is uncommon on those south of the 38th parallel. Therefore, spring turnover does not have the full recirculating effect in southern impoundments.

Many hydropower dams have outlets at the bottom, and water released from the outlets is below 70° F. throughout the year, enabling trout fisheries to be established downstream.

New reservoirs test the adaptability of stream fish, as the environment may change from a shallow, turbid river to a deep, relatively clear impoundment. Native stream fish do not completely fill the new and diverse aquatic habitat. Many stream minnows cannot adapt and disappear, but gizzard shad and bullheads undergo population explosions. The bullhead bonanza lasts only 2 or 3 years, but shad may continue to increase until their abundance reaches detrimental levels.

In theory, maximum crops of catchable fish may be expected on a sustained basis only from expanding populations rather than stable populations. This is the most logical explanation for the excellent fishing experienced during the first 3 to 6 years of impoundment. Expanding, fast-growing bass and crappie populations fulfill the angler's dreams.

But the new reservoir bonanza can also be re-created in old ones by eliminating or drastically reducing the stable, slow-growing populations and restocking with sport fish.

Rapid early growth of populations in new lakes is due primarily to low fish density and high availability of food. Barring excessive siltation or turbidity, the standing crop of fish slowly increases over the years due to the constant inflow of nutrients. An increasing proportion of the standing crop, however, is made up of suckers, drum, and others, and the overcrowding of all species results in slower growth.

Population samples from over 100 reservoirs in the Midsouth averaged 185 pounds per acre, but since only two-thirds of the fish are usually recovered in samplings, the average standing crop is near 280 pounds per acre. This may range from 20 pounds in infertile waters to 750 pounds per acre in impoundments draining rich farmland.

Forage fish, primarily shad, make up about 40 percent of the population. Sport types, including largemouth bass, crappie, and other sunfish, white bass, trout, walleye, and catfish total about 30 percent, with the remaining 30 percent represented by carp, buffalo, suckers, gar, drum, and other "rough" ones.

An average reservoir supports about 80 pounds of sport types per acre, and at least 50 percent of the crop can be harvested by anglers each year without jeopardizing future production. Therefore, the current average yield of 17 pounds per acre can be doubled without endangering the population.

Computer analysis of various environmental factors which influence crop and harvest in over 200 reservoirs by the Bureau of Sport Fisheries and Wildlife's reservoir research program yielded these cause and effect relationships:

(1) Standing crop and harvest increase as minerals dissolved in the water (total dissolved solids) increase; however, when mineral content (primarily salts) exceeds one part per thousand, crop and angler harvest begin to decrease.

(2) As reservoirs age, the take decreases, but shad increase.

(3) With lower rates of water exchange (flow-through), harvest and total standing crop increase in hydropower reservoirs.

(4) With increase in relative shoreline length of reservoirs, standing crop and harvest increase.

(5) With increase in average depth and water level fluctuations, standing crop decreases.

The study also revealed that a hypothetical impoundment which would produce the highest angler catches would be 2 to 6 years old, have a dissolved solids content of 200 parts per million, an average depth of 20 feet, a relatively long and irregular shoreline, a low water exchange rate, and a long growing season.

Nearly every management technique used on natural lakes has been tried on big impoundments. Stocking, provisions for spawning sanctuaries, special rearing ponds and cover and spawning devices, planting of aquatic vegetation, and rough fish removal have not produced the desired effects in some instances.

Some outstanding management accomplishments, however, have been chalked up. Year-round open-season fishing was first applied on reservoirs and has greatly increased harvest; introductions of various sport species have added greatly to the angler's stringer; and intensive control of rough ones has improved fishing in a few reservoirs.

The principal methods now include introduction of new species, maintenance stocking of rainbow trout, walleye, and threadfin shad, water level fluctuation, rough and forage fish control, and installation of devices to concentrate and increase the catchability of crappie and a few other species.

Remarkable success has often been achieved by introducing white bass, crappie, walleye, northern pike, and rainbow, brook, and lake trout in reservoirs where they were not originally present. Constant stocking of rainbow trout is required, as they do not spawn successfully, but growth is usually excellent, and increased fishing success results.

The most promising introduced sport fish in reservoirs is the striped bass. This giant relative of the white bass has become established in impoundments in the Carolinas, Virginia, and California, and several inland States are now attempting to establish reservoir populations.

In an experiment, biologists stocked marine fish in some salty west Texas reservoirs, and the growth of flounder and red drum was phenomenal; however, they did not reproduce and continued replacement from the gulf would be required to maintain populations.

The threadfin shad, a diminutive cousin of the gizzard shad, has provided spectacular food to boost sport fishing production after being introduced in southern and western impoundments. Its superiority as a manageable forage fish

238

The lonely peace of sunset.

has been widely acclaimed, due to its small size, summer-long spawning, short lifespan, and susceptibility to winter kill, and to its suppression of the larger gizzard shad. In reservoirs, where extended cold temperatures cause complete mortality, threadfin must be restocked each spring, with successive hatches during the summer providing a banquet for bass and crappie.

Fish have enormous reproductive potential, producing more offspring than the water can possibly support if all survive. Young fish must suffer extremely

239

Urban boys learn fishing, thanks to a sportsman's organization.

high mortality or overpopulation and stunting will occur. Stunting often occurs in reservoirs, indicating a need for more efficient predators, so biologists have introduced largemouths, white bass, striped bass, walleye, northern pike, flathead catfish, and even gars in efforts to increase predation.

Thirty-one States now manage impoundments for combined production of warm-water fish and trout. Where deep waters never exceed 70° F., and dissolved oxygen levels are above 3 ppm, trout now contribute to a "two-story" fishery, with bass and crappie living in the warm upper story and trout in the cooler lower level. The trout are also found in surface waters in the cooler months, but are normally in and below the thermocline during the summer and early fall.

Trout grow from 6 to 11 inches per year in reservoirs where such forage fish as threadfin shad, alewives, or smelt are available. Four- to six-pound rainbows are now rather frequently caught in southern reservoirs.

During late summer, trout will migrate to cold, oxygenated levels near the dam. Catches by night angling are usually highest during this period, when their feeding activity is concentrated in the thermocline.

Reservoirs with annually fluctuating water levels often provide better fishing than those with stable levels. Drawdown usually occurs during the fall and winter, while spawning takes place during or after filling in the spring, so that nest builders are not jeopardized. Fall drawdown concentrates the population and increases predation by adult fish. The

240

exposed bottom dries out and cracks open, organic decomposition is stepped up, and certain fertilizer substances are released; when the bottom is reinundated in spring, these substances are available as nutrients for plankton.

When fish are concentrated by extreme drawdown, unbalanced populations can be eliminated by chemicals more economically. By carefully timing a brief spring drawdown, the eggs of carp, squawfish, and others which spawn in very shallow water can sometimes be destroyed.

On the other hand, uncontrolled fluctuations have harmful effects. Prolonged drawdown caused by severe drought or extreme annual drawdowns, inherent in the operation of many irrigation reservoirs, are examples.

Efforts to eliminate rough fish to improve fishing have met with little success in reservoirs. To be effective, netting and seining must be intensive, directed at all undesired species. The sizes and kinds requiring control often have little or no market value.

Since more efficient methods are needed, large trawls, trap nets, and electric devices are being tested. New selective chemicals may provide optimum control.

The major fish competing with the more highly sought for species like bass and trout include carp, squawfish, chub, buffalo fish, carpsuckers, and drum. As

Pan-sized trout and snowy slopes.

more is learned about these, some biological control method which limits reproduction may be discovered. Economical biological control would be much preferred to mechanical or chemical methods.

Population studies sometimes show that gizzard shad make up 50 to 80 percent of the total standing crop. In fertile waters, young shad growth is fast. At the end of the first year, however, they are too big for most predators to swallow, and they usurp nutrients and living space in competition with other fish and apparently suppress the growth and numbers of the desired sport species.

To alleviate this problem, reservoir managers apply dilute concentrations of rotenone to selectively kill shad, and immediately following treatment, fishing gets better and reproduction of sport fish the following spring generally improves. Drum and carp are also often killed during the selective treatment. Treatment costs range from $2 to $4 per acre. The effects usually last about 3 years and must be repeated at intervals to maintain desired population levels.

Heated, floating fishing docks first appeared in Oklahoma impoundments in 1950 and have since revolutionized winter fishing in the Midsouth. For example, 60,000 anglers used heated docks during a 3-month period on 19,000-acre Fort Gibson Reservoir, representing 90 percent of the total fishing effort during the winter. Crappie dominate the catches, but white bass, largemouth bass, catfish, and other species are also caught.

Dock fishing continues year-round, with some air conditioned, carpeted, and having a cafe, bait shop, and television. Anglers are seated in comfortable chairs around one or more wells inside the dock. Submerged cedars and bags of food are suspended under the docks, so that crappie are concentrated for the angler.

The construction and annual refurbishing of submerged brush shelters also concentrate fish such as the crappie for the angler. Brush shelters are anchored and positioned to avoid exposure during drawdown.

In the winter, warm water discharged from steam plants on impoundments attract fish; increases of only 2 to 3° F. can concentrate great numbers and afford excellent catches.

The use of boat-mounted lights as fish attractors has been practiced by night anglers for years; more recently, lights have been placed underwater while fishing for crappie and trout in clear reservoirs. Current tests of colored lights of varying intensity may prove rewarding.

Nearly all of the large impoundments have been built for purposes other than angling, so in some, the power or irrigation operation schedules are not designed to enhance fishery resources. Havoc is wreaked by dams that block the spawning migration of invaluable salmon and other anadromous fish. High water temperatures, fluctuating discharges, inadequate fish passage devices, reduced spawning area, and hazardous conditions for the migrating offspring have combined to reduce the salmonids.

Most reservoirs, however, have greatly increased fish production and angler catches over preimpoundment days. As more is learned about their biology, different plans for operating them to improve sport fish production will be developed. It is probable that operations will be increasingly modified to improve angling. Research, followed by workable management plans, will produce a better sport in the coming years.

242

Up through the ice—a flopping rainbow.

Tailwaters

by Donald W. Pfitzer

Tailwater is the end product of any dam, constructed for whatever purpose, where anglers can probably catch the greatest variety of fish on the greatest variety of tackle from a single point. Many times fishermen have greater success for the hours angled than in any other type of freshwater. Even if tailwater is a byproduct of another water-use purpose, it is an important part of the fishing scene of America; there is hardly a stream in the country that does not have some type of dam on it—for flood control, navigation, hydroelectric power, irrigation water, or recreation.

FISHING, GREEN RIVER, WYOMING

WITH A FEW EXCEPTIONS, the water below those dams—the tailwaters—are fair to excellent places to fish. Just as in the older, smaller mill dams, the large impoundments often block seasonal migrations, or for other reasons concentrate large numbers of fish below them.

Tailwaters are of two types: those that are cold throughout the year, and those that are warm during the summer. There are many variations within these two types, but the temperature is important for it determines the sort of fish that will be produced. The cold one may change a creek with a warm-water fish population into a fine trout stream in an area where these fish were never before possible. A warm tailwater, as you would expect, supports various warm-water fish—and some support almost as much fishing as the reservoir. The numbers and kinds of fish are controlled by the original stream and by the type and purpose of dam.

The man who fishes below dams may, in one place, catch a mixed string of crappie, white bass, and sauger; at another place, bluegills, largemouth bass, carp, and channel catfish; at still another, an 80-pound blue catfish. He may then move only a few miles to another tailwater and take a limit of 18-inch rainbow trout.

When a dam, regardless of its type, is built on a river, the entire ecology of that stream is altered. The first and most noticeable change takes place in the reservoir. The dam thus results in conditions much different from the former river and may result in many more hours of fishing or other recreational opportunity for the community around it. The more subtle changes, however, occur in the river below.

If the dam produces a deep reservoir with great storage capacity and if the water is taken from deep within the impoundment, a cold tailwater results. If, on the other hand, the reservoir is relatively shallow with a small storage capacity, or if water is drawn from near its surface, the stream below will be warm during the hot season.

Deep reservoirs, like natural lakes, stratify during spring and summer; that is, their water is composed of layers with different temperatures. The surface is warm and corresponds to air temperature; deeper water is cold, while a layer called the thermocline between these two zones is composed of cool water. Thus, discharges from the deeper zone mean tailwaters that remain cold for many miles below the dam. Of course, during winter all of the reservoir is cold.

The first of the high dams which discharged cold water were Hoover, completed on the Colorado River in 1935, and Norris Dam, constructed by TVA in 1936 on Clinch River in east Tennessee. Fishery management activities did not come to the Hoover Dam tailwater until the early 1950's. Immediately after impoundment and operation, however, the Norris Reservoir and tailwater area came under close scrutiny by fishery biologists. Dr. R. W. Eschmeyer and other TVA biologists found fishing to be good in the tailwater for the first few years after impoundment, but this initial flurry of fishing began to wane. They realized then that the native species in the river could no longer spawn and continue the population.

The biologists, for example, found crappie below the dam, during the period from July to September, that had not spawned (crappie normally spawn during the spring months). They also

Grandfather is feeling proud this afternoon.

discovered that sauger were carrying eggs from the preceding season and could no longer spawn. Beside being too cold for the crappie and sauger, the water temperature was too cold for smallmouth and largemouth bass, rock bass, walleye, and other river fish to carry out all the biological functions necessary for continuing the population.

In the years that followed, this process was repeated every time a high dam was completed and discharged cold water. By 1950 there were throughout the country a dozen dams discharging cold water—representing more than 300 river miles converted from warm- to cold-water streams. Most of these were in Tennessee, below dams constructed by TVA. An Army Corps of Engineers' dam in Arkansas on the North Fork of White River had changed a section of that famous river system into a cold-water stream.

Eventually, through research and management, biologists found that trout would survive in some of the colder streams, when stocked in large numbers as fingerlings 3 or 4 inches long. Their growth was phenomenal in many of the tailwaters: at the rate of an inch or more per month. Thus the former large warm-water streams were now the scene for flyrod and dry-fly fishermen, who took trout where no trout existed before—and much bigger ones than small mountain streams could produce.

Excitement among anglers began to run high, and by the mid-1950's, tailwater trout fishermen were a new but numerous breed. Most began with the conventional trout fishing tackle, but they discovered that riverbank fisher-

247

Waters below municipal impoundments can be managed for good fishing.

men who had never before tried for trout were catching them on all manner of bait, from earthworms to canned corn. Even bread brought trout in some streams.

A little country store on the Watauga River in east Tennessee, in the community of Siam, had never sold a loaf of whole-wheat bread—until trout fishing in the river became popular. Then it seemed that rainbows could be taken better on whole-wheat than white bread. Overnight, the Siam store began selling more whole-wheat than all other bread put together. It was used in the form of dough balls like those for carp. But instead of the carp and suckers these anglers had been used to, they were catching 20-inch rainbows.

On the small Cheoah impoundment, which is the tailwater of large Fontana Dam in western North Carolina, fishermen became frustrated because they could not catch the large trout they saw feeding on tiny midges at the surface. They tried their tiniest fly patterns, presented in the most delicate manner possible on the finest leaders, but still the trout ignored their efforts. The water was too clear to get close to the fish.

One day an angler who was resting in his boat after giving the trout all he had, began throwing bits of bread from his sandwich into the water. A slow current in this small impoundment carried the bits away; when they had drifted further

Sometimes a boat is the only way to get to the best spot.

than he could cast a flyline, he noticed trout taking the floating chips of bread. Using light spinning tackle, he tied a number 12 hook to his monofilament and attached a piece of bread, so it would float like the previous pieces. Then he scattered a few more bits of bread around and allowed his line to drift. At the right distance from the boat, the trout again began taking the bread—and a large one took the crumbs with a hook in it!

Very quickly the standard equipment used to fish this lake for a weekend was five loaves of bread, a small boat, a light spinning rod, and a large landing net. Limits of large trout became common.

Hardware also found its way into the tailwater trout scene. A 7-mile tailwater below Dale Hollow Dam in middle Tennessee had been stocked with fingerling rainbow trout in 1951. By 1953 biologists knew from population samples that the fish were growing well, but the local people, who had never fished for trout, were not catching them. One afternoon the biologist floated the fast-moving stream, casting to the bank with copper spoons. Within a few casts a new method for tailwater trout fishing had been found. The local people were told, and soon most of the fishermen in the little town of Celina, Tenn., who had a boat and motor, were floating down the Dale Hollow tailwater for 3 or 4 miles and motoring back, only to repeat the operation several times in an afternoon. They were catching big trout—rainbows and browns—on copper spoons retrieved fast.

The fishermen on this stream knew the conventional trout fishing methods, but they soon learned about bread and canned corn, the yellow variety. During the peak of the late spring and summer fishing season, more trout are caught on kernels than any other bait.

From California's Lewiston, Trinity, and Shasta Dams to South Carolina's Lake Murry, there are now more than 50 excellent trout tailwaters. The wading dry-fly purist, the adventuresome white-water float fisherman, the quiet-water float angler, and the bank fisherman with worms or kernel corn—all find trout in the cold tailwaters. On the White River in Arkansas and the Little Tennessee River in east Tennessee, elaborate charter float-boat trips are available to tailwater trout enthusiasts.

In the tailwaters, trouting is usually best when the discharge from the dam is low. During full power discharges from hydroelectric dams, fish are scattered and angling is difficult. Early mornings and weekends are usually best because of lower water at these times. Tailwater trout are usually limited to rainbows and brown.

In sharp contrast to the cold tailwaters, warm-water conditions below the large navigation, flood control, and hydroelectric dams offer a wider variety of species and fishing conditions. More than 200 such dams occur across the country, with the most popular and productive on large mainstream rivers like the Tennessee, Missouri, Tombigbee, Santee-Cooper, Red, Arkansas, Apalachicola, and Chattahoochee.

It is in the tailraces of large dams, such as Kentucky, Pickwick, Wheeler, Chickamauga, Watts Bar, and Fort Loudon on the Tennessee River, that literally thousands of pounds of fish are caught each year. This is repeated in varying degrees below Gavins Point on the Missouri River, in South Dakota and Nebraska, Denison Dam on the Red River in Texas and Oklahoma, and below the dams on the Arkansas River.

250

Rainbows don't reproduce in tailwaters, so stocking is needed to assure angling success.

The family can relax beside the water—but should pick up the litter on leaving.

Old mill dams have their tailwaters, too.

Below the mainstream dams on the Tennessee River, where records have been kept for a number of years, more than a half million fishing trips are made each year to 10 tailwater areas. One of the most heavily fished is the tailwater of Kentucky Dam located near the mouth of the Tennessee River, before it flows into the Ohio. The sauger migrates into this area, coming by the hundreds of thousands each winter and congregating below Kentucky Dam, where they meet the first barrier in their upstream spawning run. The run reaches its peak at this point in the river in December, but fishing for sauger remains good in the tailwater throughout the late fall and winter.

Variety is the spice of fishing in the big river tailwaters. At Kentucky Dam, as the sauger run begins to wane, white bass and crappie fishing picks up in spring. This is followed by catfish in late spring and summer, while bluegill, largemouth and spotted bass, drum, and other species such as carp fill in the gaps the year round.

Most of these large tailwater areas are easy to reach and to fish. Stone riprap put on the banks to prevent erosion also provides an all-weather surface for fishermen. At the Kentucky tailwater and in some other places, concrete berms have been installed to help anglers get to the water and make fishing safer. There are places to launch boats which, along with motors, may be rented at most of the larger tailwater areas. This is true throughout the Tennessee River system of dams and most of the other major rivers across the country.

Pickwick Dam and tailwater is the site for an annual catfish derby. Each summer Savannah, Tenn., conducts a festive program around the excellent catch of blue catfish that occurs below the dam during the summer. The peak is during June when thousands are caught, with prizes for the largest. The record cat is over 100 pounds, and many over 25 pounds are caught each year.

The favorite method of angling for large catfish is to float from the dam downstream using cut shad or shad guts as bait. Many fishermen use heavy salt-water tackle, which is necessary to land these strong stubborn fighters.

Perhaps no place in the fishing world offers the bank or cane pole fisherman a more rewarding trip than do the warm-water tailwaters. Success is virtually assured, and the variety and size of the catch makes the angler return time after time. During the coldest weather, when few fish the reservoirs, an ardent tail-water angler can fill his string with fine game fish.

But not all tailwaters produce a good fishery. Some provide fair action for a couple of years after the dam is completed, only to go sour and produce virtually nothing in following years. In most of these cases the cause can be attributed to the design of the dam and the attending operational patterns of water flow, storage capacity of the reservoir, stream characteristics below the dam, or other factors that can be modified prior to construction of a dam.

A true success story is in the making on dam design and operation. The multiple level intake ports, which permit selective water temperatures and quality to be discharged into the tailwater, were recommended by the Bureau of Sport Fisheries and Wildlife biologists for several areas as early at 1957, and were installed in the first impoundments in Kentucky during the next few years. Since that time much effort and research has gone into the methods of modifying the design of a dam to improve the water quality.

Regulated minimum flows to protect the fishery during periods of no power demand at the dam have improved or completely rejuvinated some tailwater areas. It is the great fluctuation in the water flow below some dams that eliminates the fish population, but great strides are now being made to correct this problem.

Fishing is possible during the colder months.

Natural Lakes

by John B. Moyle

Anglers working natural lakes use a great variety of equipment and methods, including worm and minnow dunking, deep trolling, and flipping dry flies, to catch both cold- and warm-water fish, large and small. But however they fish, they should know about the lakes they are on, for no amount of electronic equipment or other specialized gear can replace the knowledge of the physical and chemical features of these waters. With such knowledge, a good catch is more likely, and thus the sport and its enjoyment are improved.

ARCTIC GRAYLING

AMERICAN ANGLERS are fortunate to have so many natural lakes to choose from; there are at least 70,000 larger than 10 acres, with at least 50,000 of them regularly fished by more than 20,000,000 anglers. By 1985 the total fishing them may double. Often the anglers also camp, boat, or swim. And the hike or fly-in to the "inaccessible" lake also is particularly rewarding.

Each lake is unique, an object of beauty and utility in its own way and in its own setting. The smaller one, like Thoreau's Walden Pond, is an "earth's eye," while the larger ones, surrounded by hills, plains, or mountains, present many aspects throughout the year. They may be quiet sheets of burnished gold in the sunset or rough, rolling, angry waters in times of storm. In the winter, in the North they lie as still white expanses, when the ice is blanketed by snow.

There are wilderness lakes and those in prairie farm and range lands. The arctic tundra has some as does the desert country, where they may be surrounded by glittering salt flats.

In the North and at high altitudes the shorelines are lined with spruce, pine, and aspen, and in the South by bald cypress, tupelo, and sawgrass. Some, such as those in Alaska, are seldom visited, while others, such as Placid and Saranac in the Adirondacks of New York, have long been famous as summer and winter resorts. There are rural and city lakes, and some, such as Minnetonka in Minnesota, are centers of large suburban areas.

Before the coming of the white man the Indians knew, used, and respected our lakes, fishing in them, traveling over them, and often living upon their shores. Many have names that the In-

dians gave them, either in original form or translated, or are named for tribes that lived upon their shores—Winnebago, Cayuga, Erie, Klamath, Okeechobee, Winnepesaukee, and Gogebic; Quam-butch-e-mages-muglies in the wilderness country of northern Minnesota and Memphremagog in northern Vermont. Chargoggaggoggmanchaugagoggchaubunagungamaug in Massachusetts is of doubtful Indian etymology, and happily for those inquiring the way to it, is also called "Webster."

Others have been named for their size, shape, color, use, kinds of plants and animals found in or near them, rivers feeding them, or scenic features of the surrounding country. Yellowstone Lake is one of many examples. The names of many commemorate persons and events of all degrees of importance. In New York, for example, Lake Champlain bears the name of Samuel de Champlain, one of the founders of French Canada, who discovered it in 1609. In historical contrast, neighboring Lake George bears the name of an English King, George II.

Throughout the northern lake country many were once links in the water routes traveled by early voyagers and fur traders, and often their names add a French accent to the landscape— names such as Traverse, Lac qui Parle, and Superior, which was originally Lac Superieur, that is, the "upper most" Great Lake.

Lakes are scattered throughout the United States, but they are especially abundant where the landscape was shaped by continental glaciers of the last ice age. They are common in the rolling and often poorly drained topography left behind upon the retreat of the last continental glacier—the Wis-

An alpine lake has the charm of lonely beauty.

consin ice sheet of Pleistocene time—about 10,000 years ago.

This great moving mass of ice, rocks, and soil originated in the highlands of Canada and pushed southward to the Missouri and Ohio River Valleys and along the Atlantic coast as far south as northern New Jersey. Thousands of lakes lie in the rolling hills or moraines, marking haltings of the forward movement of the ice. Other thousands are found in the more level stretches of glacial soil between the glacial hills, and in the outwash plains of soil deposited by water in front of the melting ice.

The northern area of lake-dotted glacial soils extends from the Dakotas on the west, through Minnesota, Wisconsin, Michigan, New York, and New England, and reaches as far south as Iowa, northern Illinois, Indiana, Ohio, and New Jersey.

Within the glaciated region, lakes were formed in many ways. In some places, long systems of morainic hills formed dams that impounded large lakes—Mille Lacs Lake in Minnesota is such. Melting of ice masses, buried in the soil left behind, formed many "pit" or "kettle" lakes.

257

A northern pike satisfies even this "old pro."

In rocky regions, especially in the Far North, the glacial ice, using the stones it carried as cutting tools, gouged lake basins in the underlying rocks. Often strings of lakes lie in the valleys through which great rivers carrying water from melting ice once flowed.

Some lakes also are but remnants lying in depressions of the basins of once huge glacial lakes—Lake Bonneville in the Great Basin, of which Great Salt Lake in Utah is a remnant, and Lake Agassiz in the upper Midwest, now represented by Devils Lake, N. Dak.

In mountainous regions, many lakes have been formed by the action of smaller local glaciers and are abundant at higher elevations in the Rockies and the Sierra Nevada, often occupying glacial cirques. In Colorado alone there are 1,576 less than 10 acres and in Oregon about 700.

Lakes have also been formed by damming of large rivers by deltas of tributary streams, Lake Pepin in the valley of the Upper Mississippi River being one. Lake Okeechobee in Florida is a remnant of a shallow sea that once occupied a much larger area, including the Everglades. Reelfoot Lake in Tennessee was formed when the earth's crust sank 5 to 20 feet, following the

Channel catfish grow large in some of the warmer lakes.

Happiness is a good guide.

New Madrid earthquake of 1811–12. Crater Lake in Oregon, one of the world's more scenic wonders, lies in the crater or caldera of all that is left of an ancient and extinct volcano—Mount Mazama.

Lake Tahoe, the pride of California and Nevada, was formed by slipping or faulting rock layers in the Sierra Nevada. The beautiful Finger Lakes of New York lie in ancient river valleys that existed before the ice age, but which were gouged out by glaciers. There are also lakes—common in Florida—that lie in sinkholes and depressions formed by the dissolving and carrying away of limestone rock.

Oxbow lakes on flood plains are cut-off segments of old river channels and lakes of river deltas. And others were formed by landslides damming streams, by lava flows, and by wind erosion. Chubb Lake in Quebec occupies a pock-mark made when a huge meteor hit the earth. Salton Sea in southern California was once part of the Gulf of California and now lies about 285 feet below sea level. The origin of some, such as the many oval "bays" of the Atlantic Coastal Plain, is still a matter of conjecture.

Our lakes range in depth from only a few feet to 1,932 feet (about one-third of a mile) in Crater Lake, Oreg. All are warmed by the sun, and the gains and losses of heat through the year cause varying temperature patterns within

260

them. These temperature patterns, which usually include layering or stratification of water according to temperature, and at times, circulation of the water in them, have a great effect upon the life in the lakes and upon the angler's catch.

Typically in deep northern lakes, the upper waters become considerably warmer in summer than the lower waters and are separated from the lower colder waters by a transition zone, called the thermocline, in which the water temperature drops rather rapidly—usually about 0.6° F. per foot. The upper warmer layer circulates throughout the summer, but does not mix with the lower layer.

In fall, however, the surface cools and becomes denser and heavier than the lower portion, and then sinks, and the lower warmer water rises, causing the entire lake to mix. A similar overturn and mixing occurs in spring when the ice melts, and the denser and heavier water under the melting ice sinks to the bottom.

During these fall and spring periods of mixing, oxygen gas, which has been added to the upper level by wave action and life processes of plants, is distributed throughout the lake, and there is plenty from top to bottom for fish, even in deep lakes.

In the summer when the water is layered or stratified, conditions in the depths may change. If the lake is highly productive of plant and animal life, there is a continuous rain or fallout into the lower colder waters of tiny plants and animals (plankton) that have lived out their short lifespan in the upper waters. Decay of these in the lower level uses up the dissolved oxygen stored there, and thus the lower waters may not have enough oxygen in them for fish. This is why the lower level of deep fertile lakes—the so-called eutrophic lakes—will not support trout and why fishing deep will produce no fish for the angler's stringer.

By contrast, if the lake has relatively small crops of tiny animals and plants in its upper waters in summer and there is little fallout of these to decay in the lower waters, the oxygen will remain high in the depths all summer. In the oligotrophic lake of this kind, trout and related cold-water fish are at home in the deep water.

Besides lakes that stratify into well defined temperature zones or layers in summer and less markedly in winter and then mix in fall and spring, some lakes have other temperature patterns. In large windswept ones that are fairly shallow—usually those less than 40 feet deep and several miles across—the water may be mixed by waves throughout the summer, and because of this have fairly uniform temperatures and ample oxygen from top to bottom. In these the entire bottom is productive of food and hence fish, including walleye, northern pike, and sturgeon.

Very large, deep northern lakes that do not freeze over in winter may mix only once a year—in fall—and circulation continues throughout the winter. The Great Lakes (except the western end of Lake Erie) are of this type, as are some of the Finger Lakes in New York. Depth itself, even though other conditions in the water are favorable, may limit the distribution of fish. Lake Superior, for example, which attains a depth of 1,302 feet, has few fish below 500 feet.

Everyone knows sea water is salty and freshwater is not, and those living in arid regions are well acquainted with the bitter, slippery taste of alkali water. Be-

Shielded from wintery winds on a big lake.

tween these there are lake waters of almost any gradation of chemical quality. In general, however, lake waters are of three chemical types: those in which carbonate salts, especially bicarbonates of calcium and magnesium, predominate (carbonate waters); those in which sulfate salts, especially magnesium sulphate, are most abundant (sulfate or alkali waters); and those in which chlorides, especially sodium chloride, predominate (chloride or saline waters).

Most of our lakes are carbonate waters, ranging from those very low in carbonates (and dissolved salts of all kinds) and commonly called soft waters to the hard waters high in carbonates.

Soft-water carbonate lakes are characteristic of areas of ancient igneous rocks, such as granite and basalt, and areas of sandy and often forested soils with ample rainfall. Lake waters of the extensive area of ancient rocks called the Canadian Shield, extending from Canada into northern Minnesota, Wisconsin, and Michigan, are of this type, as are many of those in New York and Maine and on the sandy Atlantic Coastal Plain. Many waters of Oregon, Washington, and Alaska, and many alpine lakes also have soft carbonate water.

Such waters—since they are usually low in dissolved salts of all kinds, including plant nutrients such as phosphorus and nitrogen salts—produce quite small crops of aquatic animals and plants.

In the shallow waters of such relatively infertile lakes, usually only a sparse growth of submerged aquatic plants occur, and these often form tufts or rosettes of leaves. The water is usually clear or brownish in forested regions. Although usually only small crops of free-floating microscopic plants and animals occur in soft waters, desmids—wonderfully ornate green algae of many kinds—grow best in them. Blue-green algae, causing blooms and scums in harder and more fertile lakes, tend to be scarce.

Fish yields to the angler in soft carbonate waters are usually low, frequently below 2 pounds per acre of water per year, but the quality of the fish taken is high—usually trout.

Hard-water carbonate lakes are characteristic of areas of deep glacial soils, especially those containing considerable amounts of lime. They are found also in limestone regions, such as central New York. Smaller lakes of this hard-water type—those up to 150 acres—commonly have a vigorous growth of submerged and floating leaved aquatic plants that form a weedy zone extending from the water's edge to a depth of about 10 feet or more. This weedy littoral zone is highly productive of fish foods, such as aquatic insects, and larger kinds of free-swimming invertebrates, such as water-fleas (microcrustacea).

In this weedy zone there is an abundance of both forage fish, such as minnows and darters, and of game fish, especially largemouth bass, crappies, other sunfish, and in the North, northern pike. Perch, bullheads, and other fish may also be common.

These hard-water carbonate lakes are usually the eutrophic type, with little or no oxygen in the deeper waters in summer, and hence, no fish at the lower depths. But the yield of fish to the angler is usually high from the lake as a whole. In the Northern States, frequently 30 or more pounds of fish per acre of water are taken each year. Farther south, where the growing season is longer, the annual fish crop landing in the angler's creel is often considerably higher.

Larger hard-water carbonate lakes in the North, in which the water does not stratify in summer, often have good populations of larger game fish, and provide good fishing for walleye, northern pike,

and muskellunge. But the yield to anglers is usually less than 10 pounds per acre per year—often around 5. Submerged aquatic plants are often quite scarce in such large lakes because of heavy wave action.

Shallow hard-water carbonate lakes circulating all summer are especially prone to have growths of blue-green algae, sometimes scumlike nuisance blooms, if they receive fertilization because of the activities of man, or if they have large populations of carp and other rough fish continually stirring bottom soils. It is not uncommon, if rough fish populations are not controlled, for large shallow lakes in fertile farming country to have 400 or more pounds of rough fish per acre plus 100 pounds or more of game fish. Crappies and bullheads are often the commonest game fish.

Near the edge of the Great Plains lakes, the hard carbonate waters grade into shallow lakes with sulfate salts predominating. This change is brought about both by changes in soils and underlying rocks, especially the occurrence of Cretaceous and other rocks rich in soluble sulfate salts, and the greater aridity of the climate which causes minerals in the water to be concentrated by evaporation. Usually an increase in sulfates is accompanied by an increase in magnesium, but there are sulfate waters in which sodium and potassium are the predominate metallic ions—lakes such as those found in the Sand Hills of Nebraska. In very dry regions, such as the Carson Sink area in Nevada, waters may become saturated with sulfate salts, which are deposited as gypsum.

Many lakes with sulfate waters are quite shallow, and may provide fishing only intermittently. For example, of 169 natural lakes in South Dakota only 25

263

provide sport fishing on a sustained basis, and 95 provide it only in about 2 years out of 10, because of winter kill or lack of water.

But where such lakes are deep enough to sustain fish, they usually have good populations of both game and rough fish. In lakes of this type, bullheads, perch, northern pike, and crappies are often abundant, and the introduced carp may thrive to the extent of being a perpetual problem to fish managers. Submerged water plants of kinds that tolerate alkali water. such as sago pondweed, are often abundant. Frequently these shallow fertile lakes become quite green in summer from growths of blue-green algae.

The third water-quality type, the chloride or saline lakes, are found mostly in arid regions of the more Western States. Two well known examples are Great Salt Lake in Utah, which has a salt content about six times that of the ocean, mostly sodium chloride, and in which no game fish live; and Pyramid Lake, Nev., which is less saline and contains fish. Salton Sea, Calif.—also saline—has been stocked successfully with marine fish. Several saline lakes in Louisiana, the largest being Lake Pontchartrain, are connected with the Gulf of Mexico. There are also lakes in the Great Plains with water high in sulfate and chloride salts, of which Devils Lake, N. Dak., is an example. If shallow, these are of little value for fish, but are much used by waterfowl.

For plants and animals to thrive, lakes must have adequate concentrations of vital nutrients, including phosphorus, nitrogen, iron, and trace elements. A shortage of any one of these can limit the productivity of a lake.

The shape of the lake basin is also important, as productivity is usually inversely related to depth—the shallower the lake the more productive of aquatic life, including fish. Also, small lakes are often more productive than large lakes, since they usually have a larger proportion of shallow water.

The type of bottom soil, especially in the shallow water of the littoral zone, is also important; most productive lakes have soils with a considerable amount of organic matter.

From the long-term geological point of view, lakes are but temporary features of the landscape. All are gradually becoming more fertile, and raise increasingly larger crops of aquatic plants and animals, as time goes on. As the scientist who studies them—the limnologist— puts it, lakes change from oligotrophic to eutrophic, finally filling and becoming land. Many have disappeared in this way in the past. In most places this natural process of aging need not worry us a great deal, for the natural extinction is a very slow geologic process—a matter of thousands or tens of thousands of years.

Activities of man, however, sometimes have caused silt and plant nutrients to flow into lakes, where they increase the growth of submerged plants and the free-floating algae, causing water blooms and scums, and hastening the filling of the basin. This speeding up of eutrophication, or aging, is a serious problem in some areas and is becoming increasingly common. Lake Erie is a well-known example of a lake where the kinds of fish that long inhabited it have been almost eliminated, largely because of the effects of municipal and industrial wastes upon the lake.

Increase in the rate of aging of a considerable number of lakes, both in Europe and America, are known to have

Peace under the cypress.

been brought about by factors of human origin. There is runoff from tilled and fertilized agricultural lands, and an inflow of sewage effluents that are rich in plant nutrients, even though the sewage has been treated so it is no longer a public health hazard. Also, there is drainage from areas in which livestock are concentrated, along with runoff from streets, lawns, and gardens. In shallow lakes, stirring of the bottom by rough fish and even by large outboard motors may increase algal growth.

All of these practices either add plant nutrients to water or aid in keeping them in circulation and available to aquatic plant life. Lakes that have little water flowing from them are especially apt to be injured by excessive fertility, because little is lost in outflowing water.

Fertility in waters helps fish, and within limits is natural and necessary, but too much fertility can cause objectionable waterweed and algae problems and can change the character of a lake and the kind of fishing it produces. Much research work is being done on how to slow down the aging process—work that is essential, because both the human population and demands for recreational

use of waters are growing. Federal, State, and local agencies are all concerned. We have some answers, but many are still needed.

Here the fisherman and others who enjoy our lakes can help by understanding the needs and the complexity of eutrophication problems and supporting programs that slow down the aging. Improvement requires knowledge, effort, and money, but basic to the whole problem is an appreciation that lakes are more than water. In them there are complicated and interdependent societies of plants and animals—including fish. In them physical and chemical conditions and the life they support can and often are altered by what we do.

If we are to preserve our lakes and get the most enjoyment and value from them today and tomorrow, we who are part of the "macrocosm" of the Planet Earth must have a greater appreciation of the "microcosm"—the little world—found in every lake. If we do, and use the knowledge we gain, we can continue to rise up early in the morning and sally forth with fishing rod in hand with the expectation that angling hours will be pleasantly and not idly spent.

265

Farm Ponds

by Verne E. Davison

*My grandsons—Sidney and Charles—are grown now.
College students, they spend a good deal of their leisure fishing the deeper
waters of impoundments; they can handle sophisticated
fishing equipment and boats. But whatever proficiency they have now can
be traced back to the farm ponds of their youth.
Back when the boys were about six and nine, I was a technician helping
plan, build, and manage farm ponds in Mississippi and Alabama,
so I often took them along on my trips and taught them the pleasure of
dropping a line into those placid waters.*

FARM POND FISHING

THE PLEASURE they experienced in catching their first bluegills and largemouths on worms, crickets, and minnows in one of the thousands of ponds near Jackson, Miss., is a precious memory for me. Then when they graduated to flies and plugs—well, I can only smile in appreciation of their joy. Lines, hooks, rods, reels, bait casting, boating—all were learned by both of them on the farm ponds.

And their experience is by no means unique, as about 20 percent of today's more than 30 million licensed anglers enjoy fishing in farm ponds. Many of them—children and adults, males and females—first cast a line and learned how to catch a fish in these waters.

Far too few in America have the privilege of being near an unpolluted body of water where the art of the angle can be practiced. Often farm ponds are the only nearby places where many can go to catch fish. When properly managed,

these water holes yield more fish per hour than unmanaged natural waters.

The rippling surfaces of the ponds have added beauty to the landscape and value to the land around them. They are used for watering livestock—and for swimming, boating, fishing, fire protection, waterfowl habitat, and sometimes to irrigate gardens or fields. Fringe benefits of camping, picnicking, and bird-watching have added zest to the days that people have spent in fishing along their banks.

These benefits are assured for a long time, if landowners take particular care in managing these ponds. There are fish ponds 1,000 years old in Indonesia, and water technicians in the United States say ours can last just as long, if water-weeds are controlled and silty floodwater is not permitted to enter.

An attractive aspect of good pond management is that it can be carried out by the owner in his spare time. Fer-

Farm ponds have their naturalness, too.

A plug is irresistible to two bass.

tilization of the water, or the use of commercial feeds, increases the pounds of fish in the pond. Fees charged for using the pond can bring in extra cash.

Fishermen save time and money by working the ponds that are only a few minutes and miles from home or office. They can fish 2 hours in the coolness of a morning or evening on summer days, during the afternoon comfort of warm winter days, or between showers in April—and be home in time for the next meal, or get to work on time.

For the farmer and his paying guests, costs and returns relate directly to pounds of fish produced and caught and services provided, such as fishing, parking, and picnicking.

Fee fishing is good business for pond owners, fishing customers, and their communities. For this service, I estimate that fishermen pay out about $30 million annually.

Wise pond owners obtain help from experienced sources about the kinds of fish that can be grown satisfactorily in the water they impound. There are about 20 kinds that can be stocked or occur accidentally in farm ponds, but many fail for one reason or another to produce enjoyable fishing.

Water temperature is a crucial factor in stocking and management. Ponds are classified as cold, warm, or subtropical in the United States.

Cold-water ponds are best suited for brook, brown, cutthroat, and rainbow trout. A cold-water pond seldom warms above 70° F. in summer months. It may or may not freeze over in winter. Suitable waters occur and are impounded in most Northern States and Alaska, at high alti-

Begin modestly with bluegills, then move up.

tudes in Mountain States, at low altitudes of the Pacific States, and wherever cold springs or large wells provide waters of 60° F. or colder (even in the South).

Rainbow trout are the most commonly available for stocking cold-water ponds, but brook trout are also used regularly in the Northwestern States, and cutthroats—if they are available—are suitable where rainbows are stocked. Brown trout prosper in waters slightly warmer than those most suitable for the other three.

The four trout grow well when water temperatures are from 45° to 70° F., but they also feed, at least enough to be caught through holes in the ice, at the 32° to 39° F. temperatures that occur when ponds are frozen over.

Stocking rates are decided by the pond owner. Food supplies naturally available in ponds usually are sufficient to grow and support at least 50 pounds per surface acre, and some ponds produce 100, 150, or even 200 pounds per acre. The wise owner keeps a record of his actual annual yield for a few years, so he can stock correctly according to the productive capacity of his pond.

Trout, of course, do not spawn in ponds; therefore, the owner restocks every year, or at intervals of 2 to 3 years. To stock correctly, he estimates the number of pounds of fish for his pond, then buys a number that will reach the size

A soothing end
to a long day.

270

Bullhead are a boy's pride.

he wants—4 ounce, 5 ounce, 8 ounce, or larger—by the time he plans to start fishing.

The pond's carrying capacity can be increased much above the natural food supply by using manufactured fish feeds in a pelleted form. In this way 1,000 pounds or more per surface acre can be produced, regardless of poor, moderate, or high availability of aquatic worms, larvae, shrimp, and insects.

This is the way for owners to produce the most profitable trout fishing and best use the water resource. By daily feeding of only 2 to 4 pounds of pelleted feed to each 1,000 pounds of fish, each pound produces about one-half pound of delightful trout—and their color and taste are superb.

Warm-water ponds are those in which water temperatures rise to 60° to 70° F. early in the spring and remain regularly above 70° F. throughout the summer months. Pond owners who want to grow

fish without frequent restocking, stock with bluegills and largemouth bass—the most successful combination thus far. They can substitute redear sunfish for about one-fourth of the bluegill stocking.

Experience in thousands of warm-water ponds provides conclusive proof that the purposeful or accidental addition of other warm-water fish is poor business. Almost any other kind of sport fish added to the largemouth-bluegill-redear pond either fails to survive or causes poor fishing within 2 to 5 years.

Largemouth and bluegill fishing yields only 15 to 50 pounds of fish per acre annually—in ponds of average fertility—but owners increase the yields to 150 or 200 pounds per acre by following a correct plan of fertilization.

Warm-water pond owners who prefer a fish that will not reproduce successfully stock with channel catfish—a species of good sport fishing quality and excellent taste. They buy the number they want from farmers who grow them for sale in farm hatcheries.

Channel catfish are fed commercial pelleted fish feeds to produce 1,000 pounds or more per surface acre. Catfish ponds with only 100 to 500 pounds of fish per acre do not yield good fishing.

Catfish are fed in the same manner as trout, but one important difference is recognizable—catfish grow best in water temperatures between 70° and 90° F., slowly between 60° and 70° F., and little if any below 60° F. So the owner learns his pond's seasonal water temperatures and calculates the number of favorable growing days it will provide.

Fishery research in Southern States indicates that blue and white catfish may be as successful as channel catfish in warm-water ponds. But farmer experiences with these fork-tails only began in the 1960's, so it may be a little too early to predict the degree of success possible.

Three other catfish—black, brown, and yellow bullheads—prosper in warm-water ponds, but they also spawn repeatedly and usually overpopulate the water seriously. However, if a weedless pond is maintained with largemouth bass, the bullhead fingerlings are soon caught by the largemouth.

Green sunfish is a widespread native species that easily invades warm-water ponds, unless the owner carefully avoids the possibility. They often hybridize with bluegills, producing an offspring that confuses the fisherman who wonders what kind of fish he has caught, as the hybrid has color variations related to both parents. The green type usually fail or upset the fish population in the pond.

Others that likewise fail include the warmouth, rock bass, smallmouth bass, black crappie, and white crappie. If they do well for a year or two, they then upset the largemouth-bluegill population and soon cause poor fishing.

Buffalo, carp, goldfish, mullet, yellow perch, shad, shiners, suckers, and various minnows also invade ponds, but can be kept out by properly designed spillways and screens.

Carp, incidentally, can be grown rapidly and heavily in warm-water ponds by feeding the same as trout or catfish. They are strong fighters on the line, and when cooked properly—as has been repeatedly proven by guest tasters at Auburn University—they taste just as good as largemouth. The Israeli strain is a much more attractive carp that has only a few large scales, a more slender body, and a small head. It too will thrive in ponds.

In subtropical ponds, three species of tilapia from tropical waters abroad have been introduced in the United States.

Rising to get the fly in a cold-water pond.

Farm ponds are a fine place for the gang.

The male of a Zanzibar strain, when crossed with the female of a Java strain, in particular produce a surprising hybrid—one in which all the offspring are males and grow faster than the parents.

All species of tilapia, however, perish when the water gets colder than 50° F., so these tropical fast-growing fish are suitable only in pond waters with temperatures 50° to 90° F., or higher. In spite of this trait, however, a few tilapia, held in aquariums or heated ponds, can be stocked in April (at central Alabama latitudes) and their offspring can yield 500 pounds or more of sport fish before the end of October. Yes, from eggs to one-fourth pound fish in 100 days!

So there you have it—the three types of farm ponds and some of the fish managed in them. The future for all three types is very bright. Farmers and ranchers in the United States built about 2½ million ponds between 1936 and 1967. And I estimate that by 1985, an additional half million will be built. The best ones are in the upper reaches of small watersheds, well above where large reservoirs are built, but there are many remaining sites that owners can take advantage of.

This gigantic building program in process has resulted because State agencies, the Soil Conservation Service of the U.S. Department of Agriculture, and Interior's Bureau of Sport Fisheries and Wildlife have helped landowners get financial and technical assistance on how to build and stock the water holes. These agencies, whose assistance programs will continue, have also been very helpful in providing information on how to manage the ponds successfully for multiple use.

More than 2 million acres of newly created water in which fish can be grown have thus been created in the 30 years ending in 1967. I estimate that by 1985, there will be about 1 million additional acres established. About 12 million anglers may be using this resource by then.

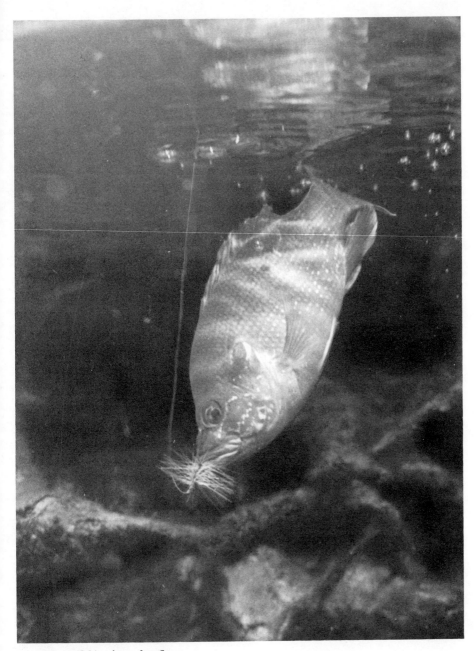

A green sunfish's view of a fly.

Estuaries

by Lionel A. Walford, John R. Clark, *and* David G. Deuel

Several things combine to give special biological value to estuaries, apart from their beauty and recreation aspects. For the salt marshes which characterize estuaries are extraordinarily fertile, producing nearly seven times as much organic matter per acre as the water of the Continental Shelf, twenty times as much as the deep sea, and six times as much as average wheat-producing farmland. It is no wonder that creeks meandering through the marshes are superlatively rich feeding grounds for fish and wildlife. For this reason alone, estuarine waters are excellent nursery grounds for coastal fish.

CRABBING, TEXAS COAST

Thomas Point Light in Chesapeake Bay—anglers' rendezvous.

IN ADDITION, their shallowness generally bars the entry of larger carnivores that frequent the deeper waters of the estuary and the ocean beyond. Their wide bays and meandering marsh creeks also add enormously to the area of the shallow water nurseries.

Species such as bluefish, weakfish, flounders, croaker, and spot reproduce in the open sea. The times and places of spawing are all determined by the destination of the young fish, as well as by the temperature requirements for incubation and growth. The eggs and larvae, drifting with the sea currents, are carried toward shore. The path of their drift may be a very short distance or hundreds of miles. In any case, the fry ultimately find their way into an estuary and then to a suitable habitat. This may be a particular type of bottom such as rocks, sand, or gravel; or it may be vegetation such as seaweeds or marsh grasses.

Estuaries differ greatly in form, occupants, and conditions of waters from place to place around our coastlines. Thus people see them differently, according to where they live—Georgians as boundless expanses of marsh, Washingtonians as deep cool sounds, New Yorkers as wide shallow bays. Differences and similarities are brought out by reviewing the major coastal sectors of the continental United States shoreline.

The North Atlantic coastal sector extends from the rocky coast of Maine to the sandy shores of Long Island along 7,980 miles of tidal shoreline (measurement includes islands, bays, sounds, lagoons, and tidal rivers to head of tidewater or where waters narrow to less than 100 ft.). North of Portland, Maine,

278

the bays are deep and fiordlike. There are no barrier beaches or large lagoons, and marsh development is confined mostly to the edges of tidal rivers. Where the bay shores are protected from ocean waves, broad mud and sand flats become exposed with the ebbing tide. Clear, cold Gulf of Maine waters fill the bays, making them small pockets for ocean life.

South of Portland the rocky bays give way to shallow lagoons protected from the sea by barrier beaches of sand thrown up by ocean waves and currents. Fringing marshlands become wider; but only at Long Island do they become more than a mere suggestion of the broad marshes lying to the south.

Of all the fish that take advantage of the North Atlantic estuaries, none is more widespread than winter flounder. This familiar flatfish feeds on the worms, mollusks, and small crustacea such as shrimp and crabs that abound over the bottom of estuaries. Anglers take winter flounder from boats, bridges, piers, and from shores throughout the North Atlantic estuaries and south to Delaware Bay. In 1965 they caught 20 million of them in North Atlantic coastal waters.

In summer the flounder move into cooler deeper parts of bays or offshore onto the Continental Shelf, but they return inshore in fall to feed. They may remain there or again move offshore to hibernate in the mud for the winter. In early spring when the water warms to about 40° F., winter flounder again become active. They feed, spawn, and by late spring leave for deeper water. The New England estuaries thus serve not only as feeding places for winter flounder much of the year, but also as the major

Trolling with gulls for company.

The throw-netter gets mullet, but he must have skill.

nursery grounds for their young.

Most other fish of the northern coastal area, however, make long seasonal migrations. For example, each spring multitudes of striped bass migrate northward from the Middle Atlantic region along the coast to populate the shores and bays of southern New England and the river estuaries of northern New England. In Massachusetts, for example, with the incoming tide, bait fish such as menhaden and silversides follow the rising tide into the tidemarsh creeks to feed upon the abundance of microscopic plants and animals. Striped bass then make their way into the flooded estuary to feed in turn upon the bait fish.

These New England visitors, which for some reason are mostly females, sometimes winter over in northern rivers, but usually return to the Middle Atlantic region in the fall. They spend most of their life in saltwater, but then go up rivers to spawn. Anglers are reported to take over 10 million a year in the North Atlantic area.

Two other anadromous groups of recreational value, the shad and alewife, are caught only as they pass through the estuaries and rivers as adults on their way to freshwater to spawn. After the young leave the rivers they disappear into the sea and are not seen again until they return for spawning. Smelt are anadromous too, but even the adults are confined mostly to estuaries and near-shore waters. Their young move down to the estuarine nursery grounds when about 1½ inches long.

Another popular North Atlantic species, the summer flounder, is a seasonal visitor to the northern coast. The adults live far offshore and to the south at the edge of the Continental Shelf in winter, but close to the coast and in the bays in summer. They spawn over the Continental Shelf in the fall, and the young drift south with the ocean currents for many weeks before swimming inshore to enter their nursery areas, principally in the Middle Atlantic region. Anglers caught 12 million of them in the North Atlantic region in 1965.

Many fish usually caught in deeper bays and sounds or offshore benefit from the outward flow of nutrients produced in North Atlantic estuaries. Oceanic groups like cod, haddock, and pollock abound in bays along the Maine coast, although they have long since deserted densely settled areas like Boston Harbor where the early settlers found them abundant.

Valuable bait types found in North Atlantic estuaries at young or adult stages include herring, menhaden, killifish, and silversides. Also clams, crabs, worms, and other forage items grow in abundance on the bottoms of estuaries, supplying large stores of food for fish and bait for anglers.

From the Hudson River to Florida's Palm Beach, there is a sharp contrast to the rocky coast of New England—a nearly level plain composed largely of sands and gravels. Sand barriers and barrier islands enclose many bays such as Barnegat Bay, N.J., and large sounds such as Albemarle and Pamlico, N.C., and fringe the coasts of South Carolina and Georgia. Subject to the forces of sea and wind, these sand islands continually change in shape, size, and even position. Storms may cut through new inlets or close up old ones. But with all this dynamic action, the marshes and lagoons behind remain fairly stable.

Chesapeake Bay and Delaware Bay are remarkable features of the Atlantic coast. Apart from their great size, their tributaries are tidal all the way to the rocks of the fall line; and the estuarine zone can be followed for miles around them, marshes occurring as far inland as Philadelphia and Baltimore.

This sector of coast lies between temperate and subtropical regions. In addition to its endemic transitional fish, it is visited by those migrating from the South in summer and from the North in winter. Thus during summer you may be surprised by an occasional tarpon, jack, or pompano as far north as New Jersey and New York; and during the winter by cod fairly close to shore as far south as Chesapeake Bay. But even within this transitional area, you will find differences in the composition of marine life north and south of Cape Hatteras.

Some Atlantic game fish spawn in the estuarine zone or so close to the inlets that the young are virtually delivered to their nursery grounds. Notable among these are winter flounder, spotted seatrout, and weakfish.

Several Atlantic coast fish run up rivers into freshwater to spawn, but one fish—the American eel—does the reverse. It comes from the sea at a very young stage, spends almost all of its 5 to 20 years of life in estuarine areas or in freshwater, sometimes astonishingly far inland, and when mature returns to the sea. Then it disappears from sight, travels out into deep water beyond the Continental Shelf, east of Florida and of the Bahamas, south of Bermuda. There it spawns and dies. The eggs hatch, the young drift for a month or two, reach the coast by spring, and somehow find their way through inlets to estuaries all along the coast from Mexico to Canada.

After a period of metamorphosis and growth, the sexes of eels tend to separate, most of the females working their way up into freshwater, the males remaining in bays and tidal creeks. The eel is, of course, a true fish, with fins and scales, and is an excellent panfish. Anglers catch about 4 million of them a year, fishing with rod and line, mostly at night, using small fish, shrimp, clams, or worms for bait. Small eels are excellent as live bait, the hook being inserted in the lower jaw and out the upper jaw. Larger ones, up to about 18 inches long, rigged for trolling, are effective lures for striped bass, bluefish, snook, and billfish.

The shad, also an anadromous fish, enters bays and estuaries along the Middle Atlantic coast, appearing as early as January in Florida and Georgia, March in rivers tributary to Pamlico and Albermarle Sounds, A p r i l in the Potomac, and May in Delaware. They seem to pause in the brackish estuarine waters before resuming their long journey upstream; and during that time, which may last several weeks, anglers find excellent sport trolling, casting, or jigging from small boats.

Immediately after spawning, which may be hundreds of miles upstream, the spent and emaciated fish return to the ocean, while the young fish stay in the rivers to go down to the sea in the fall.

Among the several anadromous fish native to the Atlantic coast, the striped bass is beyond question the object of the most passionate affection by anglers. More has been written about it than any

Snook are a favorite in Southern waters.

282

other shore fish; yet it remains unpredictable and in many ways mysterious.

Little can be said about the stripers without using qualifying expressions like "evidently," "apparently," and "more-or-less." Although classified as a single species, it is evidently composed of a number of populations, each of which is more or less associated with a particular river system and marked by distinctive features of habits and appearance, which can be extremely subtle and hard to describe, let alone measure.

Some populations of stripers, say those at the southern and northern extremes of their Atlantic coast ranges, seem to be wholly river fish. Elsewhere, as in the Chesapeake area, there are local populations that divide their year between estuarine or bay feeding and wintering grounds and river spawning grounds; while there are other populations which after spawning, migrate out to sea and along the shore. The distances traveled grow progressively longer with age.

The southern Atlantic shoreline of Florida is one of transition from coastal barrier islands to coral islands and reefs. The Florida Keys, extending 150 miles southwest of mainland Florida, separates the shallow water of bays such as Biscayne bay, Barnes Sound, and Florida Bay from the deeper waters of the Atlantic Ocean. South of Miami the estuarine area is characterized on the Atlantic coast by coral reefs, and on the gulf coast by mangrove forests which extend north to the vast swamps of the Everglades and the Ten Thousand Islands area.

Although many northern species are seasonal visitors to this area, most of the fish here are subtropical. Many more species occur about the Florida Keys and the southeast tip of Florida than either along the Atlantic coast or the northern Gulf of Mexico.

The shores of the Gulf of Mexico are low, sandy, and marshy. Most estuarine areas there are quite shallow and have resulted from the formation of offshore bars parallel to the shore. The delta of the Mississippi River, which extends to within a few miles of the edge of the Continental Shelf, contains countless islands and many bays, coastal marshes, and coastal lagoons. The river carries large quantities of silt, organic material, and nutrients into the gulf.

The coast of Texas is characterized by narrow barrier islands and reefs that cut off long, narrow coastal lagoons parallel to the coast. These lagoons are connected to the gulf through only a few narrow inlets, with the result that there is little circulation between them and the open gulf. The lagoons, fed by rivers, are subject to wide ranges of temperature and salinity, the extremes of which may result in mass mortality of fish. Several are hypersaline, the most notable being Laguna Madre, a 115-mile long lagoon in southern Texas. Laguna Madre receives limited freshwater and has only one narrow opening to the gulf. Salinities as high as 10 percent have been recorded there.

Shrimp are abundant throughout the Gulf of Mexico coastal area. They spawn in offshore waters of the gulf, and within a few weeks the young move into the estuarine areas. They remain there for 2 to 4 months, and then return to the open sea. They are an important item in the diet of many species of fish in the estuary as well as in coastal gulf water.

The spotted seatrout is one of the most important fish throughout the Gulf of Mexico as well as along the South Atlantic coast. Its favorite food and the most widely used live bait is shrimp. These fish also feed on live fish and crabs. The entire life cycle of the sea-trout is spent within the estuary, and the infrequent seaward movements of this species result from the occurrence of un-favorable temperatures (less than 50° F.) or salinity (less than 0.5 percent)

Seatrout spawn in coastal bays and lagoons from March through Novem-ber, and the young fish live in shallow grassy areas. Except for fish over 6 pounds, the seatrout is a schooling fish. The best seatrout fishing is during spring and fall, but they may be taken the year around on both natural and artificial bait by boat and shore fishing, from docks, piers, and bridges. Early morning hours are usually the most productive.

Black drum are dependent on estuar-ies during their juvenile stages and are found all along the gulf coast. Spawning occurs in the spring in estuaries and along gulf beaches. The young fish feed on worms, crustaceans, and fish, and al-though the adults are primarily mollusk feeders, they also eat shrimp, worms, algae, and fish. The best fishing for black drum is from January through March. Anglers fish from boats, piers, jetties, and the surf, using clams, crabs, or shrimp. Although the black drum reaches 140 pounds, the average size in gulf waters is 3 to 6 pounds.

The Atlantic croaker and the red drum are favorite inshore sport fish in the Gulf of Mexico. Both spawn in fall and winter along the open beaches of the gulf, and the juveniles are found in the estuaries. The adults of both are found in the estuary as well as in shallow coast-al areas.

Although croaker are caught year-round, the best fishing is from July to November. They feed on crustaceans,

mollusks, and fish, and the most popular baits are shrimp, clams, crabs, and small fish. Since croaker is a bottom feeder, bottom fishing, either still or casting, is the most productive.

Young red drum feed on copepods, amphipods, and shrimp, while adults feed mainly on crabs, shrimp, and fish. Red drum are taken on live bait, cut bait, spoons, and plugs, and are caught surf casting, trolling along the beach, or from piers, jetties, and docks. Best fish-ing in gulf waters is from October through March.

The crevalle jack is a popular inshore fish which is caught the year round in gulf waters, although the summer months are most productive. Spawning occurs offshore from March to Septem-ber, and the juveniles move into the estuaries for sanctuary. This species feeds on shrimp and other invertebrates and is caught on live or cut bait, plugs, spoons, and flies. A hard fighter when hooked, crevalle jacks are caught around bridges and pilings and on flats. Larger fish, up to 40 pounds, are taken along ocean beaches.

The tarpon is one of the most spectac-ular game fish caught in the Gulf of Mexico. Although it spawns offshore, the young move into brackish water, bayous, and lagoons, where they feed on inverte-brates and various species of fish. The adult is carnivorous and spends part of its life in estuarine areas. Tarpon are sen-sitive to cold water and leave the inshore areas to avoid low temperatures.

Although tarpon are taken through-out the year in gulf waters, peak fishing is in spring and summer. Their large size—often over 100 pounds—and jump-ing ability when hooked make them much sought by anglers. They are taken by boat and shore fishing using live or dead bait, such as mullet, shrimp, or crabs. Trolling plugs or spoons and also fly fishing are popular.

The bonefish, like tarpon, spawn offshore, and the young occur in estuarine areas where they feed on invertebrates. They are a shallow water species which frequent tidal mud flats, feeding on small fish, shrimp, squids, and mollusks, and are noted for their long runs when hooked. Although they are caught the year around in the Florida Keys, the summer months are most productive. Fishing is best on the shallow water flats by casting or fly fishing, either when wading or boating. Live bait, such as shrimp or crabs, and artificial lures are used.

The North Pacific seafront, south of the tundra-bordered shores of northern Alaska, is rocky and steep along much of its length, comparable only to that of Maine among Atlantic States. Pacific rivers typically discharge cool water into deep bays or directly into the ocean. In these bays and sounds, tucked in behind rocky headlands and around the river deltas, there are limited alluvial lowlands and tidal flats; but the only extensive coastal plains are the tundra expanses of northern Alaska that slope gently to the sea. At Point Conception, Calif., a change from north to south temperate life zones occurs, hence a change in the species composition of the fish fauna.

The North Pacific coastal sector embraces 38,000 miles of tidal coastline—31,000 in Alaska and 7,000 in Washington, Oregon, and northern California. But along this coast there is much less shallow, protected estuarine area than along the Atlantic coast.

The one North Pacific estuarine system that is similar to Atlantic estuaries occurs in San Francisco Bay area where the Sacramento and San Joaquin Rivers flow together into Suisun and San Pablo Bays. These two rivers do not run directly from mountain slopes to the sea, as do many Pacific rivers, but rather wind slowly through the extensive lowlands of the Sacramento-San Joaquin Valley, becoming warm and nutrient-charged on their way to the sea, as many Atlantic rivers do while flowing through the Atlantic coastal plains.

With few bays and sounds and shallow, protected estuarine areas along the North Pacific coast, it is not surprising there should be few species that have a critical link in their lives involving estuaries. Of more than 30 groups of saltwater fish which we usually consider dependent on estuaries to some degree, only three—salmon, smelt, flounder—have species native to the North Pacific.

The most highly prized fish of the North Pacific coast are the salmon, which spend short but critical parts of their lives in coastal waters. Five Pacific species appear in coastal waters twice in their lives: once as juveniles migrating from freshwater spawning and nursery areas to the open sea, and once as adults migrating back into their natal rivers to spawn. The estuaries through which they pass have great importance in their lives as places where the transition is made between freshwater and saltwater phases. The three species of interest to anglers—chinook, coho, and pink—are caught in estuaries (including bays and sounds) as well as along open coasts.

Anglers meet the salmon along the paths of their migration from the time they reach the coast until the fish are safely into freshwater at which time they cease feeding. Angling for them is usually done from a boat, in the ocean, straits, passes, sounds, bays, and river

285

Flounder are caught in many inlets on the East coast.

mouths, but some salmon—particularly coho—are taken in streams where one may fish from banks.

A close relative of the salmon, the steelhead trout, is also a popular anadromous game species. This sea-run variant of the rainbow trout behaves much as a salmon and occurs from California to Alaska. The young spend 1 or 2 years in streams before going to sea. They stay in the ocean for a few years until they mature and then, unlike the Pacific salmon, return regularly to rivers to spawn every year thereafter.

An important flatfish, the starry flounder, occupies shallow waters of the estuaries and ranges across the estaurine zone from open coastal waters on up into tidal rivers and even into freshwater lakes. The starry flounder is a bottom fish found on mud, sand, and gravel bottoms from Alaska to southern California. Spawning occurs in the shallow coastal areas that also serve as nursery grounds. Starry flounder eat mostly small shellfish from the bottom but do take some small fish in their diet as they grow older; clam siphon tips comprise a large fraction of the diet in California waters. Starry flounder angling is done mostly in bays by still fishing using natural baits dropped to the bottom.

The many species of smelt found along the North Pacific coast remain near the beach most of their lives, feeding on minute life in the water. They are caught along the beach mostly with hand-held nets. Many smelt deposit their spawn along the sandy shores of the open coast. Two species—the American smelt and the eulachon—migrate through estuarine waters on their way to spawning grounds in Pacific rivers.

The shad, brought to the Pacific coast from the Atlantic in the last century, has thrived well in its new surroundings.

286

Initial plantings of shad were made in the Sacramento and Columbia Rivers in 1871. First runs of mature shad entered the Sacramento River in 1877, and became a market fish in the San Francisco Bay area within a decade after the original transplantation. Having spread out from the original plantings, it is now established along 3,000 miles of Pacific coastline from southern California to Cook Inlet, Alaska. They are fished in rivers or near river mouths with light tackle.

Striped bass, introduced in the San Francisco Bay region in 1879, gave rise to a productive commercial fishery from about 1890 to 1935. Then legislation was enacted to reserve the species for game fishing. California law now forbids selling, exporting, or importing striped bass. Pacific coast anglers fish for them near the mouths of rivers, in slow-moving streams, and in sloughs. In the San Francisco Bay region, they spawn in the spring and summer in fresh waters of the Sacramento and San Joaquin Rivers and their deltas. The young occupy the rivers and upper estuary and move toward the bays as they grow older.

We have seen that the United States is well endowed with estuarine areas remarkable for the abundance of aquatic life, including marine game fish, which they nurture. The estuarine zone ranks among America's great natural resources, a national treasure which should be enjoyed and respected. But people have treated estuaries barbarously, using them as dumping grounds for refuse, factory wastes, and domestic sewage. They have allowed large areas to be ruined, some by land fill projects to make real estate, others by mining. Another desecration is dredging out channels for navigation and putting the spoil out of the way, with more thought to convenience than to preserving the valuable shellfish habitat which it smothers.

Although conservationists have been decrying mistreatment of the estuarine zone for many years, their efforts to correct it have met with subtle resistance from many quarters.

There are arguments that conservation stands in the way of "progress," a specious argument. Progress may be inevitable, but not at the expense of long range public interest. Men must learn to design the human uses of land and waters in accord with ecological principles to fit man's activities harmoniously into the vital environment of our estuaries.

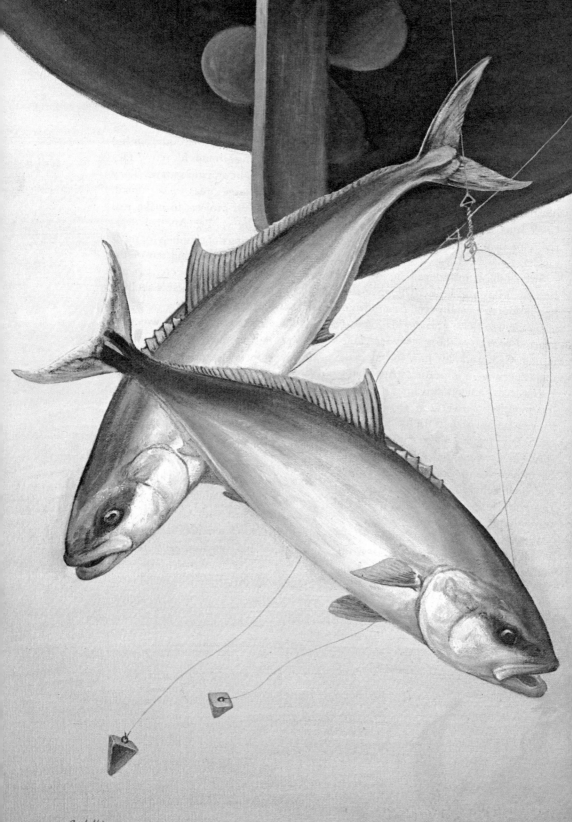

Bob Hines

Along the Coast

by David H. Wallace

*With such a variety of fish and such extensive coastlines,
it is not surprising that so many million Americans wet their lines
in angling on coastal waters. In the New England and
Middle Atlantic areas, they pick up near the shore such prizes as
striped bass and the bluefish. Further south and in the gulf,
tarpon, drums, and red snapper take the bait. On the West coast, bonito,
striper, salmon, sculpins, and halibut are prized sport fish.*

YELLOWTAIL

ONE OF THE MORE FAMOUS coastal fish is the striped bass. Although native to the Atlantic coast, eggs and larvae of stripers transported to the Pacific coast in the late part of the 19th century survived to establish a tremendous recreational fishery there. Saltwater fish are generally not considered to be exclusively game fish. However, the striped bass is many sportsmen's choice for an exception to this generalization. It has captured the imagination and challenged the skill of the saltwater angler to such an extent that it is frequently called the "King of the Coast."

Stripers are anadromous, coming in from the sea to brackish and freshwaters to spawn. On the Atlantic coast, they spawn in estuaries from North Carolina to Connecticut, while the major spawning grounds on the Pacific are in the Sacramento Delta area. Adults spend a substantial part of their life in brackish rivers and bays. Indeed, striped bass seem almost timid in their ocean movements. Their ocean habitat is generally confined to a relatively narrow band extending only about 10 miles from shore.

Sexual maturity of striped bass is reached in males at the end of the second year, when they are from 10 to 14 inches in length. Females mature several years later, when they are 18 to 22 inches in length, and weigh from 4 to 6 pounds. Young fish spend the first couple of years in the estuaries, but in their third year some of them start to make extensive migrations along the shore.

There is a northward movement from North Carolina, the Chesapeake and Delaware Bays in the spring after spawning to as far north as the Maine coast. These migrants spend the summer in the area from New Jersey to Maine, with a return southern migration in the fall.

In California, stripers are most abundant in the Sacramento River system. Since these fish were introduced on the West coast, they have become a major recreational species, yielding several million pounds annually; and commercial fishing for them there is prohibited. Similar laws have also been adopted by several Atlantic States to preserve them exclusively for the sportsman.

Stripers are taken by casting in the surf, trolling and chumming from boats, and under some circumstances, by bait fishing on the bottom. The availability of the species and the fact that it grows to a large size in its several habitats are the main reasons for its great popularity. The maximum size taken by hook and line is just under 75 pounds, although records show commercial catches of individuals up to 125 pounds.

Along the Atlantic coast, the bluefish is noted for its fighting ability. While it does not exceed 25 pounds in weight, sportsmen claim that pound for pound it is the best fighter of any species from Massachusetts to Florida. They winter in the Florida area, but disappear from those waters in spring as they migrate north. Spawning takes place at sea off the Middle Atlantic States. The young work their way into the estuaries, where they grow to a size of 7 to 10 inches by early fall. The southern migration then starts, and the migratory cycle repeats itself.

Bluefish are caught casting in the surf, chumming or trolling from boats, and the young are taken in the estuaries, using live minnows as bait. One of the most exciting experiences possible is to be drifting in a boat through a tide rip when the blues are biting. Gulls wheel overhead and squeal their shrill cries, as they watch in the water for crippled bait fish injured as the blues rush through the school feeding ferociously. As the gulls dip to pick up their tasty morsels of fish, the blues strike the jigs, spoons, feathers, or other lures with great force.

The line is peeled from the reel at a great rate, until the angler is able to turn the fish and gradually work it toward the boat. Blues fight so furiously that even after being boated they frequently thrash about in the boat biting wildly. Woe to the careless or unwary angler who allows his hand to get in the path of these sharp teeth.

While striped bass and bluefish are considered the elite of fish caught in the surf along our Atlantic coast, most saltwater fish are caught still fishing on or near the bottom from boats, piers, or docks.

This type of bottom bait fishing is the hard core of the recreational fisheries along all our coasts: Atlantic, gulf, or Pacific. Anglers by the millions, ranging in age from 3 to 93, enjoy this kind of saltwater fishing. Piers, large party boats, private boats, and small rowboats provide access to the fishing grounds.

Fancy rods and reels are not essential. Fishermen use a wide variety of equipment, from simple cane poles to sturdy rods with expensive reels bearing quality lines. And regularly the fish oblige, whether they be pollock in New England, croaker in the Chesapeake Bay, spotted weakfish in Georgia, drum off Louisiana, or rockfish off Oregon.

According to a Bureau of Sport Fisheries and Wildlife survey in 1965, 1.4 billion pounds of fish were caught in saltwater, with 62 percent of this total taken still fishing at or near the bottom. Only in the Gulf of Mexico and near southern California did the catch by

A good cast into the surf.

trolling exceed that made by still fishing.

In the South Atlantic and Gulf of Mexico, many sportsmen select the mighty tarpon as the most prized coastal game species. Even the offshore billfish are no more spectacular in their efforts to shake loose a lure. Fishing for tarpon from small boats approaches the finest in sport. The big silvers, once hooked, "come out of the water like a Polaris missile," as one fisherman described it. Spectacular leap follows leap, with violent head shaking in frantic efforts to shake loose the spoon or feather, and with a great splash each time as a fighting fish falls back into the sea.

Not all tarpon fishing is confined to boats, since these beauties can be caught at times from piers and bridges. The Florida Keys are favorite spots for this type of fishing, but tarpon are abundant in many areas along the gulf coast and the Florida east coast as well.

Standard tarpon equipment is a stiff rod, 60-pound test line on a 4/0 reel, 5/0 hook, and 10 to 15 feet of wire leader. Once equipped, you are ready to do battle with the proud silver of the South. However, if the struggle is successful, and the fish is brought to gaff, remember the tarpon is not prized for food. Prize specimens are mounted for trophies, but more and more sportsmen are releasing the fish to fight another day.

Another silver beauty, the coho salmon, shares with chinook the favor of sportsmen in the Pacific Northwest. These anadromous species spawn in the freshwaters of the Columbia River and numerous other streams along the California, Oregon, and Washington coasts. After spending their early life in the streams and rivers, they make extended migrations seaward. After several years of feeding and rapid growth at sea, they move inshore again, heading back to the stream of their origin. As they approach the coast, they pause in their migration to feed so that they can withstand the final rigors of their surge to their spawning grounds.

Along the coast, fishermen await the return of the salmon. Action begins slowly in June, accelerates in July, and reaches a peak in August when the main run reaches the estuaries. Thousands of boats—from tiny skiffs to large cruisers—brave the high seas over the bar at the mouth of the Columbia.

"Mooching" is the popular way to fish, using herring or similar fish as bait. The line is peeled off the reel and allowed to drift away on the current. No weight is used, which leaves the baited hook suspended near the surface.

Coho salmon from 8 to 15 pounds strike with lightning speed and—without any sinker to hamper them—present a challenge to any angler who is willing to do battle with light rod and line.

Bigger chinook salmon are on the move at the same time, their red markings distinguishing them from the light silvery cohos. Their fighting ability also sets them apart. Chinooks grow to a much larger size—40 to 50 pounds—but smaller ones in coho-size range are worthy foes to any sportsman.

While drifting bait fishing has its strong advocates among the salmon devotees, trolling is also a common method, and frequently halibut also are caught in this way.

"I must down to the sea again . . .
the lonely sea and the sky."

Today's anglers and yesteryear's wreck.

Some prefer one tarpon to forty of anything else.

The Pacific halibut, a flatfish of the flounder clan, is widely distributed along the coast from Oregon to Alaska. Since it grows to a large size and bites readily, it is a popular game fish as well as a basis for one of the most important commercial fisheries. Halibut are unique as one of very few ocean fish shared by more than one nation, and currently under scientific international management.

Depleted some 40 years ago, the halibut population has been restored through regulations of the crop of mature fish harvested each year. The result has been a stable, successful commercial fishery, and excellent angling for sportsmen. In Alaska, where Dolly Varden trout and coho fishing in the surf is popular, halibut are tremendously abundant and big. A 50-pounder is considered a baby, and no sportsman fishing for halibut is satisfied until he graduates to the 7-foot, 200-pound class.

While the halibut is Mr. Big as far as the North American flatfish are concerned, there are many species of flounders on all our coasts which are the basis of a tremendous recreational fishery. Our anglers catch about 74,000,000 pounds of flatfish annually. More sportsmen try for this group than any other, and with excellent success.

Whether he fishes from boat, from a pier, or casting off the shore, the novice angler has an excellent chance to make good catches of flounders. The gear needed is simple—a light rod and reel, 20-pound test line, a hook, and a sinker. All kinds of baits from bloodworms to fish attract the flounders. Little skill is needed on the part of the angler to set the hook. Catches of 20 to 40 winter flounders per man-day are not unusual around Cape Cod, Block Island, or in Long Island Sound, during late winter or early spring when this species moves inshore for spawning.

In the same general area, the summer flounder is available readily to the sportsman. In Great South Bay, a body of water 30 miles long and 5 miles wide on the south shore of Long Island, anglers take about 1,000,000 annually. This is only one small area within the range of this fish, which is distributed from North Carolina to Massachusetts.

But State fishery agencies are concerned about this species. For example, in Great South Bay, the number of fish taken by anglers dropped to less than 200,000 fish in 1967. The life history has been studied, and the migration patterns worked out by fishery biologists of several East Coast States. But thus far, no coordinated regulatory program has been developed.

South Atlantic and gulf sportsmen are dependent generally upon four groups of fish: the drum family, which includes croaker, spot, weakfish, spotted seatrout, black drum, and red drum, many taken from Chesapeake Bay to Florida and from Florida to Texas; and the groupers, grunts, and snappers.

These species are basically bottom feeders and are generally caught still fishing, either casting from the shore or from anchored or drifting boats. The croaker and weakfish for many years were generally available, but some 15 years ago both declined in abundance.

Some observers believe that the decline came about from over fishing by the commercials and sportsmen. Others feel that environmental factors adversely affecting the survival of the eggs and larvae at sea brought about the drop in production.

The spotted seatrout and other drum along the gulf coast continue to be abundant and available in considerable quantities to the sportsmen. The red and black drum are prized as fighting game fish along the South Atlantic coast, while the red drum is a mainstay of a dedicated group in the gulf. Red snapper also is a sought-after species because of the relative ease of catching by hook and line and because it is delicious to eat.

Sport fishing along the Pacific coast supports a large party-boat industry, as well as angling from specially constructed fishing piers, particularly on the southern California coast. This development of pier facilities involving State and local government has fostered great interest in recreational fishing there.

Both rockfish and scorpionfish belong to the largest family of fish from California waters, and some 50 different

295

Razor-clam diggers on the Washington coast have their own techniques.

species live off that coast.

Bonitos make up the greatest number and poundage caught by sportsmen off the California coast, although yellowtail and jack mackerel are popular. The Pacific bonito sometimes grows to 25 pounds, but most weigh between 3 and 12 pounds. The best fishing time is in the summer and fall. Bonito are excellent fighters and have voracious appetites. Once a school is aroused, the fish will take almost any bait or lure tossed their way. Live anchovies and sardines make the best bait for still fishing; chrome and feather jigs and plastic squid are most effective for trolling.

Scorpionfish are most abundant in rocky areas along parts of the Pacific coast. While caught in great quantities,

they are not noted for fighting qualities. They take a hook baited with squid and lowered to the bottom. The lack of fighting ability is somewhat compensated by their fine textured white flesh, which is mild in flavor.

Thus, the sportsman along the coasts of the United States has a variety of species to choose from: at least 100 which are taken by hook and line. Some are caught near the surface, while others prefer a bottom habitat. Some take only a moving lure, while others are interested in a baited hook that is relatively still. Anglers can find just about any kind of fishing that might suit their fancy somewhere along our shores.

But even coastal species which for many years have been present in abundance need to be husbanded and protected. Extensive research programs must be mounted to obtain biological information as a basis for management programs, and practical mechanisms must be evolved for conservation of those species which make interstate coastal migrations.

Little progress has been made in this direction. Each State has been jealous of its right to regulate the taking of fish while they are present within its borders. Most States have been unwilling to delegate regulatory authority to interstate agencies so that individual species may be managed throughout their range. But with the influx of foreign fishing vessels, just outside our 12-mile fishing limit, added to our own intensive fishing, a number of the bottom species may soon be over fished. We must develop sound interstate programs so that we will be in a better position to negotiate effectively on conservation and sharing the catch with other countries which may fish off our shores.

Unlike the pollution and physical destruction taking place in our streams and estuaries, coastal waters are relatively pure; however, we must be vigilant to make sure that pollution does not increase to the point where our coastal environment becomes unsuitable for reproduction and survival of the young.

Fishery habitat improvements have been made on freshwater streams for many years, but such concepts are new in saltwater. Artificial saltwater reefs offer one technique to attract and congregate fish to a given area by supplying a place of shelter, and sources of food for bottom feeders. Reefs have been tested and studied intensively by California biologists, with several other States committed to programs of artificial reef development. New York biologists are fabricating structures of discarded automobile tires and concrete to serve as "fish houses." Maryland is using oyster shells for the same purpose and testing various other materials.

Most biologists working on these projects believe that artificial reefs do not themselves increase fish abundance. Their major accomplishment is to concentrate species at fixed locations, where they are more readily available to anglers.

But despite these efforts, there is a need for more funds for law enforcement, research and management personnel, environmental preservation, and habitat improvement. Such funds are not readily available, since most programs are financed by direct appropriation of general funds from Federal or State treasuries. The big leap forward in marine conservation will take place when our saltwater sportsmen are ready and willing to pay a fee for their recreation to finance programs designed to improve fishing.

A few States have already acted to license saltwater fishermen. With increasing taxpayer pressures to hold down public spending, a source of funds becomes of paramount importance, if the scientists and the fishermen believe programs are justifiable in terms of specific needs.

The supply of fish along the coast is not limitless. We must husband the resource so that it is maintained at a high level. Sound research and management are essential ingredients for future good fishing.

Out to Sea

by Donald P. de Sylva

*Deep-sea fishing is a great sport—because it is an avocation
where the "amateur" may break records at any time. The world's record
for Atlantic blue marlin, for example, was successively
shattered during the past 10 years by persons who had hardly fished at all.
It was held (briefly) by an intransit Air Force
sergeant passing through San Juan, Puerto Rico; he was looking for
something—anything—to kill an otherwise boring afternoon,
waiting for a plane at the airport. So he went fishing. Before the
afternoon was over he had established a new
world standard— a 756-pound blue marlin. You don't necessarily have
to invest a half-million dollars to catch a huge fish.*

FISHING AT SEA

CHARACTERISTICALLY, the sport in deep-sea areas is known as "blue-water" angling, because most of the large, pelagic (open-ocean) species occur in the cobalt-blue waters of Florida, the Bahamas, and the Caribbean; the deep steely-blue waters of Hawaii, Pacific Panama, or North Carolina; and the dirty-blue waters far off New England, Long Island, or Peru. The inshore, green or greenish-blue waters generally do not harbor the giants which are targets for the sportsman who already has everything, but wants the ultimate in large fish. Of course, there usually is no clear dividing line between blue and blue-green waters or offshore-inshore habitats, and some species, such as the white marlin and barracuda, seem to be equally at home in either area, depending upon time of year and geographic locality.

Usually blue-water species are not found inshore, even during the early part of their life cycle, and inshore fish do not leave their coastal lairs. Possibly depth, water clarity and chemistry, taste, and food are the factors keeping these animals in their respective habitats, but there are probably many unknown reasons, still to be studied and evaluated by scientists.

Another peculiarity of blue-water fishing is the angler himself. He is patient, persistent, and not easily discouraged. Before World War II, the deep sea was virtually the domain of the full-time diehard sportsman who lived only for the day when he could get out to sea. Or it was a plaything of the wealthy, the recluse, or the eccentric. But this has changed for many reasons, and the deep sea is no longer the sole possession of a given clan.

Now the blue-water angler can be anyone with time and a little money, but most important, much perseverance to carry out a consistent program of angling, which may be considered almost a profession even for the amateur. Blue-

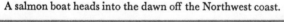

A salmon boat heads into the dawn off the Northwest coast.

water fish are notoriously hard to find and unpredictable. But there are 20,000 to 30,000 anglers in the United States who are dedicated to the blue water, dutifully returning to the sea each season with high hopes that his blue marlin will be a record.

Perhaps for the same reasons that *National Geographic* has captured the imagination of millions, deep-sea angling has been long alive in the hearts of land-locked boys from Minnesota or Iowa. Philip Wylie's stories of Crunch and Des, as they prepared for a mighty tuna tournament off Coral Cay in the Bahamas, or legion articles in fishing magazines about Salty Bill, the swordfisherman from Cuttyhunk, bring vivid recollections to mind during a cold winter's night far from sea. Reading these episodes, we vicariously pictured ourselves hauling in the mighty bluefin. And most of us thought that dreaming was as far as we would ever get. But times have changed, and the landlocked boy from North Dakota now can save for and spend his vacation angling at a rather low cost, for the same fish he once read about.

Deep-sea fishing is largely confined to tropical and subtropical waters, although many species normally found close to the Equator regularly migrate poleward in late spring and summer, following the warm-water drift from equatorial regions, but returning toward the Equator in the fall. Accessibility to warm waters generally decreases as one goes farther toward the poles, because the warm currents are farther offshore. Thus, while the Gulf Stream flows from 3 to 5 miles off the Florida shore, off New Jersey it may be 100 miles. And on the Pacific coast, the cold California current, wedging in from the north, hugs the Cali-fornia coast and forces warm water from the south to offshore.

In the Western Hemisphere, proverbial hotspots for deep-sea angling are the coast of southeast Florida, adjacent waters of the Bahamas, and the northern Caribbean Islands. Important ports include Key West, Marathon, Islamorada, Miami, Fort Lauderdale, Pompano Beach, Palm Beach, Stuart, and myriad fishing docks in between. In the Bahamas, Bimini, Cat Cay, Walker Cay, Chub Cay, West End, and Eleuthera are some of the famous spots repeatedly written about in fishing magazines. Havana, once a famous sport fishing port, is now only a memory of Ernest Hemingway's pen, but white and blue marlin still abound off there, and the Cubans, including Fidel Castro himself, still thrash the water for these gamesters.

Nearby Jamaica boasts superb fishing for blue marlin on its north coast, as do the islands of Hispaniola and Puerto Rico. In addition to blue marlin, hordes of white marlin, sailfish, yellowfin and blackfin and skipjack tuna, wahoo, and barracuda abound in offshore waters. And the steep Continental Shelves of these islands make it a short run—as little as 15 minutes—from the dock to the 1,000-fathom curve.

The Virgin Islands, currently holder of the world record Atlantic blue marlin—814 pounds—also boasts excellent angling for all kinds, besides fine reef fishing closer in. The Windward Islands are still little explored from the angler's standpoint, but wherever the ardent fisherman dares he wins in these islands, for an abundance of large game fish is found at certain seasons in the passes and about the currents that swirl among these emerald isles.

Between the Yucatan Peninsula and

301

The tuna's "little" but the fight was fun.

the Colombian coast, the area is poorly known from the angler's standpoint, as well as from the scientist's. What little fishing that has been done—largely off British Honduras—has produced species typical of the Florida coast. The angler can expect to find roughly the same species all over the tropical western Atlantic Ocean, that is, from North Carolina to Brazil, although these species will readily move out of these confines during the months of extremes in water temperature.

The coast of Venezuela is particularly rich in deep-sea species, even though the water along this coast is not deep blue, but greenish. The plankton-rich area usually attracts one of the largest concentrations of white marlin ever experienced by the angler, as well as sailfish, tuna, bonito, barracudas, and dozens of other smaller species. To the east, little fishing has been done between Cumaná (Venezuela) and Trinidad, although some good fishing is reported off Trinidad (as well as off nearby Tobago

302

and Barbados). The Guiana coasts southward to south-central Brazil are a disadvantage to blue-water fish, because the heavy runoff of the muddy Amazon and Orinoco Rivers is not to the liking of such fish as marlin, tuna, and dolphins, and the angler must go many miles from shore to find them. However, this runoff occupies a very shallow layer, and Japanese commercial fishermen, setting hooks off the muddy Amazon, report that they catch yellowfin tuna just below this muddy layer.

South of Brazil along the Patagonian Shelf, schools of tuna and dolphins and concentrations of marlin have been reported. But the wide Continental Shelf here necessitates that the angler travel far from shore to catch these deep-sea fish.

Returning to the Northern Hemisphere, north of Florida the Gulf Stream moves offshore at Cape Kennedy, coming close in again at Cape Hatteras, N.C. Fishing for blue-water species between these capes is often spotty and uncertain, although anglers with long-range vessels have had considerable success running offshore 60 to 100 miles.

But Cape Hatteras is itself a superb fishing area. Shoaling off the bottom at Diamond Shoals, a hazardous landmark for shipping, causes mixing of the water and turbulent currents. In this area, dolphin, tuna, marlin, swordfish, amberjack, and bonito abound, once one navigates the hair-raising Oregon and Hatteras Inlets.

Farther up the coast, during the summer from the Virginia capes to Cape Cod, white marlin, little tuna, bluefin (school and giant), blackfin and skipjack tuna, dolphin, and wahoo drift about in varying concentrations. The coasts of Maryland and New Jersey annually attract hundreds of boats during white marlin and tuna tournaments, and occasionally a big blue marlin snaps the light line of an unsuspecting angler.

The eastern end of Long Island is famed for white marlin, swordfish, bluefin tuna, and mako shark—all great gamesters—but in recent years, fewer have been caught. Giant bluefin run in late summer from Block Island and Point Judith, R.I., up past Cuttyhunk, Provincetown, and Ipswich, Mass., and then drift north to Nova Scotia in early fall. Most runs of giant tuna, white marlin, dolphin, and bonito north of Florida begin in late June and end abruptly about the third week in September.

On the Pacific coast, deep-sea fishing for tuna and marlin is best known from off Avalon, southern California, the tip of Baja California, and into the Gulf of California. Acapulco and Mazatlán, on the mainland coast of Mexico, produce large numbers of striped marlin and sailfish, as well as a number of smaller fish such as bonitos, dolphin, and the inshore roosterfish, in addition to the common inshore and reef fish.

To the south, little professional angling occurs until one reaches the Pearl Islands of Panama and the famous area just to the south, Piñas Bay. Reports are not unfounded of schools of sailfish or dolphin so common that they are a nuisance, and marine life in this area is among the richest in the world. Gorgona Island, off the Pacific coast of Colombia, has lots of very large sailfish, numerous black and striped marlin, yellowfin tuna, dolphin, and bonito, but this part of the world, in spite of its good fishing, lacks adequate tourist facilities.

Further south, off the Ecuadorian coast, are found large black, blue, and striped marlin, sailfish, tuna, and occa-

After an immense struggle of fish against man, the prize falls limp.

sionally swordfish. Peru, especially off Cabo Blanco, is noted for its big swordfish, giant black marlin (the present world record of 1,560 pounds comes from here), yellowfin and bigeye tuna, and giant swordfish. The 2,200-mile long coast of Chile holds as wide a variety of fish resources as one could desire, but few facilities are as yet available. The north-central area has good quantities of swordfish, including the present 1,182-pound world record (from Iquique), large yellowfin and bigeye tuna, striped marlin, and a few large dolphin. In the south-central parts, swordfish, bigeye tuna, and albacore are common, but are not sought extensively by anglers.

Except for a few major centers of angling famous around the world, most areas far from North and South America are still virgin, waiting to be utilized by local and foreign anglers. Notable areas of excellent fishing include the Azores, southern Spain, off Denmark and Norway, Malta, parts of southeast Africa (Natal, Tanzania, Kenya), eastern Australia, New Zealand, and the Hawaiian Islands. But one can safely assume that any reasonable warm-water area of proper currents and food supply, with potentially good angler accommodations, is a likely area for the development of a good sport fishery resource.

Blue-water sport fish have several traits in common. They are extremely fast swimmers—some perhaps can exceed 40 or 50 mph. Their vision is excellent, and they rarely feed by smell. Save for the great barracuda, which can be found nearly anywhere, nearly all deep-sea game fish spend their entire life in blue water, although some may be caught at the edge of coastal areas. They are generally found in offshore currents, and are sought near current and tide rips and near patches of drifting weed, particularly where the weed is located along a rip.

While most anglers fish for blue-water types at the surface, the paradox of this

304

What do you do with a bonnet shark?

is that most pelagic ones spend their lives in subsurface waters, occasionally deeper than 100 fathoms. Here they seek small bonitos, tuna, squids, small shrimp, and the thick soup of small drifting organisms which comprise the plankton. They also spawn in these waters, and the young grow up in them, feeding on the plankton, and themselves being eaten by other game fish.

The giant of the big-game species is the broadbill swordfish, which grows to nearly a ton. The present world record on hook and line is 1,182 pounds, from Chile. Broadbills are also caught by anglers off Long Island, New England, and the Maritime Provinces of Canada, in the Mediterranean, and off Portugal and southern California. But they are never really common, and a broadbill is always a prize. Some are taken occasionally, usually unintentionally, by anglers in Florida and the Caribbean, while deep fishing or drifting. Commercial fishermen have taken broadbills on hand lines hundreds of feet below the surface—many in tropical waters.

Black marlin vie with swordfish for size. The world's record, from Peru, weighed 1,560 pounds, and larger ones have been reported taken by commercial fishermen. Blacks are taken from Chile to Panama, around Hawaii, New Zealand, Australia, Tahiti, and other western Pacific Islands, Ceylon, and East Africa. None has yet been authenticated from the Atlantic Ocean.

A close relative is the blue marlin, which grows to over 1,000 pounds in the Pacific, and has been logged in at 845 pounds in the Atlantic. These are more common than black marlin, and in some places like Jamaica and Puerto Rico, occasionally become abundant. The Bahamas, Cuba, Pacific Panama, Hawaii,

southern Florida, and western Mexico usually yield nice catches of blues.

White marlin are smaller but scrappier; they seldom grow over 100 pounds, and the record of 161 pounds has not been approached for years. But they are very common in some areas such as Venezuela, Cuba, the Bahamas, from Long Island to Virginia, and in the northern Gulf of Mexico. They also occur in southern Spain, but relatively little angling occurs in the eastern Atlantic, so little is known about their true abundance.

Closely related to the white is the striped marlin, found only in the Pacific and Indian Oceans. A scrappy fighter, putting on great exhibitions of leaping and tailwalking, it averages about 150 pounds.

Sailfish are found all over the world, but the exact number of species is not known. A Pacific form grows to at least 250 pounds, while the largest Atlantic sailfish taken on hook and line was 141 pounds, from West Africa. Most caught around Florida are less than 80 pounds, but like the white marlin, the small size is more than compensated by the fighting qualities and spectacular leaps. Sails abound in southern Florida, Cuba, the blue waters of Central America, and Venezuela. In the Pacific, they travel in schools off Panama and Mexico, while some are caught around Hawaii, Japan, the Philippines, Australia, India and Ceylon, and East Africa. They are less common about islands and more concentrated along the mainland, where they occasionally come in from blue water to green or even dirty water.

Closely related to the white marlin are the rare spearfish from the Mediterranean, western Atlantic, and Pacific and Indian Oceans. They resemble

This record jewfish was caught by a woman.

sailfish but have a long, low dorsal fin instead of the characteristic high sail. Their habits are similar to the marlins, but they are more restricted to the high seas, far from land.

Tuna are also a prize of big-game fishermen, and the bluefin ranks highest in popularity. They grow to over 2,200 pounds, but the world-record hook-and-line catch was just under 1,000. These giants migrate vast distances across oceans, apparently swimming hundreds of feet deep. Their migrations are poorly known, but scientists are starting to unravel some of these mysteries. These great game fish are primarily taken off New England and Nova Scotia, the Bahamas, England, Norway and Denmark, the Mediterranean, Australia, and California. All tuna are eagerly sought by commercial fishermen, and wherever they operate there are bound to be opportunties for sport fish catches.

This is especially true of yellowfin, which are eagerly sought by anglers and offer a tremendous potential. They are abundant in the eastern Caribbean and the Gulf of Mexico, Bermuda, Pacific Panama, Hawaii, some of the western Pacific Islands, the Indian Ocean, and especially off West Africa.

Blackfin tuna are small members of the family, travel in huge schools, and can be caught on light tackle. Similarly, skipjacks seldom grow over 25 pounds, and offer good angling sport on the high seas. Other species are the little tuna of the coastal Atlantic and the black skipjack of the eastern Pacific. These average about 5 pounds and are good sport on ultralight tackle.

Perhaps the most beautiful game fish is the dolphin; its golden-hued, blue-spotted body changes color at every turn, and it gives the most exciting leaps, twists, and turns an angler could ask for. They are common in all warm seas of the world, and a good angler on a good day can catch several hundred. The average size is about 5 pounds, but they commonly exceed 30 pounds. The world record is 82 pounds.

Wahoo are relatives of the tuna, and swim as fast as anything in the sea. They grow to over 150 pounds, and are exciting to catch, but rarity makes them an accidental catch in most places, although they are occasionally common in the Bahamas.

Close relatives of wahoo are the king mackerel of the Atlantic and the seerfish of the western Pacific and Indian Oceans. The king mackerel grows to over 80 pounds, while seerfish exceed

150. The latter are somewhat more of a coastal fish, and are usually found off the edge of the very deep reefs. Sometimes they travel in huge schools, and an experienced angler can catch a hundred small ones in a day.

One of the most underrated fish is the great barracuda. In the tropical Atlantic and Pacific they grow to 100 pounds, are common, and when caught on the proper light tackle will leap and fight as well as any other game fish. Anglers generally hold them in scorn because they bite the tails off expensive baits trolled for marlin and tuna. Off California, the Pacific barracuda is caught by the thousands by avid anglers working from drift or party boats.

Also caught in large numbers in the Atlantic is the sporty, hard-fighting amberjack. In the Pacific, anglers go for the yellowtail. Like the king mackerel, these jacks are not truly blue-water species but are taken from the edge of the deep reefs inshore to shallower waters. They are generally taken while slow trolling or still fishing, in contrast to most deep-sea fish which are caught by fast trolling.

Sharks are being sought as game fish by an increasing number of anglers. In many parts of the world there are shark derbies and contests, which have the twofold purpose of providing sport and reducing the shark potential. Species such as the great white, mako, and spinner leap from the water and make long, strong runs. The International Game Fish Association lists the mako officially as a game fish. They are caught all over the world in tropical, subtropical, and temperate waters, although none are ever common.

Some sharks, such as the lemon, silky, smooth dogfish, hammerhead, dusky, and soupfin, are more common and are sought by anglers.

The secret of big-game fishing, as in any angling, is to match the tackle to the fish. A valiant but small bonito weighing 5 pounds has little chance against a bluefin tuna rod and 130-pound test line. Blue marlin, swordfish, and bluefin tuna are usually sought using braided or monofilament line, with rod and reel to match. For such large fish, light tackle would be a reel of from 6/0 to 9/0, 30- to 50-pound test line, and a 12- to 16-ounce rod. Heavy tackle comprises a 12/0 reel, 130-pound test line, and a 24- to 30-ounce rod. For smaller species, such as sailfish, white marlin, and striped marlin, light tackle includes reels of 2/0 to 4/0, a line test of 12 to 20 pounds, and a rod of 6 to 9 ounces. Heavy tackle consists of a 6/0 reel, 30- to 50-pound test line, and a rod of 16 to 18 ounces.

Smaller species such as small tuna, bonito, dolphin, barracuda, and little sharks may be successfully taken using heavy and light spinning tackle or bait-casting tackle, and for the ultimate in skill and enjoyment, a flyrod. The Rod and Reel Club of Miami Beach sponsors a 10 to 1 Club, in which a citation is given to persons catching a fish 10 or more times as heavy as the breaking strength of the line. Hence, the tendency for sportsmen is to fish with lighter tackle for greater sport and to tax the angler's skill.

Most anglers fishing an unknown area will check with local tackle stores, guides, and bait dealers to learn of local customs. Selection of proper bait may pose a problem, and local bait stores should be consulted. For deep-sea fish, the most popular angling method is to troll the bait at the surface directly from the rod tip or to skip it from an out-rigger pole. Some anglers prefer to tow a bait just under the surface. This works better for many tuna, amberjacks, and king mackerel, and may be better for all species under some conditions. Proper rigging of the bait is a must, for the continuous pounding will soften it and tear it from the hook.

Popular baits for swordfish, big marlin, and bluefin tuna are bonito and small tuna, squid 15 to 20 inches long, mullet, bonefish, small Spanish mackerel or barracuda, and large ballyhoo. Each must be specially rigged, which is an art in itself. For small marlin, sailfish, and barracuda, good trolling baits are ballyhoo, small mullet, squid, and eels, while small tuna, king mackerel, and amberjacks can be taken on a strip bait cut from the belly of a tuna or bonito, and on spoons and feathers with or without a strip bait attached.

Coming into popularity is the live-bait method, using a live jack, pinfish, or any small hardy species which tends to swim deep when put on a hook. This method is extremely successful for sailfish, king mackerel, and amberjack. Occasionally, live baits are fished from kites from the vessel.

Deep-sea fishing by the novice is best done by contacting the local charterboat association or Chamber of Commerce and hiring a boat for the day. Prices range from $50 to $250 a day in the States for a good boat, including bait, tackle, lunch, and the crew's knowledge. An average price might be $90 per day, and this is for four to six persons—a real bargain for the enjoyment of a boat ride, even if you catch nothing. If you specifically request it, most captains will take you out for a marlin, and if nothing is caught by noon they will change

tackle and troll for small species.

Boats range from 25 to 65 feet if designed for blue-water fishing, and are usually quite comfortable. The captain is a dedicated professional who takes pride in his ability to locate and catch fish. Some blue-water anglers hook up outriggers to larger outboard-powered boats or the inboard-outboard type (outdrive) boats, but these tend to be cramped for a day's trolling. The angler, whether he fishes from a luxurious 60-foot yacht or from a 19-foot outboard, generally must go great distances at considerable expense to catch his fish, which finally may cost him several hundred dollars a pound.

The future of blue-water fishing is generally a good one. Better boats and tackle are being built at more modest prices, and an increasing number of ports over the world are realizing the economic return of big-game angling to the community. Facilities for boats and chartering are improving. Presently there seems to be plenty of fish to go around, but many scientists are concerned over the future.

Fortunately, most high-sea fish are not affected by man's ruin of the coastal environment through pollution, although insecticides and radioactive wastes have already been found in high-sea tuna. Possibly the food of some blue-water fish is adversely affected by man's contaminants, but it is too early to know.

Much basic research is needed on the life histories of these open-ocean species, and some anglers have suggested that a token license of even a dollar would help finance knowledge about these precious resources. Also needed are catch-and-effort records of individual anglers, so that scientists can work out conservation programs.

Logbooks maintained by anglers would help to determine what some anglers and scientists feel is a real threat to blue-water angling—the sudden increase of commercial fishing on the high seas by many countries. Marlin, tuna, swordfish, bonitos, sharks, and others are being taken in huge numbers on long-lines, drift-lines, harpoons, and seines. But concrete data and research are needed to determine if there is any serious overfishing.

Presently the Bureau of Sport Fisheries and Wildlife, the Bureau of Commercial Fisheries, Sport Fishing Institute, International Game Fish Association, and the United Nations are all deeply concerned with the problem, though more data and research are needed. Hopefully, man will be too intelligent to deplete this resource as he has certain estuarine and coastal areas.

The return home—a good time to savor the day's achievements.

311

The mystery of rolling seas—always a challenge to the adventurous

MAN TRIES HIS HAND

Genesis

by Paul E. Thompson

If there really is a little of the "Old Adam" in each of us,
then deep in our subconscious is a certain nebulous, primeval feeling.
For in Genesis, Adam was specifically given dominion—
or domination—over the fish and wildlife of his earth. I don't know what
he did with this power, but ever since, his descendants have been
trying to do something. There have been little successes here and there,
but if Adam was around about 4000 B.C., there must have been
some failures too. It was Virgil in 70 B.C. who cautioned his countrymen,
"Yield not to adversity, but press on more bravely";
a charge to conservationists as timely now as ever it was.

UTAH SPORT FISHERY RESEARCH, LAKE POWELL

SOMETIMES it seems that truly there is nothing new under the sun, and just as truly it is hard to find the beginning, the genesis, of attempts to manage fish for human enjoyment and profit. Before the exodus from Egypt—1500 B.C.?—the "fish in the river died and the river stank." If it was pollution it was somehow cleared up, and there were fish in the river again. Unfortunately, Moses left no recipe for pollution abatement for posterity. Sometime later Moses brought up clear, clean water from underground, but there's no record that he raised fish in it.

The Chinese certainly had fish hatcheries as long ago as 500 B.C.—it's all written in their history. They liked to fish for sport too, and some were the purest of the pure as anglers. The story comes down from an early dynasty of the angler on the bank of a fish pond with his baited hook dangling a foot or more above the water—to give the fish a sporting chance.

We know the Chinese were selecting the best species for stocking their waters and selecting prime specimens for broodstock. They fertilized their ponds, controlled predators and unwanted vegetation, fed the fish, and provided suitable places for them to spawn. They developed an art of fish management, and carried it with them from country to country and down through the generations.

If the Pacific coast Indians and Eskimos came across a land bridge from Asia, at some far distant time, they didn't bring fish husbandry with them, but they did bring along a primitive understanding of fish conservation. Their reed-woven basket traps, set in stake fences in the salmon streams, could catch every migrating fish on the run from the sea

to the spawning grounds, but they didn't. The traps were lifted at intervals, during the season of the run, to allow "escapement" and reseeding. The aborigines didn't learn that in college, suggesting that fish management is partly compounded of good observation and good common sense. The fishermen who have followed have been forced by law and regulation to do likewise.

The earliest conservation or "management" measures were most likely restrictions and prohibitions brought on by alarms about declining catches, or by the power of the emperor or despot to set aside waters for his exclusive jurisdiction and use. Thus, the royal fish ponds and the king's trout streams, which persist in fact or in legend to this very day. This kind of treatment of fish and fishermen set the pattern for generations, and influences us in this one.

It is popular to call it the Puritan Ethic—all the innumerable Do Nots—but it started long before the Puritans: you cannot fish here—you may not fish now—you will not use that method—that kind of bait is illegal. So early fish management, from the dietary laws of Leviticus (not Genesis this time) and the edicts of the Pharaohs and the Asian kings and emperors, was mostly a compendium of restriction, prohibition, regulation, and calculated inefficiency.

True, there was a concurrent art of husbandry or fish culture that sometimes included penning fish for later use. And certainly there has been some transplanting of fish from one place to another for many centuries.

Anthropologists and archeologists have demonstrated the enormous mobility of the world's people even in prehistoric times. I suggest, what with people moving over long distances to visit each

Chemical controls for unwanted fish species are used in preparation for restocking with desirable species.

other for romantic, friendly, or hostile reasons, that fish got moved around with them. Thus, even the practice of the last 100 years of bringing in exotics, like carp, brown trout, and tilapia, and transplanting domestic species, like striped bass, shad, and rainbow trout, is not really new. It was a management practice that had its genesis in the very dim past.

If one lives long enough, genesis leads eventually to revelation, and so from "in the beginning . . . ," it has come to pass that fish conservation and fish management have moved or are moving (but oh, so slowly) toward the light. If the light is still something less than 100 watts, there are omens of the brighter day to come. Prohibition is giving way to

deregulation, exploration, and manipulation. Preconceived notions still hold sway in some quarters, but using science to promote sport fishing is the growing fashion.

If we pass glibly over the negatives of pollution and population explosions, and concentrate instead on the positives of fine fishing potentials, we can better see where we are since genesis. No use kidding ourselves, we don't know much yet. (So what? That shouldn't give us fishermen, fish biologists, or general conservationists pause, if we just stop and think that humans in general don't know much about themselves, their surrounding, or anything else.)

Trouble with managing fish for perpetuation has arisen because of folklore,

For several thousand years, people have been trying to improve fishing by stocking
—sometimes successfully, often failing—but this means is modern.

pure ignorance coupled with smug assumptions about them, pure selfishness, and conflicts among water users for water.

Ever since Ulysses went fishing for survival and Loki, the Norse demon, fabricated the first fish net and changed himself into a salmon, fish mythology has been hard to beat. There are nice fish and evil fish; there are pretty fish and

ugly fish; there are good-eating fish and inedible fish; and there are useful fish and trash fish. The great schools of some fish are inexhaustible. A spawning season is off limits. A desirable species over there is just what we must have over here. The individual fish doesn't count. One kind of fisherman is more righteous than any other kind. And so on.

Personal preferences, prejudices, and

318

tastes, colored by grandfather-to-father-to-son tales, enhanced by old and recent storytellers, exaggerated by advertisers and other exploiters of human credibility—all have had too much influence on conservation actions. But I admit that all of this kind of thing has made a part of our lives more colorful than a mere drab recital of facts and figures.

The biology of fish can be fascinating too, even though it deals with facts. Many fish have narrow oxygen and temperature and spawning preferences or tolerances. Little wonder that American shad, transplanted in the 1880's to the Mississippi River near St. Paul from Chesapeake Bay, never did move down to the Gulf of Mexico and back up the river to spawn and provide the predicted good fishing, coming and going. Or that stocking sunfish in natural lakes where they already occurred did not improve angling at all.

Until the landmark biological work on TVA reservoirs, fishermen and conservationists alike passively accepted the ancient idea that regulation of open seasons, creel limits, and minimum sizes—all essentially negative—was morally good for fishermen and fish, if not good for fishing. Then—Eureka!—anglers were encouraged to fish anytime, anywhere, for anything right up to their own full enjoyment and use without waste. They were even told how and where and how deep to fish at different times of the year. A modicum of biological knowledge made a revolutionary change which gradually, over two decades or more, has influenced warm-water fish management countrywide—and for the better all around.

One of the last best hopes for plenty of fishing for more fishermen is in the great impoundments of the country. As natural waters have been polluted or have disappeared into culverts or diversion channels or have otherwise been diminished in size or quality, reservoirs have been built to store millions of cubic feet of fishable water. Desperate fish managers have stocked them with everything from African tilapia to marine striped bass. (Sorry I couldn't say Zebra fish so as to have a neat A to Z.) Research and management experiences have suggested ways angling can be improved or perpetuated in the big reservoirs.

But researchers and fish managers don't call the shots. The water managers do, primarily for power, flood control, irrigation, and municipal water supply. Some progress is being made toward accommodation among the water managers and fish managers to enhance the fish and fishing.

Fish management has had its fads and fancies among professionals as well as among laymen. Some of these persist, but gradually there is developing what someday will be a science, which by logic and experience and successful demonstration will be able to override the well-intended mistakes and gropings of the past.

Gone is the fancy that water is water wherever you find it, that a trout raised in the cold, alkaline water of a hatchery can be dumped into a stream receiving acid mine wastes with any chance of success. Gone is the fad for hit-and-miss transplantings.

The incident which should have killed the notion, but did not, is revived every decade or so by storytellers. Livingston Stone, a New England pioneer in fish culture and a most energetic human being, accumulated an assortment of live fish and shellfish, placed them aboard

319

Biologists take bottom samples to see how rich in food the waters are.

a railroad "fish car," and headed for San Francisco Bay. When a Nebraska railroad bridge collapsed en route, the whole collection was stocked in Elkhorn River—tautogs, lobsters, and oysters from the ocean, and catfish, eels, shad, yellow perch, and brook trout from fresh waters of the eastern seaboard. Stone survived the trip successfully—more successfully than most of his cargo. That was in the 1870's, but the fad persisted long after the beginning of the 20th century.

Nostalgia sometimes has an influence on demands for fish transplants. The way United States troops and civilians are distributed around the world, in military, aid, Peace Corps, and diplomatic services, has made the difference. The boy who fished for largemouth bass at

home has grown up, moved halfway around the globe, and wants to fish there for bass. The pacification officer in South Vietnam thinks our channel catfish is one of the greater needs there. Most of the requests ignore the fact there is no dearth of catfish or other good sporting species in most parts of the world. A little local knowledge is a fine thing.

With the rise of speedy calculators after World War II, and the rise of statisticians and analysts with them, there came an idea that fiddling with fish themselves was a waste of time and energy. Reduce everything to a formula, develop a jargon—population dynamics, instantaneous fishing mortality, etc.—and the problems of resource management are solved. That wave of the future has ebbed and taken its place as a reasonable part of, but not a replacement for, the total animal biology.

Then, the fashionable seeking for a meaningful all-purpose measure of "productivity" of waters held sway for a long period. Its appeal, perhaps, has been that it is or sounds terribly basic, and thus profound. The Danish technique of studying productivity with ^{14}C, the isotope of carbon, makes the whole thing even more keyed to the nuclear age. Primary productivity cultists, combined with more recent biologists enamored of energy flow measurements from one trophic level to the next in pond, lake, or estuary, have left their marks in the literature of ecology.

But when these results of scientific endeavor are eventually put in proper perspective—with the "statistics are everything" and with those of the animal-oriented biologists, physiologists, and behaviorists—then we shall have come a long way from genesis and shall have that elusive, sure science of fish management. It will take the best brains to achieve that synthesis.

Until that utopia is in view, the brightest hope for reasonable fish management and good fishing in perpetuity—that means forever, I think—lies with the States. The U.S. Fish Commission was founded in 1871. Twenty-one States and one territory had fish commissions in 1870, when California's was named, or earlier. By 1879, 35 States and Wyoming Territory were "managing" their fisheries in one way or another. California's first year appropriations and fees amounted to $11,322.17, but the Commission spent only $7,759.04. Its income rose to $14,436.05 within 8 years, but expenditures fell to $7,599.51, perhaps because the Federal Agency was stepping

Electrical shockers that stun fish enable biologists to learn the varieties present in a stream.

The first representation of fishing in North America; 1585 watercolor of North Carolina coastline by John White, who arrived with members of the "Lost Colony" but returned to England.

up its shipments of fish into California at little cost to the State.

Beginning in 1876, the first fish commissioner of Iowa got the idea of rescuing fish from pools and lakes cut off from the Mississippi River as the spring flood-waters receded. The idea was a natural for official and public appeal, and caught on in the upper Mississippi River States. After all, "rescue the perishing" has been a part of the Judeo-Christian ethic for centuries and in Midwest hymnals for many decades. While most fish rescue work had died out about the end of the thirties, there was still a little here and there in the middle fifties.

The new era for the States began in 1951, when Congress set aside excise taxes on fishing tackle for apportionment to the States, Puerto Rico, and Guam according to a relatively simple formula. The changes were visible in many disadvantaged States almost overnight. Careers in fishery science not only were possible but sought after. The politics of State office holding diminished. A snowballing effect is apparent in retro-spect. New public fishing waters and improved access to old waters encouraged sales of more fishing licenses, brought in more revenue. State colleges produced professional fish managers who, after State employment, brought about better public understanding of the facts of fish life. More fishermen mean more problems for the managers, but the professionals can handle them more constructively.

We have come a long, long way since Genesis in attitudes and in applications of our still small bank of knowledge. It will be another century before people can deal effectively with the large questions of interstate and international fish management, the manipulation and control of fish populations in reservoirs, the enrichment of barren waters, and the too-rapid eutrophication of natural lakes. Sport fishing will then be the beneficiary, and the promise of Genesis will be fulfilled: man will truly exercise dominion over the fish and waters for his enjoyment.

Fishery Science

by Robert E. Lennon

*The period between World War II and 1965 must be recorded
as the era when fishery science came of age in the United States, for more
research has been accomplished in the past two decades to find
out how to manage fish than in all the previous years of wildlife history.
Larger funds are now available for research than ever before,
both from special taxes and from Federal or State appropriations; larger
numbers of students are being graduated by the
universities to conduct research; and more research is being
conducted by Federal, State, and private agencies.*

FISHING FOR SALMON

W HAT IS THE RESULT of it all? The result has been a determined effort to find the ways to save a resource from destruction in America, so that many millions can continue to use it for satisfying recreation.

Before describing some of the insights being uncovered by the new research efforts, I would like to briefly describe four milestones in this postwar era. The first has to do with the establishment of the Sport Fishing Institute, the second with the so-called Dingell-Johnson excise tax, the third with the decision by Congress to appropriate direct funds for concerted research efforts, and the fourth with the training of specialists in fish management and research.

The Sport Fishing Institute was established in 1949 by manufacturers of fishing tackle and accessories, outboard motors, boats, and other sporting goods used by anglers. It was organized to help improve sport angling, by promoting research in biology, by publicizing conservation, and by providing professional service to official agencies and key citizen groups. About 25 percent of the institute's annual budget is devoted to fishery research, much of it in the form of fellowships, cash, or equipment to researchers in universities and other institutions.

Thus more than 150 manufacturers of angling equipment have gone on record in behalf of research and wise use of the resource.

The Federal Aid in Fish Restoration Act, passed by Congress in 1950—the so-called Dingell-Johnson Law—did more for sport fishing than any previous Federal legislation. It required that funds from a 10 percent excise tax on fishing rods, reels, creels, and artificial lures be turned over by the U.S. Treas-

ury through the Bureau of Sport Fisheries and Wildlife to the States and territories under a prescribed formula for projects beneficial to sport fishing. The result has been the completion by State wildlife agencies of many sound conservation measures.

One feature of the D–J Act is a provision that the States match the Federal money on a 25–75 basis; that is, the State pays 25 percent of the costs of an approved fishery research or management project, and D–J money pays 75 percent. Since the States obtain most of their fishery funds from the sale of fishing licenses, the angler obviously is paying for the improvement of his sport through the purchase of both tackle and licenses.

The D–J funds apportioned to the States each year support a great amount of work on conservation. The States received more than $75 million in D–J money in the period 1952–67, which, with their own contribution of $25 million, provided more than $100 million for much-needed fishery work.

There are, however, many interregional, interstate, and international problems in sport fisheries which are not investigated under the D–J program. Recognizing that, Congress expanded Federal investments in fishery research and management. In the past decade, the Bureau of Sport Fisheries and Wildlife has constructed 14 research laboratories (making the present total 19). They are staffed by biologists, chemists, physiologists, bacteriologists, parasitologists, and other scientists.

The objective of these laboratories was the determination of new insights for fish managers. Answers were sought for such questions as: How can the natural environment be managed to improve the

Viewing chambers enable investigators to monitor upstream migrations.

productivity of sport fish? How can hatchery fish be produced more efficiently and used more effectively? How can habitat be protected? How can fish that are "pests" be controlled effectively?

Concerning the fourth milestone, there was a shortage of trained fishery workers that was hampering research and management activities. There just weren't enough skilled personnel to carry the new fishery science to the lakes, rivers, estuaries, and marine waters that were in need of attention.

Congress recognized the shortage and passed Public Law 86–686 in 1960, "to facilitate cooperation between the Federal Government, colleges and universities, the States, and private organizations for cooperative unit programs of research and education relating to fish and for other purposes."

The Bureau of Sport Fisheries and Wildlife was given funds to establish cooperative fishery units at specified colleges and universities, in cooperation with host schools and State wildlife departments. The first unit was activated in 1962; by 1968 there were 23 units in operation.

The cooperative fishery units are manned by biologists who teach college and graduate courses in fishery sciences, direct student research projects leading to master's and doctor's degrees, and conduct their own research. The units therefore contribute a pool of trained biologists to meet Federal, State, and private needs in working on fishery problems.

These four milestones, and probably a few factors missed, have done much in the past 25 years to help fishery biology become a science—a young science with a long way to go, but vigorous and on the move. Many mysteries in fish and aquatic ecology remain to be studied, but we now have the men to tackle the research. Eventually they will turn up more insights on how to manipulate populations of game fish to improve fishing.

Sound management of fish requires first that we know as much as possible about each species. Where does it prefer to live? What does it prefer to eat? Where does it go to spawn? How does it behave in the face of increased pollution, increased pleasure boating, and other water uses?

Our biologists have begun to use electronic tracking apparatus, underwater television, minisubmarine, and scuba gear to scrutinize the resting, feeding, schooling, migrating, spawning, and other behavior of fish in lakes and oceans. Dry chambers constructed under streambeds are used to observe the behavior of stream fish. The causes of fluctuations in fish populations, for example, may show up during such studies.

Nor are the insides of living specimens ignored by researchers. New developments in anesthetics and surgery make it possible to open up fish, examine organs, sample tissues, and sew up the animal again. Also live fish can be catheterized to collect samples of urine that are analyzed to detect effects of drugs, pesticides, or pollutants on the kidney.

Blood samples are taken from living fish and analyzed as an aid to diagnosing diseases or to evaluate artificial diets.

Plankton samples reveal life-supporting capacity of waters.

Behavioral changes caused by chemical agents can be detected in the laboratory.

Analyses of certain fractions of blood also help biologists to distinguish discrete races or populations of fish within a given species. Such information on races or populations will enable biologists to manage the fishery and protect any of its discrete segments from overexploitation.

Water temperatures receive a lot of attention from fishery scientists, since fluctuations are known to influence the appearance or disappearance of game fish along the Atlantic, gulf, and Pacific coasts and even the survival of young. Vast areas of coastal waters are involved in the studies, and biologists have mounted infrared detectors in aircraft to measure surface temperatures rapidly and accurately. Knowing the preferred temperatures for fish, the biologists can predict with increasing reliability where the fishing for bluefish, albacore, striped marlin, and other species is best at certain times.

The biological influences of varying water levels in reservoirs are also being studied. The fluctuations of levels in reservoirs are usually more drastic and frequent than in natural lakes, especially if the impoundment exists primarily for hydroelectric production, irrigation, or flood control. Biologists are learning how to capitalize on the fluctuations to maintain good fishing.

Lowering the water level at certain times, for example, may reduce the spawning success of unwanted species or perhaps increase predation on over-abundant or stunted varieties. Or the water level may be raised at an appropriate time to enhance the migration and spawning of other fish.

Some progress has been made in scheduling the changes in lake levels which are beneficial to sport fishing with the industrial or agricultural demands for the water.

The artificial rearing and stocking of both fresh- and salt-water game species by private, State, and Federal institutions are important to the maintenance of fishing and get much study. The selection of fish for rearing and stocking,

Skindiving gives a first-hand view of underwater conditions.

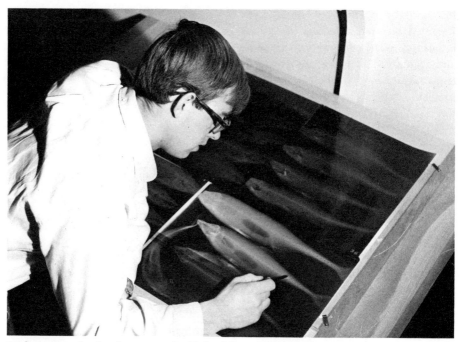

Students are trained under cooperative Federal-State fishery programs.

however, is no longer haphazard. A lot of research effort may go into the selection of a game fish which may give the best results in certain lakes or streams.

And once a species is selected, additional effort is devoted to choosing an appropriate strain. Rainbow trout, for example, come in a variety of strains, just as strawberries or tomatoes do, and it is often extremely important to plant the proper breed to obtain satisfactory results.

Fishery managers at the moment do not have as many strains of known characteristics and performance as they would like, since this is a relatively new concept in fisheries, but progress is evident.

Several laboratories are investigating species, strains, and hybrids of game fish to find and develop those which may perform better in wild waters, withstand warmer or polluted waters, be resistant to pesticides or competing species, grow faster, mature earlier, be more vigorous and sporting, or be more available to anglers. The chances are great for perfecting strains or hybrids which are tailored to present day needs.

The rapid invasion by "trash" fish into new waters or reclaimed waters is a widespread problem which biologists would like to solve effectively and economically. Considerable research is centered, therefore, on the design and operation of fish-proof barriers. Electric barriers (impenetrable electric fields in the water) arrest upstream movements of sea lampreys in some tributaries of the Great Lakes. Mechanical barriers of several designs show promise for use in small streams and in the outlets of lakes. Self-cleaning types have been devised to eliminate difficulties with waterborne debris, and they work well when not subject to severe flooding or ice action.

On the other hand, it is often desirable to facilitate the movement of fish up and down rivers, over or around dams. The matter of providing fish ladders and fish passages was at first oversimplified, and many of the structures built years ago failed to serve the purpose. They may have looked nice to people, but the fish ignored them.

Scientists then began to study the fish themselves to determine how they orient themselves to currents and falls when migrating up or down stream, what velocities and volumes of water are excessive or acceptable, and what time of day fish prefer to pass through ladders or fishways. It also became necessary to find out just how and where a fish initiates his jump to surmount a falls.

Actually it is a rather precise point if the jump is a long or high one. The depth and configuration of currents are important to successful jumps, and resting periods and places may be needed between difficult jumps. The results of extensive observations, made on fish in streams and in pilot facilities, brought about improvements in the design and operation of fish passages.

But to sportsmen, the reclamation of lakes and streams with toxicants is one of the more spectacular fish management procedures. Overpopulating species are killed in large numbers, and stocked game fish fill the niche.

The first treatment of a lake with a chemical to kill stunted fish occurred in 1914. The practice grew slowly in the next 20 years because the chemical was difficult to use well, as it also killed food-fish organisms and aquatic plants.

By 1950, however, the renovation of lakes with toxic chemicals was acknowl-edged to be a promising management practice. Much remains to be done in perfecting chemicals and techniques for use on large scale in lakes and streams.

Fishery managers desire most to have means for selectively removing "weed" species from waters, while leaving game fish unharmed. For example, they would like to remove carp selectively from the many waters where the species interferes with the sport fishery or waterfowl production. Trout angling in many waters can be improved if suckers, minnows, and other fish can be brought under control.

The tough and adaptable goldfish became established in some lakes and warrants control. The green sunfish sometimes disrupt largemouth bass-bluegill ponds. Squawfish are voracious predators on small salmon in West coast streams. Hordes of stunted and scrawny yellow perch may take over a lake. Gars, too, may be so abundant in places that they are detrimental to other fishing.

The older chemicals used as fish toxicants lacked selectivity. Moreover, the toxicants were usually obnoxious to all fish and tended to drive them to seek every possible avenue of escape from exposure. For this reason, attempts at reclaiming lakes and streams were often less than satisfactory because target fish found temporary escapes and survived.

Investigators are now working on toxicants which impart no odor or color to the water and do not repel fish. They also seek chemicals which affect only certain species. No less important is the research on the proper formulation of toxicants to enable fishery managers to hit target fish effectively, at those times of the year when the fish are congregated in certain parts of lakes or streams for spawning or feeding.

Fishery research must consider some of the nostalgia about the past in planning for the future.

The idea is that carp, green sunfish, suckers, and other locally undesirable fish may be controlled by poisoning the adults, eggs, and young at spawning sites in several successive years, instead of expensively treating an entire lake or watershed at once. Or a special formulation of toxicant may enable a manager to kill rough fish in the upper layer of warm water of a lake in summer without harming game species in the deep, colder water.

The researchers are not neglecting possibilities of integrated controls that might involve attracting and holding target fish in a certain area with one chemical, until they are affected by a second chemical which will anesthetize, sterilize, or kill them. In waters where bullheads are problems, an irritant might be used to cause them to come out of the mud and be exposed to a toxic chemical.

There is no lack of ideas for combining chemical and electrical tools, or chemical and biological tools, to manipulate populations of fish.

There have been, therefore, some remarkable insights in sport fisheries in the past two decades. Implemented by funds and research, they are helping fishery managers keep pace with the growth of sport fishing. The future of the sport looks brighter because funding for research, training of specialists, and applications in fishery management are expanding from year to year. We can be confident that the young and flourishing fishery science will generate exciting new insights to enhance the resource, and thus increase the pleasures of sport fishing.

Man-Made Fish

by Roger E. Burrows

The words "man-made" have the connotation of something being artificial or handcrafted, but in fishery science this is not quite so. We start out with one of nature's creatures—a fish—and seek to improve it through careful breeding, proper diet, disease control, and controlled environment, then attempt to introduce it into the wild in plentiful numbers for future harvest by man. The greatest man-made changes in fish have come about through selective breeding to improve hatchery production.

BIG HOLE RAINBOW AND BROWN

Hatchery fish are tested for their ability to survive in the wild by swimming against the current in stamina tunnels.

BROOD STOCKS have been developed which have greatly increased egg production over wild stock. Some have been induced to spawn earlier or later and grow more rapidly than their forebears. Disease resistance, usually to one specific disease, has been bred into some varieties to produce a more viable race. Others have been developed which have lower vitamin requirements and greater tolerances to unfavorable environmental conditions than their wild brethren.

But despite these successes in careful breeding to improve hatchery production, we are still faced with this sad fact: Often hatchery fish do not adapt to a wild environment. Sometimes losses are great during the adaptation period. Our research therefore is also aimed at carefully scrutinizing both fish and environment to determine what is causing the fish kills.

Our genetic studies, meanwhile, have also resulted in the hybridization of sev-

338

eral species of warm- and cold-water fish. Several of these crosses were made with the specific objective of producing a species which would be better adapted to meet the requirement of a particular habitat in the wild.

The splake, a fertile hybrid cross between the brook and the lake trout, has proved to have many of the traits sought for in a lake fish. It grows faster, matures more rapidly, and spawns in the same type of rocky reefs as the lake trout. It is now being stocked extensively in Lake Huron and many of the smaller northern lakes. Other such hybrids should issue from future research.

Successful crosses have been developed in the pike family to introduce hybrid vigor and possibly extend its range across our country. We are proceeding with extensive experimentation with many types of catfish to develop a hybrid that grows faster for fish farming.

Most crosses are sterile, and we have used this to advantage in farm pond management. Here the productivity of a species like the bluegill, which is stocked as forage for largemouth bass, may cause an imbalance in the predator-prey relationship and a stunting of the population. The planting of a sterile hybrid forage fish helps to keep such ponds in balance for longer periods.

But we are only beginning to exploit the potential of genetics. Fish with three to four times the growth potential of present strains are not too far distant. The trophy fish of today may become commonplace in the future. All the desirable qualities of a species can be accentuated and propagated.

Man has long had a good idea of what fish eat in the wild. This knowledge has been put to use in one of man's principal methods of capture: hook and line fishing. Once fish have been placed in confinement, however, natural food is no longer available in sufficient quantity to meet the demand, and substitutes have had to be developed.

Poor nutrition definitely alters any animal. Inadequate diets can produce mass mortalities, and marginal diets can produce fish with such impaired capabilities that they have little or no chance of survival after release. Research laboratories are determining the vitamin, amino acid, fatty acid, and mineral requirements of most species of fish which are extensively cultured. With this knowledge, we are formulating and testing diets which more nearly meet the requirements of the animal while it lives in captivity.

Variations in diet composition can be used to speed up or retard growth rates, and thereby alter the life cycle. The size of both Atlantic and Pacific salmon fingerlings determines the year at which they migrate to the ocean. Slow-growing ones may migrate in their second or third years, fast-growing individuals in their first year. Longer rearing in freshwater results in lower adult survivals. Diet is one factor which is now used to accelerate growth rate and induce early migration.

Diets containing insufficient calories to allow for adequate fat storage result in fish with low energy reserves, and therefore little opportunity for adaptation to a wild existence. An increase from 4 to 8 percent fat in chinook salmon fingerlings resulted in a doubling of adult survival. Chinook salmon fingerlings, however, when fed hard fat from cattle and hogs, develop high levels of cholesterol in the blood and degeneration of the liver, spleen, and kidney tissues, which result in anemia and even-

339

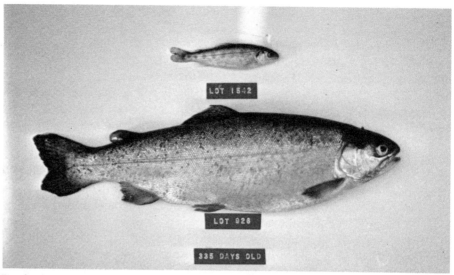

In selective breeding, fish of the same age reared under same conditions
vary in size because of inherited differences.

tual death. Elimination of raw meats and hard fats from the diets improved salmon runs in the Northwest. So we must consider the type of food to feed the fish.

The basic nutrition requirements of fish are well on the way to being established, with adequate diets now available. Perhaps the greatest improvement in this field has been the development of pelleted rations which allow control of the protein and caloric intake. In this way we can control growth and energy reserves and tailor fish to meet many specific situations in the wild.

We still have much to learn about the presence or effects of infections. The larger gill and body parasites are relatively obvious under microscopic examination, but the recognition of latent internal infections is very difficult. Latent infections lie dormant with no recognizable symptoms displayed by the fish until placed into an unfavorable environment, then the disease explodes in epidemic proportions. Other diseases which

are tolerated in favorable habitat may result in unexpected mortalities under stress of high or low water temperatures, or of pollutants.

We can evaluate the obvious in terms of immediate mortalities; the presence of insidious diseases, however, may be impossible to diagnose. Our approach in this instance is to try to impose resistance either by breeding or immunizing.

We have developed treatments for the control of certain epidemic diseases. More important, we are testing methods of immunization for several diseases. Such developments offer the possibility of protecting hatchery-reared fish from the diseases which they may encounter in the wild environment. Immunization to a disease also prevents the possibility of a latent infection of the disease from destroying or decimating a hatchery population after release.

In the area of environmental control, we now know that the rearing of fish is best accomplished in a favorable tem-

340

Environmental factors like temperature can also be varied to speed or retard growth of fish in same age-class.

perature range. Optimum as opposed to marginal rearing temperatures have a startling effect on growth. Chinook salmon fingerlings, for example, with an increase of 15° F. in water temperature, from 40° F. to 55° F., will respond with a threefold increase in the percentage gain, from 50 to 150 percent per month. All other things being equal, the larger the fish at release the better the chance of its survival to harvest. Sockeye salmon fingerlings twice as large at release have three times the number of returning adults.

Fish culturists are aware of the advantages of favorable temperatures for fish rearing, but until recently, the costs of heating and cooling the quantities of water required for hatchery operations have been economically unfeasible.

In 1965, we developed a practical method for reconditioning hatchery water for reuse. The reuse of water makes possible temperature control within the system. With controls, it is possible to produce the best temperature regimen for the species to be reared.

Hatchery rearing may create other environmental conditions which can alter fish traits. Overcrowding of the rearing ponds can produce polluted conditions in which the oxygen is depleted and the metabolic waste is accumulated in the ponds. Under such conditions, the fish are stunted, low in vigor, and are particularly vulnerable to disease infection. The situation is further aggravated by the reuse of water without reconditioning. Such fish have at least two strikes against them when released.

We have identified the factors which limit production in rearing ponds and have defined these limitations in terms of the available oxygen, density of fish, and waste accumulation. We are now in a position to stock ponds to their optimum rearing capacities without overloading.

The water velocity created by the several types of rearing ponds in use also

341

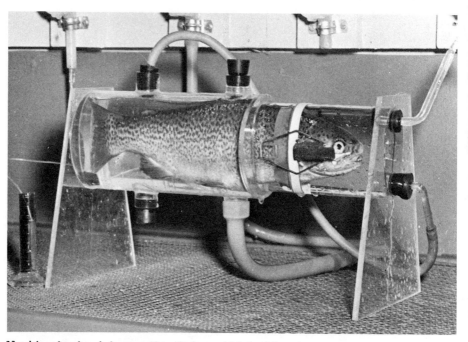

Nutrition chambers help researchers find out which foods benefit the fish most.

Fish recover from surgery performed under hospital conditions to find out how specific organs are affected by certain diseases.

changes the fish. Ponds which have little or no water velocity produce sluggish fish which are poorly adapted to a stream environment. The situation is comparable to conditioning a thoroughbred for racing by keeping him in a box stall with no track exercise or training and then expecting him to perform competitively in a race.

The significance of exercise is easily demonstrated. We have developed a new type of rearing pond which increases fish stamina. Such fish have a greater ability for survival to adults in the wild.

If the quality of the fish is altered by poor nutrition, disease, and unfavorable environment, then there must be changes in the animal's physical, physiological, and chemical characteristics. Knowing what the changes are helps us determine the type of fish we have. Fortunately, we have developed equipment and techniques that enable us to

Biologists working to breed a superior fish start with superior specimens from nature.

measure a significant number of such alterations.

For example, the physical performance capabilities can be measured by several types of exercise chambers. Tests in such chambers indicate that a nutritional deficiency which creates an anemia results in lower stamina. Also, any nutritional deficiency or external parasite which causes swelling or fusion in the gills results in impaired performance. And enviromental conditions such as ammonia exposure which create a gill irritation result in reduced performance.

A reduction in muscle tone due to lack of exercise is best measured in the stamina tunnel, but there are other physiological and chemical changes which can be related to poor performance and may be measured directly.

Fish blood has many significant measurable characteristics. The number of red cells, their compacted volume, and the amount of hemoglobin they contain are all measures of types of anemia. A high percentage of small, immature red cells in the blood is an indication of a vitamin C or E deficiency. Additional vitamin deficiencies also may be determined by chemical analyses of the red cells. The blood plasma may be analyzed to determine the amount of protein, glucose, cholesterol, minerals, and meta-

The splake is a man-made fish—a cross between lake and brook trout—
with rapid growth and excellent sporting qualities.

bolic waste products. The plasma proteins may be further analyzed to determine the amounts of albumin and the several globulins.

The chemical analysis of the fish body to determine the amount of protein, fat, ash, and water present is one measure of the effect of diet on the animal. Variations in the chemical composition of the fingerlings can be correlated with performance in the stamina tunnel and with survivals after release.

But one question we are often asked is this: How well will our man-made fish thrive in man-altered environments? We already have an approach and a partial answer to this problem. For example, when temperatures move into the lethal range of a species in the wild, the species is eliminated. Therefore, if we cannot alter the temperature of the habitat, we seek to improve the species at hand by breeding more tolerant individuals, or we supply a temperature-tolerant species that is equally acceptable.

Wastes also present problems, as certain species of fish and individuals within a species are less tolerant than others to chemical or organic pollutants. We try to capitalize on the tolerance of some individuals, by breeding entire races from these few to survive in areas containing moderate amounts of wastes.

People are becoming more aware of the dangers of pollution, and legislation is being enacted to control this problem. Realistically, I think we can expect some thermal, chemical, and organic pollution to be with us for some time to come. It is, however, likely that we can breed desirable races of fish that will tolerate moderate—but not extreme—alterations in the environment and still develop.

Deforestation and irrigation practices dry up streams during periods of fish spawning and egg incubation or reduce stream flows and create intolerable temperatures. Through selective breeding, we can alter the spawning time of many species to conform to periods of more favorable conditions.

Much remains to be done, but I believe we are using the right approach.

344

Fishery research has not withdrawn into an ivory tower but is dynamic—actively developing the facts and methodology required for the production of fish designed to meet the requirements of specific environments. Only through man-made fish can our fisheries meet the rising demands placed upon them by pollution and by the greater harvests to be made by our expanding population.

Old Fish in New Homes

by Howard A. Tanner

*Clear in memory is the story I heard as a child
of cowboys in the 19th century using a battered coffeepot to
transfer a few golden trout from a tiny
headwater stream across a low pass to another willow-lined stream. Then
there was the account of Missouri's first fish commission's attempt
to transplant rainbow trout. It seems that the chief fish warden,
after having announced that he would achieve great results
for fishermen, dumped buckets of rainbow
into the warm, muddy Missouri River.*

GOLDEN TROUT OF THE WEST

THERE ARE many other such stories, but these two are enough to illustrate how haphazard and without any sound planning were many early American efforts at transplanting fish.

Some oddities still persist today because of such early introductions. For example, the high mountain area at the head of the Rio Grande River, known as the San Luis Valley, with many mild to moderately thermal artesian wells and springs, contains the Asiatic tench. How it got there, we still don't know. The fish is of little or no interest to residents, many of whom are unaware of its presence.

Confined to two or three neighboring lakes near Colorado Springs, Colo., the grass pickerel resides. This little pike rarely reaches 14 inches anywhere and is almost certainly there as a result of mistaken identity. Some early fish culturist must have thought the fish he moved with much effort and expense was the northern pike.

Of such early attempts, we have a few records and know of the consequences of some transfers of fish into new areas, particularly during 1860–1895. It was, for example, during this time that the carp was successfully moved from Europe to our East coast, heralded as a "wonder fish," then bred and dispersed westward with great enthusiasm—only to prove to be more of a nuisance than a boon.

The California Fish Commission was particularly active in bringing in new fish, with at least 31 species having been introduced into the State in the 20 years following 1870. Many were intended for food, but the angler was not forgotten by such imports as striped bass, muskellunge, northern pike, crappie, walleye, Atlantic salmon, brook trout, brown

The carp was hailed as a great food fish when introduced from Europe in the 19th century. Enthusiasm later waned but was revived by archers and other anglers.

trout, whitefish, yellow perch, large- and small-mouth bass, and bluegills.

Included here were the dramatic successes of the striped bass and American shad. From a planting of less than 500 fingerlings in the Sacramento Delta, striped bass quickly expanded to a combined sport and commercial fishery producing several millions of fish annually. The striper moved first throughout San Francisco Bay, then northward as far as Coos Bay, Oreg., and well southward along the California coast. The success

Brought from tropical regions for aquariums, the walking catfish has gotten into natural waters and is able to spread by moving overland. Accidental transplants are a threat to balanced fishing.

of the American shad was only slightly less dramatic.

Repeated but unverified reports of sporadic die-offs of "whitefish" in Cheeseman Reservoir, a Denver water supply impoundment on the South Platte River, led me to set nets there in the mid-1950's. The reservoir at that time was closed to the public. My sampling yielded 11 lake whitefish of several age classes. Curiosity as to origin led me to the archives of the Denver Water Board, where a brief notation explained that soon after construction of the reservoir (early 1900's) "whitefish" had been planted to "control algae." This species had remained there largely unknown for over 40 years, and to the best of my knowledge is still there today.

Incidentally, the movement of fish was not all east to west. The beautiful rainbow trout was probably confined to the Pacific drainage of North America when first discovered, but since then its popularity as both a food and game fish led to its introduction into freshwater and anadromous habitats throughout the earth. Today it dominates the world commercial trout production.

California golden trout are so well established in the Wind River Mountains of Wyoming that Wyoming produced the world's record.

The Sacramento perch, greatly depleted in its original California range by a combination of competition from introduced fish species and of habitat alteration, was transplanted with consider-

The sea lamprey became a destructive agent for Great Lakes fish by entering through man-made Welland Canal bypassing Niagara Falls—a disastrous, unplanned transplant.

349

From an original transplant of 400 striped bass in a California bay,
the population of this species has grown to several million.

In season dipnetters go for smelt, an oceanic herring-type fish that has adapted well to Great Lakes waters.

widely dispersed cold-water lakes, and is present now in more than 20 States.

Sometimes fish and other denizens of the water world are permitted to spread accidentally. The construction of the Welland Canal, for example, in the early 19th century allowed creatures to move from Lake Ontario into the other four Great Lakes, which until then were effectively protected by Niagara Falls. Several species have since penetrated the upper lakes, the most infamous being the sea lamprey, a parasite that found difficult going in Lake Erie and did not reach the upper three until the 1930's. But once there, it decimated lake trout, whitefish, herring, burbot, and several other fish species. All relations between species were severely upset, and with the chief predators removed, the prey species suffered from excessive survival.

There were at least two other harmful introductions into the upper Great Lakes as a result of the Welland Canal: the alewife and white perch. Of these two, the alewife is the one that is to date truly significant. It was detected in the upper Great Lakes by the mid-1930's but was a fish of unusual occurrence until 1955–64, when it gained enormous abundance, particularly in Lakes Huron and Michigan. Since 1964 it has clearly dominated fish populations in Lakes Huron and Michigan. It is abundant in Lake Superior in only a few shallow, warmer areas. It can be demonstrated as detrimental to many native species.

The white perch has achieved significant abundance in Lake Erie. Its presence is generally regarded as undesirable, and its spread throughout other portions of the upper Great Lakes is viewed with apprehension.

An earlier man-made introduction into the Great Lakes that has had a

able success into saline lakes of western Nevada, western Nebraska, eastern Colorado, and perhaps elsewhere as well. This is a highly desirable sunfish (not a perch), reaching up to 4 pounds in weight. Its ability to survive in the highly mineralized lakes has led to its favorable consideration in States with such waters.

Several of the Pacific salmon were also widely introduced across the country, often failing. But the landlocked sockeye filled a useful role in many

A good sport and table fish, capable of tolerating a wide range of temperatures, walleye have been widely stocked in reservoirs and streams.

serious effect on fish populations is the American smelt. In the early part of this century an attempt was made to transplant the landlocked Atlantic salmon. The smelt was recognized as an important food species for the Atlantic salmon, and so it was introduced simultaneously into Crystal Lake, Benzie County, Mich.

Here the landlocked salmon disappeared, but the smelt thrived and spread to all of the upper four Great Lakes. Smelt runs of major proportions and large scale die-offs started—including the catastrophic one in 1943, when a windrow of dead smelt extended for hundreds of miles along Great Lakes beaches.

The smelt today is reasonably important as a commercial fish and no doubt is in certain circumstances important as a forage fish. However, its voracious behavior as a predator on small fish has long made it suspect, and many consider its presence unfortunate.

Other early and deliberate introductions into the Great Lakes included the West coast steelhead and the brown trout from Europe. Both of these fish, while highly regarded and contributing seasonally to sport fishing, cannot be considered of major numerical or poundage importance. Their presence in the upper Great Lakes seems assured, and their compartively high value will bring other efforts to expand their numbers.

It is also a matter of record that several representatives of the Pacific salmon were frequently introduced into the Great Lakes. While some of these produced identified survivors, none thrived, and all eventually disappeared, except that pink salmon are found rarely in Lake Superior. This introduction was made during the late 1950's, and while it has survived for several generations, its permanent place in the upper Great Lakes is not yet assured. It must be considered insignificant in its present numbers.

Two of the more interesting introductions into some of the many reservoirs built in this country in the 20th century have been the threadfin shad and striped bass. The threadfin is a rapidly reproducing forage fish (provides food for other fish) that frequently does well in warmer reservoirs, particularly in the Southwest where forage species have been absent or seriously inadequate.

A few successful reservoir introductions include white and largemouth bass, lake and rainbow trout, walleye, golden shiner, bluegills, redear, channel and flathead catfish, and even crayfish and shrimp.

The huge farm pond building program underway in the United States has permitted large-scale introductions of trout, largemouth bass, bluegills, tilapia, and catfish.

Recently a noteworthy effort was made at the Salton Sea in inland southern California—a very difficult environment for fish. This body of water, created by water used for irrigation, which then accumulated in an undrained depression, is extremely salty. Evaporation and less waste irrigation water is making it even saltier. However, a fish population in this desert country and in this body of water was highly desired.

And biologists of the California Game and Fish Department succeeded. Some of their efforts were by trial and error, but they did establish a good recreational fishery. It was first necessary to find marine invertebrates capable of living there. Sandworms were found to thrive. Then several fish known to exist in sea waters of high salt content were tried. The corvina survived in good numbers, using the sandworm as food supply, and now there is fishing where none existed before.

But the largest scale introduction and probably the most successful one in America began in the fall of 1964, when the Michigan Conservation Department made a series of new fish introductions into the Great Lakes (a program I was happy to be part of). The first four fish to be considered were the sockeye, coho, and chinook salmon, plus striped bass. Only the first three have as yet been introduced.

Some of the background leading to this decision is extremely important. International sea lamprey research and control and the lake trout rehabilitation programs were coordinated and directed by the Great Lakes Fishery Commission. On the United States side, these programs were carried out largely through contracts to the U.S. Bureau of Commercial Fisheries. The scourge of the sea lamprey after 15 years of arduous labor was, by 1964, coming under control. The international lake trout stocking program of the Great Lakes Fishery Commission had produced substantial recovery of lake trout stocks in Lake Superior. The first lake trout plantings were taking place in Lake Michigan.

There were established traditions which led to the assumption that the Great Lakes fisheries, having always been managed for commercial harvest, would be returned to similar objectives.

The newly reorganized Michigan Conservation Department, however, led a change in policy. Michigan had never before played a significant role in the fishery management of Great Lakes waters, even though the State had 3,000-plus miles of shoreline and regulatory authority over 74 percent of the U.S. waters of the upper three Great Lakes. The State had the most to gain or lose in any Great Lakes fish management undertakings. The decision by its conservation department was to reorient all fish management of the upper Great Lakes to the development of recreational sport fisheries. It was this change in management objectives that led to the introduction of the now famous coho salmon.

The absence of adequate predator fish populations and the decision in favor of recreational management objectives were significant considerations that guided the selection of the coho, but other important considerations entered into this introduction. The enormous abundance of the alewife provided assurance that the voracious coho would have an adequate food supply. Fishery biologists who would have liked to include in their repertoire of management tools the possibility of introducing new species were by then deeply concerned over the potential damage of any introduction. They knew as a general rule, however, that no one had ever brought about serious trouble by introducing any member of the salmon family.

Other factors relating to this introduction are these. The total technology available for transplanted salmon populations became adequate only since 1959. The adequacy of West coast technology had been clearly demonstrated by 1964, and the skills and techniques available there could readily be applied to the Great Lakes situation. A careful review of the literature showed numerous examples, both in North America and in Asia, where salmon had been successfully established, at least temporarily, in freshwater.

Furthermore, the Pacific Northwest was for the first time reporting surplus coho eggs. These factors, plus the negative conviction that lake trout offered far less than an optimum management potential for recreational fishing, led to the introduction of the coho. The generosity of Oregon and later Washington and Alaska is recognized. It should also be pointed out that Ontario was the first to introduce sockeye into the Great Lakes. The Province has also under serious consideration introducing masu salmon from Japan.

Michigan's first coho eggs were obtained in January 1965. Roughly 850,000 fish survived to planting from this first million eggs. These fish were stocked in the spring of 1966 as smolts weighing 1 ounce. The coho were

About 18 million pounds of channel catfish are stocked each year in fee-fishing ponds.

Tilapia from Africa are very fast growers in some of our southern waters.

released in Platte River, near the town of Honor in Benzie County and in Bear Creek, a tributary of Manistee River in Manistee County, near the town of Kaleva. In addition to these two Lake Michigan tributaries, coho were released in the lower reaches of Big Huron River, a Lake Superior tributary.

These three releases produced a precocious jack run of some 10,000 fish to the release sites in the fall of 1966. The average weight of fish in this precocious run was in the neighborhood of 3 pounds. This is larger than the typical West coast jack, and the size, numbers, and small percent of straying nurtured the growing excitement that has accompanied all phases of this introduction.

In the late summer of 1967, as the salmon approached the mouths of the Manistee and Platte Rivers, sport anglers harvested about 50,000 coho. A total of about 245,000 coho were accounted for from the original planting of 850,000

fish. This survival, which reached 36.8 percent in Lake Michigan, was truly astonishing to everyone. The fish caught by sport anglers in the lake averaged nearly 15 pounds, with some individuals exceeding 20 pounds.

To view with some appreciation the intensity of public excitement over the salmon in the Great Lakes, remember that fishermen, most of them novices to salmon angling, caught over 5,000 on several different weekends. This many large high-quality game fish had simply never been experienced by any group of Midwest freshwater fishermen.

The first chinook salmon introduction, under the leadership of Dr. Wayne Tody, the chief of the Michigan Conservation Department's Fish Division, went into Lake Michigan in May 1967.

It is now apparent that Michigan, assisted by other States and the Province of Ontario, will proceed to a full scale effort to stock at somewhere near op-

356

timum rates the upper three Great Lakes with several species of salmon, presently the coho, chinook, and sockeye. Growth and survival of these fish continue to be extraordinary. Their feeding habits are predominately the alewife, and the basis for a new balance seems at hand between predator and prey species in the Great Lakes, with management oriented toward a fantastically productive sport fishery.

Assuming that initial successes and high values are maintained, the reconstruction of Great Lakes fish population structures, through introductions of fish selected for their recreational potential, appears at this writing, to offer the most outstanding success since the introduction of the striped bass in San Francisco Bay in the 1870's.

The experience in the Great Lakes with coho demonstrates that there are times and places where the transfer of fish to another locality is both appropriate and a highly promising fish management technique. But I wish to close this chapter on a cautionary note. The accidental intrusions, like the sea lamprey into the Great Lakes and manmade introductions like the carp, led to disastrous consequences. Millions of dollars are still spent annually by conservation agencies to control these undesirables.

It is true that the culture and movement of fish species is much easier to accomplish today because of technological gains, but we must be mindful of consequences. Transfers should be made only after careful investigations by competent fishery ecologists. Only through such careful studies can we find out whether sport fishing will be enhanced or hindered by introducing old fish into new homes.

A New Look at Hatcheries

by Harvey Willoughby

The operation of fish hatcheries and the use of hatchery fish are as old in the United States as fish management itself. But the hatchery of today is undergoing startling changes in looks, function, and the underlying philosophy regarding its part in the conservation of our fish resources. Once considered a tool of politicians, hatcheries were for years held in low esteem by many biologists who cited instances where the wrong species were planted in wrong places under wrong conditions.

CHINOOK SALMON AT SEA

After on-site studies of Lake Powell, hatchery workers decided the best way to stock the Arizona-Utah impoundment was by plane, with fry riding the watery spray down to the lake.

THESE SCIENTISTS tried to sound the warning that planting fish was often not the answer to poor fishing. The approach seemed so logical to laymen, however, and for this reason was so attractive to politicians at all levels, that the warnings went unheeded.

Caught in the middle of this controversy was the fish culturist. Exposed to the opposing arguments of scientists and sportsmen's groups, he continued to raise fish, knowing that those which were properly used would improve sport fishing, and with the hope that those which were improperly used would at least do no harm.

Finally there emerged a new scientific discipline—fishery management, with biologists trained in chemistry, physics, biology, ecology, ichthyology, limnology, and population dynamics, and in a unique position to test and evaluate methods for managing the fisheries of this country. As the results of testing, creel census evaluations, and lake and stream inventories were analyzed, a new understanding of the role of hatcheries in fishery management began to emerge. Instead of resulting in closure, as many purists had predicted, hatcheries have assumed greater obligations and responsibilities, and have gained the respect of most fishery managers.

Fish rearing as practiced in this country is usually classified into two types: pondfish and salmonid culture. The pondfish type is generally extensive because of the relatively large acreages required to rear the fish in ponds on natural food. Trout and salmon culture, on the other hand, is intensive because large numbers of fish are reared in a small area.

As a means of comparison between the density of fish in natural waters and fish reared in hatcheries, one might ponder the fact that an average yield for a natural lake or pond would be in the neighborhood of 100 pounds of fish per surface acre. In a warm-water hatchery this yield can be increased five-fold on natural feed alone, and twenty-fold where natural food is supplemented with manufactured feed. In trout hatcheries, where fish can be held in close confinement and raised entirely on prepared feed, a yield equivalent to a quarter million pounds per surface acre is commonplace.

The most common species reared at pondfish stations are large- and small-mouth bass and other sunfish such as bluegills and redear, as well as catfish, northern pike, walleye, and striped bass.

The pondfish culturist is basically an ecologist. His job is to maintain optimum opportunities for fish to spawn and grow under seminatural conditions. He hopes to improve upon nature by increasing the survival rate of the fish and to rear very large numbers by increasing the productivity of the pond.

Survival rates are improved by eliminating competition from other fish and holding cannibalism to a minimum by preventing a size spread of the fish in the pond. In order to prevent a size spread it is essential that the fish spawn at or near the same time. This is achieved with channel catfish and striped bass by injecting the female with hormones causing them to spawn at a predictable time, usually within a day or two. Under natural conditions, spawning occurs over a period of several days or even weeks.

The eggs of striped bass are stripped from the female by hand and immediately fertilized with sperm from the male fish, and then they are placed in incubating jars supplied with flowing water where they hatch in 3 or 4 days. Catfish are paired. One female and one male are confined in an aquarium or holding pen until spawning takes place. The egg masses are then removed, placed in hatching troughs, and gently agitated to assure water circulation through the mass until they hatch. It is relatively easy to get huge numbers of active, healthy fry from a few brood fish by these methods. A 5-pound catfish will produce up to 10,000 eggs, while a 5-pound striped bass will produce 300,000 eggs.

Controlling the spawning and survival of pondfish such as largemouth bass is a more exacting task. To date, manual spawning of these species has not been widely practiced. The alternative has been to place sufficient adult bass in a pond with the hope of getting 20 to 30 spawns per acre of water. When all factors are favorable, success is realized. When sudden cold spells cause the water temperature to drop sharply, the male bass, whose task it is to guard the eggs and keep them swept clean and aerated, will abandon the nest, and the brood is lost.

For years fish culturists have been searching for a means of delaying the spawning of bass until the possibility of the temperature dropping below 65°F. is remote. The solution to this problem was found only when another but heretofore equally perplexing problem was solved—that of positively distinguishing between male and female bass.

While most fish can be identified as to sex by some physical characteristic, largemouth bass have defied such identification, and fish culturists have had to guess at their sex, except immediately before spawning time. With the discovery that their sex could be determined with the use of a biopsy needle or an otoscope, populations of male and female could be identified and separated. Since bass will not spawn as long as the sexes are kept in separate ponds, spawning could then be scheduled late enough in the spring to assure success.

The next step, to increase the reliability of hatchery production of both large- and small-mouth bass, will come when the spawn of these fish can be collected and cared for in the hatchery much as catfish are. Limited success in this direction has been achieved by placing nylon-felt mats in the ponds to serve as a place for the fish to deposit their eggs. Experiments conducted at the warm-water fish culture development center at Marion, Ala., during the past several seasons, has indicated a promising preference for use of the mats by the spawning bass. After the eggs are laid, the mats are removed and placed in hatchery tanks where fish culturists can give them the required care and protection to assure a high rate of survival.

A principal limitation to higher yields of warm-water species in hatcheries has been the problem of providing them with natural food. To accomplish this, ponds are fertilized to encourage the production of microscopic plants, which utilize energy from the sun to convert chemical elements into complex foodstuffs. The order of events is for the microscopic plants, called phytoplankton, to combine the fertilizing nutrients into cellulose, fats, and protein. The phytoplankton are the primary converters in the development of the food supply for microscopic animals called zooplankton. The zooplankton are eaten by insects and small fish, which in turn are eaten by larger fish.

Such intensive fertilization of ponds can produce up to 500 pounds of fish from an acre of water in a single season. When this 500 pounds of fish is composed entirely of such desirable species as largemouth bass, fishery managers have at their disposal significant numbers of predaceous fish for both improving recreational fishing and for bringing into balance stunted overpopulations of such fish as carp and gizzard shad.

The new technique in pondfish culture is to go several steps further than nature could in the production of pre-

A careful check is made for ripeness before inducing spawning by Atlantic salmon.

daceous fish. We have already discussed methods used to secure millions of young fish through control of spawning and care of the young. The next step, in bypassing nature's order of things, is to feed the fish directly.

With catfish, and apparently striped bass, direct feeding can be easily accomplished. Both species readily adapt, whether the food is chopped meat or fish or specially formulated dry pellets. Consequently catfish production throughout the South and Midwest is soaring to tremendous heights. Striped bass culture is likewise showing great

promise, although the production of this species is still in the developmental stages.

Efforts to hand-feed largemouth bass have often been discouraging, but progress continues, and recent reports from the National Fish Hatchery at Marion, Ala., tell of production of 5-inch largemouth bass by supplemental feeding with conversion ratios of 1.4 pounds of food to produce a pound of fish. With developments like these, and production figures of 3,000 pounds of fingerling fish per acre, warm-water game fish production promises a bright future for the

363

Craig Brook National Fish Hatchery in Maine specializes in restoring runs of Atlantic salmon in New England rivers.

recreational potential of America's inland waters.

Trout and salmon have been intensively reared in hatcheries for a hundred years. The discovery that these fish could be spawned by hand and their offspring raised on prepared feed permitted a degree of control, only now beginning to be exploited by fish culturists. Despite the fact that trout and salmon culture is an old art, tremendous advances are still being made in the rearing of these fish.

One of the basic advances in trout and salmon rearing is in the area of nutrition. Fish diets are now compounded as carefully and scientifically as diets for domestic animals. Pioneered by research into the basic nutritional requirements of fish, then developed and put into use

by fish culturists, modern hatchery diets are compounded to meet the requirements of each species and size of fish and the peculiarities of the environment in which they are reared. Mechanical fish feeders are coming into widespread use and are taking over the role of feeding the precise quantities of feed at prescribed intervals. The more advanced of these devices monitor water temperatures and adjust the daily ration accordingly.

To stay fully aware of the condition of his fish, the modern hatchery manager routinely performs clinical blood tests, takes weights and measurements, and even exercises the fish in special chambers to test their stamina. Where the pondfish culturist is basically an ecologist, the trout and salmon culturist is a

Grayling is one of a wide array of fish that are spawned for hatchery production.

physiologist. He must know the requirements for space, for the physical and chemical components of the water, and the nutritional requirements of the fish. Through careful control of these factors, each pound of trout or salmon raised may require as little as 1.2 pounds of food. Growth rates can be calculated with utmost accuracy. Through precise feeding, care, and good recordkeeping, the fish culturist can forecast the size of the fish months in advance, and thereby adjust the production schedule to meet the management need.

When fish are closely confined and crowded, far beyond the densities at which they would be found in the natural state, maintaining an acceptable environment is very important. Water in a trout or salmon hatchery must be between 32° F. and 70° F., relatively free of toxic metals such as zinc, copper, and manganese, and from excessive levels of such gases as nitrogen and hydrogen sulfide. Oxygen levels must be maintained above 5 ppm, and ammonia should not exceed 0.2 ppm for long periods of time. If the water quality criteria are met, most salmonids can be crowded to the point of being solidly packed in the rearing tank.

A dramatic demonstration of this was seen at the Benner Springs Experiment Station, Pa., a few years ago when Keen Buss hatched a number of brook trout in glass jars. Supplied with an ample flow of water and fed adequately, these fish grew until they completely filled the jar. They were so densely packed that it became impossible for them to move in any direction to get food. Their only recourse was to open their mouths and wait for water currents to bring in the food. Even under these conditions the fish remained healthy and continued to grow normally. The point to remember is that the flow of water was adjusted so as to maintain the necessary oxygen levels and remove the waste products of metabolism. This coupled with the food supplied by the hatcheryman met the basic requirements of the fish.

Water supplies, both entering and leaving a fishpond, must be monitored for their chemical content. Sufficient oxygen must be supplied by the incoming water to permit the fish to use the food. The relationship between food eaten and the oxygen required is so constant that many fish culturists calculate the oxygen content of the water entering a pond as a means of determining the carrying capacity.

While oxygen is usually the first limiting factor in the hatchery environment, it is not the only one. As oxygen is used to break down foods for energy and growth, byproducts are formed. Prominent among these are carbon dioxide and ammonia. Carbon dioxide poses few problems for it can easily be removed by

365

In restoring runs of steelhead in Northwest rivers, hatchery workers built hatching channels beside the streams and stocked them with eggs.

aeration. Ammonia, however, is another matter, and is very difficult to remove by mechanical means. Thus, when water is reused from one fishpond to another, it can be aerated to renew its oxygen content and to remove the carbon dioxide, but ammonia continues to accumulate, and soon reaches toxic levels.

A recent development in the use of bacterial filters, which convert free ammonia to more tolerable nitrates, has opened up possibilities for a tenfold increase in the quantity of fish that can be reared in a given water supply. Thus the limitations upon hatchery production continue to be reduced, and the capability of hatcheries as a useful tool in fishery management continues to improve.

Controlling fish diseases is a continuous task in fish hatcheries. Here, where dense crowding creates suboptimum conditions, populations must be constantly watched for signs of infections, malnutrition, or environmental stress.

Therefore, biologists specifically trained in fish disease control are employed. They use the same diagnostic tools as their counterparts in human medicine. Blood analyses, biopsies, and bacterial cultures are routine procedures to keep tabs on the health and condition of fish at hatcheries. Sophisticated instruments monitor the quality of the water, and up-to-the-minute indexes of weight gains or losses are posted.

Fish diseases are found to run the gamut from parasites, one species of which can attain a length of 3 feet, to viruses so small that a magnification of 750,000 diameters is required to cast even a shadow of their shapes.

When specific diseases are identified, appropriate treatment might include

Millions of fingerlings pass through hatchery scales and trucks on their way to stocking in a variety of waters.

such measures as the administration of approved drugs and antibiotics, quarantine, special diets, or vaccination. Thus, even though extremely crowded in comparison with wild populations, the state of health and life expectancy of a hatchery fish, whether a catfish or an Atlantic salmon, is much better than that of its wild counterparts.

Changing needs of fishery management often dictate a change in program direction or techniques in fish culture. An example of this is the multipurpose diversion canal and salmon spawning channel being constructed in connection with Tehama-Colusa water diversion project in northern California.

Promising to be one of the largest fish cultural installations on the North American Continent, the Tehama-Colusa spawning channel is planned to provide spawning habitat for 60,000 chinook salmon annually by 1985. These fish presently ascend the Sacramento River to spawn, and like all Pacific salmon, die after spawning is completed. The Tehama-Colusa Canal will provide prime spawning gravel in which these fish can deposit their eggs. Access to the spawning channel will be controlled to allow optimum numbers to lay their eggs at one time. The eggs will incubate in the canal, and the resulting young fish will live and feed there until they are ready to migrate to the sea.

When the spawning channel reaches full capacity, up to 60 million salmon will begin life in this man-made habitat. They will migrate to the ocean to live and grow. Three to seven years later they will return to the Sacramento River as vigorous fighting game fish and also valuable, nutritious food. Some individuals may weigh 65 pounds, and where 1 pound of fish left the spawning channel,

50 pounds will return. Most of the returning fish will be captured by either sport or commercial fishermen before they reach Tehama-Colusa, but sufficient numbers will reach the canal to assure perpetuation of the run.

Operation of the spawning channel is both an engineering and a fish cultural challenge. The engineering challenge will be in operating the mammoth traveling bridge which will service the canal. The bridge will span the canal, and travel its length via motorized carriages running on rails along the sides of the canal. It will serve as a working platform from which biologist and engineers can manipulate both the fish and their environment for optimum production.

For example, an underwater viewing chamber will be suspended from the bridge to permit biologists to observe the movements and behavior of the fish. Elaborate gravel cleaning devices will flush deposited silt from the channel after each spawning season. Young fish will be sorted, counted, and representative numbers marked as a means of evaluating the contribution of the spawning channel to the Pacific salmon fishery.

These and other changes that have taken place, during the last few years in fish hatcheries, reflect an emerging scientific approach to the ancient art of fish culture. A more profound change, however, is occurring in the basic philosophy of hatchery operation. This change reflects not so much how hatcheries are operated as why. The hatchery manager of today submits his production schedule to the critical eye of the fishery management biologist. It is this specialist who determines what part hatcheries will play in the management effort, or indeed if hatchery fish are even needed. When this determination has been made, and if hatchery fish are required, then the management biologist and the fish culturist work together to schedule hatchery production to meet the management need.

For example, when Lake Powell on the Colorado River was impounded in 1963, biologists had a stocking plan ready. The warm upper layers and the shallow bays were thought to be warmwater fish habitat, while the cool lower layers were considered suitable for trout. The reservoir was immediately stocked with huge numbers of largemouth bass and trout, to provide this new impoundment with desirable game fish, before less desirable species became too numerous. The plan was carried out on schedule, and the result was excellent angling for both bass and trout the following year.

Similar efforts have resulted in other outstanding successful projects in the last decade, including the introduction of Pacific salmon into the Great Lakes, the creation of "two-story" fisheries in many large reservoirs, and increasing returns of salmon and steelhead to West coast streams. Thus it is apparent that fish hatcheries, with over 100 years behind them, are now innovating on the basis of scientific research—not political pressures—and are producing fish to meet the needs of American fishermen. They are a primary tool in the fishery manager's kit.

Federal hatcheries provide for more than 40 million additional fishing visits on public and Indian lands.

MONEY TO BE MADE

Benefits Spread Far and Wide

by Richard H. Stroud

*An obviously rapid growth of population, plus increasing
participation by our citizenry in all kinds of outdoor recreation,
is an American phenomenon. This is demonstrated in our
traditional recreation of fishing and hunting by records for annual sales
of sporting licenses, records dating before World War II.
The first National Survey of Fishing and Hunting, sponsored by the
U.S. Bureau of Sport Fisheries and Wildlife, clearly
confirmed strong participation. It also revealed as early as 1955 that
angling expenditures must henceforth be reckoned in the billions of dollars.*

LAKE TROUT

PARTLY AS A RESULT of these findings, the Congress established a temporary (1959–1962) Outdoor Recreation Resources Review Commission to recommend a national program to accommodate future needs. The Commission issued 27 definitive study reports, three (Nos. 7, 19, and 20) providing pertinent data concerning fishing. A second (1960) and third (1965) National Survey of Fishing and Hunting bore out the continued strong growth of angling participation, and firmly established sport fishing as a significant element in the national economy.

A nationwide detailed survey of the habits and preferences of Americans engaged in outdoor recreation was conducted in 1960–61 by the U.S. Bureau of the Census. The survey (ORRRC Study Report 19) determined that about 35 percent of the U.S. population, 12 years of age and over (133 million), fished at least once during the period June 1960 to May 1961. These 47 million anglers fished an average of 11.9 days per year, with participation rates being highest in the South, and lowest in the Northeast. Fishing was found to be the preferred outdoor activity among 33 percent of the population.

The tabulated data revealed that about 26 percent of all fishing activity (man-days) occurred in the spring, 47 percent in summer, 18 percent in the fall, and 9 percent in the winter. Fishing participation during the winter was 16 percent in the South, compared to 4 percent in the Northeast, 6 percent in the North-Central States, and 7 percent in the West. There were about 3,700,000 persons who fished during the December-January-February period in the north-central and northeast regions; undoubtedly, the great majority were ice

fishermen. The study estimated that total annual man-days of fishing during 1960 equaled about 560 million (more recent data indicate that they had increased to 678 million by 1965).

A comparison of data from the three national surveys of fishing shows a strong growth trend for fishing participation in the United States that greatly exceeds that of additions to the general population. Such statistics, useful in helping to predict future demand, do not indicate possible influences of other forms of outdoor recreation on fishing activity, nor the motivating effects of current trends toward more leisure time, paid vacations, and higher incomes.

To provide some of those data, which are vital to sound planning for the future, the temporary Outdoor Recreation Resources Review Commission sponsored a special study of demand factors among American adults (18 years or older) by the University of Michigan Survey Research Center. The resulting study report (No. 20), which furnished the hardcore data for the basic ORRRC Report, revealed that 20 percent of all those interviewed had fished "often" (5 or more times), and 18 percent "a few times" (1 to 4 times) during the year 1959. On this basis, nearly 43 million adults wet a line during that year.

The report authors also ranked outdoor activities according to "involvement," based separately on prompted and on spontaneous mentions of activities of the interviewees. Fishing was found to be one of the most "involving" activities. The survey also attempted to define the extent to which people would like to increase their participation in the future, as a means of determining potential needs for facilities.

It would appear from these various

374

Various kinds of powerboats have become closely allied with angling.

data that facilities will have to be increased not only in accordance with population growth and to relieve present overcrowding, but also to allow for some rise in participation rates.

Interviewers first asked the people, "How do you usually spend most of your leisure time?" in order to focus on the regular day-to-day leisure patterns. Fish-

ing was the most frequently mentioned of all active sports; conclusion: ". . . swimming, hunting, and especially fishing seem to be of the greatest importance and salience. . . . That one out of six Americans spontaneously mention fishing in the context of questions asking about activities they engage in 'quite a lot,' would seem to attest to the impor-

375

At tournament time, beach buggies line up along the dunes.

The Bureau of Sport Fisheries and Wildlife published in 1966 the third of a series of National Surveys of Fishing and Hunting. It reported that 28,348,-000 habitual ("real" or "substantial") anglers—those folk 12 years or older, who participated at least three times, or who spent at least $5 during the year—devoted 522,759,000 recreational days out fishing and spent $2,925,304,-000 on their preferred means of outdoor recreation. In addition, 3,241,000 youngsters of ages 9 through 11 years also fished during some portion of 28,-265,000 recreational days in 1965. Thus, during that year, well over 31,589,000 habitual anglers 9 years or older fished during a total of more than 551,024,000 recreational days.

These data exclude the millions of angling youngsters under 9 years old and the added millions of incidental anglers of all ages—those fishing less frequently than some part of 3 days or spending less than $5 during 1965—who collectively complete the overall total of angling participants estimated by the Sport Fishing Institute.

One among every 10 women and girls in the general population fishes, while one among every three men and boys fishes; one among every four anglers is a woman or girl.

Primarily because of various traditional legal exclusions (too old, too young, property owners, disabled servicemen, aborigines, specified waters, etc.) only 59 percent of all habitual anglers 12 years or older were licensed in 1965. These include those various categories of saltwater fishermen who are now licensed in some manner in eight coastal States (Alabama, Alaska, California, Louisiana, North Carolina, Oregon, Texas, Washington).

tance of this recreational activity."

The report concluded with an analysis of camping, observing that proximity to water sport facilities is an important factor to consider in planning the location of additional camping areas; three-fourths of the campers interviewed went fishing.

The total number of angling participants, including those individuals of any age, who fished only occasionally, and/or spent little or virtually nothing in the process, was estimated by the Sport Fishing Institute to have been about 55 million during 1965!

An estimated 601,000 U.S. anglers fished in Canada (up 37 percent since 1960), some 138,000 fished in Mexico, and 57,000 fished in other foreign countries in addition to fishing in U.S. waters.

Freshwater supported 426,922,000 recreational fishing days of effort by 23,962,000 habitual anglers. They spent an average of $89 per person during the year or $4.98 per day. Saltwater supported 95,837,000 recreational fishing days by 8,305,000 habitual anglers. They spent an average of $96 per person in 1965 or $8.34 per day. Freshwater fishing generated $2,125,652,000 of gross business activity, compared with $799,-656,000 generated by saltwater fishing.

The overall total of angler expenditures for necessary goods and services (nearly $3 billion) was comprised of expenditures for: (1) primary fishing equipment—rods, reels, lures, tackle boxes, lines, landing nets, etc. (11.0 percent); (2) auxiliary equipment—boats, motors, boat trailers, camping gear, coolers, cameras, etc. (26.9 percent); (3) food and lodging—in excess of what would normally have been spent staying at home (15.2 percent); (4) transportation—largely out-of-pocket costs of operating motor vehicles, plus some travel on common carriers (14.7 percent); (5) fishing licenses and privilege fees (4.5 percent); and (6) bait, guides, and miscellaneous expenses (27.7 percent).

Among the 8,305,000 habitual saltwater anglers, some 4,486,000 fished exclusively in estuaries and coastal marine waters; the remaining 3,819,000 fished extensively in inland freshwaters as well. Over half of all saltwater anglers (4,-178,000) and of total marine angling activity (55,950,000 recreational days)

occurred on the Atlantic coast where annual angling costs, averaging $79.27 (about $5.92 per angler day), were lowest. Roughly one-fourth of all saltwater anglers (2,084,000) and marine angling activity (22,390,000 recreational days) occurred on the gulf coast where annual angling costs, averaging $84.50 (about $7.87 per angler day), were intermediate between East and West coasts.

The nearly one-fourth of saltwater anglers (2,043,000) and one-fifth of marine angling activity (17,497,000 recreational days) remaining were found on the Pacific coast. There, angling costs averaged $143.11 for the year (about $16.71 per angler day). The comparatively high costs associated with fishing in the Pacific Ocean were directly related to the larger, more seaworthy fishing craft required for the blue-water fishing prevailing there.

Boating, indeed, is so intimately involved with fishing generally as to be virtually synonymous during most of the time for a strong majority of boat users.

Many anglers begin with cane poles in still or sluggish waters.

377

To get a good taste of the wild, the angler comes equipped with tent, boat, and tackle.

A 1958 study of the marine market, conducted by Sindlinger and Company, Inc., New York City, for Popular Boating magazine, found that fishing was the most important specific use for boats. Some 14.7 million people were estimated to have used boats for fishing, 12.1 million went pleasure boating and cruising, 1.7 million were "interested" in water skiing, and 1.4 million used boats in duck hunting.

These estimates included extensive duplications of activities among individual boat users; this factor was recognized but the extent of multiple counting was not determined. Among the readers of Popular Boating magazine, with 331,000 boats in ownership in 1958, about 83 percent of boat owners indicated they used their boats for fishing.

A 1962 report of boating activity in

Oregon tended to substantiate the findings noted above, as well as extend them. In Oregon, over 86 percent of all boats under 21 feet (95 percent of all pleasure boats registered) were engaged in fishing at least part of the time during 1961. Over 47 percent were used over half of all boating time for fishing, while only 14 percent were not used for fishing at any time. With respect to larger boats, again, only some 14 percent were not used for some fishing at any time.

Fishing was the principal use reported (over half of all boat time involved) of the small boats, whether in rivers (46 percent), lakes and reservoirs (53 percent), or coastal waters or ocean (84 percent). Larger boats (over 21 feet long) were used for fishing 10 percent of the time in river situations, 35 percent of the time on lakes and reservoirs, and

378

78 percent of the time on coastal waters or ocean. All of the larger boats located in marine waters were used to some extent for fishing.

A special study of angling was prepared by the Bureau of Sport Fisheries and Wildlife for the Outdoor Recreation Resources Review Commission (Study Report No. 7), with advice and assistance from the Sport Fishing Institute. A major conclusion was that the number of anglers would probably increase 50 percent by 1976 and 150 percent by the year 2000. The U.S. population, by comparison, was estimated to increase by only 30 percent and by 98 percent, respectively, over 1960 figures. By century's end, the total of fisherman days was expected to be about three times what it was in 1960. (Results of a 1965 study of summertime outdoor recreation by the U.S. Bureau of Outdoor Recreation suggest, however, that this may prove conservative.) Then-current trends indicated, in round figures, that 63 million anglers would devote 1,300 million man-days of recreation to fishing in the year 2000.

The angling study team determined, among its many other important findings, that the average daily catch per angler was about 1.3 pounds of fish in freshwater and about 7 pounds of fish in saltwater (5 pounds on the Atlantic and gulf coasts; 15 pounds on the Pacific coast). Using these data, it is possible to calculate that total catch of fish by those anglers accounted for by the third National Survey of Fishing and Hunting was approximately 1.36 billion pounds in 1965. This consisted of about 644 million pounds of freshwater fish and about 716 million pounds of saltwater fish.

If we count the fishing of all anglers,

Tired of the struggle, a fortunate few fly in for relaxation.

regardless of their ages and frequency of fishing—about 50 million additional angler days—some 62 million pounds of freshwater fish and 42 million pounds of saltwater fish must be added. This brings the total sport catch to about 1.5 billion pounds, the vast majority of which were undoubtedly eaten by their captors. By comparison, the equivalent U.S. commercial catch of edible food fish fluctuates annually around 1.7 billion pounds, thereby indicating the substantial, if secondary, contribution to the national diet made by sport-caught fish.

It is equally possible, using these same data, to relate the gross expenditures of sport fishermen to their catches per angler day of fishing. It becomes clear,

379

Before lines can be wet, there's the chore of setting up a gravel-bar camp.

Wheels play a greater part in fishing than we generally recognize.

when this is done, that fishermen are voluntarily paying about $3.83 on the average to catch each pound of fresh-water fish they harvest. It becomes equally clear that anglers similarly expend an average of about $1.11 for each pound of saltwater fish they take along the Pacific coast. Correspondingly, they are paying about $1.30, on the average, for each pound of saltwater fish they harvest along the East and gulf coasts.

The ORRRC angling study report concluded that the heavy fishing demand expected to materialize in the future can be met with only slight reductions in the present average catch. New reservoirs are expected to add 10 million surface acres by 2000, doubling present impounded waters; these new waters will supply about one-third of the expected increase in fisherman-trips. Improvement of existing waters through better management, combined with the capacity of existing waters to absorb more fishing effort even without improvement, is anticipated to meet an additional one-third of increased demand. Marine waters can absorb the remaining one-third, provided that estuaries are not damaged or rendered unfit as spawning and nursery grounds, and anadromous species are not blocked by more man-made structures.

Essential requisites are that siltation and pollution must be prevented and controlled more effectively, fishery research must be expanded to provide bases for improved management, and the problem of getting adequate funds for these conservation programs must be solved.

At least 75 percent of the angling activity in 1960 occurred on public waters, and this percentage is expected to rise in the future.

The full economic significance of sport fishing in America is only partially revealed by findings from the three successive National Surveys of Fishing and Hunting made thus far. For example, a Special Study Committee sponsored by Resources for the Future (composed of geologists, biologists, engineers, agricultural economists, and general economists) undertook a sophisticated economic analysis of the benefits from different, often conflicting, uses of water in New Mexico. The study, published in 1963, found that water utilized in New Mexico for fishing and related recreational activities (camping and picnicking) adds $200 to $300 per acre-foot to the economy of that State.

By comparison, an acre-foot of water used by agriculture adds only $50, while the value added by industry is from $2,000 to $4,000 per acre-foot. This study, undertaken to determine the best possible uses that might be made of New Mexico's share of the San Juan River water, allocated water for agriculture, recreation, and industry in eight different proportions, and the future values of each allocation were projected. This required that present values of water be determined; of special significance were the economic values attributed to fishing, camping, and picnicking. Other water uses (for agriculture and industry) are normally emphasized to the detriment of recreational facilities.

Fishing, according to Committee Chairman Nathaniel Wollman (University of New Mexico), "is an activity that includes but goes beyond the acquisition of fish." Consequently, in a novel variant on customary philosophy, the surface area or stream length was used as a physical measure of the recreational resource of "fishing," rather than the number of fish awaiting capture or fish creeled. The value-added per acre-foot of new water allocated for fish and wildlife was estimated from the amount of such water, the total traffic in fisherman-days, and the value-added that could be attributed to the average fisherman-day. Being an intangible, the value-added for fishing was measured indirectly from the "fee" paid by the consumer for a day's fishing—the "fee" including food, shelter, transportation, equipment, and use of water.

In New Mexico, total expenditures per fisherman-day in 1962 amounted to $11.93 (resident, $9.93; nonresident, season, $19.02; nonresident, 5-day, $31.93). The percentage breakdown of angler-expenditures for fishing (exclusive of license fees) was as follows: ve-hicles, 25.5 percent; food, 16.5 percent; transportation, 15.5 percent; boats and motors, 12.7 percent; camping equipment, 9.8 percent; fishing tackle, 7.8 percent; lodging, 6.5 percent; special clothing, 2.2 percent; horses, etc., 1.1 percent; fees, 0.5 percent; other, 0.6 percent; and "bribe of wife," 1.6 percent.

By integrating fishing days per season, fishing intensity, amount of water, and amount of money spent per fisherman-day, the value-added per acre-foot of water in New Mexico was calculated to have been $264—a measurable contribution to economic welfare.

All in all, it is evident that sport fishing is a major element of outdoor recreation and tourism, that it generates a substantial amount of gross flow of dollars through the national cash register,

Boats come in a variety of sizes and styles.

and that it will probably expand three-fold to fourfold by century's end, not counting inflationary factors.

It may also be concluded that a considerable fraction of the gross expenditures by anglers generates substantial new income to large numbers of Americans engaged in the manufacturing and service industries that cater to angler demands throughout the Nation.

The extent of new income thereby created is no doubt approximately indicated by results of a statistical study of tourist expenditures conducted by Dr. Lewis C. Copeland, University of Tennessee. He showed that 9 million tourists spent $230 million in Tennessee in 1960, which total amounted to 6 percent of all retail trade in the State that year. The study emphasized the booster effect of tourist trade upon Tennessee business.

Dr. Copeland stated, as one conclusion in his report, that "every dollar spent by tourists [in Tennessee] generates 32 cents income for someone in Tennessee." It therefore requires, he said, "the visitation of [only] 85,000 tourists [to create] income of $294,000—[which is] the equivalent of the yearly income from the average [Tennessee] industrial plant." We have noted with respect to nationwide angling that gross expenditures attributable to fishing averaged $4.98 per day for freshwater and $8.34 per day for saltwater during 1965.

I would conclude, therefore, upon applying Dr. Copeland's 32 cents-per-dollar formula noted above, that each day's fishing by anglers nationwide probably generates something around $1.59 and $2.67 new income, respectively, to those Americans who serve in some manner the many needs of sport fishermen for a wide variety of durable goods, expendable supplies, and personal services they use when fishing.

Cash-and-Carry Fishing

by Willard T. Johns

*If you expect to catch fish every time you go fishing,
you're doomed to a frustrated existence. For, neither natural reproduction
nor hatchery-produced fish can insure a strike with every cast,
even in the most remote wilderness waters. For fish cost money, and there
are not enough of them (or of dollars) to provide unlimited catches
for every angler within easy distance from his home. This is especially
true for trout, which require clear, cool water of a
quality fast disappearing in or near our large metropolitan areas.
So many anglers have accepted "cash and carry" fishing—
an operation managed to assure a catch with a minimum amount of
time, effort, and skill for everyone paying a fee.*

FEE FISHING STREAM

THERE IS no simple or single definition for cash and carry fishing; it comes in many different forms. In many types, of course, there is some "cash" and some "carry" involved. Take party or charter boats, for instance. For a fee paid to the owner or operator of the boat, you are entitled to come aboard and be carried out to the fishing grounds, usually in saltwater along our coastlines. Millions of sportsmen enjoy this kind of fishing every summer, but it all depends on luck, skill, and the ability of the "skipper" as to whether or not your party or charter boat brings home fish.

Then there are the operators who charge for the use of facilities, such as fishing piers, boat launching ramps, or boats, which they own. But, again, you pay your money, and you take your chances on catching fish; the cost or fee is fixed, regardless of the number of fish you catch or don't catch. Even a wilderness fly-in or the employment of a fishing guide is a type of fee fishing, inasmuch as you pay for equipment and services provided to make your trip more enjoyable and possibly more successful. But, there is no guarantee that you will catch fish. Many sportsmen have had to smile and bear the experience of seeing their hard-earned dollars disappear in a storm that prevented them and their guides from fishing on a lake too rough for safety or a stream too high for successful fishing.

From the standpoint of guaranteed success, cash and carry fishing should be defined on the basis that you pay for the fish you carry home, rather than for the privilege, facilities, or guidance involved in catching them.

Years ago, and to this day, one type was membership in a private club. For $50 or $100 or $1,000 per year, a club member was able to fish a stretch of stream or a lake heavily stocked with lunker trout, and even more heavily posted against trespass by the general public. It was, and is, a very exclusive, highly expensive, but usually quite satisfactory way to go angling. Many clubs raise the fish in their own hatcheries; others purchase them from commercial hatcheries.

For those who can afford it, or for those lucky enough to be invited as a guest of a member, this is undoubtedly the sport of kings. There are thousands of such private clubs throughout the country; more will probably be formed in the years ahead.

But for the majority of America's anglers, such membership is beyond their means. For them, other types of cash and carry fishing are becoming increasingly popular.

Although this type of fishing comes in almost as many varieties as soups on the supermarket shelves, it is basically provided in two ways—either by private individuals offering a service and product for profit, or by local and State government agencies offering a fishing opportunity above and beyond what is commonly found in open waters. Both charge a fee; both may require a State fishing license. Generally, however, the operator is allowed in many States to conduct his business regardless of whether or not his customers are licensed fishermen.

First, let's look at the commercial establishment. One study made in 1961 showed there were about 1,500 such pond operations in the United States, with Pennsylvania having the greatest number, 238, and California next with 186. Most of these had been started after World War II, and undoubtedly the

386

Fishing is possible day and night on the charge-for-fun pier lit by electricity and moonglow.

total number now operating throughout the country is considerably higher. In that year, however, 55 percent handled trout only, 16 percent warm-water species, and 29 percent both. Operators usually charge 10 cents per inch of fish caught and kept, or $1 to $1.50 per pound. Many operators required that all fish caught be kept, regardless of size. Trout were typically stocked at 1,000 to 2,000 per acre, and were from 7 to 15 inches long. Most catch-out pond operators had less than 3 ponds, total-ing 4 acres, with annual incomes of under $3,000.

"Most of the folks who come here," I was told by one operator, John E. "Bud" Gingrich, of Richland, Pa., "have never fished before. In fact, I've been surprised to find that even among those who have had some fishing experience, 7 out of 10 never before caught a trout." Gingrich owns and operates Limestone Springs Trout Farm, Inc., a combination trout hatchery and fishing facility near Meyerstown, in the heart of the Penn-

The charterboat can well be worth its modest cost.

sylvania Dutch Country.

Limestone Springs offers both pond and stream fishing, in a beautiful setting, under surprisingly natural conditions. No admission fee is charged, but for every trout you carry home, the cash cost is $1 regardless of size or weight. The water is clear and cool (Limestone's water supply system produces a constant flow of 15,000 gallons per minute, at an average summer temperature maximum of 56 degrees, a winter temperature of 44 degrees); the trout are brightly colored and full of fight, and the average size runs between 10 and 14 inches. There are no restrictions on type of lure; during a recent visit I saw everything used from cheese to 22 dry flies. There is no closed season; Limestone is available 365 days each year. The only regulation is that you must keep every fish you catch.

Most of the 9,000 people who fish at Limestone Springs, according to Gingrich, live within a 50-mile radius of the

facility, although there have been visitors from as far away as New England. Even the New Englanders must be surprised to find their native square-tails in such a place, complete with deep green bodies mottled in black with bright scarlet spots, fins, and upper bellies.

"We're now stocking brook trout almost entirely," Bud told me. "Most people seem to prefer them over rainbows and browns. They look better, and they taste better. Rainbows seem to become shy of so many lines and lures passing over them each day, while the brown trout is just too smart for the average angler."

Before becoming a fishing operator, Gingrich was in the florist business. On the day I visited him, he was sitting quietly beside one of the rearing pools in the hatchery which supplies trout not only for his pond and stream, but also to other clubs, private waters, fishing derbies, or fee areas throughout the mid-Atlantic region. In introducing myself, I asked what he was thinking about in such a quiet, dejected manner.

"I was just thinking about getting back in the florist business," he answered. Then he pointed to the rearing pool behind him, which was completely devoid of fish or water. "Last night some debris got into our water supply system and raceways. It finally lodged over the intake for this pool, and I've just lost more fish than I care to think about."

There are other problems in trout farming and fee fishing. One of the most unusual, at least at Limestone Springs, is depredation on fingerling fish by blackbirds. Bud told me that several years ago blackbirds caught an estimated 29,000 fingerling trout out of a rearing pool which originally contained 65,000. Even as we were talking I could see several helping themselves to a few young trout, carrying them off in their sharp beaks to feed their young or themselves.

Despite his losses, Bud Gingrich was greeting visitors to his operation with a smile, later that day. He got into this business, he had told me, because he liked to fish, and because he liked to see other people become interested in the sport. For Bud Gingrich, an avocation had become not just a vocation but a sincere desire to help people find an enjoyable, healthy, and satisfying form of outdoor recreation. Many of those he was helping that day were fathers, bringing their children outdoors to teach them the basics of fishing and to give them a thrill that would last a lifetime—the thrill of catching their first trout. I couldn't help but feel that, even though Meyerstown is a long way from the wilderness streams and lakes of Potter County or the Arctic Circle, this little backyard setting was giving rise to a new generation of anglers every day of the year.

Government operated fee fishing lakes or streams are becoming increasingly popular in a few of the States which have tried them. Lake Murray, a 150-acre San Diego, Calif., water supply reservoir, is a good example. The lake once furnished sufficiently good largemouth bass and bluegill fishing to support 7,000 days of angling annually. Visitors were charged a daily fee of $1 for patrol and sanitary services.

Then in 1959, trout were stocked in the lake. By 1961, attendance increased to an astonishing 50,000 angler-days, in spite of a two-third reduction in the length of the open season. The catch jumped from 7,000 to 50,000 pounds of fish. Catches averaged nearly a pound of trout per angler-day. The entire operation was financially self-supporting with no increase in fees, because increased attendance spread the costs over a broader base.

At the other end of the line—across the Nation in Virginia—the State's Commission of Game and Inland Fisheries operates several pay-as-you-go fishing projects. Among them is a 4-mile

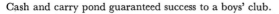

Cash and carry pond guaranteed success to a boys' club.

Operators include largemouths and bluegills in many fee fishing waters.

stretch of Big Tumbling Creek on Clinch Mountain. During 5 months of operation in 1964, anglers caught well over 44,000 (86 percent) of nearly 52,000 trout released in the stream. The take-home catches averaged two or three trout per day of angling. In addition to having an appropriate State fishing license, fishermen were charged a $1 daily fishing fee.

In Missouri projects have been equally as successful and attractive to trout fishermen. The State, of course, has very little, if any, open water suitable to trout production or stocking—the chief reason the Missouri Conservation Commission decided to provide cash and carry trout fishing in the first place. According to fishery superintendent Paul G. Barnickol, there were about 25,000 anglers when the first season opened on the State's four trout management fee areas in 1949–50. By 1959–60, 139,041 had used the areas. Over 234,000 pounds of creel-sized trout (one-half pound or larger) were released in these four areas in 1959. Releases were made the day before opening, and each day thereafter.

Fee fishing is not restricted to trout, however. Untold numbers of farmers

have opened their farm ponds to the public, often charging a daily fee to cover maintenance and stocking costs or to realize a little additional income in their overall farm operation. Untold thousands of fishermen, young and old, have found that it is good fun to catch largemouth bass and bluegills at some nearby farm pond. And in some parts of the country, that lowly, wonderful creature—the catfish—has become the center of attraction at some cash and carry lakes.

Down in Alabama, for example, fishery biologists at the Auburn Fisheries Experiment Station are sold on the suitability of channel catfish for some managed ponds. They stocked a 12.4 acre lake in February 1958 with 2,000 3-inch finglerlings per acre. These little cats were fed pelleted fish food daily at rates varying from 5 to 25 pounds per acre. The pond was opened in September—8 months later—when the catfish averaged 0.7 pound each. In the following year, 579 fishermen caught 1,292 pounds of channel catfish, 37 pounds of largemouth bass, and 27 pounds of other fish per surface acre. A daily fishing fee of $1 was charged, so the average price of catfish to the angler was 46 cents per pound. They caught 62 percent of the catfish stocked. Deducting costs for fertilizer, feed, fingerlings, and labor, the experiment netted $112 per acre.

Cash and carry fishing obviously can be profitable, and it can be fun. For the urban dweller, hard-pressed for time, transportation, and finances, to make a fishing trip to the Nation's famous angling meccas, a fee fishing lake, pond, or stream within a few hours drive may be the answer to their dreams.

"Of course," says Alex Calhoun, "personal standards for acceptable fishing conditions vary considerably." Calhoun is chief of the California Department of Fish and Game, Inland Fisheries Branch, and he was speaking to the U.S. Trout Farmers Association at its annual convention in Las Vegas in 1967. "We all know purists," he continued, "who will fish only with flies, on scenic, uncrowded waters. But many urban anglers these days are eager to catch large, desirable fish under rather unnatural circumstances."

If you're one of the latter, cash and carry or fee fishing is probably the most economical, easiest, and quickest way to do it. For that reason, the future for these types of operations is bright. It will be impossible for State and Federal agencies to provide that kind of fishing for the Nation's growing army of anglers. All their hatcheries put together can't fill America's millions of surface acres of fishing waters with the number and size of fish—at least not at present or foreseeable license fees. And the days when naturally produced fish, especially trout, can satisfy all of the anglers all of the time are gone forever, especially in or near our large metropolitan centers.

Fee fishing pond—simple tackle, easy-to-catch fish.

The Bait Industry

by Gene L. Letourneau

*That little earthworm the "complete angler" once depended upon
has grown into a giant as sport fishermen have elevated bait into a
major industry. Only a few years ago Arkansas producers
were using over 13,000 acres of ponds for raising only golden shiners—
and this wasn't enough! Another couple of thousand acres produced
fathead minnows, goldfish, and Israeli carp which are also used for bait.
Although Arkansas is perhaps the center for bait fish culture,
Missouri, Texas, Oklahoma, Ohio, Arizona, California, and Louisiana
produce large numbers of minnows, at least partly because of the
scarcity of wild bait fish. Nature just doesn't produce enough to
satisfy the demand. In some States wild bait fish
have been so seriously depleted that regulations now protect them.*

BAIT AND TACKLE SHOP

THE 1966 PRODUCTION of bait fish in Arkansas amounted to 3 million pounds worth $5,325,000. The gross return per acre for golden shiners was $300. Goldfish returned a higher gross, estimated to be $1,000 per acre. Gross per acre returns for rice in 1966 was $191, for oats, $35, and for irrigated soybeans, $70.

One reason for the widespread production of bait fish is the scarcity of wild ones. There aren't enough to satisfy the demand.

Thus bait production can be a profitable business. To cite another example, a producer moved into an area near Sacramento, Calif., dug 100 ponds, and stocked them with golden shiners and fathead minnows. In one season he was unable to supply the demand.

One also gets a good idea as to the returns from bait from the fact that in Maine diggers of sandworms and bloodworms were paid $1,327,210 for their labors in 1967.

In 1964 about 85 million live shrimp and 520,000 pounds of dead shrimp with a combined wholesale value of $1 million were sold by the bait industry in Florida.

On the Texas coast that same year, in Galveston Bay alone, over 850,000 pounds of shrimp with a retail value of about $1 million were taken for bait.

In southern California, with its large population of sport fishermen, bait becomes so scarce during peak seasons that it is necessary to import longjaw mudsuckers, a saltwater fish, from Baja California. This movement of live bait to areas of critical need can cover vast distances. For example, baitfish are shipped into southern California from points as far away as Texas and Missouri. The export demand has been so great that some watersheds in Utah are virtually depleted of small suckers and minnows.

Actual production figures are not available for many States, but California has one of the better documented bait industries. In 1966 more than 13.5 million pounds were taken from the coastal areas. Nearly all of this catch was anchovy. About 160,000 pounds con-

Some like to seine their own bait.

Marine worms can be had up and down the east coast.

Golden shiners are the basis for a large bait industry.

sisted of other species such as Pacific herring, jack mackerel, squid, and sardines.

New Hampshire, a State always on the ball when it comes to sensing the needs of anglers, didn't wait for complaints about availability of bait. It published a list of bait dealers on the seacoast who usually have a steady supply of clamworms, as well as shrimp and alewives. Copies of the list are available free to anglers from the Concord-based department.

Availability of bait at dockside has improved greatly within the past few years, with the construction of modern marinas and better supervision of them. It is a rarity to find a popular landing without a good supply of bait used locally. Modern transportation has made it possible to express worms from Maine to the Pacific coast or shrimp from Alaska's inland passage to Montauk Point in New York overnight.

Wisconsin and Michigan anglers prefer local species of bait fish for walleye, northern pike, and muskellunge. Resident anglers at Moosehead Lake, Maine's largest body of water, stick by native shiners for trout, salmon, and other large fish.

Clams—soft, hard, and sea—are used primarily for bottom species by salt-

water anglers from Maine to Virginia. Shrimp is the favorite from the Carolinas southward throughout the gulf and is used on everything from weakfish to tarpon.

Seaworms, both sand and blood, are a favorite bait for most small game fish and used from Maine down through Delaware. The seaworm now also is becoming popular in the Chesapeake Bay area, and Hal Lyman, publisher of *Salt Water Fishing* magazine, says that the demand is exceeding the supply.

This probably brought about the 1967 strike of Maine diggers. According to a veteran digger, "It became obvious that the returns for labor were not adequate." When he started several years back, diggers were getting $2 per hundred worms. An average low tide "dig" totaled from 1,000 to 1,500 worms. Normally only one tide can be used as darkness precludes working both.

The strike boosted the diggers' pay to $3 a hundred. Demands for the Maine worms have increased so fast that the supply has shown signs of diminishing. The worms, according to this digger, are running smaller (they must be at least 4 inches in length).

The Maine worms are usually packed in boxes of 250. In 1967 California anglers began asking for them. As a

395

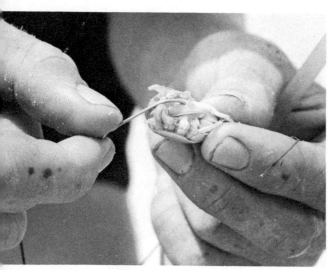

Mole crab is a good bait for surf fishing.

result some retailers were getting a dollar for 20 of them.

Value of the worm harvest in 1967 was set by the Sea and Shore Fisheries Department of Maine at $834,826 for bloodworms, $492,384 for sandworms.

Cut bait runs the gamut all over the East coast, ranging from herring used for cod to mullet for nearly everything that swims below the Virginia capes. These bait fish also are used whole for both big and small game species.

From north to south on the Atlantic, the most popular baits seem to be herring, mackerel, mummichogs, mullet, balao—all of which are plentiful except the balao. The latter also is a popular bait as far north as Newfoundland and south to the Bahamas. The balao are being flown from Florida and command a good price anywhere. They also are popular in Bermuda where the sport fishing industry is growing them in a spectacular manner. Both balao and mackerel scad, however, can be caught off that island.

Mullet, cut or whole, and shrimp are preferred baits for everything from tarpon to redfish on the gulf coast. Sardines and anchovies are favored in California for yellowtail and albacore. For Pacific salmon of all species, herring (either whole or cut) are widely used.

Supplies of anchovies and sardines on occasion are short when the demand is high. Herring are usually available, and one handler has packed them in Maine to ship to the Pacific coast.

Eels, live or frozen, the whole critters or skins, have become a popular striped bass bait in the Northeast and are also being used offshore for big game fish.

Squid, mackerel, small bonito are used when available, but these are mostly localized baits used for such species as the tuna, marlin, and sailfish.

The process of stripping large bait fish for skip bait has become popular in sailfish or marlin waters, and almost any species of small fish is used for this purpose.

Veteran saltwater fishermen prefer fresh bait, but the day when they could run up to a dragger and get a well full of ground fish to use as chum is about over. Anchovy (known there as hog-

Mullet, crab, and clams are standbys for bait in many areas.

mouth fry), smelt, sand lances, and menhaden, incidentally, are popular chum material.

The bait business is becoming better organized in many sections of the country. The producers are uniting for better returns, and handlers are getting the bait to the consumers when it is needed.

Lack of publicity for outlets, however, is a definite weakness. For example, whether you're on the Maine, New Jersey, or Carolina coast, you're lucky if you spot a sign indicating where bait can be purchased. A series of advertisements in local newspapers would be of great help to the anglers.

Coastal anglers take it for granted that someone at the dock will know where to get bait. Generally, in populated areas, this is true, but it doesn't hold from coast to coast.

Freshwater situations are entirely different. The sporting-camp operator is usually the bait dealer. He must have a source of supply of hellgramites, bait fish, frogs, grasshoppers (in season), and worms, both earth and night crawlers.

Admittedly not all bait outlets make money on the product. I know some who carry baits just to satisfy regular customers and rely on sales and rental of tackle and boats and other equipment for their profits.

Then too, it is not easy to enter the bait field, particularly as a producer because know-how is hard to come by. States should follow the lead of Arkansas by providing knowledge on fish culture, particularly the raising of bait. They should also offer tips on better handling, storage, and marketing procedures.

There are some bait fish that can withstand rough handling and remain alive, but research should also be conducted to

Nightcrawlers help catch almost any kind of fish.

turn up more that can live through the rigors of processing for marketing.

In addition, certain bait fish pose a threat to other fish when released into lakes, ponds, and rivers. We thus also need research to turn up more varieties that will not become a nuisance. In the meantime, some States have banned the use of certain live bait fish in some of their waters.

This has increased the demand for processed bait fish, especially smelts, which are favorites with landlocked salmon and brook, rainbow, and brown trout.

397

Shrimp are readily available even from supermarkets—universal saltwater bait.

Michigan's great success with coho salmon undoubtedly will result in increasing demands for bait, but the situation there is well in command as alewives, on which the salmon feed, can be obtained at dockside.

Smelts and some other bait fish can be processed easily even by a novice. In the Northeast, smelts are placed in jars in a solution of one part formaldehyde to four parts of water. Adding a dash of alcohol (any kind) will help keep the bright colors of the fish longer.

Incidentally, after the smelt spawning run in the spring in some lakes there is a fairly large smelt kill. Most large fish will not feed on the dead or dying smelt, yet they will strike the processed smelt trolled as sewed-on bait.

This is the exception to the rule. Usually, you cannot fool all the fish all of the time with any kind of bait.

PROBLEMS TO OVERCOME

Threat of Technology

by Michael Frome

*One of the more revealing records of the damage to water and its
fishery is found in the Midwest. Sixty years ago, Dr. Victor Shelford,
an ecologist at the University of Chicago, conducted a survey
of fish in small streams in the Chicago area; he carefully identified
exact localities and species he collected.
Fifty years later, Dr. Rezneat M. Darnell, of Marquette University,
visited all of Dr. Shelford's stations on one of the small streams near
Waukegan, the Dead River, hoping to determine the
natural changes in the stream in half a century.*

RED DRUM AND CROAKERS

HIS STUDIES of Shelford's records and museum collections did not reveal so much of the natural changes as they did the deterioration of an aquatic environment through human encroachment. Fifty years ago the stream flowed through a forested area which paid out its water gradually and maintained a rather even flow. The water was clear and supported a population of fish characteristic of such environments. Today it flows largely through treeless suburban backyards. Following heavy rains the stream rises to torrential flow and subsides just as quickly afterwards. During summer drought the upper reaches dry up completely.

Farther down, the streambed contains a series of disconnected pools, receptacles for effluent from nearby cesspools. Organic material from the cesspools greatly reduces the oxygen supply of the water and creates a malodorous health hazard. Where roads cross the stream, one encounters the conglomerate human trash that characterizes the age of technology. The downstream section flows through a park, but human handiwork is evident in many subtractions from (and a few additions to) the original fish fauna.

Not all the changes can be laid directly to man, simply because there is not enough knowledge of the complex interactions involved. But wholesale elimination or reduction of native species is obvious. The change can be termed, at best, the substitution of a pollution-tolerant, garbage-feeding community in place of the original clean-water community.

The same story is being repeated in many other localities in America—in the name of progress, profitability, "increasing the tax base," attracting industry, and a thousand other explanations that serve a few and go unchallenged by the many. In most cases, no one is watching. The tragic history of the symbolically-named Dead River has found its way into the records of civilization. "It must stand somewhat alone," as Dr. Darnell has written, "as a monument to human extravagance, a wretched byproduct of the American way of life."

There are countless brooks in the cities and some still flow, but technology has shown the way to encase each, in a culvert or completely within a submerged concrete pipe. By the same token, highways constructed to the highest technical standards also have been endowed with culverts that block fish passage. Siltation resulting from dredging and filling for new roads has destroyed fish habitat; and the widening of stream channels by highway builders has created warmer shallower water.

Pollution induced by technology comes in many forms, but a group of the more formidable ones are the industrial wastes—acids, alkalies, heavy metals, and heat—which are toxic to fish. They are discharged into streams and lakes by a variety of industries, sometimes virtually untreated. Steel mills, paper plants, mines, refineries, food processing plants—you name them, any of a multitude of enterprises going full steam and growing in America—generate thousands of tons of such wastes.

Different poisons are continually turning up. The industrial discharge of mercury into waterways for example, forced more than 20 States to impose fishing curbs in 1970.

Industrial wastes like these caused at least half the 9 million fish-kills in 1966. Kills by municipal discharges

A 1970 Louisiana off-shore oil well fire and subsequent spill threatened fishing and waterfowl along the mouth of the Mississippi.

Green areas show dying mangroves resulting from diking, dredging, and filling in a Florida estuary. In this infrared aerial, red means healthy vegetation.

these wastes produced overenrichment, reducing oxygen to a level at which fish cannot survive.

Eutrophication is a natural process. Spread over many centuries or millenia, the gradual accumulation of nutrients and sediments ages a lake and ultimately extinguishes life within it. It is said that a lake has a normal lifespan of about a million years. In the past decades, however, the aging process has been accelerated by man's helping hand.

At the beginning of this century, for instance, the condition of the Great Lakes was not much different from that when the last glaciers receded about 11,000 years ago. The lakes were teeming with fish. Today Lake Erie may be beyond retrieval—well on its way to becoming virtually a ghost lake, filled with debris and detergents, devoid of useful freshwater life. Lake Michigan is well on its way to the same fate. Even if all human polluting activity stopped at once, it might take 500 years to restore Lake Erie to its condition of 25 years ago, and 100 years to restore Lake Michigan—if they can be restored at all.

There are many varieties of trout in the country, all requiring clean, cold waters for survival, but uncontrolled hydraulic mining, pouring silt into receiving waters, has eliminated many trout streams.

In the Pacific Northwest, millions of dollars have been spent to aid anadromous salmon and steelhead trout to reach their spawning grounds in the mountains and for their offspring to return to the Pacific Ocean. Erosion silt, however, generated by logging operations and mining wastes on both private and public lands, work against these efforts. Trout and salmon waters have been destroyed or rendered marginal.

were second, and agricultural operations third. More than 11½ million fish were killed in 40 States in 1967, an increase of 21 percent over 1966. Industrial pollution again led in the number of kills and dead fish reported—139 cases with more than 8 million fish eliminated. Agricultural operations moved into second place ahead of the cities.

In one devastating swoop, a million fish were killed by mine drainage in Pennsylvania, when heavy rains washed mine acid deposits into the Allegheny River. In Florida, another million perished when Lake Apopka received effluents from a citrus processing plant and drainage from farms containing pesticides and fertilizers. Nutrients in all

Water temperature exerts a profound influence on aquatic life. Uncontrolled high water temperature—"thermal pollution"—is one of the contemporary threats. It acts to kill fish by deactivating enzymes and stimulating production of toxic materials within the bodies. It bars movement of migrant fish. It prevents production of desirable game species and completely alters the ecological life community of a stream.

For example, the Columbia River has been warming steadily, due possibly to the retention of water by increasing numbers of dams or possibly to the discharge of nuclear waste heat from the atomic reactors at Hanford, Wash. Whatever the cause, the river-warming process has stimulated the spread of columnaris, a formerly rare, but deadly, bacterial fish disease. Consequently, mortalities have been extensive among salmon climbing toward ancestral spawning grounds.

Now additional proposed construction of nuclear power plants would raise water temperature of the Columbia to 85° F., at least 5° above the maximum that salmon and steelhead can tolerate for even a few hours. The prospect for the anadromous fish is far from bright, unless Oregon and Washington soon agree that the temperature of the Columbia must not be allowed to rise over 68° maximum.

A 2-year study is now underway by the Department of the Interior on the biological effects of thermal inputs into the Columbia, marking one of the first broad investigations into all aspects of this factor on the aquatic environment.

In some cases a slight increase in water temperature may be beneficial to fish and fishing, but we are now moving rapidly into the era of large nuclear

Pollution is as close as your front yard.

power plants, which discharge far more waste heat, or thermal water effluent, than anything in conventional steam plants today. No substitute has yet been found that equals water for cooling purposes, and virtually all the large freshwater flow sites have already been tagged for possible use.

Although many questions are still to be answered about thermal pollution, it is conceivable that artificial cooling lakes or recirculation of water in air-cooled towers before discharge could reduce or eliminate pollution; there is no reason why technology cannot be employed to protect as well as to endanger the fishery resource, but there is no time to be lost.

Unfortunately, the trend of the times is more typified by the authority granted by the State of Florida to a private util-

405

Pollutants, including domestic and industrial wastes, are responsible for large fish kills.

ity company to construct a nuclear power plant on the shore of Biscayne Bay, an important estuary for marine life forms, and an exceptional source of sport and commercial fishing. Construction and operation of atomic powered generating plants, incidentally, is licensed first by the U.S. Atomic Energy Commission. However, control of water pollution arising in such plants is not presently clearly established and is only being considered by Congress.

Like thermal pollution, the full effects of many pesticides are not known. But no intensive research is required to recognize that improperly applied pesticides cause spectacular mass deaths of fish, as well as delayed damage to reproductive capabilities of fish, birds, and mammals. The unsolved mystery is the ultimate impact on mankind of pesticide

residues lingering in soil, water, air, and animal tissues.

Before World War II pesticides were nonpersistent, being derived from natural organics, such as pyrethrins which come from dried flowers of chrysanthemums and nicotine-sulfate from tobacco-type plants. In recent years, however, the skills of technology have enabled 8,000 firms to produce a wide range of chemical compounds—variously called insecticides, rodenticides, herbicides, fungicides, and fumigants for use on farm, forest, and garden—for which the American public pays over a billion dollars a year. Pesticides today are in every major river system of the country. They have reached the polar regions and distant parts of the most distant ocean.

Fish life is very sensitive to pesticides. The pesticide may enter unicellular or-

406

Waste organic matter has developed excessive growth of bacteria that are causing fin rot in bluefish.

ganisms at the base of the food chain and gradually accumulate through the biological systems. Or the poison may enter the body of a fish through the gills. It then may act on the blood, the nervous system, or on other organs. Small fish are eaten by large fish, large fish are eaten by birds, such as the osprey and eagle, transmitting the poison to the top of the aquatic chain. Pesticides may not kill on the first go-round, but they may appear in milk and eggs or accumulate in animal fat.

In one celebrated case, in order to control a troublesome hatching insect at Clear Lake, Calif., the water was treated with insecticide called DDD to yield a concentration of 0.02 parts per million. Presently plankton accumulated residues at 5 ppm. Fish ate the plankton and concentrated DDD in their fat at levels up to 2,500 ppm, but they did not die. Grebes and diving birds fed on the fish and died—the concentration in grebe tissue was 1,600 ppm.

Losses of birds can hardly escape notice, unlike great kills of plankton. Nevertheless, laboratory tests show that chlorinated hydrocarbons—DDT, dieldrin, toxaphene, lindane, chlordane, aldrin, and heptachlor—at a concentration of 1 ppm can decrease plankton growth and reproduction by 50 to 90 percent, thus wiping out an entire crop of food at the base of the aquatic chain.

Pesticides have become voting members of the marine and coastal community. They cast their ballots whenever man exercises direct application to control mosquitoes, flies, and weeds in marshes and bays. They arrive like carpetbaggers, riding the rivers and the

407

winds. They overrule some of the most valuable species of fish and shellfish—one part of DDT in a billion parts of water will kill a blue crab in 8 days; such other estuarine creatures as shrimp, mollusk, salmon, oysters, mussels, and clams are also highly sensitive.

In all ways, estuaries are undergoing the most intensive exploitation. The sheltered coastal bays, shallow sounds, creeks, mudflats, sandflats, and marshes—the life community where river currents merge with the tides of the sea—are being banished to oblivion by dredging and landfills in order to make way for industrial sites, massive real estate developments, navigation channels, oil exploration, marinas, military bases, and garbage dumps.

Estuaries are immensely productive. They mix freshwater with mineral-rich seawater and organic products of underwater decay. The fertility of the estuarine zone is evident in its large populations of wildlife: song birds, shore birds, waterfowl, and mammals.

In addition, most species that provide much of saltwater fishing spend at least part of their lives in the estuaries feeding on insects, mollusks, and crustaceans. Flounders, croakers, drums, shad, spotted seatrout (a top ranking fish in South Atlantic and gulf coast waters), striped bass, even young barracuda, and tarpon are dependent on the coastal bays, lagoons, and tidal rivers for spawning or feeding or temporary shelter in their rhythmic migrations to the sea.

Thus, we really should appreciate the tidewater marsh; the long, fertile tidewater bordering the Atlantic, in particular, stands out as one of America's natural treasures, fully comparable to the Great Barrier Reef of Australia.

However, tidal wetlands are ridiculed by special interests, their technologists and apologists, as "wastelands" and "cesspools." Thousands of precious miles have been destroyed along the Atlantic and gulf coasts, while California has lost two-thirds of its estuary habitat.

San Francisco, as an example, was the most important fishing port on the West coast at the turn of the century, the home base of the famed whaling fleet that roved the Pacific, as well as of the oystermen who farmed the bay. Even as recently as the early 1930's, it ranked as the most important commercial port. Oysters were harvested annually in amounts ranging between 10 to 15 million pounds and softshell clams up to 300,000 pounds. Since then an estimated 83 percent of estuarine area has been destroyed in San Francisco Bay. The oysters, the clams, the links in the food chain of life for fish are now gone.

The largest bay in Texas, at the mouth of the Trinity River at Galveston, has been a major center of sport fishing, and the source of 85 percent of all oysters harvested in Texas. This bay, too, is endangered. A combination of five companies is in the midst of the largest dredging operation in the Nation—if not the world—a 7-year program designed to clean out the reefs of oyster shells for use in cement, road building, and chemical industries, and threatening a future of sterility for Galveston Bay.

In Florida, the vogue among developers is to build new land for "Venetian-type" housing projects. The fill for the land comes by drag lining estuarine bottoms. In Tampa Bay, dredge and fill operations were authorized over the protests of the National Audubon Society, conservation organizations, and the Bureau of Sport Fisheries and Wildlife.

408

The magnificent coho fishery created in Lake Michigan by successful transplants is being menaced by pesticides.

After 10 years of drag lining, the bay was found to be seriously affected. And the feeding grounds for one of the most important colonies of white ibis left in North America was undermined.

The Department of the Army has jurisdiction over navigable waters, assigned to it by a law of 1899, and the Army Corps of Engineers thus has the responsibility for issuing permits for dredging, filling, and excavation. The Department of the Interior, however, carries the responsibilities to control and prevent pollution in the Nation's waterways and to conserve the Nation's fish and wildlife resources. After a lengthy sequence of disasters, marked by technological primacy and unilateral decisions by the Army Engineers, the two Departments reached agreement in 1967 to coordinate their efforts. The agreement provides the mechanism for consultation between the Departments, for advice to be provided by fish and wildlife and pollution tech-

nicians; although the Corps continues to have the final word, the threat of technology appears to have been tempered with balance and reason.

The Estuary Protection Act, adopted by Congress and signed by the President in August 1968, affords the means to inventory and define the fundamental values and potentials of all estuaries, whether for wildlife, recreation, minerals, or development. It provides for Federal, State, and local cooperative action to protect, conserve, and restore estuaries. It is a promising major forward step in the age of mechanization.

The Estuary Act demonstrates what can be done, once we recognize that technical knowledge no longer guarantees social advancement, that we must reckon with the consequences of technology. Some good things are being done—the record is not all bad. Fish ponds in the South are producing as much as a ton of fish per acre of water.

409

We are raising fish in rice-growing areas, and farming oysters and shrimp. Reservoirs and lakes are being stocked with carefully selected organisms to fill out a food chain as fishing has become an increasingly important feature in management.

And passage of the Water Quality Act of 1965, with provision for establishment of water quality standards for interstate and coastal waters, irrespective of the sources of pollution, has marked the beginning of a new era in water management. But the major challenge lies ahead.

"Our technology has outpaced our understanding, our cleverness has grown faster than our wisdom," Dr. Roger Revelle declared, while serving as chairman of the National Committee for the International Biological Program.

"Because of our limited understanding of the relationships among living things, we are limited in our ability to predict the effects of technical change, or to help the technologists conserve the values and utilize the abundance of the world of life. Our goal should not be to conquer the natural world, but to live in harmony with it. To attain this goal we must learn how to control both the external environment and ourselves. Especially we need to learn how to avoid irreversible change . . ."

Our superstandard of living may require super sources of energy, as we are often reminded, but there is now no way out except the firm exercise of discipline over production. The discharges of sewage and chemical wastes, dredging, diking, filling of wetlands, pesticides, construction of supertankers that allow for superdisasters—these and other interventions are destroying the life and richness of natural waters.

410

Above all, a good fishing stream can be maintained only with a steady flow of clean, clear water. To keep the waterway clean requires wise land use and management. When soils erode down a hillside into a stream, when pollution destroys water quality, fishermen suffer along with all other users.

Thus, science and technology must transcend the boundaries of river systems and drainages. They must embrace the physical, chemical, and biological qualities of land and water, the moral qualities of man, coordinating demands and demanding restraint where needed. Technology need not be a threat; it can be a boon in the true progress of civilization, providing it honors the integrity of the life community.

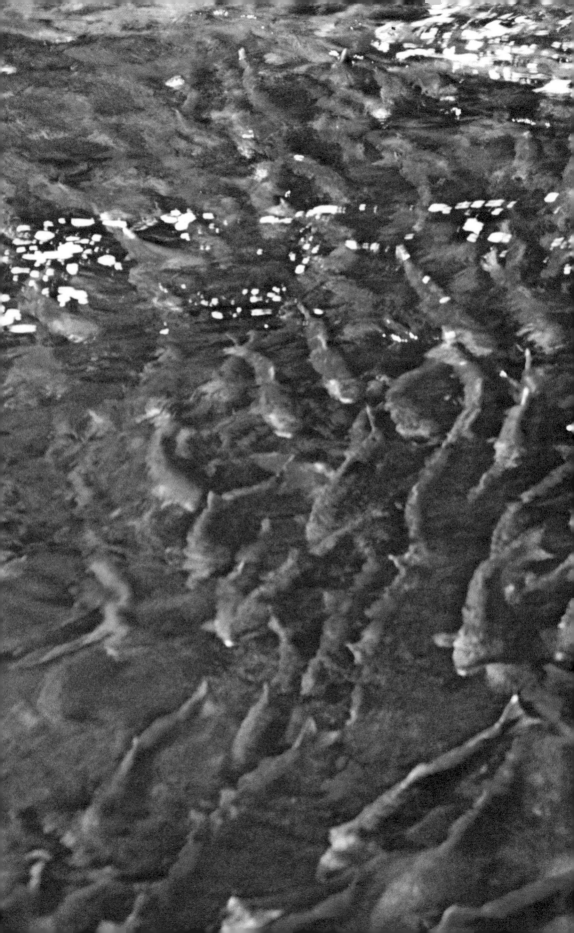

A Fish Looks at Multiple Use

by Willis King

Like the air we breath and the soil beneath our feet,
water is vital to our existence; and like the other resources, it is
subject to many, diverse uses, some of which consume it,
while others do not degrade its equality. It may be changed physically
or chemically, sometimes for good, sometimes for worse,
thereby affecting all living organisms that dwell within and depend
upon it. So far, multiple use has not drastically altered
the oceans; they are still a place for sustained growth of many fish,
as they are still relatively unpolluted (except for coastal areas and
despite occasional spills of oil or chemicals).
But few of our inland waters or estuaries have remained as they were
when white men invaded the North American Continent.

MIGRATING SOCKEYE SALMON IN ALASKA

WITH SETTLEMENTS along the water courses and the coastal areas, rapid population increases, and growing industrialization, changes in environment were inevitable. Many of these changes have not been favorable to fish.

For example, migrating salmon, striped bass, or shad entering the mouth of a river or an estuary almost certainly face critical conditions. Estuaries are perhaps the most delicately balanced of aquatic environments. Man and his governments have been negligent in protecting these waters, and often destructive. The Soil Conservation Service estimates that 1 billion tons of soil in the United States alone are annually washed from the place of origin downstream by flowing waters, often choking mouths of rivers, covering gravel beds, and filling marshes with smothering silt. Silt and mud in the water prevent fish foods from living and the fish from finding its food and reproducing.

Even more insidious is the practice of making an estuary the depository of pesticides and chemicals released or applied on the watershed hundreds of miles upstream. Fish kills in the lower Mississippi River in the winter of 1963–64, estimated at 5 million, were traced to a deposit of endrin in the Memphis, Tenn., area. The chemical was dumped into a tributary without thought of downstream effects on fish and aquatic life. It found its way into the river and was picked up by feeding fish. Thus using the waterways for disposal of untreated chemical wastes or using the chemicals without considering their effects on the water and aquatic life can be lethal and is intolerable.

The high real estate value of water front property, plus inadequate laws and regulations to protect it, have in recent years led to a loss of more than 7 percent or 568,800 acres of estuaries important to fish as spawning sites, as nursery areas, and in the production of food organisms. Preempting the shorelines, building various structures, dredging, and filling bring changes and losses of habitat that so far we do not know how to replace.

To striped bass, for example, an estuary is all important. The shallow waters just above the brackish zone are the nursery areas where small fish feed during their first summer. Adults live in the estuary, except when they are on their spawning migration up a nearby river, or when the occasional fish takes to the ocean for distant travels. The marginal zones of shallow waters, with their usual beds of vegetation, are extremely important as producers of insects, crustaceans, and small fish—the food supply for larger fish.

Where man has filled the estuary with mud, pesticides, industrial chemicals, and wastes, or covered the banks with debris and bulkheads, the numbers of fish that the water will support must certainly decline. If conditions become bad enough, fish can no longer use the area, and that population eventually disappears.

As a salmon, striped bass, or shad heads upstream it may find smooth swimming and reach the desired spawning area. Chances are, however, it will find man has put obstacles in its path. In fact, few of our major rivers are without dams. Some of the dams may rise only a few feet, while others present impassable heights of several hundred feet. This does not imply that all dams are bad; certainly our way of life requires multiple use. Water must be stored for generating electric power, irrigating crops, navigation, flood control, domestic

To arrive at upstream spawning areas, salmon have to overcome many barriers, including man-made obstructions.

or industrial use, and recreation.

Resource managers have learned to construct passageways which permit fish to reach waters above many dams, but not all fishways are successful, as biologists and engineers will attest. At best, only a portion of the adult fish make a successful passage. Managers also try to help by actually collecting and hauling the fish to other streams or by taking them above dams by various mechanical means, but this is expensive and not always feasible. Thus, while some salmon and shad runs have been saved, many more have been lost.

As a last resort, fish hatcheries are built and may keep alive a valuable run of fish. In West coast streams, for ex-

ample, some of the returning salmon even enter the water supply and tanks of the hatchery where their lives began. This arrangement can be helpful in hatchery operations, but it destroys some of the romance of natural history.

Migrating fish may encounter a zone of oxygen-deficient water caused by domestic sewage and other organic and chemical wastes entering farther upstream. The condition can often be predicted, and measures can be taken to relieve the oxygen demand so as to allow the fish to get through. Nature may relieve the condition in time by increasing the river's flow through rainfall or melting snow.

All conflicts are not yet over for the

upstream migrant. On many streams fish will find diversion of water into irrigation canals, for industrial use or city water supplies, and for a host of other uses. Some of the diversion dams are barriers, but because they are usually not very high, passage may be provided over them. But blocked passage or destroyed spawning beds can be the final blow to a long upstream struggle. Gravel is needed for new highways and buildings, and often the streambed is the most economical place to obtain it.

In California, a 1960 study on the Sacramento River found that an acre of spawning gravel could support 730 chinook salmon worth $20 each, or a total of $14,600. Few acres of gravel, when converted to masonry or building blocks, are worth that amount.

Placer mining for gold has damaged 203,000 acres of stream habitat in West Coast States, and is continuing to a lesser degree.

Some destruction of spawning areas may be necessary, but an informed public will weigh the values and influence the decision as to which streams should be mined and which must be protected.

Upstream watershed areas are immediately affected by various land practices including surface mining, farming, and lumbering. Farming, for example, that does not include sound soil conservation practices, like terracing and contour plowing, often means soil is deposited in the streams and spawning areas destroyed. This also may result from the practice of clear-cutting all trees without leaving a corridor along the stream.

A survey made in 1962 showed more than 65,500 miles of streams were unusable for fish as a result of pollution, erosion, diversion of water supply, and

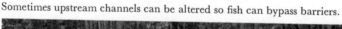
Sometimes upstream channels can be altered so fish can bypass barriers.

Some fish ladders achieve their purpose; some don't.

other causes. This is 7.2 percent of our total stream mileage in the United States.

A few years later, another survey showed that pollution of streams by acid drainage from coal mines alone made biological deserts of 6,000 miles of streams. By 1967 surface mining of all types adversely affected 13,000 miles of streams.

Small fish moving downstream from a spawning area to the sea encounter many of the same problems that met adults on their upstream migrations. Multiple use of water faces them mile after mile. Those that reach the ocean are fortunate—and few.

It is, however, possible for engineers, industrialists, biologists, and politicians to get together and agree on plans for a river which will permit the resident fish to survive, and migrating fish to reach their destination. This was done on the Roanoke River in North Carolina about 12 years ago in a determined mutual effort to save the striped bass in that river. A group of 11 representa-

tives of private industries, State and Federal Governments, and local citizens, worked out operational criteria which would provide minimum safe conditions for migration, spawning, and survival of the fish. Thus far the plan has worked, with only one or two serious accidents which killed some fish.

The resident fish, meanwhile, that occupy a limited water area such as a natural lake or pond, encounter multiple use of that water just as much as anadromous fish that travel hundreds of miles upstream. Consider a city water supply reservoir of 500 acres. City managers are often quick to explain that domestic supply is the primary function served by the reservoir. The water taken from it already has served many uses and will satisfy many more—for people to drink, to wash the dishes, to supply several industries, and to carry away their wastes. For the water stored in the reservoir, there is likely to be stiff competition.

Probably a few score ducks and other water birds will spend part or all of their time on the water resting, nesting, or

417

feeding. Muskrat and beaver may inhabit the shore; swallows feed on insects emerging from the water; ospreys feed on the fish; and frogs fill the spring air with their choruses. Such wildlife uses do not ordinarily make the water less suitable for fish.

Often society claims the privilege of seeking recreation on the protected waters of the reservoir. Boats are used, some by those who merely like to be on the water for esthetic or romantic reasons; some want to fish. In fact, even though carefully regulated, fishing may be intense on a reservoir of this size. Often the larger fish and the predator species, which are needed to maintain a balance, are highly sought by anglers. This may result in an overabundance of small fish or less valuable species.

Furthermore, it may not be in keeping with the primary purposes of the reservoir to add fertilizers or carry out other management practices to increase the fish crop; or it may not be feasible to add chemicals to control overabundant or undesirable water plants. Inability to apply good fishery practices on water areas which are intensively used often limits further use of the water and denies full recreational opportunities.

But people have not yet exhausted their demands on reservoirs of this type. They like to use high-speed boats and motors which, while actually harming only a few fish, disturb feeding and spawning activities, especially in the shallow waters. Wave action may wash away banks and bring silt into the waters.

Recreationists may go one step further and share the environment with the fish. Swimming does not ordinarily disturb fish, although use of scuba may affect fishing, especially if the divers drive away or remove fish from favorite spots. Water skiing brings more conflicts for the water area, affecting people more than it bothers the fish.

Fish that live in such a reservoir lead a precarious existence, yet generally manage to reproduce, grow, and provide some recreation. A will to survive and high reproductive potential make fish an important part of the natural scene and provide an attractive form of multiple use—fishing.

In larger reservoirs, fish life is hazardous, too. Reservoirs providing water to drive turbines for electricity may have fluctuating shorelines. Daily slight fluctuations may not be serious; steeper fluctuations adversely affect the production of bottom-dwelling organisms which fish require for food. Likewise, excessive fluctuations may expose the spawning beds of largemouth bass and other sunfish, preventing successful reproduction.

Incidentally, fluctuations performed in a manner recommended by biologists may help control undesired fish, such as the carp and gizzard shad. Carp tend to overpopulate and roil the water, eat or destroy plants desired by waterfowl, and take the space that could be utilized by more desired species of fish.

But seasonal fluctuations in water level may be helpful or harmful, depending upon the time of the year and extent of the drawdown. Winter drawdown, to create new storage space for anticipated flood waters in the spring, concentrates all the fish in a weed-free environment, thereby letting predators feed on surplus forage fish. This management tool is especially helpful in the South in reducing excessive numbers of small shad and bluegill. Thus, fishing often improves following periodic winter drawdowns. Seasonal lowering of the water

Access areas are built at impoundments to achieve multiple use.

is also an excellent way of controlling excessive plant growth in the middle latitudes of our country.

On the other hand, summer drawdown may be an excellent waterfowl management tool, but can interfere with spawning and growth of fish. Often it is necessary to establish priorities in managing water resources, and fish may not always be favored.

New uses of fish habitat are continually arising. In recent years the use of water to cool nuclear reactors and steam-powered electric generating equipment has become widespread. Water temperatures just below the outlet may be several degrees higher than elsewhere in the reservoir or river. In the winter higher temperatures serve to attract fish, and fishing may be good in the warmed water. But in the summer, temperatures higher than normal may encourage growth of algae that choke waterways and foul nets and water intakes. Some of the algae whose growth is favored may give undesirable tastes and odors to the water and to the fish and shellfish that live in the affected

419

Fishing anyone?

area. Higher temperatures may bring on conditions of low oxygen or high carbon dioxide, which are adverse to fish life.

Even in natural lakes, multiple use has become the rule. An old disease with a new name—lake eutrophication—has caught on. This is simply premature aging of a natural body of water.

Instead of the slow gradual deposit of organic materials on the lake bottom coming from decaying plants and animal tissues, including the single celled organisms, there has been a speed-up of the filling-in process. This may include silt and mud carried from the shore and adjoining lands by surface runoff, or it may result from the excessive addition of nutrients. Such nutrients stimulate the growth of aquatic plants to such enormous amounts that their remains accumulate at a faster than normal rate.

Nutrients may come from fertilizers placed on the watershed to grow crops, or they may reach the lake through overflow from septic tanks or inadequately treated sewage.

The rapid rise in development of vacation homes on waterfront property has brought tremendous problems in sewage and waste disposal. Because many of the lowlands about the lakeshore cannot retain the additional liquids, the nutrient-laden waters flow to the lowest point.

Some lake waters are nearly sterile, and the addition of organic material up to a certain low level is helpful to fish

420

life; too much brings problems. As a result, the fish faces reduced living quarters and depleted oxygen supply, and man faces loss of quantity and quality of water, as well as a suitable place to fish.

In small man made ponds, multiple use reaches an extreme level. There is competition for the water for crops, livestock, extinguishing fires, boating, and swimming, as well as space for fish to live and grow, and a watering place for wildlife.

But biologists know better how to manage small ponds than they do other aquatic environments. The water supply can often be controlled in volume and quality. The fish population can be replaced if it is lost, stocking is not too difficult or expensive, and the effects of mistakes in judgment can often be compensated or a new start made. A well located, constructed, and managed pond is a fine example of multiple use at its best. Fish play a prominent role in this use, and are the basic reason for constructing 75 percent of the small ponds in this country.

Fortunately, streams flow clear from most of our State and Federal public lands, especially the national forests, parks, and wildlife refuges, despite multiple use of the land and water. But human use of these lands is rising, so good management must continue to assure water quality, and thus save the streams as well as the fish life they support.

Well, that's the story—both good and bad—of how multiple use affects the fish. How many of the old fishing holes that we enjoyed in our youth still exist?

Fish are one of the best indicators of how well our water resources are being managed. Given bad management, the fish will die and man's existence also could be jeopardized. Water resource managers must make possible multiple use, and still maintain quality in the aquatic environment. And it is the responsibility of the public to insist that this be done. Wise use—not abuse—must be the rule.

Frustrations

by George Laycock

*Close to the serious angler's heart lies a cherished vision
of a mountain brook, or a remote and lonely lake, far from the maddening
pressures of the city. He dreams of escaping the crowds and
finding release from tensions and troubles, freedom from the conflicts
of the everyday world. Wandering into that idyllic setting,
he casts a carefully aimed plug, or sets a fly upon the rippled surface.
Gone are his troubles and far away his problems.*

NORTHERN PIKE

F THIS SOUNDS too good to be true it's because the fisherman is filled with frustrating problems promising to make the fishing of the future less and not more attractive. There are competitors for the shoreline and the surface as well as the water, gallon by gallon. There are despoilers and diverters, dammers and drainers, and polluters of wide variety.

And what will it be like if progress and growth as we know them continue? This means towns, parks, industries, resorts, docks, and private cottages and clubs strung out all along the shores of waterways. It also means people vying for the water without regard for the angler.

Consider one of the prime nuisances and competitors—the water skier. I agree that not all water skiers are stinkers any more than all stinkers go water skiing. But the fact remains that enough water skiers are ill-mannered (it doesn't take many) to put this problem on any list of angler complaints.

Early in 1968 the *New York Conservationist* printed a pathetic appeal from one of its harassed readers who had come face-to-face with this problem. Scandaga Lake, he explained, has about 25 miles of shoreline, but near the southwestern shore there lies a cove some 300 feet across and 12 feet deep. "We fish there a lot for smallmouth bass," he said, "pike, large bullheads, and recently, rainbow trout. Sometimes it's a lot of fun. This particular day there were some 20 boats anchored there."

Then bearing down upon them came a boat which, except for its faster speed, reminded the writer of the Staten Island Ferry. "It passed us like the 20th Century Limited, and then these skiers each took a different route through the anchored fishermen. We all ducked to keep our heads from being sawed off by the ropes. Those in small boats came up bailing. . . ."

There are too few public waters where a suitable answer to this problem has been found. Administrators have attempted to work out plans to permit fishermen a degree of freedom from water skiers' activities. Zoning is one such answer. On large reservoirs it is sometimes advisable to set aside sections of the lake for skiing, and limit it to these zones. There can also be corridors or travel lanes assigned where powerful boats may use higher speeds reaching their skiing areas.

Some administrators favor regulations prohibiting skiing from shore, as well as a "no wake" rule for waters within 100 yards of shore. It is also sound to consider rules limiting the seasons and time of day when water skiing is permissible. Rules sometimes advocated for this include no skiing before Memorial Day, and then only between 10 a.m. and 5 p.m., leaving the more productive fishing times undisturbed.

There is little excuse for permitting large motors on small lakes, especially those smaller than 500 acres. There is,

Upstream.

A frustration to any angler.

however, always some delegation trouping into the appropriate public offices to demand that the rules be relaxed.

One such group in a Midwestern State appeared before the State game and fish commission, accompanied by a minister of the gospel. He announced that first he would lead the group in prayer, whereupon he did offer a loud and eloquent plea that the Almighty endow these policymakers with the wisdom to see the need for added horsepower and water skiing. Thereafter, the lake was zoned, and although some of it was open to the big boats, part of it was restricted to smaller fishing boats.

Prayer is undoubtedly preferable to the solution chosen by one aging Kentucky angler who could not adjust to the

Outdoorsmen across the country are witnessing such signs.

425

Where do we park the boat?

invasion of his favorite impoundment by a growing band of water skiers. His answer: A .38 caliber revolver lay in a corner of his tackle box. "We got cures for everything else," he said, "from tobacco worms to horse flies. This here pesticide really works against water skiers. Of course," he added grinning broadly, "I never aim right at 'em. Just over the top of 'em. And sometimes you don't have to shoot at all."

There must be a better answer—one both legal and socially acceptable.

Recently snowmobiles have earned condemnation from ice fishermen on northern lakes. Michigan fishermen complain that the snowmobile drivers race back and forth over the ice, scaring fish, and reducing the catch. In due course there may be a solution worked out to alleviate this conflict.

Even canoeists, who themselves seek wilderness and pursue a quiet sport, sometimes plague the fishermen. Certain streams in Michigan, famous for their trout, have in recent years become raceways for canoes. There may be no answer except zoning of such streams, because not only do canoes spook the trout, but they also, on occasion, knock anglers from their feet.

Skindivers can also pose a problem.

426

One pair of divers can so disrupt a popular fishing area that most of the fish are scared away. The divers often are themselves fishermen, with deadly dart-guns. They have the advantage of seeing the fish.

Swimming is another frustration. Many large areas along all coasts are crowded with swimmers, until there simply is no room for the fisherman for hundreds of miles along waterways during many fair weather days.

Some fishermen find fault with such wild competitors as the kingfisher, osprey, eagle, pelican, tern, and heron. But careful food studies by biologists have frequently revealed that the fish consumed by many of these birds are species the fishermen ignore anyhow.

For example, the brown pelicans, in trouble themselves along much of their native coastal range, live primarily on menhaden. And the eagles and ospreys are so rare that the sighting of one may be cherished by the fisherman more than the catching of a pan-sized trout. So don't worry about the wildlife—people are the main problem.

There is the inevitable competition, and sometimes conflict, with the commercial fishermen who set their nets and hooks in bays and estuaries, along the seacoast, and out to sea. It is frustrating to the angler to see large quantities of fish, large and small, taken so easily, especially when he may be having a hard time catching just a few of his favorite croakers, bluefish, mackerel, stripers, or other sea bass.

Recently, there has been a large influx of foreign long-line operators from Canada, Cuba, Russia, Japan, Spain, and Norway along our coasts. This is an added frustration to those anglers who seek swordfish, sailfish, marlin, and other groups which frequent the offshore outside territorial waters.

But perhaps the biggest problem plaguing the fisherman is lack of access to fishing areas. Shorelines of streams, lakes, and seacoasts are crowded for hundreds of miles with various establishments. There has been a rush to the water by entire towns and cities, industries, resorts with hundreds of hotels, docks and piers, private cottages and clubs, and even parks. Farms have grown in size and now encompass entire water-

Nature's fish catchers get frustrated too, but this anhinga didn't.

The contemplative sport of angling.

ways. Everyone wants water, but few respect the needs of the angler. The net result is that the fisherman often can't get to the waterway legally, even if it is suitable for fishing.

Then there are commercial operations draining and filling areas, building seawalls and other abutments, driving piles, and constructing homes along the waterways.

For example, at Boca Ciega Bay, bordering on St. Petersburg, Fla., a third of the water body was removed from use for angling. This once splendid sport fishing area is now a residential site, as developers dredged the bottom and extended the shoreline for building lots. In addition, the bay originally contained many shallow grass flats ideal for spawning, feeding, and cover for many fish. This habitat was destroyed permanently.

And we can't ignore sewage treatment

plants. All towns are building them along the waterways (even though they seldom treat the sewage 100 percent). This may be a source of pride for towns and water pollution abatement experts, and we still need more and better ones. But such a plant sometimes stinks up an excellent fishing area, until you have to cast with one hand and hold your nose with the other.

Industries flock to waterfront sites. Often they siphon off water to create a reservoir, then up goes the no-trespassing sign. A few now and then open up the reservoir for—as they proudly say— "multiple use." This may mean crowds with boats and water skis, and so fishing is a lost cause again.

Road builders sometimes decide the easiest and cheapest way out is to follow a stream. They not only alter the shoreline with such things as culverts and

428

bridges, but they also dredge for fill material. They may remove ground cover along the river allowing silt to wash into the stream.

A favorite place to dig for sand and gravel is the flood plain—which can affect the fishing. In other instances this becomes a "good" location for a city dump.

And so the list of frustrations goes on and on, until the future of angling looks less and less promising. The answer may rest in better planning. One oldtimer told me that the only planning that's going to help is planned parenthood. I don't believe that. Resource-conserva-

tion planning would be a boon.

If our inadequate planning continues, the fisherman has just begun to feel the squeeze. It's bound to get worse. But sometimes only slight changes in planning or zoning would give the angler a place in the scheme of things.

No one person can be expected to have solutions to the growing list of frustrations faced by anglers. The answers begin with recognizing the problems and reaching agreements with nonfishermen that the rights of the angler are important considerations as we go on "improving" the landscape.

Aim for Quality

by Ed Zern

*All of us have known times when fish were so abundant
that catching them became a bore, if not actually a chore. I once forfeited
3 precious (and prepaid) vacation days at a Canadian camp
after 55 successive casts of a wet fly produced 55 brook trout,
and headed back to the Pennsylvania Poconos where I could
fish hard all day and catch four or five finicky brown trout, or none.
So let's recognize that quantity, in angling, is simply
a variable in the equation that defines quality angling, and that unless
one is fishing for the market, or trying to keep
a clutch of Cub Scouts titillated, quality is all that matters.*

BROOK TROUT

IT SEEMS to me that the quality of any sport fishing depends on several factors, and of course one of these is quantity; it's hardly conceivable to speak of quality fishing in totally fishless water, and we've touched on the ennui induced by overabundant, easily caught fish. Between these extremes there's a wide range, and the fact that we may find sport and enjoyment almost anywhere within it is part of the charm of angling.

I've written elsewhere that if an omniscient guide led me to a beautiful mountain stream and said, "Bub, there are trout in every pool and riffle of this crick, but nary one over ten inches," I wouldn't fish it. If he added, "Come to think of it, there's one old buster somewhere in this two-mile stretch, or maybe two, but there hasn't nobody raised them all season," I'd start climbing into my waders. Which is to say: Without some element of mystery, and the possibility, however faint, of latching onto leviathan, there can't be quality angling.

Nor can there be quality fishing without quality habitat, in both the ecological and aesthetic senses. I know a limestone stream in Pennsylvania that produces enormous "hatches" of fat, luscious stoneflies, and as a consequence also produces enormous brown trout. Experts come in droves to fish it for trophies, and angling writers have penned reams in praise of it—and brother, you can have it. It's a murky, often muddy brook flowing through meadows between littered banks trampled to gumbo by the boots of fishermen. In the name of stream improvement, local anglers have hauled sections of concrete sewer pipe and old open-end oil drums and anchored them in midstream, to increase the flow of water through the venturi-tube principle. It has all the bucolic charm and pastoral beauty of a sink full of used dishwater, and despite its big, heavy trout it can't, in its present unloveliness, produce true quality fishing.

Well then, let's suppose we've found a wild and beautiful river of deep, bedspringless pools and swift runs, with strong, streambred trout in numbers and sizes to provide excellent sport if and when they're moving. Let's suppose it's a grand day in early June, with a good hatch on the water and trout rising freely. Let's suppose you've spent five minutes cautiously working your way into position to cast a homemade dry fly to a two-pound rainbow, picking off natural red quills as they drift by the boulder that gives him cover.

You're about to make your first cast when out of the rhododendron along the bank, and into the water, plunges another angler. Grunting a grudging greeting he sloshes through the shallows, making waves guaranteed to put down every feeding fish for at least an hour, and disappears upstream.

When you've found another pool and several rising trout and have carefully waded out to a casting position, there's a splash in the middle of the pool—and again every fish runs for cover. This time it's a novice fisherman with a shiny new spin-casting outfit, and the splash was a two-inch pickerel lure he had plopped into the water from the bank behind you. He's pleased with himself. "Beat you to it didn't I?" he says with a friendly grin—and you realize that conceivably, deep down, he may be a fairly decent human being; the simple-minded slob just doesn't know any better.

You realize, then, that there can't be quality fishing without quality fishermen—that today, with millions more

432

A quality environment for fishing.

people having the leisure, the money, and the inclination to go fishing, thousands of neophytes take to lakes and streams every year without the faintest notions of elementary angling courtesy or the basic traditions of sportsmanship and sporting ethics. And while sharing a stream or lake with them at close quarters, you aren't likely to enjoy real quality fishing. In time, of course, they'll learn, but as each one graduates—as you and I once did—from the ranks of the unwitting boors, two newcomers may take his place.

Perhaps the solution is compulsory courtesy courses, akin to the safety courses now required of new hunting licensees in several States.

But I think the most important ingredient of quality angling, even when all the other requirements are met, is the angler himself. For only the sportsman who brings to the water, along with his gear and tackle and bait or lures or flies and license, a love of the sport of angling rather than of merely catching fish . . . an eye for the beauty of unspoiled countryside or unpeopled wilderness . . . an ear for the symphony of running water and the song of birds . . . and a

Boy Scouts learn ethics along with technique on a fishing pier.

Angling ethics imply a decent respect for the environment.

looking along the river or lakeside. But these are peripheral and largely accidental; we can't do much about a falling barometer or a surly farmer (made surly, probably, by the vandalism or thoughtlessness of other "sportsmen") or an absence of visible wildlife.

But we can, happily, do something about some of those other, more central things that make for quality angling.

We can do everything in our power to preserve or restore quality habitat for the fish we seek: unpolluted water in unspoiled surroundings. We can urge that money now spent on biologically senseless but politically expedient warmwater fish hatcheries and stocking programs be spent instead on habitat improvement. We can join at least one local and one

Those who know must teach.

A healthy habitat means healthy fish—and healthy humans.

heart for rejoicing at being a part of nature's eternal happening . . . will be capable of knowing the meaning of quality in angling.

I've stated my case here in terms of trout fishing, because that's the kind I mostly do, but these conditions for quality angling apply to cane-pole fishing for bluegills in a Louisiana lake, bullhead fishing in an Iowa farm pond, Atlantic salmon fishing in a New Brunswick river, trolling for walleyes in a TVA impoundment, or steelheading in an Oregon river. Only the terms of reference are changed, and none of the values. And quality angling is always a matter of values rather than numbers of fish.

Oh, there are other considerations that affect the quality of a day's fishing: the weather, water conditions, the tackle we're using, the friends we're with, the fellow-anglers we meet on the water, the farmer with whom we trade small talk after stopping to get permission to cross a field, the wildlife we see by luck or

Trophy reel brings back memories of successes—the way fishing enriches many in their later years.

national conservation group working for clean, unpolluted waters and the maintenance of natural areas. We can recognize as friends and allies all the conservation-minded people and organizations in our community—because the battle for clean waters is one we can't win alone. We can cajole our Congressmen with cards and wires and letters, reminding them politely but pointedly that we count on them to reflect, in their legislative activity, our concern in clean water today and tomorrow.

We can do something about the quality of anglers on the water we fish, by making sure that we, ourselves, observe the elementary rules of stream courtesy and sportsmanship as well as the formal fish and game laws.

We can support our own State's conservation department in its effort to solve the enormous problem of providing angling for an exploding population while recreational and industrial demands on water resources multiply like mice. We can go along with fly-fishing-only and trophy-fish-only experiments that may point ways to partial solutions. We can remind ourselves that a trained fishery biologist isn't likely to have all the answers, but he almost certainly has some of them and is worth listening to.

We can, in short, be something more than fishermen: We can be good sportsmen, active conservationists, and responsible citizens. If enough of us are, perhaps our children and their children will enjoy quality angling.

435

To the desert we turn for a different type of fishing experience—on one of the Colorado River man-made lakes.

THE FUTURE

Good, Bad, or Indifferent?

by John S. Gottschalk

*If Izaak Walton would look down at the angling world of
the 20th century, he would sigh in satisfaction—that his fishing exploits
took place three centuries ago! The uncrowded banks of
the river Dove, where the only distraction was the mooing of distant cows,
would seem to him (as to us) a piscatorial philosopher's paradise.
He would be speechless in amazement at what has happened to his chosen
pastime since he last lectured his "gentle scholar"
on the art, science, joys—and minor perils—of all things piscatorial.*

BARRACUDA AND REEF FISH

B ET IF A GHOSTLY Walton examined the motives and techniques of today's anglers, he would find them little changed from his own time. And therein glows a ray of hope for the future of angling. Human nature does not change; the allure of fishing will tempt tomorrow's anglers as it does today's. Herbert Hoover put it well: "The reason for it all is that fishing is fun and good for the soul of man."

Now we come to our vision of the future, the challenge placed on our generation if fishing is to continue as a major factor in the outdoor life of Americans. Many predictions concern themselves wholly with the how and where of angling, ignoring broader issues that will be key factors in determining the quality of our future angling. Let me state here that the sport is inevitable and will continue indefinitely; how good it will be depends on whether we improve the water resource and fishery management techniques and whether we intensify research to gain new insights for our fishery managers. Let's first discuss the water resource.

As America has grown out of its colonial background, we have carried with us a national irreverence for our natural resources, born of our ancestral need to conquer the wilderness. Nature's gifts existed in such abundance that today's priceless natural assets were then considered obstacles to survival or at least to "progress." Forests were cleared for cornfields, swamps and marshes became wheatfields and onion patches. Rivers were dammed and channeled to provide man a measure of control of water.

Only in the last 25 years have we recognized that there is a limit to our essential resources, and that human existence rests upon man's ability to equalize his use of resources on the one hand with his stewardship of them on the other.

A basic problem is that production for economic affluence carries with it the wastes that are an integral part of the production process; unless wastes are reckoned with, they are also a destructive agent. Thus, pollution of our water is an expression of man's productive capability carried on without recognition that we are operating in a closed system demanding that all matter be accounted for.

This would apply in general to any resource, but we have entered a period in which competition for water is growing rapidly. Planners have projected this competition in statistics predicting with alarming overtones the shortages we may expect in the next 50 years.

Consider those water development projects that have long since left the imagination of planners and moved onto the drawing boards or into pilot-plant models. We see Government and industry engaged in a cooperative effort to convert sea water into drinking water, and striving to reduce the cost so that converted water can be used for municipal requirements. In water deficient areas, herculean efforts are made to prevent loss of moisture into the atmosphere by canalization of river systems, by development of chemical films to reduce evaporation losses from reservoirs, and even by elimination of vegetation that is often of great value for wildlife — because vegetation's process of converting sunlight and chemicals into food puts much moisture into the atmosphere. Our future water problems are dramatized by proposals to convey water from the Northwest into heavily populated areas of the Southwest.

440

Fishery research, partly financed by excise taxes on equipment, considers environment as well as fish.

It is clear that we face a growing shortage of water in America. This partly has been brought about by the growth of our human population, with all the demands this has placed on our basic water supply. The personal needs of individuals will amount to much more as our population exceeds 300 million in another quarter-century.

But of all the ways in which man has misused water, the worst is in considering streams, lakes, and estuaries as receptacles or transmission systems for our wastes. Probably more water is ruined in the United States by pollution than by any other cause, a phenomenon that continues despite the efforts being made to find means to cope with this problem.

Abundant, cheap energy has been responsible, in large measure, for our civilization; man's ingenuity may have been the underlying cause, for his technological ability to harness energy sources has been the primary factor that has led to our affluent life in the second half of the 20th century.

This energy production has required a great deal of water. Most of our demands today are met by electricity, produced either in single or multipurpose hydroelectric projects. While it may be argued that the water loss from such projects in minimal, there have been serious, and sometimes devastating, resource dislocations produced by giant water impoundment projects.

Almost every kind of power production (including that from fossil fuel plants and those fueled from nuclear piles) generates heat in such quantity that a substantial part of the water

Prospects look good that future anglers will continue to experience the joys of casting along a stream.

needed for cooling is wasted. Most of the wastage is to the atmosphere as vapor. Fossil fuel plants in the past were small enough that their water-warming tendency had only local and temporary effects, but with the advent of immense nuclear power stations, efficient only in production sizes on the order of 10 to 20 times as large as coal-fired plants, thermal heating becomes serious. This, too, represents a source of competition for water, an essential resourse base.

Past irrigation projects have been largely located in the arid West, but recent years have seen the same techniques used in other parts of the country that experience periods when rainfall is insufficient to guarantee optimum crop production. Thus, irrigation has become a national rather than a regional competitor for water.

We have occasional water crises today, but we will be in continuous crisis by the turn of the century. Competitive situations will exist between communities, between elements of our social structure, between industries, and between various recreation pursuits, including types of fishing.

So we must develop a conservation philosophy—actually a conservation ethic—that requires sophisticated concepts of allocation if there is to be water available for recreation. Waste control will have to be accepted as normal, particularly in cities, where control must apply not only to waste products, but to prevention of water wastage in any form. Our technology will have to make possible complementary uses—those that take the same water but at different periods, and those that permit simultaneous use of the same water for two or more purposes.

Achieving rational choices of water use is a problem to which little thinking has been applied because we have not yet recognized the issues as critical. If a

442

trout stream is diverted to storage in a reservoir for irrigation of sugar beets, objections are usually overruled because there are other alternatives for fishermen—although other alternatives for agriculturists were not explored. But as competition for water increases, means will have to be developed from an economic and political point of view for consideration of all reasonable alternatives.

Who must insist upon other alternatives? An alert citizenry, of whom the hard core will have to be anglers, insisting that these decisions shall not be made in an atmosphere of ignorance, or that special, local interests are not given paramount consideration in the distribution of what is now, and will become more so, America's primary resource—water.

Concerning improved fishery management techniques, let us agree at once that this includes increased production of the fishery resource for human use. While the primary necessity for anglers is insuring fishing opportunities in the future, improving fish production is nearly as important. By increasing our understanding of how to produce more fish in a given volume of water—growing two fish where one grows now—we can increase the productive capacity of existing waters and improve the fishability of waters that may, in the future, be subject to reduced quality or more intensive use for purposes other than angling.

Increased commercial harvest on the world's oceans will require international agreements protecting sports fishing.

443

Our ability to develop fish husbandry from its relatively primitive status to a scientific undertaking is an essential requirement for the future. We have made progress in this area in the past quarter of a century, but we will have to increase our knowledge manyfold to keep pace with future competition for water. Our knowledge base must grow not only in terms of hatcheries; we must learn more about lakes, streams, and ponds.

Hatchery operation in the United States has shown an interesting evolution. Beginning with the advent of fish culture here 100 years ago, dependence upon hatcheries as a panacea for depleted fisheries reached a high point in the midtwenties. As we learned more about natural factors controlling fish populations, hatcheries and stocking went under a cloud that is pretty well cleared away as fishery managers increase their sophistication in matching hatchery output with management needs.

Nowhere has new ability to manage fisheries with hatcheries been more successful than in the handling of anadromous fish on the West coast and in the Great Lakes. The coho salmon has had great success in both areas after transplants. On Lake Michigan coho fishing became literally a craze in the late sixties, with over 125,000 fish taken by anglers in less than 3 weeks during the fall of 1968. While many old ideas about the value of stocking have been disproved, it is now clear that a viable species reared in a hatchery can contribute much to outdoor recreation by providing the incentive for an angler's quest.

Much has been learned about lakes, streams, ponds, and reservoirs, but the changing character of all these waters— plus increased demands upon them for competing uses—requires intensified effort to understand the complicated biological, chemical, and physical factors controlling fish production. Monitoring systems are required to tell the fishery manager facts about the habitat itself and to inform him of the reaction of desirable species to changes in the environment. Knowledge is needed to determine how and under what conditions management tools can be employed, and these tools must be strengthened and improved.

Essentially fishery management is nothing more than making decisions aimed at realizing a given objective, the decisions based on information gained through scientific study and experimentation. The fishery manager must not depend for guidance on guesswork, superstition, public opinion, or political pressure. In the future, even more than today, management will demand expanded knowledge and artistry in the application of that knowledge, plus a warehouse of sophisticated equipment beyond anything we are using today.

But we must recognize there are still hundreds of miles of fishable streams, thousands of acres of lakes and reservoirs not accessible to the public. Until a few years ago, access was not a problem, because other public fishing was available in sufficient quantity. Recently, considerable effort has been expended to open up such areas, but probably more of these places are being restricted than are made available, because such sites are often sold at high prices. Where once a few cabin owners populated a remote lake, chances are that the lake is now surrounded by a summer resort with restrictions on access, or with such heavy other use that the public doesn't want to fish there. Greater effort will have to be

Pollution can no longer be tolerated.

made to equalize pressure by extending the usefulness of waters now in private or quasiprivate status.

Fishery management still has far to go before it achieves the needed finesse in manipulating populations of fish and angling waters. An anology may be drawn between future fish management and modern agriculture. A farmer takes a hundred acres of what was once timber or grassland and, by the application of technology, eliminates those plants (and in some cases animals) that might compete with the crop capable of yielding a profitable production. Years of research in agriculture schools and world-wide searches have yielded high-producing crop strains. The farmer also has a variety of chemicals to control pests (plant and animal) or to stimulate production by supplementing natural inorganic nutrients. Something of this sort will become true for fish management.

Better use of game fish, better control of "weed" species, and enhancing the environment to produce more food for the fish population are several areas of potential development in sport fish conservation. Varieties offering the most in terms of production for outdoor recreation must be favored at the expense of those species which are noncontributors.

Our technology to date tells us the fewer species of fish in a given body of water, the greater the potential production. But we know from experience that only in rare instances is it possible to manage for a single species or even a fish population of a few species. Variety may be desirable to satisfy the differing needs of the angling community: Small children might like to catch large bass but their ability to do so is limited, so in ponds where there are mixed anglers, catfish and sunfish may have to be produced to take care of junior anglers. This is possible while producing bass or pike to reward the adult anglers.

In other situations, the food chain relationships of the water may be such that there must be a higher percentage of prey species to sustain a rapidly growing population of predator fish at a population level high enough to reward the angler.

Studies and projects aimed to help manage and produce desirable fish populations have been underway for some years, but we are just beginning to make advances that will someday provide a firm basis for the management needs of tomorrow.

The same can be said about our knowledge of how to cope with the control of undesirable species. Use of toxic chemicals to control undesirable fish populations has been prominent in many programs for at least 25 years, the goal being to eliminate those species competing directly with more desirable fish for food or habitat space, or preying directly on game fish at some stage in their life. Often up to 98 percent of the poundage of fish in a given lake is composed of species making no contribution to anglers or as food for sport fish. While we have achieved some sophistication in control methods, we must accomplish much more to meet the future needs of American anglers.

Methods of fertilization must be developed to take into consideration the problem of "aging" of waters. Sometimes it may be necessary to rejuvenate lakes by eliminating some of the nutrient material added to them in the form of sewage effluents.

The management of catch itself—that is, the control of populations by removing appropriate fractions to promote the best sport fishery—will also become more important.

In another 25 years, fishery managers will be applying the results of studies on genetics. New as they are, experiments in selective breeding have already shown an ability to produce strains of fish better than of the stock from which the selections were made. Several State fish and game departments are actively engaged in stocking hybrids, including sunfish that do not overpopulate as readily as their wild kinfolk. One commonly used hybrid, the splake (a cross between lake and brook trout) is being planted in many areas of North America because of its rapid growth and excellent sporting characteristics.

Additional emphasis must be placed on adequate management of estuarine areas and coastal waters which have added much to our fishing. Because of improved boats and motors and the concentration of human populations near the coastlines, more anglers are turning to marine environments. The increase has been such that at least one-fourth of all our fishermen use the oceans.

Our coasts and estuaries, far from being the inexhaustible resource they were once considered, are a delicate part of our outdoor environment. We cannot continue to treat bays, sounds, and coastal regions as a cesspool for industrial America and still retain them as the source of much recreation in the future.

Management techniques are available for handling much about the estuarine and coastal fisheries; yet, one of the largest problems—how to deal with the interstate nature of most species found along our coasts—has not yet been resolved. Until a way is found to treat a particular species as a conservation responsibility throughout the whole of its range, we will never be able to deal effectively with our coastal fishery resources.

We have the potential to increase concentrations of sport fish off our coasts, and much more can be developed with additional studies. But our near-shore marine waters will continue to be an important source of recreation in the future, only if society as a whole recognizes the need to treat these resources as though they are not expendable.

This Nation has had a long-time interest in technical fishery problems; the American Fisheries Society was organized in 1870 as the professional association of fishery workers and is one of the oldest scientific organizations in America. This interest has produced a substantial body of scientific information about this segment of our renewable natural resources. Fishery managers, however, are in the same position as any other technical group faced with America's rapid population increase: Facts developed over the years are no longer adequate to keep up with the demands for "progress" and demands for protection of resources needed by a greatly increased human population.

As our population continues to expand, more dependence will have to be placed upon knowledge gained from scientific studies of three essential components of our recreational fisheries: the fish, their environment, and the people who in one way or another are dependent upon fish populations. The future will bring unprecedented pressures upon the natural habitats, long the locale of specific fisheries, and will greatly complicate the problems of adjusting resource use to meet the needs of future citizens.

The need for more knowledge is accentuated by the realization that within 30 years, 9 out of 10 Americans will be living in cities. It is impossible to estimate the effect of an urban existence for most of our people, yet it is obvious that many of today's city tensions will become increasingly critical if opportunities for relaxation and recreation are not immediately available. Something like Walton's "contemplative sport" will be a prime need for tomorrow's citizens. Projections by Marion Clausen of the amount of time people spend in leisure activities show a continuing growth, with

If housing, resort, and industrial developers continue to take over estuaries, sportsmen will lose many fish-rich areas.

about 38 percent of the time of all people being devoted to leisure activities by the year 2000.

With this kind of an outlook, we must have studies to determine present and predict future characteristics of fishing interest. We need to know what the goals of fish management should be, if we are to provide the inner satisfactions that

447

Americans living today associate with angling. Our responsibility may be to "cut down the time between bites," but this generality will not provide a base on which to build for a tomorrow when the desires and actual needs of people may be different from what they are today. Thus it behooves fishery researchers to look beyond the fish and to concern themselves with the angler.

Our study of the angler ought to try to anticipate what he thinks about when he has a satisfying day afield. Is he only interested in bringing back a full creel? Is his primary objective to break a record? Is he satisfied to catch a few fish and find the rest of his reward in being outdoors? Shouldn't we—as Ed Zern suggested in his chapter—in addition to quantity, also focus on quality?

We need to find out why an angler decides that one fish is more desirable than another, and whether he can have his attitudes changed. Why is it, for example, in the Northeast and the Northwest, where trout and salmon have been popular for generations, many anglers reject the so-called "spiny-rayed" species? Throughout the Middle West and South, "spiny rays"— the black basses and other sunfish and catfish—are highly prized.

We need to know much more about crowding on fishing streams. Many people look upon angling as an opportunity to get away from other people, yet any opening day of the season near large centers of populations will find mobs competing for elbow room at popular fishing places. Is fishing the recreation in these instances, or is it merely an excuse for the kind of recreation that comes from a social event involving close proximity and interaction?

What makes an angler tick? We will have to find answers before we can be certain of what to plan for future fishing potential. This will require an entirely new kind of research for the fishery manager, who must finally come around to learning how to manage people in the process of managing fish.

But the scientist still has a large job ahead if he chooses to focus on fish and their environments, on much deeper and broader comprehension of the way fish live and what nature requires that they have as a minimum for existence. As we must study the behavior of fishermen, we must study the behavior of fish, too.

Little is known about how fish react to different kinds of stimuli, yet many new stimuli are introduced into their habitats every year. Behavior is frequently a reflection of some physiological change, and thus it will be necessary to perfect our knowledge of the biology of fish.

Despite a great deal of information about many fish, there is still much that is unknown. Some species have been studied intensively, but even these have information gaps that must be filled before we can carry out management in a completely knowledgeable way. Many others, particularly oceanic species, became subject to scientific study only recently. With better vessels, better methods for observation, and better techniques for determining lifespan and migration, much can be done to understand the life cycle of these little known denizens of the seas.

It is equally important to understand the characteristics of the groups of various species and the total populations that make up all the components of any given fishery. "Population dynamics" is the term applied to the study of changes

Closed-circuit television monitoring of fish migration is an example of sophisticated technology coming into use.

not readily identified.

It is easy to see why a favorite spawning marsh or bay is no longer effective if it is converted into a dumping ground for trash. It is much more difficult—yet just as important—to learn how the introduction of a minute amount of some chemical substance affects the egg or larval stages of fish and their food organisms. Food, shelter, other associations, and behavior of fish—all are affected when the environment is modified.

We normally think of changes in the environment as destructive, but under some circumstances physical and chemical changes improve habitat. In other situations it is desirable to find ways of modifying the effects of man-induced changes in the environment to reduce damages or even to increase benefits. Considerable effort, for example, is being expended on the upper Sacramento River to provide artificial spawning beds in an irrigation canal to help take the place of natural spawning areas rendered useless by the construction of a large water storage and irrigation project.

that take place in fish populations and that provide us with the means of describing these populations. Thus, it is through population dynamics that we can estimate how many are available in a given fishery. We must predict at what size fish should be harvested under varying conditions; we must forecast whether a fishery is expanding or declining; we must identify geographical areas that will profit or suffer from changes in the fish population.

As humans make changes in water areas, the environment of our fisheries also changes. Factors that have controlled population levels in the past may change; indeed, such environmental changes as the introduction of pollutants may simply destroy the population. Thus, we need to know the tolerance of aquatic organisms, including fish, to gross changes of their environment and also to more subtle changes

In summing up, I believe that what enough people have wanted and needed over the years, they have generally been successful in obtaining. This outlook prevails for angling in the future; however, we will not automatically succeed. Success requires wide public interest, support, and attention, together with wise administration and dedicated efforts by fishery managers and researchers, if the potential of the future is to be realized.

Most of our efforts in the past and probably in the future will be dependent upon some kind of governmental program, probably at both State and Fed-

449

Informing political leaders and mass communicators of the fishery environment is an essential part of management.

eral levels. This means that the interests of the citizen fisherman are more deeply involved with governmental programs than are some other aspects of our future. The public will have to maintain constant vigilance to be assured that government programs for protecting the environment are supported at a level needed to maintain the kind of environment fish will need. Programs of research and related fishery management must likewise be supported at realistic levels of financing if all of the possibilities that lie ahead are to be achieved.

This kind of support is something that all programs require. But if we are to do justice to our fishery resources, there must be citizen support in another area. A number of policy shifts are required as a basis for continuing progress in the development of our fisheries.

First, these must be recognized as a national resource of significant proportions. The values of these resources have been taken for granted in the past and often ignored in the competition for joint water use.

Second, we must establish a system for evaluating our resources which gives recognition to the impact of recreation in American life and provides a means of equating the intangible assets of a livable out-of-doors with the more measurable benefits related to products that can be bought and sold in the marketplace.

Third, the enhancement of fishery resources must be recognized as an intrinsic aspect of the management of water development projects.

Fourth, fishery management must be based primarily on information obtained by scientific methods rather than on ill-founded opinion or politics.

Fifth, we must realize that protec-

450

tion of the environment is absolutely essential to the achievement of the ultimate potential from any renewable resource. The environment cannot be allowed to deteriorate or be destroyed lest we do irreparable damage to the fisheries and other necessities of our existence.

We are gradually recognizing what must be done in the future. We have demonstrated this by the increased public concern about the destruction of the environment and the insistence on protection for important parts of our natural scene. Belatedly, we have begun the big job of restoring our anadromous fisheries—the runs of salmon that once flourished on the East and West coasts.

Intensive efforts are going forward to reclaim the Great Lakes from the doldrums into which these fisheries were plunged with the advent of the sea lamprey. Efforts to improve the fishery potential of our large reservoirs are continuing apace.

In spite of a past of relentless destruction of fishery resources and general public apathy, we are now moving toward an era of significant progress. No one can predict the future with assurance, but based on the interest and concern shown by Americans in what happens to their natural resources, I believe that there will be fishing for fun for as long as we want it.

Authors

Anne H. Bosworth is a deep-sea angler and conservationist.

Roger E. Burrows is Director of the Salmon Cultural Laboratory, Bureau of Sport Fisheries and Wildlife.

Homer Circle is an outdoor writer.

John R. Clark is a marine fish researcher with the Bureau of Sport Fisheries and Wildlife.

Verne E. Davison is a farm pond expert and biologist for the Department of Agriculture.

Donald P. de Silva is affiliated with the Institute of Marine Sciences, University of Miami.

David G. Deuel is a marine fish researcher with the Bureau of Sport Fisheries and Wildlife.

John Dobie is affiliated with the Minnesota Department of Conservation.

Charles K. Fox is an angler and outdoor writer.

Michael Frome is an outdoor writer.

John L. Funk is affiliated with the Missouri Conservation Department.

John S. Gottschalk former Director of the Bureau of Sport Fisheries and Wildlife.

Curt Gowdy is a national television sports commentator and lifelong angler.

Clarence P. Idyll is affiliated with the Institute of Marine Sciences, University of Miami.

Robert M. Jenkins is Director of the National Reservoir Research Program, Bureau of Sport Fisheries and Wildlife.

Willard T. Johns is affiliated with the Pennsylvania Fish Commission.

Wheeler Johnson was affiliated with the Maryland Inland Fisheries Commission and is now an outdoor editor for the Washington Post.

Carl Otto von Kienbusch has combined a lifetime of angling and business and has collected one of the finest set of books on angling in the world.

Willis King is Chief of the Division of Fishery Services, Bureau of Sport Fisheries and Wildlife.

George Laycock is an outdoor writer.

Robert E. Lennon is Director of Fish Control Laboratories, Bureau of Sport Fisheries and Wildlife.

Gene L. Letourneau is an outdoor editor for the Gannett Newspapers.

William M. Lewis is professor of zoology with Southern Illinois University.

A. George Morris is affiliated with the Missouri Department of Conservation.

Charles E. Most is an angler and outdoor writer and an information officer with the Bureau of Land Management.

John B. Moyle is affiliated with the Minnesota Department of Conservation.

Donald W. Pfitzer is an information officer with the Bureau of Sport Fisheries and Wildlife.

Craig Phillips is affiliated with the National Fisheries Center and Aquarium, Bureau of Sport Fisheries and Wildlife.

Jack Randolph has combined a military career with angling and outdoor writing.

Ben Schley is an angler and outdoor writer and a biologist with the Bureau of Sport Fisheries and Wildlife.

Rex Gary Schmidt is Chief of Audio Visual Services, Bureau of Sport Fisheries and Wildlife.

Frank J. Schwartz is a professor of zoology for the University of North Carolina and former editor of the Transactions of the American Fisheries Society.

C. Lavett Smith is affiliated with the Department of Ichthyology, American Museum of Natural History.

Richard H. Stroud heads the Sport Fishing Institute.

Howard A. Tanner is affiliated with the Michigan Conservation Department.

Paul E. Thompson is Chief of the Division of Fishery Research, Bureau of Sport Fisheries and Wildlife.

Charles H. Walburg is a research biologist on reservoirs, Bureau of Sport Fisheries and Wildlife.

Lionel A. Walford is Director of the Sandy Hook Marine Laboratory, Bureau of Sport Fisheries and Wildlife.

David H. Wallace is Director of Marine Fisheries, New York Conservation Department.

Robert B. Whitaker is an angler and an information officer with the Bureau of Land Management.

Harvey Willoughby is Chief of the Division of Fish Hatcheries, Bureau of Sport Fisheries and Wildlife.

Warren J. Wisby is Director of the National Fisheries Center and Aquarium, Bureau of Sport Fisheries and Wildlife.

Ed Zern is an angler and outdoor writer.

Contributors of Photographs

Arizona Game and Fish Department:
  Bill Sizer, 356
Boy Scouts of America:
  Ted S. Pettit, 219
Erwin A. Bauer, 25, 37B, 89B, 90T, 101, 123, 132, 258, 271, 378, 382
British Museum, 322
Bureau of Commercial Fisheries, 164, 196, 199, 207, 208; also:
  George Mattsch, 30
  John Thompson, 331
  Bob Williams, 223B, 328, 426
Bureau of Land Management:
  Jim Lee, 376
Bureau of Reclamation, 417, 449; also:
  J. R. Cotterill, 251B
  Mel Davis, 241, 249
Bureau of Sport Fisheries and Wildlife, 13, 48, 222, 329, 330, 338, 340, 355; also:
  Peter Anastasi, 116
  Glenn K. Brackett, 22, 79, 146, 324, 350, 375, 433T
  A. W. Bromley, 300
  Charles Cadieux, 360
  R. P. Dexter, 58
  Jan Fardell, 341
  Luther C. Goldman, 363, 364, 424, 442

Bureau of Sport Fisheries and Wildlife—Con.
  E. P. Haddon, 349B, 379
  Jerry L. Haut, 27T
  Eugene F. Hester, 119, 236
  Edmond S. Hobson, 69B
  W. L. Johnson, 317
  George B. Kelez, 47
  Eugene Kridler, 419
  Nick Mariana, 342 T and B
  Dave Marshall, 57, 296
  Frank R. Martin, 89T, 257, 336, 248
  David L. Olsen, 26
  Don Pfitzer, 80, 450
  Ben Schley, 5, 170, 320, 321, 367, 377, 410, 433B, 436
  Rex Gary Schmidt, 12, 20, 28, 31, 84, 85, 86, 88B, 95, 97, 110, 111, 115, 120, 121, 127, 130, 136, 140, 171, 188, 201, 212, 216T, 220, 240, 244, 251T, 259, 260, 266, 268, 270, 272, 274, 278, 286, 291, 293T, 298, 302, 312, 314, 320, 335, 370, 384, 389, 391, 392, 394, 395R, 397, 405, 416, 436, 445, 447
  Myron J. Silverman, 407
  D. L. Tennant, 88T, 425B
  Averil Thayer, 216B
Carnegie Institute:
  William H. Longley, 69T

EDITOR'S NOTE: Art in chapter 15 by Oscar
Warbach

Common and Scientific Names

Anchovies—Engraulidae

Barracuda, *Sphyraena* sp.
Bass—Serranidae
    Kelp bass, *Paralabrax clathratus*
    Red grouper, *Epinephelus morio*
    Striped bass, *Roccus Saxatilus*
    White bass, *Roccus chrysops*
    White perch, *Roccus americanus*
    Yellow bass, *Roccus mississippiensis*
Billfish—Istiophoridae
    Atlantic sailfish, *Istiophorus albicans*
    Black marlin, *Makaira indica*
    Blue marlin, *Makaira nigricans*
    Pacific sailfish, *Istiophorus greyi*
    Spearfish, *Tetrapturus* sp.
    Striped marlin, *Makaira audax*
    White marlin, *Makaira albida*
Blennies—Blenniidae
Bluefish, *Pomatomus saltatrix*
Bonefish, *Albula vulpes*
Bowfin, *Amia calva*
Brotulas—Brotulidae
Butterfish—Stromateidae
Butterflyfish and angelfish—Chaetodontidae

Cardinalfish, *Apogon* sp.

Catfish—Ictaluridae
    Blue catfish, *Ictalurus furcatus*
    Bullheads, *Ictalurus* sp.
    Channel catfish, *Ictalurus punctatus*
    Flathead catfish, *Pylodictis olivaris*
    Madtom catfish, *Noturus* sp.
    White catfish, *Ictalurus catus*
Catfish, African synodontids, *Synodontis* sp.
Catfish, sea, *Galeichthys felis*
Catfish, South American armored—Callichthyidae
Catfish, South American banjo—Bunocephalidae
Cavefish—Amblyopsidae
Characin, Mexican cave. *Anoptilhthys jordani*
Chimaeras—Chimaeridae
    Ratfish. *Hydrolagus colliei*
Cichlids—Cichlidae
Cobia, *Rachycentron canadum*
Codfish and hake—Gadidae
    Burbot, *Lota lota*
    Cod, *Arctogadus, Boreogadus, Eleginus,* and *Gadus* sp.
    Haddock, *Melanogrammus aeglefinus*
    Hake, *Merluccius* and *Urophycis* sp.
    Pollock, *Pollachius virens*

457

Damselfish—Pomacentridae
  Beaugregory, *Eupomacentrus leucostictus*
  Damselfish, *Eupomacentrus* sp.
  Sergeant major, *Abudefduf saxatilis*
Discus fish, *Symphysodon* sp.
Dolphin, *Coryphaena hippurus*
Drums—Sciaenidae
  Atlantic croaker, *Micropogon undulatus*
  Black drum, *Pogonias cromis*
  Corvina, *Cynoscion* sp.
  Freshwater drum, *Aplodinotus grunniens*
  Kingfish, *Menticirrhus* sp.
  Red drum, *Sciaenops ocellata*
  Seatrout, *Cynoscion* sp.
  Spot, *Leiostomus xanthurus*
  Weakfish, *Cynoscion regalis*

Eel, American, *Anguilla rostrata*
Eel, electric, *Electrophorus electricus*
Eel, gulper—Saccopharyngidae
Eel, moray—Muraenidae
Eel, Nile, *Gymnarchus* sp.

Flounder, lefteye—Bothidae
  Summer flounder, *Paralichthys californicus*
Flounder righteye—Pleuronectidae
  Pacific halibut, *Hippoglossus stenolepis*
  Starry flounder, *Platichthys stellatus*
  Winter flounder, *Pseudopleuronectes americanus*
Flyingfish—Exocoetidae

Gars—Lepisosteidae
  Alligator gar, *Lepisosteus spatula*
  Longnose gar, *Lepisosteus osseus*
  Shortnose gar, *Lepisosteus platostomus*
Giganthurids—Giganthuridea
Goby—Gobiidae
  Longjaw mudsucker, *Gillichthys mirabilis*
Goosefish, *Lophius americanus*
Grenadier and rat-tail—Macrouridae
Grunts—Pomadasyidae
Guppy—*Lebistes reticulatus*

Hagfish—Myxinidae
Halfbeaks—Hemiramphidae
  Balao, *Hemiramphus balao*
  Ballyhoo, *Hemiramphus brasiliensis*
Herring—Clupeidae
  Alewives, *Alosa pseudoharengus*
  American shad, *Alosa sapidissima*

Gizzard shad, *Dorosoma cepedianum*
  Menhaden, *Brevoortia* sp.
  Pacific herring, *Clupea harengus pallasi*
  Pilchards, *Harengula* sp.
  Sardines, *Harengula, Sardinella,* and *Sardinops* sp.
  Skipjack herring, *Alosa chrysochloris*
  Threadfin shad, *Dorosoma petenense*

Idiacanths, *Idiacanthus*

Jacks, scads, pompanos—Carangidae
  Amberjack, *Seriola* sp.
  Bumper, *Chloroscombrus chrysurus*
  Crevalle jack, *Caranx hippos*
  Jack mackerel, *Trachurus symmetricus*
  Mackerel scad, *Decapterus macarellus*
  Pompano, *Trachinotus carolinus*
  Roosterfish, *Nematistius pectoralis*
  Yellowtail, *Seriola dorsalis*

Killifish—Cyprinodontidae
  Mummichogs, *Fundulus heteroclitus*
Knife fish—Gymnotidae

Labyrinths—Anabantidae
Lampreys—Petromyzontidae
  Sea Lamprey, *Petromyzon marinus*
Lanternfish—Myctophidae
Lances, sand, *Ammodytes* sp.
Livebearers—Poeciliidae
  Amazon molly, *Mollienesia formosa*
  Gambusia, *Gambusia* sp.
  Gila topminnows, *Poeciliopsis occidentalis*
Lumpfish and snailfish—Cyclopteridae
  Globefish, *Cyclopterichthys glaber*
Lungfish, *Prototopterus* sp.

Mackerels and tunas—Scombridae
  Albacores, *Thunnus alalunga*
  Bigeye tuna, *Thunnus obesus*
  Black skipjack, *Euthynnus lineatus*
  Blackfin tuna, *Thunnus atlanticus*
  Bluefin tuna, *Thunnus thynnus*
  King mackerel, *Scomberomorus cavalla*
  Little tuna, *Euthynnus Alletteratus*
  Pacific bonitos, *Sarda chiliensis*
  Seerfish, *Scomberomorus commersoni*
  Skipjack tuna, *Euthynnus pelamis*
  Spanish mackerel, *Scomberomorus maculatus*
  Wahoo, *Acanthocybium solanderi*
  Yellowfin tuna, *Thunnus albacares*
Minnows and carps—Cyprinidae
  Bitterlings, *Rhodeus sericeus*

Bluntnose minnows, *Pimephales notatus*
Bullhead minnow, *Pimephales vigilax*
Carp, *Cyprinus carpio*
Emerald shiner, *Notropis atherinoides*
Fallfish, *Semotilus corporalis*
Fathead chub, *Hybopsis gracilis*
Fathead minnow, *Pimephales promelas*
Golden shiner, *Notemigonus crysoleucas*
Goldfish, *Carassius auratus*
Grass carp, *Ctenopharyngodon idella*
Mimic shiner, *Notropis volucellus*
River shiner, *Notropis blennius*
Sicklefin chub, *Hybopsis meeki*
Silver chub, *Hybopsis storeriana*
Silverband shiner, *Notropis illecebrosus*
Speckled chub, *Hybopsis aestivalis*
Spottail shiner, *Notropis hudsonius*
Squawfish, *Ptychocheilus* sp.
Sturgeon chub, *Hybopsis gelida*
Tench, *Tinca tinca*
Mola—Molidae
   Ocean sunfish, *Mola mola*
Mooneyes—Hiodontidae
   Goldeye, *Hiodon alosoides*
   Mooneye, *Hiodon tergisus*
Mormyrid, African freshwater—Mormyridae
Mullets—Mugilidae
   Striped mullet, *Mugil cephalus*
Needlefish—Belonidae
Paddlefish—Polyodontidae
Parrotfish—Scaridae
Perch—Percidae
   American freshwater darter, *Etheostoma* and *Percina* sp.
   Sauger, *Stizostedion canadense*
   Yellow perch, *Perca flavescens*
   Walleye, *Stizostedion vitreum vitreum*
Perch, climbing, *Anabas* sp.
Pike—Esocidae
   Chain pickerel, *Esox niger*
   Grass pickerel, *Esox americanus vermiculatus*
   Muskellunge, *Esox masquinongy*
   Northern pike, *Esox lucius*
Pipefish and seahorses—Syngnathidae
   Pipefish—*Syngnathus* sp.
   Seahorses, *Hippocampus* sp.
Piranha, *Serrosalmo* sp.
Porcupinefish, *Diodon hystrix*
Porgies—Sparidae
   Pinfish, *Lagodon rhonbodies*

Sheepshead, *Archosargus probatocephalus*
Puffers, *Canthigaster*, *Lagocephalus,* and *Sphaeroides* sp.

Rays, electric—Torpedinidae
Ribbonfish, *Trachipterus* sp.

Sablefish, *Anoplopoma* and *Erilepis* sp.
Salmon, trout, whitefish, and graylings—Salmonides
   Arctic char, *Salvelinus alphinus*
   Atlantic salmon, *Salmo salar*
   Brook trout, *Salvelinus fontinalis*
   Brown trout, *Salmo trutta*
   Chinook salmon, *Oncorhynchus tshawytscha*
   Ciscoes, *Coregonus* sp.
   Coho salmon, *Oncorhynchus kisutch*
   Cutthroat trout, *Salmo clarki*
   Dolly Varden trout, *Salvelinus malma*
   Golden trout, *Salmo aguabonita*
   Inconnu, *Stenodus leucichthys*
   Lake herring, *Coregonus artedii*
   Lake trout, *Salvelinus namaycush*
   Lake whitefish, *Coregonus clupeaformis*
   Landlocked salmon, *Salmo salar*
   Masu salmon, *Oncorhynchus masu*
   Pink salmon, *Oncorhynchus gorbuscha*
   Rainbow trout, *Salmo gairdneri*
   Sockeye salmon, *Oncorhynchus nerka*
   Steelhead trout, *Salmo gairdneri*
Scorpionfish and rockfish—Scorpaenidae
   Lionfish, *Scorpaena grandicornis*
   Redfish, *Sebastes marinus*
   Rockfish, *Sebastodes* sp.
Sculpins—Cottidae
Sharks, dogfish—Squalidae
Sharks, hammerhead—Sphyrnidae
Sharks, mackerel—Lamnidae
   Mako shark, *Isurus oxyrinchus*
   White shark, *Carcharodon carcharias*
Sharks, requiem—Carcharhinidae
   Blacktip shark, *Carcharhinus limbatus*
   Blue shark, *Prionance glauca*
   Bull shark, *Carcharhinus leucos*
   Dusky shark, *Carcharhinus obscurus*
   Lemon shark, *Negaprion brevirostris*
   Silky shark, *Carcharhinus floridanus*
   Smooth dogfish, *Mustelus canis*
   Soupfin shark, *Galeorhinus zyopterus*
   Spinner shark, *Carcharhinus maculipinnis*
   Tiger shark, *Caleocerdo cuvieri*
Silversides—Atherinidae

459

Skates—Rajidae
Smelts—Osmeridae
    American smelt, *Osmerus mordax*
    Eulachon smelt, *Thaleichthys pacificus*
Snappers—Lutjanidae
    Gray snapper, *Lutjanus griseus*
    Red snapper, *Lutjanus blackfordi*
Snook—Centropomidae
Sole, hogchoker, *Trinectes maculatus*
Squirrelfish and soldierfish—Holocentridae
    Squirrelfish, *Holocentrus ascensionis*
Stargazers, *Arioscopus* and *Kathetostoma* sp.
Sticklebacks—Gasterosteidae
Stingrays—Dasyatidae
    Rays, *Gymnura* sp.
Sturgeons—Acipenseridae
    Lake sturgeon, *Acipenser fulvescens*
    Shovelnose sturgeon, *Scaphirhynchus platorynchus*
Suckers—Catostomidae
    Blue sucker, *Cycleptus elongatus*
    Buffalofish, *Ictiobus* sp.
    Carpsuckers, *Carpiodes* sp.
    Redhorse suckers, *Moxostoma* sp.
Sunfish—Centrarchidae
    Black crappie, *Pomoxis nigromaculatus*
    Bluegill, *Lepomis macrochirus*
    Green sunfish, *Lepomis cyanellus*
    Largemouth bass, *Micropterus salmoides*
    Pumpkinseed sunfish, *Lepomis gibbosus*
    Pygmy sunfish, *Elassoma* sp.
    Redear sunfish, *Lepomis microlophus*

Redeye bass, *Micropterus coosae*
Rock bass, *Ambloplites rupestris*
Sacramento perch, *Archoplites interruptus*
Smallmouth bass, *Micropterus dolomieui*
Spotted bass, *Micropterus punctulatus*
Warmouth, *Chaenobryttus gulosus*
White crappie, *Pomoxis annularis*
Surfperch—Embrotocidae
Surgeonfish, *Acanthurus* sp.
Swordfish, *Xiphias gladius*
Tarpon—Elopidae
    Ladyfish, *Elops saurus*
    Tarpon, *Megalops alantica*
Tilapia, *Tilapia* sp.
Toadfish—Batrachoididae
    Midshipman, *Porichthys* sp.
    Toadfish—*Opsanus* sp.
Triggerfish and filefish—Balistidae
    Filefish, *Alutera, Cantherines,* and *Monacanthus* sp.
    Triggerfish, *Balistes, Canthidermis,* and *Xanthichthys* sp.
Trout-perch, *Percopsis omiscomaycus*
Trunkfish—Ostraciidae
    Cowfish, *Lactophrys quadricornis*
    Trunkfish, *Lactophrys* and *Lactoria* sp.

Viperfish—Gonostomatidae

Wrasses—Labridae
    Tautogs, *Tautoga onitis*

Index

464